A City Cannot B‹

MW00527175

"Sanford Ikeda made two unique contributions in his book. First, it provides a comprehensive theoretical framework for Jane Jacobs' observations about more livable cities; second, it makes a convincing assessment of the significant impact of Jane Jacobs's ideas on modern urban design and planning. Ikeda reminds us, however, that if Jane Jacobs won the battle against Robert Moses, the struggle continues between two different concepts of cities: top-down technocratic city planning as opposed to a recognition of cities as the emergence of spontaneous order as described by Jane Jacobs."

—Alain Bertaud, *Senior Research Scholar, Marron Institute of Urban Management, New York University.*

"Jane Jacobs is best known for her impact on how people view and plan cities. But she considered her economic writing her most important. Few people focus on her economics. Sanford Ikeda does it thoroughly and with great insight and is a rare voice in this area. Thus, this work is a very important addition to the application of Jacobs' thinking."

—Roberta Brandes Gratz, *Award-winning journalist and urbanist, Author of The* Battle for Gotham.

"This book is original both in revisiting Jane Jacobs's thought and in freshly contributing to urban studies, urban economics and planning theory. I believe it is the best critical presentation of Jacobs's work ever written."

—Stefano Moroni, *Professor of Planning, Polytechnic University of Milan.*

"This book masterfully articulates what many of Jane Jacob's writings can be boiled down to: that cities are, in the words of another great thinker, 'the result of human action, but not human design'. One cannot truly understand Jane Jacobs without understanding economic concepts, such as *spontaneous order*, *radical ignorance*, and *social capital,* among others. Sanford Ikeda elegantly bridges the gap between economic theory and urban planning, explaining complex ideas in an accessible way. An absolute must-read for professional planners and urbanist aficionados."

—Vera Kichanova, PhD, *Senior Economist, Free Cities Foundation, Researcher, Zaha Hadid Architects.*

Sanford Ikeda

A City Cannot Be a Work of Art

Learning Economics and Social Theory From Jane Jacobs

palgrave
macmillan

Sanford Ikeda
Department of Economics
Purchase College, SUNY
Purchase, NY, USA

ISBN 978-981-99-5364-6   ISBN 978-981-99-5362-2   (eBook)
https://doi.org/10.1007/978-981-99-5362-2

Cover illustration: © Artur Debat / Getty Images

This Palgrave Macmillan imprint is published by the registered company Springer Nature Singapore Pte Ltd.
The registered company address is: 152 Beach Road, #21-01/04 Gateway East, Singapore 189721, Singapore

Paper in this product is recyclable.

When we deal with cities we are dealing with life at its most complex and intense. Because this is so, there is a basic esthetic limitation on what can be done with cities:
A city cannot be a work of art. – Jane Jacobs.

Wise in his daily work was he:
To fruits of diligence,
And not to faiths or polity,
He plied his utmost sense.
These perfect in their little parts,
Whose work is all their prize —
Without them how could laws, or arts,
Or towered cities rise?
– George Eliot

To Alain and Marie-Agnes

Preface

Studying the writings of Jane Jacobs has enriched my understanding, as an economist, of the social cosmos. When I met the great urbanist in 2004, I was already integrating her singular insights into my teaching and professional writing. Sadly, she died two years later. While our personal connection was regrettably brief, my appreciation for her ideas has continued to deepen.

Around ten years ago, I began to think seriously about putting down, in some reasonably coherent form, what I have learned about economics and social theory from Jacobs and passed on to my students. Which is how this book came to be written. But the only good reason to add to the plethora of books out there about cities is to contribute something interesting, important, and new. I believe this book meets that challenge.

Purchase, NY, USA   Sanford Ikeda

Acknowledgments

This book has been many years in the making and has had many helping hands along the way. Accordingly, I express my profound gratitude to those named below for substantially contributing to its inspiration, development, and completion. Some names appear more than once because they have aided me in multiple ways. The usual caveat applies.

I begin by thanking Peter J. Boettke and Pierre Desrochers for prompting me to think deeply about cities in the first place and Walter Grinder for his unflagging enthusiasm and frank encouragement from the very beginning of this project until his recent death. Emily Hamilton lent careful and efficient research assistance in its early stages And Francis Morrone has long been a source of inspiration for all things architectural and urban.

The following individuals, organizations, and institutions provided venues for valuable feedback on various chapters of the manuscript or versions thereof: David Schmidtz, Mary Rigdon, and the Center for the Philosophy of Freedom at the University of Arizona; David Emanuel Andersson and Cosmos+Taxis; Anna Sachko Gandolfi, Arthur Gandolfi, Carolyn Greaige, and the Economic Freedom Institute at Manhattanville College; Larry Reed and the Foundation for Economic Education; Janet Bufton, Matt Bufton, Sabine El-Chidiac, and the Institute for Liberal Studies; Yukihiro Ikeda and Keio University; Mark Pennington, John Meadowcroft, and Kings College London; Stefano Moroni, Stefano

Cozzolino, and Politecnico di Milano; Peter Gordon and the School of Planning at the University of Southern California; Paul Mueller and The King's College; Gabriel Calzada Álvarez, Roberto Quevedo, Pablo Vasquez, and the Universidad de Francisco Marroquín; the Association for Private Enterprise Education; the Association of Schools of European Planning; the Mont Pelerin Society; the School of Urban & Regional Planning at Reyerson University; and the Society for the Development of Austrian Economics.

The Institute for Humane Studies at George Mason University sponsored an intensive two-day workshop for an earlier draft of the manuscript in November 2020, and I am truly indebted to the organizers, Greg Walcott and Stewart Robertson of the IHS, and to the participants who each read and commented on the entire manuscript. The latter included Alain Bertaud, Stefano Cozzolino, Pierre Desrochers, Edward Glaeser, Peter Gordon, Roberta Brandes Gratz, M. Nolan Gray, Sonia Hirt, James Jacobs, Vera Kichanova, Michael Manville, Sam Staley, and Joanna Szurmak.

The members of the Colloquium on Market Institutions and Economic Processes at New York University have in recent years commented on several draft chapters. I would especially like to thank Mario J. Rizzo, David Harper, William Butos, Young Back Choi, Luc Marest, J. Huston McColloch, Raoul Oreskovic, Maria Paganelli, Nathan Goodman, Justus Enninga, Otto Lehto (particularly for written comments on Chap. 9), and Alexander Schaefer.

Kaveh Pourvand organized a day-long workshop on the manuscript in October 2022, sponsored by the Center for the Philosophy of Freedom at the University of Arizona, that gave rise to many constructive criticisms from the participants who, in addition to Kaveh, included Janet Bufton, David E. Gordon, Andrew Humphries (particularly for extensive written comments on Chaps. 1, 2, and 5), Rachel Humphries, David Schmidtz, and Adriana Zuniga (particularly for written comments on Chap. 8). My heartfelt thanks to them all.

Marion Duvall of Palgrave Macmillan supplied the professional support, patient advice, and much-appreciated flexibility needed to move the manuscript to publication. My talented niece, Chieko Kagiyama, rendered all the illustrations with accuracy and alacrity. And I am deeply grateful to my wife, Jennifer Wada, for her steady encouragement over the length of this project and for her expert editorial assistance and comments, having gone over every word of the complete manuscript often more than once. I am also grateful to my son, Christopher Ikeda, for just being who he is.

The recommendations from everyone vastly improved the final version of this book. I was able and willing to incorporate a great many of them, but any errors or omissions that remain are alone my responsibility.

I thank Purchase College, SUNY, for granting leaves and release time from teaching; the Charles Koch Foundation for summer support in 2017; and the Earhart Foundation and the Mercatus Center at George Mason University for their backing early on. And I gratefully acknowledge receiving direct support for this project from the Institute for Humane Studies under grant no. IHS017036.

My gratitude and love to the decades of undergraduates who passed through my course "Cities Culture & Economy," from whom I have gained so much. I hope the feeling has been mutual. Finally, this book is dedicated to Alain and Marie-Agnes Bertaud, who have given generously of their vast knowledge and dear friendship to Jenny and me.

About the Book

Jane Jacobs is a legend in the field of urbanism and is famous for challenging and profoundly influencing urban planning and design. This book is about what we can and should learn from Jacobs's contributions to economics and social theory, which are central to her criticisms of and proposals for public policy, but frequently overlooked even by her most enthusiastic admirers. It argues that Jacobs's insight that "a city cannot be a work of art" underlies both her ideas on planning and her understanding of economic development and social cooperation. It shows how the theory of the market process and Jacobs's theory of urban processes are useful complements—an example of what economists and urbanists can learn from each other. This Jacobs-cum-market-process perspective offers new theoretical, historical, and policy analyses of cities, more realistic and coherent than standard accounts by either economists or urbanists.

Contents

About the Author

Sanford Ikeda is Professor Emeritus of Economics at Purchase College (SUNY). He is the author of *Dynamics of the Mixed Economy*, with scholarly publications in *The Southern Economic Journal, Environmental Politics, Social Philosophy & Policy, The American Journal of Economics & Sociology, Cosmos+Taxis, The Independent Review, Journal des Economistes et des Etudes Humaines,* and *The Review of Austrian Economics.* He has contributed entries for *The International Encyclopedia of the Social Sciences* and for *The Encyclopedia of Libertarianism* and has published essays in *Forbes* and *National Review Online.* His research focuses on the interconnections among cities, spontaneous social orders, entrepreneurial development, and urban policy.

List of Figures

1

Introduction

Jane Jacobs is a legend in the field of urbanism and is the subject of books, plays,[1] documentaries,[2] and even an opera.[3] She is famous for fiercely challenging and profoundly impacting urban planning and design in the late twentieth century. But this book, whose title comes from a passage in her classic *The Death and Life of Great American Cities*, is about what we can learn from Jacobs's major writings about economics and social theory. Her contributions to these areas are fundamental and game-changing for theory and policy, but they are largely neglected. I aim to rectify that.

By "we" I mean the interested reader and the admirers of Jacobs, as well as professional economists and social theorists who are probably unaware of Jacobs's important contributions to their fields of study. By her "major works" I refer to *Death and Life of Great American Cities*, *The Economy of Cities*, *Cities and the Wealth of Nations*, *Systems of Survival*, *The*

---

[1] "Boozy: The Life, Death, and Subsequent Vilification of Le Corbusier and, More Importantly, Robert Moses." See https://playbill.com/article/robert-moses-gets-deconstructed-again-with-off-broadway-transfer-of-boozy-may-1-28-in-nyc-com-125639. Accessed 6 May 2023.

[2] "Citizen Jane: Battle for the City." See https://www.imdb.com/title/tt3699354/

[3] "A Marvelous Order: an Opera about Jane Jacobs and Robert Moses." See http://mosesjacobsopera.com/. Accessed 6 May 2023.

© The Author(s) 2024
S. Ikeda, *A City Cannot Be a Work of Art*,
https://doi.org/10.1007/978-981-99-5362-2_1

1

Nature of Economies, and *Dark Age Ahead*. I will spell out in detail what I mean by "economics" and "social theory" in Chaps. 2 and 3, and in the chapters that follow, I explore in some depth Jacobs's contributions to those areas and why they are important.

1   An Afternoon in "The Annex"

I had the privilege of spending an afternoon talking with Jane Jacobs in February 2004, two years before her death at the age of 89. The meeting was arranged largely by Gert-Jan Hospers, an economic geographer currently at Radboud University of the Netherlands. It included, besides Hospers and myself, my friend and colleague Pierre Desrochers, a geographer at the University of Toronto at Mississauga, and economist Hiroko Shimuzu.

The four of us, two economists and two geographers, waited nervously for the greatest urbanist of the twentieth century and one of the most iconic and influential policy shapers of our time,[4] to answer her doorbell. As we stood on the porch of the vintage two-story house in "The Annex," a neighborhood in Toronto known for its Bohemian character, I pondered the long list of questions we had come up with at a nearby coffeehouse. The door opened and there stood before us a woman in her mid-eighties with a gray, page-boy haircut wearing a fuzzy, multicolored sweater, smiling benignly. She was leaning against a walker (she had recently broken her hip) yet was taller than I expected. I was face-to-face with Jane Jacobs, whose thoughts, words, and deeds changed the face of the modern city. That moment and the long conversation that followed is one of the peak moments of my life.

Jacobs had recently finished the manuscript for her final book, *Dark Age Ahead*, had not yet begun her next book project, which was never completed, and had just done her tax returns. Our timing could not have been better, as I later learned that while working she was extremely focused and refused to grant interviews. We had prioritized our questions because we didn't know how long we could visit and were mindful not to

---

[4] According to Planetizen, https://www.planetizen.com/features/95189-100-most-influential-urbanists. Accessed 6 May 2023.

outstay our welcome. But each time we made to leave, Jacobs made it clear she wanted our conversation to continue. We were surprised and quietly ecstatic. So over tea and cookies for nearly four hours, during which her deliberate voice never once faltered and her mind never once wandered, she cheerfully covered a variety of topics. In addition to cities, we talked about economics, social theory, and public policy, much of which has found its way into this book.

During that unforgettable meeting, I asked Jacobs where she believed her main intellectual contribution lay, and she answered without hesitation, "Economic theory!" What makes my task here both difficult and necessary is that, in my experience, those who know of Jane Jacobs, and even those who know her work well (although few economists do), tend to think of her almost exclusively in terms of her trenchant writings about and fierce activism against heavy-handed urban planning and top-down urban design; or they are rightly inspired by her commitment to people in their own communities "self-organizing" to address local problems. Some also cite her to support environmentalist causes (despite her often acerbic criticisms of environmentalists), the historic preservation of entire neighborhoods and districts (despite a paucity of published evidence of her backing the practice) or various forms of "localism" (despite the role of global, inter-city trade in her theory of economic development). Or they interpret her as concerned mainly with political theory.[5] Most are unaware of the primacy she places on her contributions to economic theory, with its appreciation for unplanned order, nor recognize the deeper social principles that undergird her economics.[6]

---

[5] For example, Nathaniel Rich wrote in *The Atlantic* in 2016: "Urban life was Jacobs's great subject. But her great theme was the fragility of democracy—how difficult it is to maintain, how easily it can crumble. A city offered the perfect laboratory in which to study democracy's intricate, interconnected gears and ballistics." I share Steven Johnson's sentiments: "Since *Death and Life*, the celebration of sidewalk culture has become the idée fixe of all left-leaning urbanists … . But the irony is that many of the same critics who cited Jacobs as the initial warrior in the sidewalk crusade misunderstood the reasons why she had embraced the sidewalk in the first place. And that is because they saw the city as a kind of political theater, and not as an emergent system" (Johnson, 2002: 94).

[6] An important exception to this is the geographer Richard Harris, especially his chapter, "The magpie and the bee: Jane Jacobs's magnificent obsession," in Page and Mennel (2017). Harris sees "major continuities in Jacobs's writings" much as I do. "She explored the social and economic aspects of this insight at different scales, and presented her conclusions so systematically that they amount to a theory of the significance of urban form. … contrary to a common perception, Jacobs's purpose was largely theoretical. It is in this light that the unitary character of her writings about cities should be viewed" (Ibid: 66).

It is perhaps an easy mistake to make since Jacobs never held an academic appointment or an advanced degree in economics. Indeed, she held no formal degree beyond a high-school diploma (Laurence, 2016). She did take courses at Columbia University that interested her, but as a non-matriculated student—"such as biology, chemistry, constitutional law, the development of legal institutions, geography, geology, patent law, philosophy, sociology and zoology" (Desrochers & Szurmak, 2017: 7)—and spent the beginning of her career amid the Great Depression working in several short-lived, clerical jobs. During World War II, beginning in 1943 and continuing for several years thereafter, she wrote articles for Russian consumption for the Office of War Information. Then, in 1952, she became a staff writer for *Architectural Forum*, where she learned on-the-job about architecture and urban planning, with help from her architect-husband Robert Hyde Jacobs Jr., but largely from her own exhaustive research (Ibid: 10–11). However, there have been other notable economists, especially before the hyper-credentialism of today, who, like Jacobs, held no advanced degree or academic position, but whose economic contributions have been widely recognized—David Ricardo, John Stuart Mill, and Henry George come to mind.

A glance at the titles of her books makes her deep and abiding interest in economics obvious: *The Economy of Cities*, *Cities and the Wealth of Nations*, and *The Nature of Economies*.[7] And in her most famous book, *The Death and Life of Great American Cities*, she describes in detail, à la modern social theory, how physical design, social institutions, social capital, and trust enable people to discover and pursue their individual plans at street level, and how doing so enables the city in which they are

---

[7] Alice Sparberg Alexiou (2006) makes a similar point in a chapter, "Economist without Portfolio," in her accessible biography of Jacobs, *Jane Jacobs: Urban Visionary*. She touches on many salient points of Jacobs's economics, though not to the extent or level of detail offered here. It also makes the unfortunate but common error of confusing Jacobs's concept of "import replacement" with the quite different and dangerous policy of "import substitution" (Alexiou, 2006: 176), which I explain in Chap. 6.

   This is also a good place to mention other works that have drawn attention to Jacobs's contribution to economics. I have indicated that there are not many, although three are particularly worthy of mention. First, Pierre Desrochers and Gert-Jan Hospers (2007) whose perspective is close to my own and emphasize Jacobs's contribution to the theory of economic development. The second by David Ellerman (2007) also emphasizes her contribution to economic development. The third is an important recent publication by Charles-Albert Ramsay (2022).

embedded to grow and flourish commercially and culturally in complex, dynamic, and unpredictable processes. She explains how innovation—in commerce, science and technology, and culture—is central to that flourishing. She explains, in a way that in my opinion rivals or surpasses most economic theorists, how and under what conditions entrepreneurial innovation takes place and how that may be undermined by attempts to central plan at the municipal level.

It is true that Jacobs boldly announces in the first sentences of *Death and Life* that "This book is an attack on current city planning and rebuilding…[and] an attempt to introduce new principles of city planning and rebuilding" (Jacobs, 1961: 3). But it is a great deal more. But her attack and the "new principles" she substitutes for the old are grounded in a profound understanding of the *economic* nature and significance of cities, and her analytical framework is built around that understanding. Jacobs makes this clear in the introductory chapter.

> While Part I is principally about the social behavior of people in cities, and is necessary for understanding what follows, *Part II is principally about the economic behavior of cities and is the most important part of this book* (Jacobs, 1961: 14, emphasis added).

It is understandable but regrettable that, despite her explicit attempts to highlight the economic core of her most-famous book, Jacobs's brilliant discussion in Part I of the "sidewalk ballet" and "eyes on the street," have attracted and sustained the most attention. And when her admirers do mention "the generators of diversity" that Jacobs sets out in Part II they typically interpret this as racial diversity (important as that is), which some critics (Schubert, 2014) have maintained Jacobs gives less attention to than she should have in 1961, and not the *diversity of land-use* that is explicitly the focus of *Death and Life* and the context from which emerges the safety and security she argues is the *sine qua non* of large-scale social cooperation (e.g., Jacobs, 1961: 144). Or they dwell on the importance of "population density," without noting that "high concentrations of people" are for her only one of the four generators of diversity that together generate land-use diversity (e.g., Jacobs, 1961: 183, 214). Or they misinterpret another condition, "mixed uses," in which her emphasis is on mixed *primary uses* that attract outsiders into an area—such as residences, offices, museums, government offices, theaters—and not, as is typically done today, on what she calls "secondary diversity" that merely serves persons already attracted into that area, such as diners, supermarkets, dry cleaners, and drug stores (e.g., Jacobs, 1961: 152, 162). But the main thrust of Part II of *Death and Life*—which explains how population density and mixed primary uses interact in complex and unpredictable ways with "short blocks" and "old and new buildings" to create the external conditions for economic development—is usually sketchily explained or ignored all together. The same can be said for Jacobs's discussion of "organized complexity," the orderly dynamism that maintains a stable interdependence among those conditions, which is the core of the final chapter of *Death and Life*, "The Kind of Problem a City Is." As I argue in Chap. 3, "organized complexity" is the conceptual complement to what social theorists call "spontaneous order" (Ikeda, 2020).

The neglect or misinterpretation of the central concerns of such a famous figure should thus be irresistible low-hanging fruit for an academic familiar with her works. At least it was for me.

2   Encountering Jane Jacobs

I became interested in Jacobs's writings around 1997. I had just published my book, *Dynamics of the Mixed Economy: Toward a Theory of Interventionism*, which was about why knowledge and incentive problems lead public policies systematically to create negative unintended consequences. I had written it at a high level of abstraction and one of my respected colleagues, George Mason University economist Peter J. Boettke, suggested I try applying the dynamics of interventionism approach to more concrete, urban problems, looking for example at why housing policies, functional zoning, and large infrastructure projects keep generating outcomes contrary to their proponents' intentions. About the same time, Canadian geographer Pierre Desrochers, who was familiar with my interest in public-policy failure, urged me to read Jacobs, whose best-known book had in fact been sitting unread on my bookshelf since graduate-school days. Encouraged by Boettke and Desrochers, I finally took *Death and Life* down and was captivated from that first declarative sentence. I was also fascinated by how Jacobs's message and style of analysis so strongly resonated with the theoretical approach I had applied to public-policy analysis in my book and with the economic framework that lay behind it: market-process economics.[8] I have since devoted more than two decades to learning from Jacobs and to integrating her ideas into my writing and teaching.

Lest my intention to discuss the economics of Jane Jacobs scare away the uninitiated, let me say that, to be honest, the field of "urban economics" for a long time never interested me. It always sounded like an area too obscure and specialized for my tastes, which ran to what a colleague once termed "big think." But for me *Death and Life* opened a new way of thinking big about the world, as it has for countless readers, in a strange but, at the same time, a very familiar way. Since this journey began, the fields I have been most closely connected with academically are urbanism and urban economics. The truth be told, however, my interest still doesn't lie in urban economics *per se* and I have never made a formal study of it, although I have read textbooks and articles on urban economics and learned selectively from concepts that are unique to the field (e.g., gravity models, central-place theory, building economics). But I am simply an economist who in mid-career became fascinated with cities as socioeconomic phenomena and who loves observing, thinking, teaching, and writing about cities. Cities are now the starting point of my interests in most areas of economics, micro and macro, and in most issues of theory and policy.

Unfortunately, unlike an urban economist, my idiosyncratic and eclectic tastes have meant that I have serious trouble explaining to people what it is that I do. The best I can come up with is the awkward phrase, "I'm interested in and write about the nature cities and their significance for cultural and economic development from the perspective of economics and sociology," which usually draws a blank stare and a quick change of subject. In fact, the best, perhaps only way I can satisfactorily explain, at least for myself, what it is I do and why I do it is to write a book like this. I blame Jane Jacobs.

As my tortuous description above suggests, I take seriously the contributions of sociology and, thanks to Jacobs, have overcome an aversion to

---

[8] For one view of "market-process," see Israel M. Kirzner's "The meaning of market process" in Kirzner (1992).

sociology prevalent among my fellow economists. I have learned important and useful things from authors such as Max Weber and Mark
Granovetter, and social theorists and philosophers such Georg Zimmel
and Adam Seligman. I have also of course learned from architects and
designers such as Léon Krier, Rem Koolhaas, Christopher Alexander and
from urban planners such as Kevin Lynch, Alain Bertaud, and many others. All of these and very many more contribute, with the usual caveat, to
the pages that follow.

That first encounter with Jacobs's work took place during a sabbatical
from Purchase College, SUNY, my academic home base from 1990 to
this day. On my return, in order to keep alive the fire that studying Jacobs
had lit, I created a new course, which Purchase's marvelous flexibility
made easy. I called it *Cities, Culture, & Economy* and I have taught it regularly since 1998. The syllabus for that course, which has evolved but
remained fairly constant over the decades, broke the course down into
several parts: The Nature of Cities, The Microfoundations of Cities, The
Evolution of Cities, Trust & Social Capital in Cities, Cities Culture &
Capitalism, The Reformist Origins of Modern Planning, Modernism &
Urban Planning, Classic Writings in Urban Design, and Current Issues
in Urban Planning. My original strategy for this book was in fact to transform that course syllabus into a table of contents for a book, but as I
worked and reworked the outline over more years than I care to say, it has
emerged in its present form, vastly different from that syllabus, but in the
same spirit.

3   What's in This Book

In terms of structure, in addition to the present chapter, Chaps. 2 and 3
constitute the introductory part of the book, the former gives an overview of Jacobs's contributions to social theory and economics in particular, while the latter introduces some of the main principles of her social
theory in the context of the trade-off between scale/design and complex-
ity/spontaneity. Chapters 4, 5, and 6 present the core theoretical framework of Jacobs's socioeconomic theory together with my interpretation.
Chapter 4 discusses the importance of diversity and heterogeneity (of

people, places, and things) in Jacobs's work and explains how coherence and complementarity can emerge from them, as well as the elements that Jacobs identifies as the generators of land-use diversity. Chapter 5 focuses on the role of social networks in providing social order in a city, which are the main sources of coherence in Jacobs's earlier work, and shows how explicitly including the concept of entrepreneurship greatly enhances the explanatory power of the social-network approach; while Chap. 6 focuses on Jacobs's argument for how a great city becomes a primary source of innovation via "import replacement" and "import shifting," and it explicitly adds elements of market-process economics to round out that argument. The final three chapters details how Jacobs's critique of urban planning and policy flow from the socioeconomic framework developed in the previous chapters. Chapter 7 looks at large-scale urban planning strategies that Jacobs herself criticizes, Chap. 8 at more microlevel policies and regulations such as zoning and housing policies, some of which Jacobs does not explicitly address, and Chap. 9 at present-day projects and proposals for urban planning and regulation, including New Urbanist and Startup Society plans. Chapter 10 offers a synopsis of Jacobs's social theory, economics, and policy recommendations and suggests areas of further study.

I hope this book offers a new and useful way to look at and think about cities, to appreciate their nature and significance for economic development and for social and cultural change, and to better see the limits of deliberate design, both private and governmental. I hope it clarifies the fundamental connection between markets and cities, and alerts professionals in economics (especially those working within a market-process framework) and in urbanism (especially among admirers of Jane Jacobs) how their respective perspectives on social institutions and processes can inform each other. And I hope it shows that Jacobs's ideas on economics and social theory are deeper and theoretically richer than most of her admirers appreciate, and how in particular it dovetails with issues of concern to market-process economics and its underlying social theory.

Finally, I should say that in addition to not being an urban planner or architect or an urban economist even, neither am I strictly speaking what you would call a "Jane Jacobs scholar" the likes of Peter Laurence, whose *Becoming Jane Jacobs* (2016) is in my opinion thus far the definitive biography of Jacobs, or of Pierre Desrochers who helped launch me on my Jacobsian odyssey and who with his encyclopedic knowledge could tell fascinating details about Jacobs's life, academic studies, and intellectual influences.[9] To be perfectly honest, I often resort to Googling to remind myself about Jacobs's birth and death dates, when and what she wrote for various publications, or when and where she lived in my own neighborhood of Brooklyn Heights. When I give public lectures, I usually have to look these up to avoid embarrassing myself in front of audiences who often know more about these things than I do.

I do think, however, that I can accurately be described as a "student of Jane Jacobs." I have thoroughly studied her major works and many of her lesser-known essays, thought and rethought, and written about her ideas, and have indeed taught them, now for most of my professional life, and have learned from her to better understand how the social world works and why. In this I can confidently say that I have succeeded as well as anyone.

After reading this book you may disagree. Jacobs is a subtle thinker though sometimes inconsistent, so it is certainly possible to interpret her writings in different ways to useful effect. I am of course confident in my interpretation, though it is perhaps not the only one possible. Different people can draw (and have indeed drawn) different lessons from Jacobs's work and so we might therefore disagree, perhaps strongly, on the meaning and especially the implications of her writings. My great hope is that, after reading this book and comparing it with Jacobs's ideas as she herself expresses them, formally in print, anyone who may still disagree with my analysis and conclusions will nevertheless agree that there is strong textual evidence to support them.

Works Cited

Alexiou, A. S. (2006). *Jane Jacobs: Urban Visionary*. Rutgers University Press.
Desrochers, P., & Hospers, G.-J. (2007). Cities and the Economic Development of Nations: An Essay on Jane Jacobs' Contribution to Economic Theory.

---

[9] See his two-part essay on Jacobs's methodology, coauthored with Joanna Szurmak, "Jane Jacobs as Spontaneous Economic Order Methodologist: Parts 1 & 2," *Cosmos + Taxis*, (2017) Vol. 4 No. 2/3: 2–59.

Canadian Journal of Regional Science/Revue canadienne des sciences régionales, 30(1), 115–130.

Desrochers, P., & Szurmak, J. (2017). Jane Jacobs as Spontaneous Economic Order Methodologist: Part 1: Intellectual Apprenticeship. *Cosmos + Taxis, 4*(2/3).

Ellerman, D. (2007). Jane Jacobs on development. *Oxford Development Studies, 32*(4), 507–521.

Ikeda, S. (2020). The Economy of Cities, Jane Jacobs's Unappreciated Classic. *Independent Review, 24*(4), 605–618.

Jacobs, J. (1961). *The Death and Life of Great American Cities*. Vintage.

Johnson, S. (2002). *Emergence: The Connected Lives of Ants, Brains, Cities, and Software*. Touchstone.

Kirzner, I. M. (1992). *Market Process: Essays in the Development of Modern Austrian Economics*. Routledge.

Laurence, P. J. (2016). *Becoming Jane Jacobs*. University of Pennsylvania Press.

Page, M., & Mennel, T. (Eds.). (2017). *Reconsidering Jane Jacobs*. Taylor and Francis. Kindle Edition.

Ramsay, C.-A. (2022). *Cities Matter: A Montrealer's Ode of Jane Jacobs, Economist*. Baraka Books.

Schubert, D. (2014). *Contemporary Perspectives on Jane Jacobs: Reassessing the Impacts of an Urban Visionary*. Routledge.

Part I

Economics and Social Theory

2

The Continuing Relevance of Jane Jacobs's Economics and Social Theory

The no-nonsense opening of Jane Jacobs's *The Death and Life of Great American Cities*—"This book is an attack on current city planning and rebuilding"—heralds the beginning of the decline of the post-World War II fascination of municipal governments with the large-scale reconstruction of cities in North America. Jacobs is one of the principal figures who, in her writings and in her activism, successfully fought the policies of a planning orthodoxy that ignored the actual values, the local knowledge, and the resourcefulness of ordinary urban dwellers.

Beginning in the 1960s, she actively challenged the widespread policy of "urban renewal," most notoriously practiced by Robert Moses[1] of New York, which frequently bulldozed the neighborhoods of the poor and politically unconnected, neighborhoods that often possessed lively community networks, and replaced them with intrusive highways, isolated housing projects, sprawling civic centers, and placeless voids that became dull and dangerous—public spaces shunned by the public. Such

---

[1] See Robert Caro's Pulitzer Prize winning biography of Robert Moses, *The Power Broker: Robert Moses and the Fall of New York* (Caro, 1975). Moses has been himself the subject of a recent play "Straight Line Crazy," in which Jacobs is also a featured character. See https://www.nytimes.com/2022/10/26/theater/straight-line-crazy-review.html. Accessed 6 May 2023.

© The Author(s) 2024
S. Ikeda, *A City Cannot Be a Work of Art*,
https://doi.org/10.1007/978-981-99-5362-2_2

heavy-handedness is less prevalent in North American urban-planning departments today. Thanks to the efforts of urbanists like Jacobs, present-day planning processes at least try to be more sensitive to the needs of local inhabitants and more cognizant of the practical importance of Jacobsian concepts such as "mixed uses," "eyes on the street," "face-to-face contact," "density," and the "sidewalk ballet." (In Chap. 8, we will discuss why even these measures tend to fall far short of intentions.)

Elsewhere in the world, however, massive, city-size projects are still being planned and constructed. Reports of the demise of large-scale urban planning and design have been greatly exaggerated, and the era of city planning and rebuilding on an immense scale is certainly not behind us. Anyone bemoaning the post-Jacobs era of scaled-down planning in America (Campanella, 2011) might take heart in these developments. And so, to the extent they ignore Jacobs's critique of twentieth century planning orthodoxy, and the social theory informing it, her arguments remain powerfully relevant.

Here are a few examples.

Zaha Hadid Architects, one of the leading architectural firms in the world, has designed an elongated mega-development of 3.6 km² (2.2 mi²), an area comparable to Midtown Manhattan, flowing like a frozen lattice through the city of Kartal-Pendik in Turkey.[2] In common with most projects of this scale, the design appeals to the eye, especially from afar, although the "parametricism"[3] of the Kartal Masterplan purportedly lends a more navigable, street-level legibility that distinguishes it from some of the others.

There are an estimated 50 mega-projects sponsored by the People's Republic of China, dubbed by critics "ghost cities" because their sprawling, pre-built residential and commercial buildings stand largely vacant.[4] One such construction in the city of Ordos, located in Inner Mongolia, is the Kangbashi district. It is one of the more populated ghost cities, currently around one-third capacity, and covers an area of

---

[2] See the masterplan at http://www.kartalkentder.org/upload/Node/38715/files/Kartal-Masterplan_.pdf. Accessed 6 May 2023.

[3] For an overview of parametricism, see https://www.parametricism.com/. Accessed 22 May 2023.

[4] Described in this article, https://www.wsj.com/articles/chinas-ghost-towns-haunt-its-economy-1529076819. Accessed 6 May 2023.

about the size of the city of Atlanta, Georgia, 352 km² (136 sq. mi). But many other of these developments remain mostly empty, still waiting for occupants.[5]

And in the northwestern desert of Saudi Arabia an ambitious one-hundred-mile-long (160 km) project called "The Line" by NEOM (New Enterprise Operating Model) is currently under construction. The dreamchild of Crown Prince Mohammed bin Salman, it is slated to cover an area of 10,232 mi² (26,500 km²), larger than the city of Chicago, with an anticipated population of 9 million. Promising "a blueprint for tomorrow," it is intended to utilize smart technology, offer an alternative to the oil industry as the country's economic engine, and become a magnet for tourists that will stretch like a giant landing strip from the Red Sea coast far into the mainland.[6]

Like the "giga-projects" of Le Corbusier, Frank Lloyd Wright, and Robert Moses, I will discuss and critique in Chap. 8, these are architectural dream-developments based on cutting-edge technology and proposed for the very near future, or, as in the case of the ghost cities, that already exist. Chapter 9 examines some of these constructions in greater detail. (In that chapter and Chap. 10, I also address the challenge phenomena such as "virtual worlds" and "the metaverse" might pose for Jacobs's emphasis on face-to-face contact.) So, although architectural styles, construction technology, and design philosophies have changed, Jacobs's criticism of modern-day mega- and giga-projects are as germane

---

[5] Some scholars of planning admire this approach.

> American planners who travel to China risk coming back equally ruined, for they learn that their Chinese cousins have effectively charted the most spectacular period of urban growth and transformation in world history. They are then beset with an affliction far worse than the "Robert Moses envy" suffered, usually in silence, by an earlier generation of American planners. Here now is a nation that makes even Moses look small. Name any category of infrastructure and China has likely built more of it in the last 30 years, and bigger and faster, than any other nation on Earth—probably than all other nations combined. Long the poor man of Asia, China is now beating us at a game we once mastered—the game of building, and building big; the game of getting things done. (Campanella, 2011: 154–5)

[6] Mohammed bin Salman's entire vision is outline here, https://www.neom.com/en-us. Accessed 6 May 2023.

as they were during the heyday of Robert Moses's urban renewal or of Le Corbusier's "Radiant City" of a century ago.

In this chapter, I begin to make the case that beyond her critique of urban planning, which I discuss throughout this book, Jacobs made valuable and relevant contributions to economics and social theory, and that the theory of society underlying both her economics and her critique of urban planning is essentially the same as the social theory underlying so-called "market-process economics," which I outline below. Subsequent chapters will flesh out that argument in greater detail.

While my focus in this chapter is mainly on Jacobs as an economist, there are several preliminary issues that need to be addressed. The first is the basic question of whether Jacobs does indeed have a social theory. The second is how her particular concern with cities sets her apart from other urban commentators and how it aligns well with the traditional concerns of economics. The two sections following briefly deal with why we should regard the city as a basic unit of economic analysis and with the meaning of public space in this study. Finally, the last two sections detail why Jacobs is a serious contributor to economic theory and especially to market-process economics.

1   Does Jane Jacobs Have a Coherent Analytical Framework?

Yes, she does. It is true that in none of her writings does Jacobs fully articulate an explicit *social theory*, that is, a coherent set of principles explaining how social order arises and is sustained at different levels of analysis, that she then systematically links to her investigations of urban phenomena.[7] But that doesn't mean a definite social theory does not frame how she views and interprets the social world.

---

[7] As I mention later, she comes close to doing so in the final chapter of *Death and Life* and the first chapter of *The Economy of Cities*.

One example of a coherent arc that runs through Jacobs's world-view is the way the central themes of her major works "scale up" over time.[8] Proceeding chronologically, in *Death and Life* (1961) she explains what I call the "microfoundations" of the way physical design interacts with human activity to promote (or hamper) dynamically stable processes at the level of the neighborhood, the city district, and the city itself, and how this in turn generates the land-use diversity that fosters urban liveliness in a successful city. In *The Economy of Cities* (1969) she presents a theory of economic development that takes those microfoundations as given and then explains how different cities depend on one another to stimulate trade and spur local innovation. And in *Cities and the Wealth of Nations* (1984), she more carefully differentiates among various kinds of settlements (e.g., innovative cities, supply regions, transplant regions) and their roles, and then examines how economic development proceeds globally, through booms and busts, taking a more "macroeconomic" perspective than in her earlier books, though still dependent on their micro-lessons.

This perspective helps explain why in that first meeting, when I asked Jacobs what she thought her most important discovery was, she again answered without hesitation, "the fractal"! Now, one feature of fractal phenomena is symmetry at different scales of analysis. For example, how a satellite image of an irregular coastline appears the same as the irregular edge of a magnified puddle of water or how the same complex patterns appear at vastly different scales in computer-generated images such as a Mandelbrot Set.[9] I was puzzled by this at the time, but I think least part of what she meant had to do with this scalability, that the dynamics taking place at the level of a neighborhood still operate, mutatis mutandis, at the level of the city, city regions, up to the complex reality of global trade.

But why doesn't she fully articulate her social theory?

I believe it is partly owing to her method of conducting research. Jacobs describes her method (Jacobs, 1961: 440) as proceeding inductively by first observing patterns in daily life, looking for "unaverage"

---

[8] As noted in Chap. 1, I recently discovered that Richard Harris has also recognized this scalability in Jacobs's work (Page & Mennel, 2017).

[9] See James Gleick's (1987) classic treatment of these phenomena.

clues to explain how those patterns emerge, and thoroughly studying reports, articles, and books on a particular subject from which she then tries to infer sensible principles to help make sense of what she has observed, read, and thought (Zipp & Storring, 2016: 317–18). In other words, she doesn't begin with a set of principles from which she deduces conclusions. Rather, her method is inductive and, as she describes it, "pragmatic." Such pragmatism, at least in Jacobs's case, means her analytical framework tends to remain implicit.

My aim, of course, is to make that framework explicit, complementing it with insights from sociology, social network theory, and market-process economics. (As I explain below, market-process economics corresponds far more closely to Jacobs's economics than do standard microeconomics and macroeconomics, which are approaches Jacobs harshly criticizes for their lack of real-world relevance, a criticism I share.) The result, I believe, is a rich socioeconomic framework, grounded in a basic understanding of how and why a great city works that will help us to better address some of the most pressing issues of the social world. I hope to highlight valuable lessons economists can learn from Jacobs about economics and urbanism, and what insights admirers of Jacobs can learn about urbanism from her economics and social theory.

To reiterate, one of my primary motivations for writing this book is to make Jane Jacobs, economist, better known, especially to those who already rightly admire her for the other contributions she has made as a public intellectual; and that most of her criticisms of urban planning and design and of various public and private policies, which have gained supporters across the ideological spectrum,[10] issue from a coherent if mostly implicit social theory. My second aim then is, as I said, to draw attention to and develop that social theory.

---

[10] For example, Adam Gopnik wrote in *The New Yorker* in 2016: "Her admirers and interpreters tend to be divided into almost polar opposites: leftists who see her as the champion of community against big capital and real-estate development, and free marketeers who see her as the apostle of self-emerging solutions in cities. In a lovely symmetry, her name invokes both political types: the Jacobin radicals, who led the French Revolution, and the Jacobite reactionaries, who fought to restore King James II and the Stuarts to the British throne."

2   What Is Different About This Book and Jacobs's Approach to Cities?

The starting point for Jacobs's analysis and the focus of much of her thought is of course the city, its nature and significance. There are plenty of books about cities. Many describe cities as engines of economic development, wellsprings of art and culture, and incubators of ideas religious, social, and scientific. There are also books about the dark side of cities and city life. But few go very deeply into explaining how and why these are peculiarly urban phenomena. Fewer still view the urban processes as expressions of "emergence,"[11] or what some social theorists describe as a "spontaneous order." That is, however, the perspective of this book and its overall contribution: *To view through a Jacobsian lens what makes a city a spontaneous order and an engine of innovation, and to trace the analytical and policy consequences of viewing it this way.*[12]

Jane Jacobs is among those few who do, indeed the outstanding one. She is probably the first to carefully examine the nature and significance of great cities to distill realistic principles governing dynamic, urban systems and then to analyze the mechanisms of economic change and the policy implications that follow from those principles. Her analysis of the relation between the design of public spaces and the social interactions that take place within them (which is discussed in some detail in Chap. 4) offers insights that complement, and often exceed, other, more credentialed scholars of urban phenomena such as Max Weber, Henri Pirenne, Georg Simmel, and Kevin Lynch. I will explore these relations and the connections between her work and modern social theorists such as F.A. Hayek, Elinor Ostrom, Mark Granovetter, and Geoffrey West in the following chapters.

---

[11] Johnson defines "emergence" as the "movement from low-level rules to higher-level sophistication" (2002: 18). I elaborate on this concept in Chap. 3, which emphasizes the feature of wholes or patterns that cannot be reduced to their component parts.

[12] Other works take a spontaneous-order approach to analyzing cities, though not so explicitly from the perspective of Jane Jacobs. For example, see (Almazá, 2022), (Urhan 2011), Alain Bertaud (2018), and the excellent collections edited by Andersson (Andersson et al., 2011, Andersson & Moroni, 2014).

But Jacobs was not the first to develop conceptual tools congenial to understanding urban processes as emergent, spontaneous orders. They have in fact been largely available for decades in the field of economics, although few professional economists today, including urban economists, have fully appreciated the urban origins of many of their standard concepts and tools of analysis. In fact, there is a tradition in economics and social theory that takes an implicitly Jacobsian view of the world in this sense. As I will elaborate in Chap. 5, it is a tradition that follows from the work of Adam Smith, Carl Menger, Ludwig von Mises, F.A. Hayek, and Israel Kirzner, which is referred to as "market-process economics." Like Jacobs, this heterodox approach to economics sees social processes as the emergent, largely unplanned, and self-regulating outcome of people who know a great deal about their local environment, though very little about the larger social order in which they are embedded, but who with the right "rules of the game" can approach a high degree of social coordination. Like Jacobs, the market-process tradition is concerned with social dynamics and how ordinary people may be able to use their own local knowledge and resourcefulness to solve the unpredictable problems they regularly encounter in their daily lives, and how social institutions such as markets and market prices help them to do so in the presence of imperfect knowledge and scarcity through voluntary, often collective, action without resort to extensive central planning. Like Jacobs, the market-process tradition finds little use for the concept of economic efficiency and static equilibrium (for reasons I discuss in the next chapter) and instead places greater importance on individual incentives, entrepreneurial discovery, and innovation to drive ordering processes, and on specific social institutions that enable these processes over time to generate economic development. In the final section of this chapter, I spell out in some detail these connections between market-process economics and Jacobs's economics.

There are also important points of difference.

Whereas property rights and economic freedom, especially free entry into and exit out of markets, are front and center in market-process economics they are, as we will see, largely implicit but no less present in Jacobs's analysis. On the other hand, whereas the market-process tradition has always emphasized the role of market prices and social institutions in economic processes, only recently have the concepts of social capital, social networks, and trust—explicit components in Jacobs's analysis—begun to play a significant part in its solution to what I call the "central question of economics" outlined, below. Nor has the market-process approach gone into much detail on the *mechanisms* and the *spatial context* of entrepreneurial discovery, including land-use diversity in entrepreneurial development, and the part that physical proximity and social networks, personal contact, and the design of public spaces play in a flourishing economic system, all of which are central Jacobsian themes.

But one thing both Jacobsian and market-process economics do have strongly in common is seeing successful social orders as those that not only solve problems, but more fundamentally as those that discover and, in a sense, create the very problems that need to be solved, and in this reciprocal fashion, drive economic development and social change. Indeed, the key to integrating the Jacobsian and market-process perspectives in a way that fills in critical gaps in each is to see that the market process and the urban process are essentially the same social phenomenon: A city is a market and a market is a city. That is what I try to do, especially in Chap. 3.

With two outstanding exceptions, who I will discuss later, mainstream economists have mostly ignored Jacobs's theoretical work.

3 A Living City Is Not a Man-Made Thing

Architects and urban planners often use the term "built environment" to refer to things such as city streets and the grids they form, buildings of various kinds, plazas, the infrastructure of electricity and water inflow and waste outflow, and areas for parks and outdoor recreation. Although each of these urban elements are consciously designed and constructed wholly or in part, usually by teams of individuals, the way they adjust to one another *over time* is not the result of an overall plan, except in the case of very large-scale mega- and "giga-projects." Buildings in a particular location—for example, offices, schools, residences, retail shops, malls, entertainment, places of worship, research facilities—are of different ages, shapes, and sizes constructed by different people for different purposes in different eras with different techniques, historical contexts, sensibilities, and knowhow. The way they all more-or-less complement one another, however, their "fit," is mostly unplanned and spontaneous. That is, just as English or any living language evolves as a result of continual and unforeseen variations in usage and context over time and in different places, a living city also evolves as structures and their uses adjust unpredictably to ever-changing circumstances. Such adjustments are, as I will treat more rigorously in the next chapter, "the result of human action but not of human design."

A living city then is not and indeed cannot itself be man-made in the sense of being designed from top to bottom. While some of its constituent parts may be meticulously constructed at a given point in time, nevertheless, their structures and usages will change in ways the original designers did not intend or could not fully imagine.

4   Why We Will Be Focussing on Public Space

Our focus is on what goes on in a city's public spaces and so it is important to understand the difference between "public space" and "private space," as used here. That difference is about the relationship between us and others who may also use the space. "Public" and "private" in this sense have nothing necessarily to do with whether the space is controlled by a government entity or is privately owned. A coffeehouse may be privately owned but is typically a public space in our sense, while CIA headquarters in Langley, Virginia, is publicly (government) owned, but it is a private space.[13]

---

[13] Public space and private space correspond roughly to Jacobs's terms General Land and Special Land (Jacobs, 1961: 262–3).

4.1   Public Space Versus Private Space

Simply put, a *public space* is a place where we are likely to encounter people who are more or less strangers to us. They include people we pass on the sidewalk for a moment and never see again, a clerk at a local supermarket, patrons in a restaurant or shoppers in a mall, a specialist to whom our primary-care physician refers us, or a new neighbor whose name we don't yet know. They range from utter strangers to what Stanley Milgrom (1977) calls "familiar strangers." They may be "socially distant"[14] from us with different linguistic, cultural, ethnic, and religious backgrounds. A pubic space is where we would not be surprised to run into people like this.

A *private space* is a place where we are unlikely to encounter such strangers. These include our home, a private club, a company office, or a classroom at the end of a school year.

Of course, at any given time, we might regard a particular space as somewhere between public and private: a coffeehouse where we talk to the barista and a few of the regular customers; a restaurant where we regularly meet friends; a museum rented out for a private gala. And some specialized spaces, such as coffeehouses or bookstores or bars, are well-known for the serendipitous encounters between strangers and the subsequent connections they may enable. Again, the distinction between public and private space hinges on whether and the degree to which we know the people we expect to see there.

Moreover, the degree to which we feel comfortable enough to be in a particular public space depends, other things equal, on how safe we feel around strangers. And the larger the size or number of public spaces in a given location, the more likely we will encounter strangers there. So, feeling safe in public space becomes more of a challenge in a city, other things equal, the larger its population. This is something we will examine closely in Chap. 4.

---

[14] We take up this and related concepts in some depth in Chap. 5.

4.2   What Goes on Within the Built Environment Can Be Planned or Unplanned

Most structures are originally built for specific activities. As a specialized space, for example, a gas station is primarily for pumping gas, not playing football, which we are more likely to do at a stadium or park. But there are other activities, such as socializing or trading or entertaining, that take place in or are facilitated by more generalized spaces, such as embankments and plazas that are used in ways that their designers may indeed have taken broadly into account ("this plaza may be used for peaceful, unspecified, public gatherings") but not planned for, strictly speaking. These generalized public spaces can have significant consequences for a neighborhood or district over time by enabling or encouraging informal contact and interaction in the presence of strangers or by accommodating multiple uses.

Within a more specialized private space, such as a corporate office, value-creating-but-unplanned discoveries ("intrapreneurship"[15]) might also take place. The focus of this book, however, like Jacobs's *Death and Life*, is on public space and the unplanned social orders that arise within it. To make matters clearer, I can illustrate our subject-matter with the help of the following matrix (Fig. 2.1):

What happens in each cell of the matrix is important to the overall social process—the dynamics of family or office relationships, for example. But we will confine ourselves mainly to unplanned orders in public space.

5   The City Is a Relevant Unit of Economic Analysis

But why focus on cities? Why not nation-states or empires (Parker, 2004)?

---

[15] "Intrapreneurship is acting like an entrepreneur within an established company. It's creating a new business or venture within an organization. Sometimes that business becomes a new section, or department, or even a subsidiary spinoff" (Somers, 2018).

	Private Space	Public Space
Planned Order	HOME	MARCHING BAND
Unplanned Order	FAMILIAL RELATIONS	MARKETS & CITIES

Fig. 2.1 Space-order matrix

An underlying principle of Jacobs's economic framework is that, like individual choice, firms, and households in standard economics, a great city or living city is a natural unit of economic analysis. That is, like an individual or business or household, a great city arises spontaneously wherever economic development consistently takes place, perhaps, though not necessarily, after an act of deliberate creation, such as the granting of a charter. But a great city doesn't automatically appear where people might happen to settle. Historically, this took a very long time. Current estimates of the age of Homo sapiens range from about 250,000 to 350,000 years, but it is only in the last 10,000–12,000 years or so that large, permanent settlements took root and the story of human civilization began. (We examine some of this history in Chap. 6.)

In contrast, nation-states are deliberate political creations of recent origin with borders that are consciously created and rigidly maintained, especially against strong economic incentives to ignore them. Moreover, cities tend to endure far longer than the states that encompass them. As James E. Vance observes, the city is "...the most long-lived of all human physical creations" while "the nation-state, which seems so powerful and fundamental today, is a late and transitory successor to the enduring city"

(Vance, 1990: 23). And while it is widely accepted that cities are the locus of social change and cultural creativity, sometimes via politics but typically via economic development, nation-states are the locus of social stasis, cultural reaction, economic protectionism, and the principal players in war and violent political conflict.[16] "Whereas nation-states tend toward revolution and radical transformation, great cities tend toward tenacious endurance and evolution" (Vance, 1990: 23).

I am not arguing that nations-states as such cannot be units of analysis for economic theory and policy or for disciplines outside of economics such as political theory. But in that case, they are essentially units of political analysis or political economy, not purely economic entities. Economists study them because (1) political boundaries create constraints on economic processes that have interesting consequences (e.g., international trade, exchange-rate movements, deadweight losses of protectionism) and (2) public choosers (i.e., those who use political means to promote their interests) want to know the narrowly national implications of various economic events or public policies vis-à-vis other nation-states. Nation-states are central to macroeconomic theory and of fiscal and monetary policy, and Jacobs is harshly critical of macroeconomics for that reason (Jacobs, 1984: 6). But cities that have emerged or that have evolved organically over time, not political entities or municipalities (e.g., the City of Los Angeles versus the urbanized area of Los Angeles), are fundamentally different from nation-states.

As I will argue in Chap. 3, it may be useful to see the study of markets as coincident with the study of cities.[17] For instance, a surprising number of concepts in economics pertain mainly to large settlements and cities. Take the following familiar economic concepts:

- Competitive markets and impersonal exchange
- The price mechanism

---

[16] Sociologist and historian Charles Tilly (1982) famously argues that "war makes states," which he characterizes as monopolies of violence and identifies with "organized crime" and "protection rackets."

[17] I develop this argument in Ikeda (2007). https://link.springer.com/article/10.1007/s11138-007-0024-2

- Entrepreneurship and innovation
- Extensive division of knowledge and labor
- Complex structure of capital
- Externalities and public goods
- Comparative advantage and efficiency

Each of these has its origin or its greatest relevance in an urban setting. In the chapters that follow, I will clarify the close connection between most of these concepts and cities. Someone (it may have been Tip O'Neill, the late US House Speaker) once said, "All politics is local." One might also say without overstatement that all economic activity is urban. Innovation and the production (and usually also the consumption) of what Adam Smith refers to as the "necessaries, conveniences, and amusements" of life happen or get their start in a city.

6 Jane Jacobs, Economic Theorist

To begin making the case for Jacobs as an economist, I would like to make some general observations about her economics. Do keep in mind, however, that my principal aim is not to summarize the entire body of Jacobs's economic work. I am mainly interested in how her work relates to and fills gaps in economics and social theory, and I will be drawing extensively from elements of her economics and social theory to construct a coherent analytical framework integrated with market-process theory. This book is therefore not meant to be a "reader friendly" version of her work or a "Jane Jacobs for Dummies." Jacobs's writings are themselves eminently reader-friendly (though certainly not for dummies). For a clear and straightforward presentation of her economics, one can do no better than to read her books.

But some brief overview is necessary to get started, so this section covers three main areas. First, a summary of Jacobs's approach to economics and her overall economic framework. Again, the best source is to read her very readable books, especially *The Nature of Economies* and, if you are a little more ambitious, *The Economy of Cities* as well as *Cities and the Wealth of Nations*. I will discuss and elaborate on most aspects of her economics and social theory in some depth in the chapters that follow. (I indicate the relevant chapters as I go along.) Second, the parts of her economic thought that I disagree with or think are her weaker economic arguments. Finally, the most time is spent establishing why Jacobs really is a serious economic theorist and not someone who simply dabbles in the subject or merely a competent amateur who has not made original and important contributions to our economic understanding of the real world.

Having established that Jane Jacobs is a legitimate economic theorist, the section following this one addresses the question of the extent to which she is specifically a market-process economist.

6.1   Jacobsian Economics

Jacobsian economics is squarely city-based. Jacobs argues that most important economic questions center on economic development and that great cities are the main drivers of economic development, especially economic development through innovation (Chap. 6). While deliberate planning by individuals, organizations, and governments each have important roles to play in allowing order to emerge in the complex patterns and processes within a great city, that order is largely unplanned, and sensitive to the scale, scope, and design of attempts, whether by governmental or business entities, to deliberately shape the city (Chap. 3).

The fuel for innovation-centered economic development is what Jacobs terms "effective economic pools of use" conveniently located so that ordinary but resourceful people may discover worthwhile ways of fitting such uses together. These potential complementarities within effective economic pools of use are themselves the fruits of the unplanned diversity of land-uses within a city, generated in the context of public spaces where myriad strangers interact with one another in peace and safety. Jacobs identifies the generators of that diversity as certain conditions within great cities—that is, mixed primary uses, the intricacy of city blocks, population density, and affordable work and living space (Chap. 4). Furthermore, strangers are the crucial and indispensable ingredient for an innovative city, where both dynamic social networks and market competition serve as organizing principles, and where tolerance and inclusivity rather than distrust and exclusivity are the norm. With those elements present, innovation and economic development can take place (Chap. 5).

For Jacobs, the keys to that development are "import-replacement" and "import shifting." The process of import-replacement consists of entrepreneurs drawing mostly on local resources—those effective pools of economic use—discovering ways to create local replacements for imported goods and services, which in turn allows locals to shift the revenues they earn from exports to purchase more or different imports (Chap. 6). Finally, poorly chosen policies for urban improvement and attempts to impose utopian visions can undermine the diversity and pools of effective use essential for innovative economic development. This is what motivates Jacobs's attack on the urban planning of her day and animates her heterodox economic analysis and policy recommendations (Chaps. 7, 8, and 9).

(Note again that in fleshing out Jacobsian economics, I will be filling in what I see as gaps with market-process concepts; I will also be fleshing out market-process economics with important Jacobsian insights. This may have the appearance of cherry-picking, but I believe I am presenting in these pages enough of Jacobs's socioeconomic ideas to give an accurate and fairly inclusive picture of her original economics and social theory.)

6.2   Where I Disagree with Jacobs

There are some economic and policy ideas of Jacobs's that I disagree with. I will point most of these out as they arise in the chapters that follow. There are two, however, that I think are worth mentioning at the outset. The first is her qualified advocacy of protective tariffs, which is not so much wrongheaded as ignorant of important realistic considerations in the political economy of interest groups. I address this in the Appendix to Chap. 6 ("On the Need for Tariffs"). The second is her vagueness on the nature of what constitutes economic value, which is worth noting because value theory is at the heart of most systems of economic thought (with important exceptions that I will mention). While important, my disagreements are not serious enough dissuade me from the utility of her socioeconomic framework.

6.3   Jane Jacobs as an Economist[18]

One way to demonstrate Jacobs's standing as a serious economic thinker, and not merely a dabbler in economics, is to enumerate some basic criteria for what it means to be an economist and then examine the extent to which she meets these criteria in her published work. But what criteria to use?

I have taught economics since 1986 at the university level. While some might regard my approach to doing economic analysis as somewhat heterodox,[19] my approach to teaching an introduction to "the economic way of thinking" departs little from the mainstream, and so I feel confident in using my own criteria to evaluate Jacobs's standing as an economist. Still, I appreciate that the reader may disagree with my criteria. To partly address this, I will first invoke the opinion of two widely respected economists, one a Nobel Prize winner, in support of Jacobs's *qua* economist.

6.3.1   Economists on Jane Jacobs

The first is Robert Lucas, the 1995 Nobel Laureate in economics. In an article, "On the Mechanism of Economic Development" published in *Journal of Monetary Economics* in 1988, Lucas states that in seeking the significance to economic development of what he terms "external human capital," he will closely follow the path laid out in Jacobs's *The Economy of Cities* (1969a) which he calls "remarkable" and "highly suggestive."

The second is the urban economist Edward Glaeser, who terms these external effects of human capital "Jacobs spillovers" and finds that they

---

[18] Here, I again mention the work by Charles-Albert Ramsay (2022), published as I was completing the manuscript for this book, which argues as I do for greater recognition of Jacobs's contribution to economics. Purely by coincidence, the subtitle of his book and the heading of this subsection are nearly identical. For a succinct and accessible treatment of Jacobs's economics, sans discussion of social theory and with a different emphasis on policy issues, one could not go wrong by reading his book.

[19] I am, as it should be clear by now, a student of economics in the tradition of Carl Menger, Eugen von Böhm-Bawerk, Ludwig von Mises, F.A. Hayek, and Israel M. Kirzner, among others, in other words "market-process economics," some details of which I will make explicit in the text.

better explain differences in labor productivity than competing concepts. His analysis and results were published in an oft-cited article, "On the Mechanism of Economic Development," in the *Journal of Political Economy* (Glaeser et al., 1992: 1126–1152).

Lucas, Glaeser, and others, including popular economist Richard Florida (2014), validate Jacobs's *insights* as having important economic implications, but they do not per se establish Jacobs's credentials as an economist. After all, some political economists cite Abraham Lincoln's dictum—"You can fool some of the people all of the time and all of the people some of the time, but you can't fool all of the people all of the time"[20]—but that doesn't make Lincoln a political economist.

Yet it would be extremely unusual for an amateur or a mere dabbler to publish in a top-tier economics journal, and Jacobs did just that in 1969 with her "Strategies for Helping Cities" (Jacobs, 1969b) in the prestigious *American Economic Review*. The article outlines the main themes of her book, published earlier that year, *The Economy of Cities* (1969a).

Next, we look now at how Jacobs approaches her subject matter in order to determine the extent to which her approach is essentially economic.

6.3.2 What Is Economics?

When I teach introductory economics, I frame the body of economic theory around a statement that I call "The Central Question of Economics":

> How, in the presence of scarcity, human and natural diversity, and imperfect knowledge, does social order emerge among myriad, self-interested strangers?

Other than the mention of "imperfect knowledge," this is pretty standard microeconomic stuff.[21]

---

[20] Public-choice economists often refer to this as "Lincoln's Law."

[21] In the final section of this chapter I explain in what way this makes my economics heterodox.

Economics helps us to understand how markets turn these challenging conditions—scarcity, diversity, ignorance—into virtues by transforming the potential inter-personal conflicts they create into useful complementarities by examining the *institutions* that enable myriad self-interested strangers to cooperate, directly and indirectly, intentionally, but mostly unintentionally. That is precisely what Jacobs does in *Death and Life*.

In economics, the institutions that usually do the heavy lifting include property rights, norms of free association and tolerance, and stable rules limiting fraud and coercion and maximizing the scope of voluntary individual action. These three factors are usually associated with the concept of "economic freedom" (Gwartnery et al., 2019). The idea of economic freedom is mostly implicit in Jacobs. However, the unplanned, large-scale street-level and interpersonal cooperation that is one of her main concerns presupposes that people own the resources (human and natural) they buy and sell in cities, that they do so without unwanted interference from others and, of course, without having to obey a comprehensive central plan. But by the same token, modern economic theory has only fairly recently begun to appreciate the role of social capital and social networks and other "invisible" social infrastructures that Jacobs pioneered in 1961 and, as she argues and that I argue in this book, constitute the broader institutional matrix for economic development.

But to what extent does Jacobs's research program address the Central Question of Economics, and to what extent is her answer to it a recognizably economic one? Let us take the following factors in order: scarcity, diversity, ignorance, strangers, and social order.

Scarcity Some view scarcity—that is, when consuming more of one valuable resource entails sacrificing some amount of another—as the starting point of economics. In a world of scarcity you have to make trade-offs. Like many prominent economic theorists in the twentieth century, however, Jacobs doesn't make this the explicit starting point or principal focus of her work. Indeed, as we will see in Chap. 3, Jacobs fought against a fixation with efficiency, which is doing something with the least sacrifice, and so by implication she fought against a fixation with the problem of scarcity.[22] From this perspective, coping with scarcity and efficiency take a back seat to innovating and reducing scarcity. Nevertheless, she is not guilty of "magical thinking" by ignoring scarcity. She clearly recognizes that trade-offs are unavoidable in the real world of scarce resources and never ignores costs in her analysis. Indeed, the failure of planners to recognize the trade-offs they incur in their urban planning is the raison *d'être* of *Death and Life*.

Modern economics teaches us that market prices reflect the relative scarcities of resources (e.g., Landsburg, 2013). When real-estate becomes scarcer, its market price goes up relative to, say, the cost of construction, and so, other things equal, developers will build taller buildings. A clear understanding of how market prices tend to reflect such scarcities and how they also help to coordinate the plans of countless people is indeed an indicator of economic intelligence. While this is mostly absent in her earlier works, by her 2000 book, *The Nature of Economies*, Jacobs clearly grasps how market prices provide feedback to buyers and sellers about the scarcity of resources. This dialog from that book is an example.

> "Price feedback is inherently well integrated," said Hiram. "It's not sloppy, not ambiguous. As [Adam] Smith perceived, the data carry meaningful information on imbalances of supply and demand and they do automatically trigger corrective responses." (Jacobs, 2000: Loc 1629)

She also understood how price regulations and subsidies distort this feedback process.

> New York City failed to abandon rent controls instituted after civilian construction was halted during the Second World War; then, as anachronisms, ironically, rent controls depressed construction. (Jacobs, 2000: Loc 1728)

And in her last published book, *Dark Age Ahead*, she points out

---

[22] In the language of economics, Jacobs was most concerned with the problem of how we push out the "production possibilities frontier" or, better, how we create brand new, hitherto undiscovered production possibility frontiers?

Rent controls helped check the avarice of profiteering landlords. Evictions for inability to meet rent increases diminished or halted. But otherwise, on balance, rent control was counterproductive, because it did nothing to correct the core problem, the lack of new or decently maintained affordable housing, the missing supply that was a legacy of fifteen years of depression and war. (Jacobs, 2004: 142)

In other words, high rents reflect the relative scarcity of housing, which fixing rents too low with regulations did nothing to address.

Human and Natural Diversity I mentioned earlier that one of the ideas Jacobs's followers often single-out is "diversity," but it is important to note that when Jacobs uses "diversity" in *Death and Life*, she is referring primarily to the diversity of land-use, rather than to racial or gender diversity. More broadly, of course, that diversity of land-use derives from the diversity of the perspectives, knowledge, backgrounds, and tastes of the people who use that land, which in turn can be traced to some extent to their economic, cultural, racial, ethnic, and gender differences. In any case, as we have seen, this diversity of land-use is for Jacobs a primary desideratum because, other things equal, greater land-use diversity in a public space creates the effective economic pools of use that fuel the discovery of value-creating complementarities.

Imperfect Knowledge If knowledge were perfect, we wouldn't really need cities (and the social networks in them). Perfect knowledge means we never make mistakes or miss any opportunities that matter. A city brings diverse people together so that they can learn and connect with one another and discover opportunities for mutual benefit they didn't know about, which is also what a market does. If everyone is perfectly aware of all such opportunities, there is no economic reason for them to gather to exchange information, in either a city or a market. The *raison d'être* of a great city and the markets and social networks that constitute it is the presence of "radical ignorance" or "not knowing that you don't know something" in the real world (Kirzner, 1973), which I discuss at greater length in the final section of this chapter and in Chap. 4. Jacobs makes this point in many ways, one of which is her observation that urban planning fails when planners lack what she calls "locality knowledge" (Jacobs, 1961), a close relation to what Nobel laureate F.A. Hayek terms "local knowledge" or "the knowledge of the particular circumstances of time and place" (Hayek, 1945). (More about this in the penultimate section of this chapter.) That lack of locality knowledge means planners' ambitions must be far more modest than the Le Corbusiers and the Robert Moseses Jacobs attacked, and more sensitive to the needs, knowledge, and resourcefulness of the inhabitants of a city.[23]

Strangers The word "stranger" appears 36 times just in chapter 2 of *Death and Life of Great American Cities*, alone, and about 41 times total in the first 100 pages of the book. Indeed, the underlying theoretical question there is precisely how millions of strangers cooperate sufficiently to generate a flourishing order? In Jacobs's own words

> The bedrock attribute of a successful city district is that a person must feel personally safe and secure on the street among all these strangers. (Jacobs, 1961: 30)

As we will see in Chap. 5, this emphasis on socially distant strangers is central to her analysis of what makes a great city creative and innovative.

Social Order Essentially, what Jacobs seeks to explain in *Death and Life* is how the interaction of individuals, all following their own plans and armed with locality knowledge, generates an unplanned but stable social order of neighborhood communities with their supporting networks. The nature of that order is, as she refers to it in the final chapter of that book, characterized by "organized complexity." The coordinating mechanisms for Jacobs are social networks and the price mechanism, as I will discuss in Chaps. 5 and 6, respectively.

---

[23] I should mention that assuming perfect knowledge is also a vice common among economists, justifiable at times when we try to see the ideal end states to which real-world forces may be tending, for example in models of perfect competition or pure monopoly. As I explain later, Jacobs's dispute with such economists is one of the things that places her in the camp of market-process economists.

Organized complexity is something economists have been concerned with since the French Physiocrats and Adam Smith in the eighteenth century, and a century later in the writings of Carl Menger (theory of the evolution of money [1883]) and Léon Walras (general equilibrium theory [1977]). Indeed, one of the on-going controversies in economics from the early twentieth century to the present day is whether central planners can deliberately and successfully construct a complex social order on a system-wide scale. This controversy is known as the debate over the possibility of rational economic calculation under pure socialism or the "socialist calculation debate" for short. One of the defining features of market-process economics is a profound skepticism about this possibility. In the final section of this chapter, I address the question of which side of the debate Jacobs falls, although the reader may have already guessed.

To be fair, however, it is possible to fully embrace the concept of organized complexity and still believe people can consciously create organized complexity. In other words, organized complexity is not the same thing as spontaneous order. But the context in which Jacobs uses the idea in *Death and Life*—for example, the sidewalk ballet, social capital, social networks, safety and trust, economic development, and her critique of ill-informed planning—makes it clear that it is precisely the unplanned, spontaneous character of the great city that she identifies as the source of a city's organized complexity.

6.4   Summary

Those who have only read *The Death and Life of Great American Cities* might easily fail to notice Jane Jacobs the economist. In one sense, as I suggested in the last chapter, most of her readers tend to focus almost exclusively on Part One of that book on "The Peculiar Nature of Cities" with its detailed study of the use of city sidewalks, memorable imagery of the "sidewalk ballet," and analysis of city neighborhoods, while overlooking the strong economic themes she develops in the rest of the book, especially Part Two on "The Conditions for City Diversity." Obviously, then, to claim as I do that Jacobs had a great deal worthwhile to say about economics is not in any way to discount her contributions to urban planning, urban sociology, and political theory. On the contrary, my overall point is that her insights in all these areas issue from a common social theory or socioeconomic framework.[24]

But to the specific question of whether it is reasonable to regard Jane Jacobs as an important economic thinker, the answer is an unqualified yes. First, she self-identifies as an economic thinker. Second, eminent economists have acknowledged her inspiration in their own work. Third, she has published in highly prestigious economic journals. Fourth, her work meets the criteria of what constitutes an economic point of view by engaging the problems of scarcity, human and natural diversity, imperfect knowledge, and how countless strangers can form a stable and complex social order. And while she doesn't employ sophisticated mathematics, the preferred tool of many though not all economists, she does construct abstract models of economic development in her characteristically idiosyncratic way (Jacobs, 1969a: 252–61). As will become more evident as we proceed, she understands the nature and significance of prices and markets, of innovation, and of entrepreneurship. Crucially, Jacobs locates these phenomena in the urban context and she uses them in her economic analysis.

7   Jane Jacobs, Market-Process Theorist

While Jacobs is often skeptical of schemes to extend government intervention, especially of course in the area of urban planning and design, and seeks solutions to problems that we would today characterize as market-based, she is no advocate of unregulated, free-market economics. She doesn't reject all urban planning and indeed favors zoning restrictions on the size and form of buildings, limited landmarks and heritage preservation, housing subsidies to developers and landlords, and, as we have seen, even tariffs to protect import-replacing activities (although she was mindful of the downsides to this policy). This, of course, doesn't

---

[24] On the other hand, as I point out in the Introduction, it would take a real effort to miss Jacobs's sustained preoccupation with economic theory and policy in her subsequent books.

disqualify her from being a market-process theorist, contrary to what many people believe, including some advocates of market-process economics, themselves. So then what are the hallmarks of market-process economics? As I have written elsewhere:

> [Market-process economists], in particular, have consistently stressed, in contrast with the mainstream of the profession, the role of social institutions, the prevalence of inefficiency and discoordination, the relative importance of processes over endstates, the centrality of entrepreneurial discovery in the market process, and the nature and significance of spontaneous orders. (Ikeda, 2007: 215)

More succinctly, the editor of *The Elgar Companion to Austrian Economics* Peter J. Boettke identifies three methodological tenets that characterize market-process or what some call "Austrian Economics": methodological individualism, methodological subjectivism, and market process (Boettke, 1994: 4). Taking these as our criteria, then, to what extent can we say that Jane Jacobs is a market-process economist?

Jacobs herself in the final chapter of *Death and Life* outlines the following ways of thinking about cities.

> In the case of understanding cities, I think the most important habits of thought are these:
>
> 1. To think about processes
> 2. To work inductively, reasoning from particulars to the general, rather than the reverse
> 3. To seek for "unaverage" clues involving very small quantities, which reveal the way larger and more "average" quantities are operating (Jacobs, 1961: 440)

It might be useful to try to relate these "habits of thought" to the tenets outlined in Boettke (1994) as closely as possible:

Methodological Individualism The building blocks of any explanation for Jacobs—for example, of safety, trust, social capital—are the actions of individuals and how, for example, the design of a public space impacts their interaction, especially when those interactions result in complex, dynamic, and unpredictable patterns and processes that take place in living and dying cities. I believe this is what she means in #3 when she admonishes us to "seek 'unaverage' clues involving small quantities." One of her jabs at urban planners is that they tend to be concerned exclusively with "statistical people" (Jacobs, 1961: 136) rather than actual, flesh-and-blood people who operate in cities and how they interact with their urban environment.

Methodological Subjectivism Moreover, one of her most-quoted phrases is "eyes on the street," which refers to the individual perceptions and observations of ordinary people in their daily lives following their own plans. How they regard others in public spaces, and their safety and trust in them, is for Jacobs the starting point for understanding why some urban environments are successful and others are not.

Market Process Certainly "to think about processes," by which she means social processes that take place over time, is consistent with the market-process concern, not with equilibrium end states, but to processes that may tend toward those end states and the patterns that emerge within those processes. And as we will see, Jacobs uses economic theory to help us understand economic development, the nature of which is dynamics and not stasis; it is an evolutionary approach in which the passage of time plays a significant role: "The constructive factor that has been operating here meanwhile is time. Time, in cities, is the substitute for self-containment. Time, in cities, is indispensable" (Jacobs, 1961:133).

Beyond these methodological characteristics, what other features of Jacobs's economics are characteristically market-processual?

Ignorance and Imperfect Knowledge This is part of the Central Question of Economics. Without going into great detail here, one of the principles of modern market-process economics is that in the real-world people never have all the relevant information they need to perfectly execute their plans (Hayek, 1945, Kirzner, 1973). As I mentioned earlier, the *raison d'être* of great cities and the markets and social networks that define them is the presence of radical ignorance (i.e., not knowing that you don't know something) and radical uncertainty (i.e., uncertainty that is inherently unquantifiable) in the real world. Moreover, absent such ignorance and uncertainty, gathering in cities or anywhere else would be largely unnecessary. One of the main ways we learn is through contact with others, and so the need for such contact disappears when there is nothing more to learn. When planners ignore this they endanger the life of a city.

Role of Entrepreneurship A central element of modern market-process economics is an appreciation of entrepreneurship as the driving force of the market (Kirzner, 2000). This includes the discovery of previously unexploited profit opportunities, particularly discoveries that generate innovation. For Jacobs (1969a: 49) innovation involving what she calls "new work" is the essence of economic development (Chap. 6). For example, her narrative in the opening chapter of *The Economy of Cities* (1969a) is focused on how the causes and conditions of the discovery of agriculture, among the greatest innovations in human history, uniquely emerge in large, diverse settlements.

Knowledge Problem As we will see, what has come to be known as "the knowledge problem" is of central concern to both the economics and social theory of market process economics. It arises when knowledge relevant to the success of a design or plan is both *dispersed* across the minds of very many individuals and dependent on the local *context* of that knowledge (i.e., dependent on the circumstances of and interpretations in a particular place and time).

While there are many examples of Jacobs's appreciation of the knowledge problem, one of the best appears in the penultimate chapter of *Death and Life*:

> In truth, because of the nature of the work to be done, almost all city planning is concerned with relatively small and specific acts done here and done there, in specific streets, neighborhoods and districts. To know whether it is done well or ill—to know what should be done at all—it is more important to know that specific locality than it is to know how many bits in the same category of bits are going into other localities and what is being done

with them there. No other expertise can substitute for *locality knowledge* in planning, whether the planning is creative, coordinating or predictive. (Jacobs, 1961: 418; emphasis added)

The recognition of the problem of local, contextual knowledge to planning of all kinds at all levels of decision-making is a fundamental principle of the social theory of market-process economics and, I will argue, Jacobs's socioeconomic framework.

Subjective Value Theory The genesis of market-process economics is Carl Menger's exposition in 1871 of the subjective marginal-utility theory of value—that value is in the eyes of the beholder—in contrast to the then prevailing objective or labor theory of value, in which economic value does not depend on subjective perceptions but is inherent in a resource or commodity. It is in this area of economic theory where Jacobs is perhaps the least market-process oriented, insofar as she is never entirely clear about what she means by value. This need not constitute a serious divergence from the market-process perspective. Why not?

Let us first recognize that she seems to assume that the reader knows what she means when she speaks of the value of something, which varies between a kind of labor-theory of value (in which the economic value of a good derives from the amount of labor that has gone into its production) to at times a more modern concept of subjective (marginal) value (in which the value of the good depends on its usefulness to someone for something). For example, when she writes about economic development, there is an almost exclusive focus in both *The Economy of Cities* (1969) and *The Nature of Economies* (2000) on the creation of jobs, or in the case of economic development what she calls "new work" that is reminiscent of the economics of John Maynard Keynes, who fashioned a "labor-based" macroeconomics (Garrison, 2000).

This conflation of work, jobs, and sometimes even energy is also evident in Jacobs's discussion of imports and exports. For example she writes: "What are exports? End products of a settlement's economy, that's what. They're discharges of economic energy" (Ibid: Loc. 782). And elsewhere: "Works of art are extreme and vivid examples of import stretching, but other kinds of producers also stretch imports" (Ibid: Loc. 852). But goods don't derive their value ultimately merely from "stretching" (a market-processian might say "lengthening the structure of production"), as important as that may be in an economy, and we cannot simply assume that what we call "art" always has value.

As a trained economist understands, imports not exports are the *raison d'être* for trade. Exports buy imports, just as the revenue from what we sell to others gives us the wherewithal to purchase things from others. Jacobs, in explaining economic development, tends to focus on the production-side and less on the demand-side of the process. But from exports to resource endowments, Jacobs seems to assume that whatever is produced or used in production *ipso facto* has value, without articulating the nature of this value or clearly identifying its source (e.g., Jacobs [2000: Loc 819]), which in modern economics is what the end users of the product *subjectively* perceive that value to be. Again, value lies in the beholder and is not inherent or embodied in whatever is beheld. I wonder if this is a result of Jacobs's focus on the details of the process of economic development, so that the idea of value gets lost in the background? This is worth dwelling on for a moment.

Jacobs (speaking through one of her characters in *The Nature of Economies*) says:

> "If exports are a settlement's economic discharges, then what are its received infusions of economic energy?" Murray asked rhetorically. "Imports! Besieging armies and blockading navies have always known that." (Ibid: Loc 795)

Imports can be seen as *inputs* for the exported *outputs*. But the ultimate purpose of trade at the level of the individual or the city is consumption. To call exports "economic discharges" then is misleading, but Jacobs does recognize that they are not lost entropically to the system "because payments for exports buy imports" (Ibid: Loc 804). And it is clear that Jacobs avoids the discredited mercantilist error, common to this day, of valuing exports over imports (Chap. 6).

She does sometimes hint at a subjective concept of value, as in this passage:

"Joel and Jenny were producing services," said Hiram. "You can't call their work of searching, sampling, assembling, and distributing 'nothing.' They were adding human capital to other matter/energy in the city conduit. What Joel, Jenny, and their salesmen added was sufficiently concrete and *useful* to purchasers of findings to be worth part of the cost of the items." (Ibid: Loc 859; emphasis mine)

Like J.M. Keynes's obsession with employment, Jacobs's focus on "new work" in the process of innovation (Jacobs, 1969a, 1969b: 49) sometimes seems to suggest a classical, labor-theory of value. And, again, in her *The Nature of Economies* it almost seems as though "energy" rather than subjective value drives the economic system.

It's a muddle.

Did she clearly articulate a theory or value in her writings? No, but in the end that is not a requirement to qualify as an economist or even a market-process economist. Self-identified market-process economists, including myself, have not done so, and neither do others whom many consider strongly sympathetic to market-process economics, such as Nobel Prize winner Elinor Ostrom.

The Role of Institutions Jacobs sees the city as a fundamental economic unit of analysis and as a collection of complementary, evolving institutions: for example, the built environment along with the invisible infrastructure of norms, social networks, social capital, and neighborhoods. Indeed, the city itself, as a whole, is a social institution. In this sense, institutions of one kind or another are certainly central to Jacobs's socioeconomic framework.

Spontaneous Order The founder of the so-called Austrian School of economics, Carl Menger, made this relevant observation regarding "new localities":

As a rule, however, new localities arise "unintentionally," i.e., by the mere activation of individual interests which of themselves lead to the above result [the unintended result, as the unplanned outcome of specifically individual efforts of members of a society] furthering the common interest, i.e., without any intention really directed toward this. (Menger, 1883: Book 3, Chapter 2, Section 4(b)

As I argue in Chap. 3, the last chapter of *Death and Life* concerns the organized complexity of cities while the first chapter of Jacobs's next book, *The Economy of Cities*, is explanation not only of how that organized complexity emerges unplanned, but the innovations that take place within it also emerge unplanned. Cities are spontaneous orders *par excellence* and spontaneous order is *the* central concept of the social theory underpinning market-process economics.

Critique of Macroeconomics Jacobs's critique of macroeconomics is scathing. Moreover, it overlaps the core disagreements that market-process economists have leveled against it.

> [W]e must be suspicious that some basic assumption or other is in error, most likely an assumption so much taken for granted that it escapes identification and skepticism. Macro-economic theory does contain such an assumption. It is the idea that national economies are useful and salient entities for understanding how economic life works and what its structure may be: that national economies and not some other entity provide the fundamental data for macro-economic analysis. (Jacobs, 1984: 29)

She thus questioned whether nation-states, unlike cites, are natural units of economic analysis.

> Nations are political and military entities, and so are blocs of nations. But it doesn't necessarily follow from this that they are also the basic, salient entities of economic life or that they are particularly useful for probing the mysteries of economic structure, the reasons for rise and decline of wealth. (Jacobs, 1984: 31)

Instead, as I argued earlier, cities are natural units of economic analysis. The book she wrote after *Death and Life* does become increasingly more oriented toward macro entities. But this doesn't make Jacobs a methodological holist any more than a microeconomist who studies macroeconomic phenomena, such as aggregate national income or economic development, from a microeconomic perspective of knowledge and incentives must be a methodological holist. The key for the microeconomist and for Jacobs is that what constitutes a satisfactory explanation of a phenomenon—whether market prices or inflation—can be traced back to the actions and perceptions of individuals. Jacobs is a methodological individualist and a methodological subjectivist, and in *Death and Life* (perhaps less so in subsequent writings until *The Nature of Economies*) this is precisely how she explains urban phenomena.

Modern macroeconomics disregards the concept of capital complementarities in the structure of production. Jacobs in *The Nature of Economies*, her use of the concept of "codevelopment" and the interdependency of economic variables in the process of economic development, as well as her discussion of "biomass" (Jacobs, 2000: Loc 708) and the complexity of the division of labor, is fully consistent with the market-process concept of complementarity through time among heterogeneous units of capital (Lachmann, 1978). For instance, one of Jacobs's characters observes:

> "Many imports, even after they're initially transformed or otherwise stretched, are then passed around some more, fragmented, recombined, recycled, and stretched further." (Jacobs, 2000: Loc 867)

As I mentioned earlier, putting her treatment of value to one side, "import stretching" in Jacobs's analysis plays a very similar role in increasing value-productivity that "lengthening the capital-structure of production" to increase the value of consumption goods at the end of the process plays in the market-process framework, explicated by Hayek. In this theory, net investment in complementary capital in an economy, other things equal, increases the number of stages of production in the system—a sort of division of labor and knowledge over time—and the overall length of the production process, which results in an increase in the value of the consumer goods at the end of the process (Hayek, 1935). (I develop the theme of capital complementarity in Jacobs in Chap. 4.)

Critique of Microeconomics Like market-process economics, Jacobs's approach to economic analysis is decidedly microeconomic, although in

The Economy of Cities, she takes a more sectoral view of the economy and of the relation among different regional urban economies. Nevertheless, in line with the "fractal" nature of her overall vision described at the beginning of this chapter, all of her economic analysis is grounded methodologically in the actions and creations of individual agents. And as I noted earlier, she clearly recognizes the important feedback role of prices (Jacobs, 2000), even though she does not articulate a well-developed theory of price formation.

In standard microeconomics, individual incentives are a driving force of the market process, likewise in *Death and Life*, Jacobs takes an individual, "street-level" approach to understanding and explaining how urban social orders emerge and operate. "Eyes on the street," as noted earlier, is a good example of her methodological subjectivism. I also noted that after *Death and Life*, Jacobs's concern shifts toward macroeconomic analysis: How do the import and export sectors interact, how do urban economies interact, how do economies develop over time, etc.? Unlike traditional macroeconomics, however, Jacobs's macroeconomics remains grounded methodologically on the microeconomic foundations established in *Death and life*.

Like market-processians, and unlike standard microeconomics, Jacobs is highly critical of the efficiency criterion, and is more focused on the processes of economic development and innovation, which is characteristic of market-process economics (Kirzner, 1973, 1997). This is because a great city is particularly geared to facilitate the discovery of overlooked opportunities, opportunities thrown up constantly, which would not exist in a city that was already perfectly efficient. (I will pursue the idea of the experimental nature of urban processes owing to imperfect knowledge in Chap. 6.) About the desirability of efficiency in a city, Jacobs has this to say:

> Cities are indeed inefficient and impractical compared with towns; and among cities themselves, the largest and most rapidly growing at any given time are apt to be the least efficient. But I propose to argue that these grave and real deficiencies are necessary to economic development and thus are exactly what make cities uniquely valuable to economic life. *By this, I do not mean that cities are economically valuable in spite of their inefficiency and*

impracticality but rather because they are inefficient and impractical. (1969a: 85–86; emphasis added)

I will develop this important argument in the next chapter.

Critique of Central Planning One of the features of market-process economics that sets it apart from other approaches is its epistemic critique of collectivist central planning (a.k.a. socialism). That critique is a direct implication of the knowledge problem and it continues to be a source of ideas and inspiration for a diverse range of research to this day, including urban economics.[25] Pioneered by Ludwig von Mises (1981[1922]) just after the Bolshevik Revolution, it focuses on the inability of a central planner to utilize resources rationally, owing to the absence of private property in and money prices for inputs (e.g., labor and capital) and outputs (e.g., consumer goods). Without money prices, it is impossible for planners to calculate profits and losses, which are the means by which they are able to tell whether they are wasting resources. Later, F.A. Hayek (1945) argued that without the signals that market prices provide, planners cannot effectively harness dispersed and contextual knowledge to coordinate the innumerable plans of multitudes of anonymous strangers in a dynamic, complex economy.

Similarly, Jacobs broke onto the intellectual and policy scene with her devastating take-down of the heavy-handed central planning at the local level à la the planner, Robert Moses, and the dubious theoretical support to such planning offered, for example, by the pioneering urban designer, Le Corbusier. She later expressed her skepticism of socialist economic planning at the national level, itself.

> Nobody places more faith in the nation as the suitable entity for analyzing economic life and its prospects than the rulers of Communist and socialist countries, nor more faith in the State as the salient instrument for shaping economies. (Jacobs, 1984: 31)

---

[25] See, for example, the topics covered in Boettke and Coyne (2015).

And we have seen that the principal obstacle to effective central planning for Jacobs, as for market-process economics, is the lack of locality knowledge on the part of the planners. She was consistent in the principles of her critique, as witnessed by this passage in her last book (which I will cite again in Chap. 7), in which she explicitly invokes the knowledge problem:

> Central planning, whether by leftists or conservatives, draws too little on local knowledge and creativity, stifles innovations, and is inefficient and costly because it is circuitous. It bypasses intimate and varied knowledge directly fed back into the system. (Jacobs, 2004: 117)

As Jacobs says in *Death and Life*, "big cities are just too big and too complex to be comprehended in detail from any vantage point—even if this vantage point is at the top—or to be comprehended by any human" (Jacobs, 1961: 121–2). While there is no evidence that Jacobs was aware of the Mises–Hayek critique of central planning, nevertheless the epistemic grounds for both critiques are essentially the same.

8   Concluding Thoughts

Jacobs's insights into urban planning and design are still relevant today and so, too, is the framework of analysis, her social theory, that informs those insights. What distinguishes Jacobs's approach from other urbanists is precisely the socioeconomic nature of that framework. Although she has no formal degree or academic affiliation, Jane Jacobs should be widely acknowledged first and foremost as an exceptional economic thinker and indeed, as we will see in the pages that follow, an important one. Moreover, Jacobs's economics lies squarely in the tradition of modern market-process economics. Economists working within other traditions, especially complexity theory, might also legitimately claim her as their own. But in terms of her general orientation, the methods she uses to identify and then address social phenomena, and the policy conclusions she draws from them, market-processians may have the stronger claim.

Finally, while there are gaps in Jacobs's socioeconomic framework that modern mainstream economics and market-process economics can fill, the following chapters will show that the reverse is also true, that Jacobs's contributions to economics and social theory fill important gaps in the prevailing economic point of view.

Works Cited

Almazán, Jorge + Studiolab. (2022). *Emergent Tokyo: Designing the Spontaneous City*. ORO.

Andersson, D. E., & Moroni, S. (2014). *Cities and Private Planning: Property Rights, Entrepreneurship and Transaction Costs*. Edward Elgar.

Andersson, D. E., Andersson, Å. e., & Mellander, C. (Eds.). (2011). *Handbook of Creative Cities*. Edward Elgar.

Bertaud, A. (2018). *Order Without Design: How Markets Shape Cities*. MIT Press.

Boettke, P. J. (Ed.). (1994). *The Elgar Companion to Austrian Economics*. Edward Elgar.

Boettke, P. J., & Coyne, C. (Eds.). (2015). *The Oxford Handbook of Austrian Economics*. Oxford Univ. Press.

Campanella, T. A. (2011). Jane Jacobs and the Death and Life of American Planning. In *Reconsidering Jane Jacobs* (pp. 154–155). Taylor and Francis. Kindle Edition.

Caro, R. (1975). *The Power Broker: Robert Moses and the Fall of New York*. Vintage.

Florida, R. (2014). *The Rise of the Creative Class: Revised and Expanded*. Basic Books.

Garrison, R. W. (2000). *Time and Money: The Macroeconomics of Capital Structure*. Routledge.

Glaeser, E. L., Kallal, H. D., Scheinkman, J. A., & Shleifer, A. (1992). Growth in Cities. *Journal of Political Economy, 100*(6), 1126–1152.

Gleick, J. (1987). *Chaos: Making a New Science*. Penguin.

Gopnik, A. (2016, September 19). Jane Jacobs's Street Smarts. *The New Yorker*. Accessed 16 October 2021. https://www.newyorker.com/magazine/2016/09/26/jane-jacobs-street-smarts

Gwartney, J., Lawson, R., Hall, J., & Murphy, R. (2019). *Economic Freedom of the World, Annual Report*. Fraser Institute. https://www.fraserinstitute.org/studies/economic-freedom

Hayek, F. A. (1935). *Prices and Production*. Augustus M. Kelley.

Hayek, F. A. (1945). The Use of Knowledge in Society. *American Economic Review, 35*(4), 519–530.

Ikeda, S. (2007). Urbanizing Economics. *The Review of Austrian Economics, 20*, 213–220.

Jacobs, J. (1961). *The Death and Life of Great American Cities.* Vintage.

Jacobs, J. (1969a). *The Economy of Cities.* Vintage.

Jacobs, J. (1969b). Strategies for Helping Cities. *American Economic Review, American Economic Association, 59*(4), 652–656, Part I Se.

Jacobs, J. (1984). *Cities and the Wealth of Nations.* Vintage.

Jacobs, J. (2000). *The Nature of Economies.* Vintage.

Jacobs, J. (2004). *Dark Age Ahead.* Vintage.

Johnson, S. (2002). *Emergence: The Connected Lives of Ants, Brains, Cities, and Software.* Touchstone.

Kirzner, I. M. (1973). *Competition and Entrepreneurship.* Univ. of Chicago Press.

Kirzner, I. M. (1997). Entrepreneurial Discovery and the Competitive Market Process: An Austrian Approach. *Journal of Economic Literature, 35*(1), 60–85.

Kirzner, I. M. (2000). *The Driving Force of the Market: Essays in Austrian Economics.* Routledge.

Lachmann, L. (1978). *Capital and Its Structure.* Sheed Andrews and McMeel.

Landsburg, S. E. (2013). *Price Theory and Applications* (9th ed.). Cengage Learning.

Lucas, R. (1988). On the Mechanism of Economic Development. *Journal of Monetary Economics, 22*, 3–42.

Menger, C. (1883[1990]). *Investigations into the Method of the Social Sciences.* Libertarian Press. Also available online: https://mises.org/library/investigations-method-social-sciences

Milgram, S. (1977). *The Individual in a Social World: Essay and Experiments.* Addison-Wesley.

Mises, L. von (1981[1922]). *Socialism: An Economic and Sociological Analysis* (Trans. J. Kahane). Liberty Classics.

Page, M., & Mennel, T. (Eds.). (2017). *Reconsidering Jane Jacobs.* Taylor and Francis. Kindle Edition.

Parker, G. (2004). Nation, Empire and city: A Geopolitical Typology of States. In *Chapter 1 in Sovereign City: The City-State through History.* Reaktion Books.

Ramsay, C.-A. (2022). *Cities Matter: A Montrealer's Ode of Jane Jacobs, Economist.* Baraka Books.

Rich, N. (2016). The Prophecies of Jane Jacobs. *The Atlantic.* Accessed 16 October 2021. https://www.theatlantic.com/magazine/archive/2016/11/the-prophecies-of-jane-jacobs/501104/

Somers, M. (2018, June 21). Intrapreneurship, Explained. *Ideas Made to Matter*, MITSloan. Accessed 8 May 2020. https://mitsloan.mit.edu/ideas-made-to-matter/intrapreneurship-explained

Tilly, C. (1982). War Making and State Making as Organized Crime. In P. B. Evans, D. Rueschemeyer, & T. Skopol (Eds.), *Bringing the State Back In*. Cambridge University Press.

Vance, J. E., Jr. (1990). *The Continuing City: Urban Morphology in Western Civilization*. Johns Hopkins.

Walras, L. (1977[1874]). *Elements of Pure Economics or The Theory of Social Wealth* (Trans. W. Jaffé). Augustus M. Kelley.

Zipp, S., & Storring, N. (Eds.). (2016). *Vital Little Plans: The Short Works of Jane Jacobs*. Random House.

3

A City Is Not a Man-Made Thing

I was once waiting in line to order coffee at one of my local coffeehouses. I observed the barista, with his dark-framed glasses, scraggly reddish beard, and hurried manner, taking orders. From a distance, I formed an impression of his personality: Blasé and probably a bit curt; someone who would rather be somewhere else. But when I came face-to-face with him to place my order, I could feel his liveliness, warmth, and efficient friendliness. My impression changed dramatically.

It's the same with cities.

From a distance, from an airplane or a drone, we notice macro features and sweeping patterns that might form our first impressions. Noticing the layout of streets or the pattern of buildings from the air, we might say something like "Oh, what an impressive skyline!" or "This place is a dump!"

For instance, New York, London, and Paris each have distinct skylines. Approaching these cities from the air is thrilling as we spot the Empire State Building dominating Midtown Manhattan, Big Ben and Parliament hugging the Thames, or the Eiffel Tower standing proud counterpoint to La Défense. But while visually striking, these landmarks hardly begin to tell the story of what we will actually experience in those cities. For that

© The Author(s) 2024
S. Ikeda, *A City Cannot Be a Work of Art*,
https://doi.org/10.1007/978-981-99-5362-2_3

we need to get on the ground and touch, smell, walk, and observe. Most places are like that, some more than others. Take Tokyo.

Tokyo's skyline is to me terribly underwhelming. Heavily bombed and burned-out during World War II and subject to devastating earthquakes throughout its history, Tokyo has as a result few tall buildings today compared to other major cities, and it's not much to see from the air either. Even as you drive in along the highway from Narita Airport, the architecture for the most part remains boxy and drab. As we enter the central city, with the Sumida River winding below, if we look between the buildings, we begin to glimpse Tokyo's vitality. But it is really only when walking the streets and public spaces—of Ginza, Shinjuku, and Akihabara, for example—do we finally experience the "real" Tokyo, the Tokyo from our personal perspective, and feel what philosopher Ken-ichi Sasaki calls the urban "tactility" beneath our feet and through our skin.

Beyond Tokyo, it's also the way we finally get to know London or Paris or any other city. We do it, as an American sports program used to say, "up close and personal." Each of us experiences a city from our personal perspective, yet somehow we are experiencing the same city; we're not just a bunch of blind men touching parts of an elephant.

The noted urban planner Kevin Lynch explains that each of us gradually forms a mental image of a city that eventually overlaps enough with the images of others to enable us to coordinate our plans. A first-time tourist in New York City navigating with a two-dimensional map with explicit street and place names might tell a friend, "I'll meet you at the southeast corner of 5th Avenue and 8th Street at 1PM." (This would be harder to do in Tokyo because relatively few streets there have names, so locating a specific place is very different from the way we do it in New York; and in central London, because winding streets change names seemingly from one block to the next, locals sometimes give directions by using walking time and landmarks.)

As we spend time in a city, we get a better feel for its environs, its inhabitants and their ways of doing things, and how we navigate changes. Our static, two-dimensional image becomes an evolving, multidimensional mental map, more detailed in some ways, fuzzier in others. Experience doesn't make this mental map less abstract, but rather abstract along different dimensions. A New Yorker then might tell her friend,

"Let's meet at the Arch in the Village at lunch time." Translation: "Let's meet under the Arch in Washington Square Park in Greenwich Village around 1pm-ish." Our image of a city changes gradually but radically with experience. While our unique perspectives make it highly unlikely that these shared images and specific points of reference are identical or even always consistent, they do allow us to navigate a complex urban environment and to coordinate our sundry plans with a reasonable expectation of success.

As well will see, one of the common mistakes urban planners make when planning for cities is to assume the process works the other way, that they can impose a deliberately constructed pattern onto a physical cityscape and then expect us to adjust our behavior to it in just the way they want us to. Sometimes that happens, but it usually doesn't, especially with big plans involving large numbers of people, no matter how breathtaking or efficient the design may appear to be...from a distance.

I believe it is in this sense that Jane Jacobs says, "A city cannot be a work of art" (Jacobs, 1961: 372).

1 The Nature of a Living City[1]

As Jacobs explains in *The Death and Life of Great American Cities*:

> Artists, whatever their medium, *make selections* from the abounding materials of life, and organize these selections into works that are under the control of the artist...the essence of the process is disciplined, highly discriminatory selectivity *from* life. In relation to the inclusiveness and the literally endless intricacy of life, art is arbitrary, symbolic and abstracted...To approach a city, or even a city neighborhood, as if it were a larger architectural problem, capable of being given order by converting it into a disciplined work of art, is to make the mistake of attempting to substitute art

---

[1] I have borrowed this useful term from the title of Roberta Bradeis Gratz's book, *The Living City* (1989). Gratz is a journalist and a long-time friend and colleague of Jane Jacobs, and continues to publish articles and books inspired and guided by Jacobs's approach to understanding cities, including most recently as of this writing *It's a Helluva Town: Joan K. Davidson, the J.M. Kaplan Fund, and the Fight for a Better New York* (2020).

for life. The results of such profound confusion between art and life are neither art nor life. They are taxidermy. (1961: 372–3, emphasis original)

How then do we avoid turning the objects of urban design into taxidermy and killing off a city by planning? I think the short answer is that we avoid it by recognizing that there is a trade-off between the scale and design for a given space, on the one hand, and the degree of spontaneity, complexity, and intricacy in the resulting social order that the design will accommodate within that space.

Now, saying that a city cannot be a work of art doesn't mean that a city cannot be intentionally beautified or that deliberate design can never enhance its appearance or improve its operation in some way. Of course, it can. But I am suggesting that the beauty designed in a work of art is fundamentally different from the kind of beauty that emerges unintentionally from unplanned interactions or through long and varied experience with the real world. The skillfully made-up look of a young fashion model and the wizened face of an elderly grandmother can both be beautiful, but in profoundly different ways.

Some cast doubt on whether beauty is a relevant norm for some great cities. Niels Gron, an early twentieth-century political writer from Denmark living in New York, explains the downside of trying to achieve it.

Before I came to this country, and in all the time I have been here [circa 1900], it has never occurred to me to think of New York as beautiful.... We expect of her power and magnificence, but not beauty.... The kind of beauty that makes Paris charming can only exist where private rights and personal liberty are or have been trampled on. Only where the mob rules, or where kings rule, so that there is at one time absolutely no respect for the property of the rich and at another time for the rights of the poor can the beauties of Paris be realized. (Koeppel, 2015: Loc. 3536)

When done on a large scale, designed artistic beauty within the ecology of a city comes with a high cost and undesirable consequences, much of it more felt than seen.

I am not saying that small is always beautiful. But there is a reason why, for most of us, mega- and giga-projects are more pleasing the farther away from them we are, while the beauty or at least the distinctive character of a great city becomes visible, as I said, up close on the street and in its neighborhoods.

When she says that a city cannot be a work of art, I believe Jacobs is thinking less about aesthetics per se and more about the phenomenon of social order generally—about how a city manages to solve the problem of getting thousands or millions of strangers to peacefully cooperate to a reasonably high degree, day after day, without commanding them to do so according to some comprehensive plan.[2] For that, we need to understand the nature of the order we see in the city. In Jacobs's words,

> It is futile to plan a city's appearance, or speculate on how to endow it with a pleasing appearance of order, without knowing what sort of innate, functioning order it has. (Jacobs, 1961: 14)

And for the same reason, I believe she would not regard a city as a work of engineering, either. Both the engineering perspective and the aesthetic perspective abstract from an organic whole; both substitute a single, guiding vision or purpose for the intricate ordering and unpredictable dynamics of a system that is the result of many minds and purposes interacting. These reasons parallel those of F.A. Hayek (1967: 100) who warned of the perils of treating an unplanned or "spontaneous order" as if it were a planned order.

The economist Richard E. Wagner (2010) draws the same distinction in his contrast between "piazza and parade." In a parade, each person follows an explicit, pre-assigned set of commands consciously choreographed by an overall planner. While any social framework—from a parlor to a park—constrains individual choice to some degree, a marching band on a parade ground is an extreme example of constrained choice. To achieve the pre-ordained pattern, no marcher may deviate from assigned movements, and individuality must necessarily be submerged as much as possible into the collective. This is not the place for unscripted action. Individuality, the freedom to differentiate oneself from the

---

[2] The respected urban planner Alain Bertaud expresses a similar sentiment when he writes: "A city is not a large building requiring a detailed blueprint before being built" (Bertaud, 2018: 354).

collective, disrupts the planner's vision and therefore cannot be tolerated. The relations among the marchers must be explicit, formal, and narrowly constrained.

People also interact with one another in a piazza, of course. Whether sitting, standing, eating, walking, or dancing, there are some rules each of us needs to follow to preserve social order. While some of those rules may be explicit and externally enforced, most are informal, tacit, and negative in the sense that they tell us what we cannot do rather than what we must do. Perhaps you are not allowed to toss trash into the fountain or play loud music or assault anyone. Anything not forbidden, however, is allowed. The scope of what you can do in this hypothetical piazza is infinitely broader than in a parade, where that which is not mandated is forbidden: "Take exactly five 18-inch steps forward, turn exactly 90-degrees to the right...."

1.1   Spontaneous Order and Organized Complexity

How to differentiate the spontaneous order of a piazza in contrast to the rationally constructed order of a parade? Using Hayek's description of an "order" (Hayek 1973: 35), I define spontaneous order as follows:

A *spontaneous order* is a set of interpersonal relations that emerges unintentionally over time and is sufficiently stable and coherent to enable independent individuals to form and carry out their plans with a reasonable expectation of success.[3] A spontaneous order has the characteristic of "unplanned emergence over time."

Emergence is the property of a complex system to form out of individual elements, where that system has properties not found in the elements considered separately, and adapts to different conditions without central control (Johnson 2001). For example, the letters L-I-V-E taken separately have their own meanings as individual letters, but putting them together as the word LIVE they take on a property, a meaning, that is not implicit or inherent in the letters taken separately. Its meaning "emerges"

---

[3] Compare with Bertrand de Jouvenel's formulation: "A collection of phenomena becomes orderly for me if and when I can tersely formulate a law of structure whereby each item is assigned the position which it holds" (de Jouvenel, 1956: 43 n3).

from combining the letters in a certain way rather than another, say, as EVIL. Unlike the word LIVE, however, a living city is emergent *over time*, a spontaneous order. I should reiterate that the "order" I am referring to here is not rigid but adaptable and allows room for people to correct planning errors, while also remaining stable enough to enable them to plan with a reasonable though, owing to imperfect knowledge, not necessarily perfect expectation of success.

Hayek describes a spontaneous order succinctly as "the result of human action but not of human design" (Hayek 1967: 96–105). Moreover, the people whose actions constitute the order need not be aware *that* their choices contribute to the order nor *how* their choices do so. Rather, these orders form when the framework of rules they operate in—for example, social norms, price signals, or grammatical rules—are such that people can successfully execute their own plans without having to think very much or at all about that framework. Examples of such orders include language, culture, legal interpretation, markets, and, of course, cities. Quite a wide-ranging list!

A memorable example of a spontaneous order appears in *Death and Life*, where Jacobs describes the daily street activity in front of her home on Hudson Street in Greenwich Village (Jacobs 1961: 50–4). The patterns she observes there, which she famously calls an "intricate sidewalk ballet," consists of several waves of many different people using the same public spaces for their own purposes throughout the day and in so doing unintentionally contribute the "eyes on the street" that supply informal public monitoring, which in turn unintentionally fosters the emergence of safety, trust, and local social networks.

Each of us operates in a host of spontaneous social orders—family, markets, science, religion, language, law—so why a special emphasis on the city?

The city, the sort of city Jacobs is writing about, the great city, the city of density and diversity, is in fact the principal locus of social change. The great city is the institutional matrix that incubates new ideas and novel lifestyles and ways of looking at the world. The family, markets, science, religion, language, law, et al. are what they are because they either originated in or markedly advanced in a great city. In fact, because of the central role of cities in the development of so many spontaneous social orders, we may view a great city as a spontaneous order *par excellence*. Indeed, a great city is a spontaneous social order that itself breeds and sustains most of the important, emergent social orders that constitute civilized society. (I elaborate on this thesis when I discuss economic development in Chap. 6.) One might say that Jacobs is so strongly and relentlessly critical of the centralized, heavy-handed urban planning of the 1950s precisely because it was an attempt to turn piazzas into parades.[4] Once again, the problem is that the essential feature of a great city is change, change that is spontaneous and unpredictable, and therefore impossible to plan for except in a very limited way.

Jacobs is no less critical of the sociologist Louis Wirth's paradigm model of a city as an elegant three-variable problem—population, density of settlement, and degree of heterogeneity—with which he argues it is possible to "explain the characteristics of urban life and to account for the differences between cities of various sizes and types" (Wirth, 1938: 18). In contrast, Jacobs sees a great city as a problem of organized complexity, which involves "dealing simultaneously with a sizable number of factors which are interrelated into an organic whole" (Jacobs, 1961: 432).[5]

The final chapter of *Death and Life* and the first chapter of Jacobs's next book *The Economy of Cities*, taken in tandem, explain first why a great city is a phenomenon of organized complexity and then how the organized complexity of a city and the patterns within it arise spontaneously from the plans of self-interested individuals.[6] In my opinion, chapter 22 in *Death and Life* and chapter 1 in *The Economy of Cities* are together the most explicit enunciation of Jacobs's social theory.[7]

---

[4] We need look no further for current examples of such practices than to Brasilia, which I will examine more closely in Chap. 7, and to the examples cited at the beginning of Chap. 2.

[5] In his outstanding biography of Jacobs, Peter Laurence speaks of "Jacobs's historic introduction of complexity science to urban thinking" (Laurence, 2006: 50).

[6] Where *The Death and Life of Great American Cities* essentially concerns the nature and significance of living cities and why appreciating this demands a radical reorientation and reform of urban planning, *The Economy of Cities* concerns the nature and mechanics of city-based innovation and economic development, in which the dynamic processes of exporting and importing constitute "two interlocking reciprocating systems" (Jacobs, 1969: 234).

[7] I elaborate on these themes in Ikeda (2020).

That final chapter of *Death and Life*, "The Kind of Problem a City Is," naturally segues into the first chapter of *The Economy of Cities*, "Cities First, Rural Development Later." The former characterizes a city as a problem of "organized complexity" that results when a number of variables interact with one another in highly complex ways to generate an orderly but unpredictable "organic whole" (1961: 432). It articulates and justifies Jacobs's approach to studying and understanding living cities as complex systems. The first chapter of *The Economy of Cities* then sets out the book's essential lesson of how organized complexity emerges, including both the city itself and the processes that arise within it, which the rest of the book generalizes to explain how urban-based economic development takes place. Contradicting received archeological history, it hypothesizes that large settlements with complex divisions of labor and not farming villages must have been the origin of agriculture. But more important than this hypothesis, which may be right or wrong, are the two narratives it contains that explain how organized complexity spontaneously emerges as the unintended consequence of purposeful, self-interested activity by resourceful traders, merchants, and entrepreneurs. The first narrative is a theory of how trade among diverse groups establishes permanent markets that evolve into true cities; the second explains how the specialties of animal husbandry and seed hybridization come about as the unintended consequences of self-interested decisions. She argues that economically sustainable development occurs through innovation of this sort and that the conditions found in large, complex, and diverse urban settlements (which is another explicit connection to *Death and Life*) are necessary for that to happen.[8]

1.2   Fellow Travelers

Far more congenial to her way of thinking than Wirth are the design theories of Kevin Lynch (1960) or William H. Whyte (1980) or Jan Gehl (2013), or advocates of the novel traffic policies of "shared space" that

---

[8] I cover the subject-matter of this paragraph at length in Chap. 6.

have been spreading across Northern Europe.[9] Each pays careful attention to how real people interact with each other and with the built environment in intricate and surprising ways. All, in their own way, appreciate with Jacobs that a city is a spontaneous order.[10]

Urbanist Christopher Alexander, like Jacobs, also appreciates the complex nature of a city. For example, Alexander's well-known essay "A city is not a tree" (1965), contrasts the structure of a mathematical tree with that of a semilattice, where he deems a tree-designed city "artificial" and a semilattice-designed city "natural." A *tree* in the context of urban design refers to a scheme in which a physical element, such as a residential block or "branch," is intended to be used only in conjunction with a specified set of other elements, such as a school or grocery store or office, in branches to which it is directly connected; and people in that "branch" are not supposed to have any significant interaction with people or elements in any branch to which it is not directly connected. It is seemingly designed according to someone's notion of efficiency so that people need only use the schools, stores, et cetera, in their own neighborhood or district.[11] On the other hand, an urban design based on the concept of a *semilattice* allows for or even encourages mobility across neighborhoods and districts; it reflects how real people use the diverse land-uses of a living city.

When visually mapped out, a mathematical tree looks like a stylized tree where the smallest branch (e.g., an office, school, or grocery store) connects to one and only one inner branch (e.g., a neighborhood) that in turn is connected to one and only one branch closer to the trunk (e.g., a district containing several neighborhoods); a semilattice looks more like an incomplete, slightly messy spider's web, where one node has multiple

---

[9] See for example, https://www.pps.org/article/what-is-shared-space. Accessed 8 May 2023. I discuss "shared space" in Chap. 9.

[10] While I find it helpful to distinguish complexity from spontaneous order (or emergence), David Colander and Roland Kupers, leading authorities on complexity theory, apparently see complexity as entailing emergence: "In analyzing a complex system you have to consider the interconnectedness of the parts together with the parts themselves, which implies that in a complex system, the whole is not necessarily equal to the sum of the parts" (2014: 13).

[11] The so-called "15-minute city" of Carlos Moreno seems to have this tree structure. See https://www.15minutecity.com/. Accessed 8 May 2023. Léon Krier's version of poly-centricism within a city also has tree-like characteristics that I will discuss in Chap. 9.

physical connections up, down, or across the network, so that people living in one neighborhood may conveniently work, shop, or attend school in several neighborhoods.

Alexander fears it is "this lack of structural complexity, characteristic of trees, which is crippling our conceptions of the city." Although real people will somehow find ways to use poorly designed physical spaces (or not), tree designs unnecessarily limit how they might adjust to unexpected changes or engage in informal intermingling and connection-making that set the stage for discovery. On the other hand, designing with a semilattice in mind opens the possibility of orders of magnitude more complexity and discovery to take place. In the planning context, this means as much as possible creating conditions or establishing parameters that permit or promote novel patterns to arise via experiment and trial-and-error, as I explain below. One implication is to avoid constructing large-scale or meticulously detailed projects, of the kind mentioned at the beginning of Chap. 2, and instead to allow those details, the "granularity" of land-uses, to emerge over time.

1.3 Complexity and Radical Ignorance

As noted, Jacobs observes that the artist *abstracts* from life, with all its "literally endless intricacy." Many architects, especially those with great ambition, seem to ignore existing intricacy and treat urban environments as a blank canvas, which, if not empty already, needs to be wiped clean, sometimes literally, to make way for their brilliant creations. That is what abstracting from endless intricacy is about. The better sorts of architect-planners try at least to consider how their constructions might fit into the existing built ecology and complement the lives of the people who, with some measure of free will, might be using them. But predicting how real people will respond to change is a pretty iffy thing, whether it is an architect or an economist who is trying to do it. That iffyness comes from two factors: complexity and radical ignorance. Let's take complexity first.

Complexity in this context arises from personal interactions that are so numerous or varied or changeable that it is too costly for anyone to be aware of all of them or their consequences. But what is complexity?

Hayek defines the *degree of complexity* in terms of the "minimum number of elements of which an instance of the pattern consists in order to exhibit all the characteristic attributes of the class of patterns in question..." (Hayek, 1967: 25). As that minimum number increases, the system becomes more complex. It takes far fewer elements to fully capture the abstract concept of a city intersection ("street X and avenue Y cross at right angles") than the actual intersection of 5th Avenue and Broadway in Manhattan, depending on the particular "Lynchian image" of that place one has in mind. Working from this definition, the more complex the phenomenon, the harder it will be to adequately describe its essence in so many words or equations. In a world with only a few variables, such as those described in a high-school algebra problem or in Wirth's three-variable equation, it is possible in principle to possess all the knowledge relevant for a complete description. In the real world, however, the number of relevant variables is far too large and changeable, the number of dynamic interactions among people too intricate, and our cognitive powers too limited to comprehend any but the smallest part or aspect of the overall pattern.

Moreover, we are accustomed to thinking of complexity as two- or three-dimensional, as in a drawing or a building. Jacobs offers the following common example of complexity along the dimension of time:

> Consider the history of the no-yield space that has recently been rehabilitated by the Arts in Louisville Association as a theater, music room, art gallery, library, bar and restaurant. It started life as a fashionable athletic club, outlived that and became a school, then the stable of a dairy company, then a riding school, then a finishing and dancing school, another athletic club, an artist's studio, a school again, a blacksmith's, a factory, a warehouse, and it is now a flourishing center of the arts. Who could anticipate or provide for such a succession of hopes and schemes? Only an unimaginative man would think he could; only an arrogant man would want to. (Jacobs, 1961: 195)

Compared to the vast complexity of a social order, intra- and especially inter-temporarily, predicting the weather is a good deal simpler.

As we saw in Chap. 2, *radical ignorance* means being unaware of information that is relevant for making a correct decision, not because the cost is too high, but because we are utterly unaware that the information even exists. For example, we might be very hungry, but walk blithely past a restaurant serving food that would completely and inexpensively satisfy our hunger. A simple solution escapes our notice because of our sheer lack of alertness. So, whether the problem is complex or relatively simple, "not knowing that we don't know" means we cannot solve the problem because we don't know the problem even exists.

Acting in the presence of complexity and radical ignorance means it is impossible to know all the relevant alternatives or to trace all the consequences of any one of those alternatives because (1) we are utterly unaware of at least some of them or (2) they are too numerous, convoluted, or remote given our limited mental capabilities *even if they stood in front of us*. The first is a problem of radical ignorance, the second a problem of complexity. As a rule, the bigger the *scale* of the changes we wish to make in the real world, or the more detailed the *design* we wish to impose on a plan of a given scale, the harder it will be to predict what is going to happen because either there are "states of the world" about which we are radically ignorant or they are beyond our cognitive abilities to grasp or calculate. (These are two aspects of what I have heretofore been referring to as "the knowledge problem," which we can designate as "epistemic problems" and "cognitive problems," respectively.)

Here I am, of course, making the distinction between radical ignorance and complexity in the context of urban planning, but it also has implications for social theory and, in particular, to economics.

One of the lessons economists learned from the twentieth-century debate over collectivist central planning—the socialist calculation debate—is that the "optimal" level and scale of central planning is much lower than we think. The local knowledge—"the knowledge of the particular circumstances of time and place" (Hayek, 1945)—that we each use to coordinate our individual plans in the real world, including our tastes, the appropriate technologies, and resource availabilities, is beyond the reach of central planners.[12] Because of this, the more they try to impose a design onto a complex social order that doesn't align with our plans, the more we will adjust to the planners' interventions in ways they won't be able to foresee, often thwarting their original intentions in the process. And beyond some relatively limited degree, if the planners succeed in substituting their designs for an emergent social order—the outcome of the myriad minds of ordinary people—the result will be significantly less complex and dynamic (and perhaps beautiful) than they intended.[13]

With respect to urban design, the larger and more elaborate a design is in relation to the social space it is trying to fit into, the narrower will be the scope of unplanned activities that it permits. That is because a construction, of any scale and design, necessarily constrains to some extent how we can use the space in and around it. Building a mid-size residential townhouse within a largely commercial block means excluding other uses of that space for at least some time even as it mixes in a new land-use to the block. Still, it changes the character of that block and perhaps also the surrounding areas in unpredictable ways. This is unavoidable for any built structure, of course, but the bigger the structure and the more complex the design elements it contains, the more the designed complexity will constrain spontaneous complexity. Constructing something that takes up an entire city block, such as the Empire State Building, places even greater constraints on what we can do in and around the building itself and the surrounding area. The impact of scaling up to a multi-block development such as Lincoln Center in Midtown Manhattan or Hudson Yards on the Far West Side is greater still; and it sets planners the daunting task either of accurately predicting the range of activities in that space people will want to engage in today and in the future or of making sure

---

[12] I will have more to say about the socialist-calculation debate in Chap. 7. See Mises (1981), Hayek (1945), and Read (1958).

[13] There is a large literature based on such an appreciation of knowledge and incentive problems that critiques macroeconomic policies, and an equally large one critiquing microeconomic regulation, but outside of an urban context. To begin with, see, for example, Ikeda (1998), Boettke (1994), and Boettke and Coyne (2015). This book, of course, focuses specifically on the urban context. And while it does address topics commonly found in microeconomic discussions, rent regulation for example, my task is to use a Jacobs-inspired analytical framework to examine topics outside the normal scope of typical economic analysis, such as the socioeconomic impact of urban design and the regulation of land-uses.

the physical structure, legal rules, community expectations, and management practices are flexible enough to allow for effective, reasonably low-cost responses to unforeseen changes in economic and social conditions.

If planners want to preserve the potential for unplanned liveliness, they will need to leave substantial room in a project for adjustments over time to its structure and use. That means, other things equal, limiting the size of the project or the number of planned elements in it. Otherwise, the level of spontaneous complexity will be overly constrained by the planners' imagination. The architect Rem Koolhaas, in assessing how the skyscraper has shaped expectations about the diversity of activities within it, also points to the role of "indeterminacy," such that the success of a building should be "measured by the degree to which the structure frames their coexistence without interfering with their destinies" (Koolhas, 1994: 85).

A city can handle endless waves of problems if the rules that govern interactions in the spaces where people interact allow the collective intelligence of many minds to discover those problems and to work out solutions for them. Good urban design therefore needs to take seriously into account a city's "invisible infrastructure"—that is, the patterns of contact, dynamic social networks, and social norms—that enable individuals to harness their local knowledge and human capital. The result will be greater complexity at a moment in time and over time. Planning should complement emergent order rather than substitute for it, and planners should keep in mind that increasing the scale of a construction cuts ever more deeply into the living flesh of a city. The challenge for the designer of a public space then is where possible to enable rather than replace the spontaneous, "street-level" plans of ordinary people, and to preserve or promote public spaces where informal contact, networking, and discovery tend to happen. Too often, scaling up and adding greater planned detail progressively drains the life and intelligence from a city. Clearly, there is an important trade-off involved.

2   What the Trade-off Might Look Like

It might help to use some simple diagrams to express all this. We can depict the trade-off between (1) the scale of a given design and (2) the maximum level of complexity and spontaneity permitted by that scale as a downward-sloping curve. The specific shape of this trade-off is unimportant for now and my goal here is not to derive testable hypotheses, although I believe that is possible to do in principle. Rather, my goal is to emphasize, reasoning from our earlier analysis, that given the epistemic and cognitive limits of the human mind, beyond some point the vision of the designer in terms of scale and level of detail begins to substitute for rather than encourage the emergence of a social order of far greater spontaneous complexity.[14]

Figure 3.1 illustrates the resulting trade-off:

The scale of a structure and the designed complexity or planned uses of the space within that structure are of course two different things.

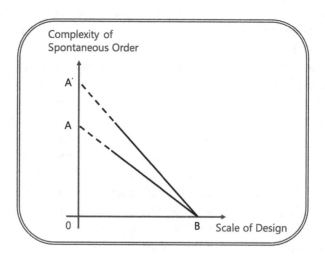

Fig. 3.1   Scale-complexity trade-off

---

[14] I should add that "unplanned simplicity" in a structure or its usage can also occur, but the consequences of doing so, such as when unnecessary walls or rules are eliminated, is to allow a greater complexity of usage over time, as Jacobs's example from earlier of the "no-yield" space illustrates.

Increasing the dimensions of a room doesn't necessarily mean the essential elements that go into its design become more numerous (e.g., floor, walls, ceiling). To keep things simple, Fig. 3.1 illustrates how scale alone impacts spontaneous complexity, keeping the number of designed elements constant. Thus, as scale increases, moving from A to B, the potential for spontaneous, unplanned order decreases. This is what happens, for instance, when a project increases from the scale of a townhouse to something like Hudson Yards.

To scale and spontaneous complexity, I am adding a third variable to incorporate Jacobs's observations on how we adjust to our environment with the passage of time. We can plan for spontaneous complexity to a very limited degree, but fortunately, the passage of real time makes it easier and usually cheaper to adjust our actions, social rules, and physical spaces to better complement our plans, again in ways that the original designers cannot foresee. For any given scale of construction, time allows us to discover uses for a space that it was not designed for and to alter the relations we can form in and around it. An entrepreneur may wish to turn a gas station into a café, for instance. With plans embodying this kind of flexibility (i.e., like a semilattice), the adjustment and adaptations need not entail extraordinary costs, and the uses that emerge will more easily increase inter-temporal complexity.[15]

In a two-dimensional image, changes in a third variable or parameter will change the position of the curve. As time passes, then, the frontier in Fig. 3.1 shifts up from AB to A'B, where point B represents the case where the structure occupies 100% of the relevant space in which we can carry out our personal plans. Again, all else equal, for any given scale, the passage of time allows us to find more ways to interact with others or to find previously unthought-of, cost-effective ways of altering the space. Koolhaas again:

---

[15] In addition to Jacobs's "no-yield space," another good example of the influence of time is William Easterly's "Greene Street Project," which traces the evolution of uses on a short block in Manhattan's Soho District over four centuries. The uses went from residential, to sex work, to garment manufacturing, to light industry, to art galleries, to present-day luxury housing. See http://www.greenestreet.nyc/. Accessed 8 May 2023.

In terms of urbanism, this indeterminacy means that a particular site can no longer be matched with any single predetermined purpose. From now on each metropolitan lot accommodates – in theory at least – an unforeseeable and unstable combination of simultaneous activities, which makes architecture less an act of foresight than before and planning an act of only limited prediction. (Koolhaas, 1994: 85)

How far A′B will shift in a given time period, as with the exact shape of the trade-off, is an important empirical question, but both questions go beyond what it is possible to explore here. We can deduce, however, that the trade-off is negative and so the line A′B, like the economist's demand curve, is downward-sloping. Thinking of the relation of time to scale and spontaneous complexity in this way helps to explain how, despite the monumental scale of Nero's Rome or of Haussmann's Paris or Niemeyer's Brasilia, time has liberated us to make spaces more useful and livable than when originally built.

What is the impact on spontaneous complexity of increasing designed complexity in a space of a given size?

Figure 3.2 depicts a possible trade-off between the potential for spontaneous complexity on the one hand, and the degree to which the complexity of the structure is planned rather than emergent.

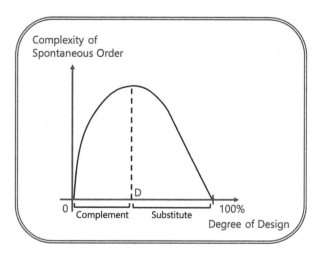

Fig. 3.2 Spontaneous complexity–designed complexity

A purely negative space, in which there are no physical design elements at all might still give rise to a spontaneous order—a proverbial "blank slate" for creative minds. But of course, no space in which people are able to act is a total vacuum. Successful action (within what will later be called an "action space") presupposes at a minimum mutually understood and followed rules of interpersonal conduct—the foundation of an invisible social infrastructure—without which we could not be confident that our plans would succeed. For example, absent mutually accepted social norms we might hesitate to enter any public space; or without commonly accepted boundaries of some kind it would be tough to build on or trade property. Thus, in Fig. 3.2, I have drawn the curve emanating from the origin—that is, where there is no design of any kind and so no spontaneous complexity—but rising steeply at first to indicate that in most cases with minimal design elements in place positive features quickly fill purely negative space. As planned complexity increases, potential spontaneous complexity reaches a maximum at D, beyond which designed complexity begins to crowd out rather than complement spontaneous complexity.

Precisely because it is not a work of art, because it is not wholly the result of deliberate design, a city can achieve astonishing and unimagined levels of intricacy and organized complexity—a deeper social order than the imposed "pretended order" that Jacobs disdained. These considerations are at the heart of Jacobs's social theory.[16]

What then is a city?

---

[16] For a view of the relation between design and complexity/spontaneity similar to mine, see the recent book by Jorge Almazán and Studiolab with the intriguing title, *Emergent Tokyo: Designing the Spontaneous City* (2022). As the subtitle suggests, while they appreciate the organic, evolutionary nature of living cities, they believe in "light planning from above and self-organizing emergence from below" (Ibid: 6) and advocate planning interventions they believe will generate complex, spontaneous streetscapes. Their urban aesthetic is heavily influenced by street-level Tokyo, and they have produced a carefully illustrated, data-driven study of certain characteristics of Tokyo: alleyways, buildings, infill, streets, and neighborhoods. They reject modernist, post-modernist, and post-critical approaches to urban planning (or non-planning), and "corporate-led urbanism." They question the belief in Japan's "cultural exceptionalism" and hold that Tokyo's design principles are transferrable to non-Japanese cultural contexts. Their recommendations tend mainly to describe desired outcomes, which I find hard to disagree with, or to address design principles private developers should follow rather than positive regulatory proposals. Indeed, finding regulatory proposals proves elusive, making it difficult to assess whether or the extent to which their approach diverges from the perspective I am taking here.

3   The City as a Spontaneous Order

Jacobs defines a *city* as "a settlement that generates its economic growth from its own local economy" (Jacobs, 1969: 161). This definition places her in the tradition of the economic historian Henri Pirenne (1952: 56), who links the re-appearance of cities in Europe after the Middle Ages with commerce, the emergence of an economic middle class, and dramatic social change. More to the point, as we will closely examine in Chap. 6, for Jacobs, the essence of economic development is *innovation*.[17]

Ancient Rome and contemporary Washington, D.C., are not quite cities according to Jacobs's definition to the extent that they consume more wealth than they produce and adopt (or suppress) rather than generate innovations. Each may "innovate" in the form of legislation and regulations that foster economic development, there is a large economic literature arguing that this has had mostly the opposite effect.[18] On the other hand, New York City is certainly a Jacobsian city because, in addition to the vast net wealth it creates for the rest of the world through trade, and the way it generates more tax revenue for the rest of the country than it receives in subsidies,[19] it is and has been the source of countless wealth-producing innovations in business and finance, in the arts, fashion, and entertainment, and in lifestyles and language. In this sense, too, Paris, London, and Tokyo are also Jacobsian cities.

It is a bit awkward, however, to deny that Ancient Rome and contemporary Washington are cities. Perhaps sociologist Max Weber's distinction between a "consumption city" and a "production city" might be more helpful (Weber, 1958: 69). Instead, however, I have found it useful to term what Jacobs strictly defines as a city as a *living city*, and to use the unqualified term "city" to refer to any large settlement where a great number of strangers peacefully interact, even if they lack density,

---

[17] Compare Jacobs's economic definition of a city with, say, that of Richard Sennett: "...a city is a human settlement in which strangers are likely to meet" (1974: 39) or of Edward Glaeser "Cities are the absence of physical space between people and companies. They are proximity, density, closeness" (2012: 6). Either would apply to a mall, a prison, or to Paris.

[18] A good place to begin would be Congleton et al. (2019).

[19] See for example https://www.osc.state.ny.us/press/releases/2020/01/new-york-continues-send-more-federal-tax-dollars-washington-it-gets-return. Accessed 24 May 2023.

diversity, or discovery. Therefore, I will use the "living city" or "great city" unless the context allows me to drop the qualifier.

Recall that many of Jacobs's admirers tend to overlook the central component of her social theory, which is that a great city and the life within it are emergent and unplanned. Steven Johnson observes an unfortunate consequence of this:

> Since *Death and Life*, the celebration of sidewalk culture has become the *idée fixe* of all left-leaning urbanists, an axiom as widely agreed upon as any in the liberal canon. But the irony is that many of the same critics who cited Jacobs as the initial warrior in the sidewalk crusade misunderstood the reasons why she had embraced the sidewalk in the first place. And that is because they saw the city as a kind of political theater, and not as an emergent system. (Johnson, 2001: 94)

Make no mistake, at any scale of a social order, there is always some deliberate design. But the spontaneity of which I speak exists at a level "just beyond" these designed elements. For example, the decision to buy from a particular supplier is deliberate, but the total market demand for that input and the pattern of responses of entrepreneurs to unexpected changes in supply are not. The architect's plan for a building may be meticulously designed with a specific purpose in mind, but how it interacts with the surrounding structures, and with the people who move in and around them over time, influencing the character of a neighborhood block, is not. These phenomena are the unintended consequences of the deliberate actions of individuals or set of designed elements.

Jacobs focusses on an urban complexity whose spontaneous emergence consists of a profound and constantly evolving intricacy.

> Under the seeming disorder of the old city, wherever the old city is working successfully, is a marvelous order for maintaining the safety of the streets and the freedom of the city. It is a complex order. (Jacobs, 1961: 50)

And once again, it is not a consciously designed complexity imposed from above, a concept utterly at odds with Jacobs's spontaneous-order-based social theory. Planning should complement or promote, not crowd out or substitute for, spontaneous complexity.

There is a quality even meaner than outright ugliness or disorder, and this meaner quality is the dishonest mask of pretended order, achieved by ignoring or suppressing the real order that is struggling to exist and to be served. (Jacobs, 1961: 15)

Like Jacobs, I see a living city as a highly adaptive system that can achieve a level of spontaneous complexity and orderly dynamism well beyond any "pretended order." Again, for the most part, cities are the result of human action, but not of human design (Hayek, 1967). They are largely emergent, self-regulating, and self-sustaining.

I say "largely" because sometimes a city, like a building, starts out as a deliberate creation by someone. But at different points in its history it may be subject to extensive redesign, reuse, and rebuilding, so that over time, it evolves in ways that no one who played a part in any of its deliberate changes could have foreseen. The original designers of the New York City subway system in the late nineteenth century could not possibly have accurately predicted how the system would evolve over the next 100 years, much less the impact it would have on life in the city. And, as we have seen, the ambitious public mega-projects undertaken at various points in a city's history—such as Haussmann's Paris—may eventually be absorbed into the urban matrix given sufficient time to adjust. A living city outgrows the design elements of its beginnings. It is a messy process, but the living flesh of a city tends to heal and grow, although no one can predict just how. (To address some readers' concerns at this point, let me say that, in Chap. 9, I will discuss examples of how deliberate design might indeed complement the emergence of complex spontaneous orders.)

Like the spontaneous orders of language, judge-made law, and markets, cities evolve in response to myriad impulses from their inhabitants. Cities thrive when we are free to interact in public spaces voluntarily with others. Flourishing cities draw together strangers seeking opportunities for profitable interactions, whatever form they may take. As I will frequently point out, what fuels innovation in a living city is the presence of people in large numbers who are socially distant[20] from one another.

[20] In Chap. 5, I explain this concept more thoroughly.

Great cities are not like towns, only larger. They are not like suburbs, only denser. They differ from towns and suburbs in basic ways, and one of these is that cities are, by definition, full of strangers. (Jacobs, 1961: 30)

These are themes I will develop more fully in Chaps. 4 and 5.

Hayek explained in his famous essay of 1945, "The use of knowledge in society," because our knowledge is limited, we rely heavily on the money prices that emerge from countless market exchanges as signals to coordinate our individual plans with one another. This ability to detect and harness dispersed and contextual knowledge enables intricate and highly complex adjustments to take place, making the market process and the price system much "smarter" than any human mind could be, even if assisted by artificial computational power. As we have seen, the knowledge problem is not computational in nature, it is rather an epistemic and cognitive problem. In the same way, the collective intelligence of people in a living city can solve countless problems by relying on the social infrastructure that emerges in an urban environment that none could discover and solve on their own.

Now, it is true that some of these problems would not have arisen but for large numbers of people with diverse knowledge, skills, and tastes packing themselves together into dense agglomerations. But these are the same conditions that foster informal contacts that ultimately turn cities into incubators of ideas and the principal sources of economic, cultural, and scientific innovation.[21] As I mentioned in Chap. 2 and will discuss at some length in Chap. 7, innovation and creativity are not needed if knowledge is perfect. And where knowledge is indeed imperfect, the innovation and creativity necessary to cope with the resulting social problems require a venue for experimentation and trial-and-error. That is what a city is.

Cities are an immense laboratory of trial and error, failure and success, in city building and city design. (Jacobs, 1961: 6)

---

[21] "The same age, which produces great philosophers and politicians, renown generals and poets, usually abounds with skilful weavers, and ship-carpenters." David Hume (1985[1777]).

But trial-and-error is characteristically messy and often dangerous. Even though the number and diversity of opportunities we find in cities significantly lowers the uncertainty and the cost of experimenting, failure and disappointment will always be part of the bargain.[22] They are always at the cutting edge of dynamic social change. Rem Koolhaas (1994: 59) put it well:

> The entire spectacle defines the dark side of Metropolis as an astronomical increase in the potential for disaster only just exceeded by an equally astronomical increase in the ability to avert it.

While he had Manhattan specifically in mind in this passage, it could apply to any living city.[23]

A city is an unintended consequence of its inhabitants following their own plans, their own dreams. And when free to do so, they will both shape and abide by norms, conventions, beliefs, and institutions—the "rules of the game"—that promote social cooperation and create wealth and innovations in ways none of them could fully imagine, let alone predict. Their choices will also nudge those norms, conventions, etc. in unpredictable directions over time.

In Chap. 2, we saw how economic freedom is implicit in Jacobs's framework. "Freedom" here also means the ability to break away from existing social networks and to make connections with new social networks. All that making and breaking, like all change, entails some amount of disappointment, even tragedy. But the payoff, the "bright side of metropolis," is greater fulfillment, innovation, and wealth. In that sense,

---

[22] I will expand on these themes in Chap. 7.

[23] This is similar to economist Ludwig Lachmann's statement in *Capital and Its Structure*:

> We are living in a world of unexpected change; hence capital combinations, and with them the capital structure, will be ever changing, will be dissolved and re-formed. In this activity we find the real function of the entrepreneur. [...] A progressive economy is not an economy in which no capital is ever lost, but an economy which can afford to lose capital because the productive opportunities revealed by the loss are vigorously exploited (Lachmann, 1978: 17–8).

This passage is also relevant to the discussion in Chap. 2 on the relation of Jacobs's thought to market-process economics.

innovation and disappointment, creativity and conflict, go hand in hand. The same human tendencies and institutional setup that create the dark, destructive side of metropolis are responsible for the bright, creative side. Trying to eliminate the dark side, to put a stop to unwanted change, or to impose rules aimed to avoid disappointment, runs the risk of causing even more profound disappointments and stifling attempts to change the status quo. In other words, taxidermy.

This is not to say that urban managers should not address noxious spillovers and dangerous practices that threaten the well-being of our neighbors, a theme I explore in Chap. 8. When planning complements productive spontaneity, ordinary people will be free to apply their knowledge, energy, and resourcefulness where they see fit, so that the forces of creation can stay ahead of the gales of destruction and the city evolves (Schumpeter, 1942).

4   Living Cities Are Not Economically Efficient

Before we can correct what we think is wrong with a city, we need an appropriate standard of what is right with it. That standard of rightness in turn depends on our understanding how the thing we are trying to fix is supposed to work. Unfortunately, when it comes to complex phenomena, finding a normative standard to evaluate what is better or worse is tricky. While standard economics might appear to be a likely place to look for it for an economic-based concept of a city, that is not the case. Like Jacobs and for essentially the same reasons, I am afraid neither mainstream macroeconomics nor microeconomics is of much help here.

Recall from the previous chapter that Jacobs is characteristically frank in her criticism of macroeconomics.

Macro-economics – large-scale economics – is the branch of learning entrusted with the theory and practice of understanding and fostering national and international economies. It is a shambles. Its undoing was the good fortune of having been believed in and acted upon in a big way. (Jacobs, 1984: 6–7)

In traditional macroeconomic theory, much important detail is lost in its focus on aggregates and averages, such as Gross Domestic Product, aggregate demand, and capital accumulation. For example, standard macroeconomic theory treats capital goods, sometimes defined as "produced means of production," as homogeneous or perfectly substitutable for one another, and makes no distinction between capital as different as, say, a hammer and a horseshoe, except that a horseshoe could be in some very abstract sense the equivalent of a certain number of hammers. The approach is too blunt to get to the level of detail needed to appreciate the complex time-structure of capital of an economy, let alone to tell us what would be necessary to promote the value-productivity of that structure (Lachmann, 1978; Horwitz, 2000).

And her regard for macroeconomics in practice is even lower.

We think of the experiments of particle physicists and space explorers as being extraordinarily expensive and so they are. But the costs are as nothing compared with the incomprehensibly huge resources that banks, industries, governments and international institutions like the World Bank, the International Monetary Fund and the United Nations have poured into tests of macro-economic theory. Never has a science, or supposed science, been so generously indulged. And never have experiments left in their wakes more wreckage, unpleasant surprises, blasted hopes and confusion, to the point that the question seriously arises whether the wreckage is reparable; if it is, certainly not with more of the same. (Jacobs, 1984: 6)

We might trace a large part of this negative assessment to her more fundamental observation, noted before, that unlike a living city a nation-state is not a natural unit of economic analysis (Jacobs, 1984: 31–32).

As we have also noted, Jacobs sees the limitations of standard micro-economics as equally severe. Take the concept of efficiency. Efforts to make cities run more efficiently, when "efficient" means something more than simply "the way I want to see things done," run up against a deep conceptual problem (Ikeda, 2010). Strictly speaking, an action is economically efficient when we can achieve a given end with the least costly of all available means. In other words, *if* we know what the most valuable end we could be pursuing is, and *if* we know what the correct value of each of the possible ways of achieving that end is, then our choices have a very good chance of being economically efficient. It would simply be a matter of matching the known, least-cost means to the known, highest-valued ends.

But if we lack knowledge of any part of that ends-means framework, if our knowledge is not perfect as to what our highest-valued goal is or the cheapest way of achieving it, it would be impossible to tell whether any particular ends-means combination is efficient or inefficient. I choose to take the train to Paris from Rome thinking it is the lowest-cost vacation destination and the cheapest way to get there, when in fact I would get a higher net satisfaction from flying to Amsterdam and vacationing there instead. I would regret my choice to travel to Paris as inefficient *only if I were aware of the superior alternative*. It is only if I know of all possible competing ends and all possible means to achieve those ends, that I can determine whether one choice is more efficient than another. We cannot compare an actual outcome with an ideal outcome if we don't know what that ideal outcome might be. It may be appropriate to speak of efficiency in Louis Wirth's ideal 3-variable city because of its sheer simplicity. But in a Jacobsian city of organized complexity, in which the city is not itself a choosing agent with a purpose of its own, the concept of an "efficient city" in the strict economic sense is completely inapplicable.

The starting point of Jacobs or of Hayek and market-process theory is that in the real world, we are aware of only a small portion of the total amount of information we need for the successful completion of our plans, and so we inevitably make mistakes and our plans conflict. Making such mistakes is obviously not efficient. Fortunately, the institutions and social processes of living cities are precisely what facilitate the discovery of such conflicts and mistakes, as well as stimulate and harness the dispersed resources needed to resolve or correct them.

To be clear, the concept of economic efficiency is valid and helpful when applied to situations where there is (1) a known and clearly specified end; (2) a known set of clearly specified alternative means to achieve that end, and where there are; (3) market prices to help people rationally evaluate the end and the alternative means. If we want to build a house to sell for a certain price, and we have the right set of inputs (e.g., labor, material, equipment, land) and the prices of those inputs, it would be possible then to make a rational, efficient decision about whether or how to build and sell it. But a living city is not a house, or a machine, or a work of art, and therefore it can be neither efficient nor, strictly speaking, inefficient.

At the deepest level, the market process and a living city are of the same nature. Neither have purposes in themselves.

And because our knowledge is imperfect (owing to the limits of our mind) and because in a dynamic world we can never fully remove that imperfection, real markets will never be efficient, and for the same reason neither will real cities be. The good news is that, with an effective process of trial-and-error, neither of them need to be. Markets and cities each embody the means of discovering and reducing those imperfections. But experimentation through trial-and-error takes us outside the realm of efficiency. To someone trained in standard economics, this sounds paradoxical. If you understand why a city cannot be a work of art, which is a superb expression of Jacobs's social theory, it makes perfect sense.

As we will see, beginning in the next chapter, a living city works by effectively combining what I call the "4 Ds," *diversity* and *density* generating *discovery* and *development*. Regarding what a normative standard consistent with promoting creative discovery would look like, I will simply say that it would focus on whether the "rules of the game" create the conditions that empower us to discover problems and to create effective solutions for them. This doesn't mean we should try to eliminate the disruptive gales of destruction. Rather, our focus should be on the enabling conditions that keep the forces of creation ahead of those dark forces, and less on how closely the outcomes we see match the ideal outcomes we can imagine.[24]

5   Concluding Thoughts

That a living city is a spontaneous order and not a deliberate work of art means there is a trade-off between the scale and designed complexity of a project and the spontaneous complexity of the social orders that can

---

[24] I take up these topics in Chaps. 4 and 6.

emerge within it, and that the passage of real time may soften the severity of that trade-off. As we will see in greater detail in the following chapters, this trade-off arises because increasing the scale and design of planned constructions impinges on spaces where creative, informal contact among strangers can happen. Design can complement those things to a point, but beyond that it begins to crowd them out. Small is not always beautiful and big is often unavoidable. That makes it all the more important to understand the impact of scale and design on complex, spontaneous social orders.

This applies as much to private projects as it does to public projects. When the designs are small relative to the surrounding social milieu, the downside of the trade-off is not very steep. The problems usually begin when budget constraints are soft and projects become mega-projects and mega-projects grow into giga-projects. At the risk of sounding ideological—Jane Jacobs somehow avoided being ideologically pigeonholed all her life—soft budget constraints are primarily the domain of governmental projects and so-called public-private partnerships: Elephantine-starchitectural-wonder-developments that require massive subsidies and guarantees too often strive for off-the-charts wow-factors that drain the life out of surrounding public spaces. Without police powers, legal privileges, subsidies, and eminent domain, could the scale and degree of design of purely privately funded developments even begin to compare to public projects in terms of potential harm to the social infrastructure? Probably not.

What I have said here applies not only to the built environment but equally to the formal rules that govern land-use and human interactions within urban spaces (Cozzolino, 2018). Rules need to adapt or permit adaptation to changing circumstances and some rule-structures, like physical structures, do this better than others (Cozzolino, 2022). Designing rules to achieve a specific socioeconomic outcome has the same tendencies as imposing a particular physical design on the social order, potentially damaging the social order in the process, although perhaps preserving the appearance of life. Taxidermy again.

I worry that in our conversations about what makes a city livable, we pay lip service to "mixed uses" and "density" and "diversity" without really understanding exactly what these mean and their importance for economic development and liveliness, which is something I will try to clarify in the next chapter. Jacobs explains how a living city fosters economic development and liveliness—for her, the two go together—by promoting the diversity of land-use and of skills, knowledge, and tastes. As we will see, no entity, private or public, can build a living city (or a neighborhood community) because it is epistemically and cognitively constrained in trying to construct the essential, self-regulating and self-refueling processes that characterize it and must emerge organically within it. In Chap. 7, I will examine cases where some have nevertheless attempted to do just this.

In the ordinary course of their activities, planners can at least refrain from doing the things that would thwart the emergence of these processes and the invisible social infrastructure that gives rise to that emergent diversity, development, and liveliness. And because I am afraid planners won't refrain, I worry that when they propose large-scale fixes for urban problems, they will do so without noticing or caring about Ken-ichi Sasaki's (1998) "urban tactility," another essential feature of the fine-structure of a living city that is the result of human action, but not of human design.

The more precise and comprehensive our image of city is, the less likely it is that what we are imagining really is a city.

What exactly is it about a living city that fosters spontaneous complexity? What are the conditions that enable the emergence of complex social order? Why do innovations happen mainly in cities? These are questions Jacobs addresses in *The Death and Life of Great American Cities* and the ones we will turn to next.

Works Cited

Alexander, C. (1965). A City Is Not a Tree. *Architectural Forum, 122*(1), 58–62.
Almazán, J., & Studiolab. (2022). *Emergent Tokyo: Designing the Spontaneous City*. ORO.
Bertaud, A. (2018). *Order without Design*. MIT Press.
Boettke, P. J. (Ed.). (1994). *The Elgar Companion to Austrian Economics*. Edward Elgar.

Boettke, P. J., & Coyne, C. (Eds.). (2015). *The Oxford Handbook of Austrian Economics*. Oxford Univ. Press.

Colander, D., & Kupers, R. (2014). *Complexity and the Art of Public Policy: Solving Society's Problems from the Bottom Up*. Princeton Univ. Press.

Congleton, R. D., Grofman, B. N., & Voigt, S. (Eds.). (2019). *The Oxford Handbook of Public Choice* (Vol. I). Oxford Univ. Press.

Cozzolino, S. (2018). Reconsidering Urban Spontaneity and Flexibility After Jane Jacobs: How Do They Work Under Different Kinds of Planning Conditions? *Cosmos + Taxis, 5*(3+4), 14–24.

Cozzolino, S. (2022, May). The Spontaneous Rules of Spontaneous Development. In *Environment and Planning B Planning and Design*.

de Jouvenel, B. (1956). Order Versus Organization. In H. F. Sennholz (Ed.), *On Freedom and Free Enterprise*. Van Nostrand.

Gehl, J., & Svarre, B. (2013). *How to Study Public Life*. Island Press.

Glaeser, E. (2012). *Triumph of the City: How Our Greatest Invention Make Us Richer, Smarter, Greener, Healthier, and Happier*. Penguin Books.

Gratz, R. B. (1989). *The Living City: How America's Cities Are Being Revitalized by Thinking Small in a Big Way*. Simon & Schuster.

Gratz, R. B. (2020). *It's a Helluva Town: Joan K. Davidson, the J.M. Kaplan Fund, and the Fight for a Better New York*. Bold Type Books.

Hayek, F. A. (1945). The Use of Knowledge in Society. In F. A. Hayek (Ed.), *(1948) Individualism and Economic Order*. Univ. of Chicago Press.

Hayek, F. A. (1964). The Theory of Complex Phenomena. In F. A. Hayek (Ed.), *(1967) Studies in Philosophy, Politics and Economics*. Univ. of Chicago Press.

Hayek, F. A. (1967). The Results of Human Action but not of Human Design. In F. A. Hayek (Ed.), *Studies in Philosophy, Politics and Economics*. Univ. of Chicago Press.

Hayek, F. A. (1973). *Law, Legislation and Liberty, Volume I: Rules and order*. Univ. of Chicago Press.

Horwitz, S. (2000). *Microfoundations and Macroeconomkcs: An Austrian Perspective*. Routledge.

Hume, D. (1985[1777]). In E. F. Miller (Ed.), *Essays, Moral, and Political, and Literary*. Liberty Fund.

Ikeda, S. (1998). *Dynamics of the Mixed Economy*. Routledge.

Ikeda, S. (2007). Urbanizing Economics. *Review of Austrian Economics, 20*(4), 213–220.

Ikeda, S. (2010). The Mirage of the Efficient City. In S. A. Goldsmith & L. Elizabeth (Eds.), *What We See: Advancing the Observations of Jane Jacobs.* New Village Press.

Ikeda, S. (2020). *The Economy of Cities*: Jane Jacobs's Overlooked Economic Classic. *The Independent Review, 24*(4), 605–618.

Jacobs, J. (1961). *The Death and Life of Great American Cities.* Vintage.

Jacobs, J. (1969). *The Economy of Cities.* Vintage.

Jacobs, J. (1984). *Cities and the Wealth of Nations.* Vintage.

Johnson, S. (2001). *Emergence: The Connected Lives of Ants, Brains, Cities, and Software.* Simon & Schuster.

Kirzner, I. M. (1973). *Competition and Entrepreneurship.* Univ. of Chicago Press.

Koeppel, G. (2015). *City on a Grid: How New York Became New York* (Kindle ed.). Da Capo Press.

Koolhaas, R. (1994). *Delirious New York: A Retroactive Manifesto for New York.* Monacelli Press.

Lachmann, L. M. (1978). *Capital and Its Structure.* Sheed, Andrews and McMeel.

Laurence, P. (2006). Contradictions and complexities: Jane Jacobs's and Robert Venturi's complexity theories. *Journal of Architectural Education, 59*(3), 49–60.

Lavoie, D. (1985). *Rivalry and Central Planning: The Socialist Calculation Debate Reconsidered.* Cambridge Univ. Press.

Lynch, K. (1960). *The Image of the City.* MIT Press.

Manent, P. (2013). *Metamorphosis of the City: On the Western Dynamic.* Harvard Univ. Press.

Mises, L. von (1981[1922]). *Socialism: An Economic and Sociological Analysis* (Trans. J. Kahane). Liberty Press.

Pirenne, H. (1952[1925]). *Medieval Cities: Their Origin and the Rival of Trade.* Princeton Univ. Press.

Putnam, R. (2000). *Bowling Alone: The Collapse and Revival of American Community.* Touchstone.

Read, L. E. (1958). *I, Pencil.* Foundation for Economic Education. See also: https://fee.org/resources/i-pencil/

Sasaki, K.-I. (1998). For Whom Is City Design? Tactility Versus Visuality. In M. Miles, T. Hall, & I. Borden (Eds.), *The City Cultures Reader.* Routledge.

Schumpeter, J. A. (1942). *Capitalism, Socialism and Democracy.* Harper Torchbooks.

Sennett, R. (1974). *The Fall of Public Man.* Cambridge Univ. Press.

Wagner, R. E. (2010). *Entangled Political Economy: A Keynote Address.* Emerald Group Publishing Limited.

Weber, M. (1958). *The City.* Don Martindale & Gertrud Neuwirth (Trans. & Eds.). Free Press.

Whyte, W. H. (1980). Small Urban Spaces. In A. LaFarge (Ed.), *(2000) The Essential William H. Whyte.* Fordham Univ. Press.

Wirth, L. (1938). Urbanism as a Way of Life. *The American Journal of Sociology., 44(1),* 1–24.

Part II

Diversity, Social Networks, and Development

4

The Paradox of Urban Diversity and Cohesion

A living city is incomparably more complex and dynamic than the most intricately designed human construct, even highly sophisticated computers and software. It is one of most complex systems of any kind. In part that is because a real city doesn't have a purpose of its own but is rather a galaxy of countless perpetually moving subsystems in which, unlike the stars of the Milky Way, each daily pursues dozens of unpredictably different purposes, with different time horizons, constantly adjusting to unforeseen changes. It is not possible to fully understand how such a system works in the same way that it might be possible to lay out in detail how a computer works, or the Milky Way. In fact, if it could fully be explained that way, it wouldn't be a living city; more man-made machine than complex social order. Again, a city is not a man-made thing.

But it is possible to identify factors that help or hinder a city's economic development. That is what Jane Jacobs does, primarily in *The Death and Life of Great American Cities*, and is the subject of this chapter.

This chapter draws in part from Ikeda (2020).

© The Author(s) 2024
S. Ikeda, *A City Cannot Be a Work of Art*,
https://doi.org/10.1007/978-981-99-5362-2_4

For Jacobs, a living city achieves greatness (e.g., Tokyo, London, New York, Paris) because its inhabitants, other things equal, are better able than smaller settlements to harness an enormous range of diverse elements. But what does Jacobs mean by "diversity," how does a city generate that diversity, and why is diversity so essential, anyway? Indeed, since homophily—like attracting like—is such a common and strong social urge, it is easy to imagine how diversity instead could be an obstacle to social cooperation. So what transforms a "bug" into a "feature" of a city, what enables complex social cooperation to emerge from the actions of ordinary people and be maintained among widely heterogeneous elements? In a world of scarce resources and imperfect knowledge, why should socially distant and self-interested strangers choose to live and work among one another?

For Jacobs the answers to these questions lie, at least in *Death and Life*, in the social networks people form when the design of public space is done right. While I have noted that in her later writings Jacobs recognizes market prices as important coordinating devices, in that 1961 book, Jacobs stresses the role of social networks and social capital as the principal cohesive forces binding all that diversity together. In Sect. 4, I will show that market-process analysis, with its emphasis on entrepreneurship and the price system, neatly complements Jacobs's focus on social networks. Together they act as dual forces for social cooperation and cohesion among large numbers of people.

1   Microfoundations of Jacobsian Economics

Jacobs notes that no city can flourish unless its residents feel sufficiently safe and secure in its public spaces. The problem is how this is possible among the myriad strangers who populate a great city without resorting to command and control. For Jacobs, the solution entails encouraging people in large numbers to use public spaces consistently throughout the day and night to foster informal contact. I interpret her solution as finding a way to encourage us to identify and utilize valuable complementarities among the strangers we encounter. Because order in a living city is largely the unplanned outcome of individual choices rather than one of imposing a preconceived design (Bertaud, 2018), grasping how a city works (short of complete understanding, of course) means approaching it from the bottom up, beginning with individual perceptions and actions.

1.1   What Does "Diversity" Mean?

I first need to clarify what Jacobs means by diversity. In *Death and Life*, diversity refers primarily to the ways urbanites use land, that is, land-use diversity. But it can refer to people, places, or things and I will be using diversity in all three senses.

The diversity of *things* refers to physical objects. Now, although the things themselves are tangible, the uses to which we put them are a matter of subjective preference. That means we can use the same physical object, such as a stone, as part of a wall or as a paperweight; and we can use objects that differ physically, such as a stone and a book, for the same purpose, for example, to hold open a door. It all depends on our ingenuity and particular circumstances we find ourselves in. Similarly, with respect to *places*, diversity refers to the different ways we perceive and use space; uses of land such as residential, commercial, sacred, and so on. Again, although a place may be tangible, we might use it for different purposes depending on our subjective goals—a high-school gymnasium at different times may be a venue for basketball or a town meeting—or different spaces may be used for the same purpose, so a restaurant or a church could serve as a wedding venue. Hence, the diversities of things and places in the sense used here primarily depend on our perceptions and preferences. Moreover, these also change over time and different people will perceive and prefer different things, contingent on knowledge, experience, and expectations.

With respect to *people*, then, diversity refers to differences in knowledge and beliefs, skills, and tastes. There are of course other significant ways people differ, but our focus will be on these. While such differences may be subjective and intangible, they are still very real. Differences in personal experience, cultural values, education, etc. can create "social distance"[1] among us, and so the challenge is to somehow transform our diversities into complementarities, potential conflict into social cohesion.

Now, Jacobs observes that in a successful city, "a person must feel personally safe and secure on the street" among strangers (Jacobs, 1961: 30). To achieve this, a city needs to rely on a self-regulating harmony of differences more than on formal policing, otherwise the budgetary costs would be far too high or, perhaps more importantly, a great deal of formal policing might itself discourage vital informal contact. Safety and security then depend mostly on unofficial monitoring by ordinary people who have different reasons for being in a public space, which is ordinarily determined by the various land-uses they find in that space.

1.2   The Generators of Land-Use Diversity

Jacobs arrives at her "generators of diversity" through keen observation, extensive scholarship, and pure genius (Szurmak & Desrochers, 2017). She concludes that to successfully generate land-use diversity, all four of the following conditions must hold and, if they do, they will interact in a logical and complex process. To be clear, for Jacobs, these should not be treated as unquestionable axioms, but should be modified or jettisoned when contradicted by the circumstances of time and place.

1.2.1   Two or More Primary Uses

Her starting point is the insight that it is vital to attract people into a neighborhood at different times of the day and days of the week.

> The district, and indeed as many of its internal parts as possible, must serve more than one primary function; preferably more than two. These must insure the presence of people who go outdoors on different schedules and are in the place for different purposes, but who are able to use many facilities in common. (Jacobs, 1961: 152)

---

[1] I define "socially distant" more thoroughly in Chap. 5.

Jacobs argues that to encourage large numbers of people to use public spaces continuously during different times of the day, there needs to be a variety of things there to attract them. This is what sets in motion Jacobs's oft-cited "sidewalk ballet" (Jacobs, 1961: 50). Once there, the tendency for people to attract more people can take hold. Jacobs calls these attractors "primary uses." A primary use then is something that gives us a reason, an incentive, to enter a neighborhood.

A residence is one common primary use. Other primary uses of urban land include, for example, an office building, a high school, a courthouse, a shopping center, a multiplex movie theater, a bus stop, a bar, a museum, or a hospital. We can probably think of many others, but keep in mind that a primary use is what brings outsiders into a neighborhood. Each primary use attracts a different group of users: residents between 6 pm and 6 am, workers between 9 am and 5 pm, theater-goers evenings and weekends, and so on. Some spaces may serve multiple primary uses, such as a good bookstore that sponsors evening readings or a civic plaza that accommodates a farmers' market on weekends when it would otherwise be empty. (I belonged to a taiko-drum ensemble that rehearses in a martial arts dojo.)

To encourage us to spend time in a public space throughout the day and week, there needs to be more than one primary use. A single use, particularly a massive one such as a sports arena or a residential complex, by dominating so much public space often precludes more than one primary use in a neighborhood. Per the arguments laid out in Chap. 3, the very large scale crowds out other potential uses. Sometimes this is unavoidable if indeed the inhabitants of a locality demand such a single massive use—or what Jacobs terms a "border vacuum" (Jacobs, 1961: 257–69)—but when the facility is not in use it tends to repel rather than attract: If people attract people, then the absence of people does the opposite. With multiple primary uses in a neighborhood—for example, a combination of residences, workplaces, entertainment venues—it is more likely that we will use the streets, sidewalks, and plazas to go about our business at different times, perhaps looking for interesting things to do, including looking at and casually keeping an eye on one another.

This influx and outflux of strangers radically differentiates a neighborhood of, say, 20,000 residents in a city of one million from a small town of 20,000. A lively neighborhood in a city brings in many more people, most of whom are strangers to one another, from the outside during the day, than is the case in a town. As journalist and author Joel Garreau (1991: 7) remarks, one sign of an area's success is if its population increases between 9 am and 5 pm. Moreover, pound-for-pound, the people residing in and attracted to a big-city neighborhood will likely seem more unusual to us by almost any measure than what we would find in a small town, because the variance of their behavior, background, and beliefs will be significantly higher. Indeed, it is precisely in the context of how a great city both attracts and tolerates extremes in human diversity that Jacobs famously writes: "Cities have the capability of providing something for everybody, only because, and only when, they are created by everybody" (Jacobs, 1961: 238).

But there are also land-uses that don't necessarily bring strangers into a neighborhood but cater to those already there because of a primary use. Jacobs calls this "secondary diversity." Examples might include a fast-food restaurant, a laundromat, a grocery store, an elementary school, or a pharmacy. Occasionally, a use that would ordinarily be secondary, a local restaurant perhaps, becomes primary if it gains city-wide popularity. Also, over time, land currently serving as a secondary use, for example a local pharmacy, might be refitted, if zoning permits it, into a primary use such as a specialty clothing shop, or if its hours of operation expands from regular business hours to 24/7 and so attract people when other shops are closed. The reverse happens when primary uses disappear, reducing local land-use diversity and making the neighborhood less attractive.

One of the catchphrases of contemporary urban planning and development is "mixed use." Developers often characterize a new project as "mixed use" when all they mean is that in addition to housing, their plans might include retail space for a grocery store and a fast-food shop. These other uses are merely secondary that likely will not themselves bring in people from outside the neighborhood or district. As a necessary factor for generating diversity, Jacobs was therefore careful to specify "mixed *primary* uses."

1.2.2 Population Density

Jacobs writes about the necessity of having a dense concentration of people in a given location in order to supply, as it were, the raw material for eyes on the street.

> The district must have a sufficiently dense concentration of people, for whatever purpose they may be there. This includes people there because of residence. (Jacobs, 1961: 200)

Without enough people to fill public spaces as they travel to work, shop, play, and so on, the informal social institutions that promote public safety and security, and the economic and cultural creativity that build upon them, will not spontaneously emerge.

Note that Jacobs lists this as only one of the four generators of diversity. (In fact, she lists it last among the four.) This is worth noting because much of the recent conversation in the urban-planning community has been about the virtues of population density,[2] as if density were an end in itself; or how once population density has reached some critical level, perhaps coaxed along by imposing green belts, the vitality and benefits of urbanism will then somehow spring up, without paying enough attention to other, equally important, factors. (This is somewhat ironic given how anti-density most urban planners were in the early twentieth century (Bruegmann, 2006) and in some cities today.) But Jacobs's concern with population density derives from her focus on land-use diversity. Population density is a virtue here to the extent that it interacts with the other three elements as a co-generator of land-use diversity. An overcrowded prison in California or the Yankee Stadium during a home game both have high population densities, but without the diversity of use that emerges from all four of the generators, neither would hardly be considered a living city, despite the large numbers of people involved.

Note also that Jacobs is careful to distinguish density from overcrowding. "Density" refers to the number of people or dwelling units per acre

---

[2] Although there is much support among some urban planners to limit densities in cities in downtown areas and in suburbs where land owners express concern about overcrowding and a decrease in real-estate values. Chapter 8 looks more closely at this issue.

or square kilometer; "overcrowding" refers to the number of people in a single dwelling unit (Jacobs, 1961: 205).[3] You can have a very high population density—the extremely wealthy Upper East Side of Manhattan has one of the highest population densities in the City of New York—without overcrowding. That is because the higher number of dwelling units per acre more than compensates for the fewer number of people residing in each unit. (Incidentally, the increase in dwellings may not be enough to offset the reduction in people per dwelling, which explains why as people grow wealthier and reside in larger units population density tends to fall even if dwellings per acre rises.) Generally speaking, overcrowding is undesirable, especially when combined with poverty, as it usually is. And it is also possible for density to be too high, especially when the physical infrastructure in a neighborhood—the sewers, streets, power grid, etc.—cannot adequately accommodate those attracted to it, a problem that typically falls to city planners to address, with uneven success (Bertaud, 2018: xiii). Another consequence of very high densities is the boring visual homogeneity that usually results because such high densities tend to require cost cutting, standardized designs (Jacobs, 1961: 213), think Le Corbusier's "towers in a park" (which is a topic in Chap. 7).

Finally, it is no mystery why population density and congestion in public spaces usually go hand in hand. Put a lot of people into a relatively small area and there are bound to be bottlenecks. High congestion, meaning a great many people using limited public space, can sometimes make life miserable with the crowds, noise, smells, and overall slowness and jumble. However, congestion is often the setting for opportunity because congestion in a great city (but not prisons or Yankee Stadium) is closely associated with a variety of people and uses of space. When the architect Rem Koolhaas speaks of the "culture of congestion" he means it mostly in a good way; that a dynamic culture arises from congestion (Koolhaas, 1994: 10).

---

[3] It is even more complicated than this since we can break down the concept of density further. While it isn't necessary to do this here, urbanists should at least be aware of the various components of "density," and there is no better expositor of this than Shlomo Angel (2020).

1.2.3   Short Blocks

> Most blocks must be short; that is, streets and opportunities to turn corners must be frequent. (Jacobs, 1961: 178)

Always look to invest in properties on a corner! That is what my business-savvy father used to tell me, which I suppose is probably common sense in the real-estate industry. From a commercial point of view, a corner has the advantage of more street frontage than a midblock unit, which means more passersby per hour. According to Joel Garreau (1991: 465), a rule of thumb for commercial success—and I believe this applies to shops in a mall as well as on outdoor streets—is to have about 17 persons per minute (1000 per hour) pass by your store during business hours. Locating on a corner roughly doubles the chances of meeting that minimum and increases your visibility. For a given area, "short blocks" translates into more intersecting streets and therefore "more corners." And while increasing the supply of corner properties would, other things equal, lower the real-estate value of corner properties, other things will not be equal if enough of us are thereby encouraged to use public spaces and so help to make it flourish.

Looking at it more from the "demand" side, Jacobs prescribes "short blocks" for a different reason; namely, short blocks promote walkability. Why? After all, 100 yards is 100 yards whether there is one street intersecting a block or none; in fact, it may increase the distance between destinations if you factor in the width of intervening streets. It is because, up to a point, breaking up a long block by one or even two streets tends to draw pedestrians (though perhaps not car-drivers or bicycle-riders) onward a little farther than the 600 feet or so that sociologist William H. Whyte (as interpreted by Garreau (1991: 464)) estimates the average person is willing to walk to a destination before getting into a car. For that reason, modern shopping malls no longer feature very long, straight, unbroken walkways. As Garreau (1991: 464–6) points out, it is a mistake for a mall-builder to let shoppers see exactly how far it is to the end of a mall, for fear they may turn around (and go back to their cars) before going all the way there. Some of the earliest malls did make that mistake, but today indoor and outdoor malls are constructed so lines of sight are limited via curves or other obstructions, stoking a person's curiosity about what may be "just around the corner." The same principle applies to a city street: short blocks lend intricacy and visual interest to public spaces. Shorter blocks mean more intersections and, as a result, more ways to get from one point to another.[4]

This is related to the concept of "granularity," in which a compound is finer-grained the more distinct elements it contains. Think about various grades of concrete or sandpaper. Applying the concept of granularity to a city street of a given length, such as Whyte's standard of 600 feet, the more land-use in that stretch the more granular it is (Price, 2015). If the entire 600 feet is one unbroken block, then it is more likely that fewer uses will occupy it than if it were divided into shorter blocks (or if a rule prohibited frontages over a relatively small size) because it is then more convenient for large investors to create buildings with extensive frontage. In the limit, a single, massive use might occupy the entire 600-foot stretch and profoundly reduce granularity, which even the addition of so-called "mixed uses" or faux variation to the frontage won't compensate for. This would be less likely if instead the street were divided into two 300-foot blocks or especially three 200-foot blocks. Adding more divisions adds more corners with one street doubling the number of corners and two streets tripling them.

Of course, this doesn't account for street widths. Assuming a standard width of 60 feet, then adding one or two streets will create blocks of 270 feet or 160 feet, respectively (Bertaud, 2018). One of the advantages of a street grid such as the one that crisscrosses Manhattan above 14th Street is that it makes plots of land more uniform and therefore easier to sell and develop (Koeppel, 2015). On the other hand, for a given street width, increasing the number of streets reduces the supply of developable real estate, which is a cost not only to profit-seeking developers but also to tax-collecting municipal governments. The cost of granularity then is less private land and public revenue, assuming the economic activity per foot stays the same on each shorter block. But Jacobs's argument is that shorter blocks promote walkability (and deter drivability), and

---

[4] Léon Krier (2007: 129): "The number of street corners is an indicator of urbanity…."

granularity enables more opportunities for diverse uses per distance traversed. Therefore, we might expect the level of economic activity per foot of frontage to increase to offset the cost of undevelopable land and so actually increase total revenue, private and public.

Andrew Alexander Price has developed a handy tool for calculating the size of an average block in each area (and therefore the number of blocks of that size) for a given number of streets and street width (Price, 2013). You can use this tool to calculate the percentage of total land in the grid devoted to streets and conversely the land available for development (subtracting municipal uses such as court houses and power plants). Price uses this tool to demonstrate that the more intricate the street grid is in terms of number of blocks per square mile the greater amount of street frontage there will be. If you divide a block with another street, you create street frontage (for various uses) on either side, even if you lose some developable real estate in the process. In Jacobsian terms that means within a given square mile of the grid, there are more land-uses and more to see and do, even if there is only one thing or use on each block. Note that not dividing a superblock but mandating smaller lots or more lots per block would also increase granularity, but following Price we can see the frontage (and corners) gained from inserting streets would increase granularity for a given number of lots per block. This aligns with the point Jacobs makes about shorter blocks. So, while Price's tool may be helpful as an indicator of a district's "walkability"[5] it is also useful for measuring what we might call "Jacobs walkability" or the potential diversity of land-use for a given distance walked.[6]

1.2.4   The Need for Old, Worn-Down Buildings

The district must mingle buildings that vary in age and condition, including a good proportion of old ones. (Jacobs, 1961: 187)

---

[5] For that, however, the federal government publishes an actual "Walkability Index" https://catalog. data.gov/dataset/walkability-index. Accessed 26 May 2023.
[6] In Chap. 9, there is a discussion of the relation of granularity (and therefore Jacobs walkability) to the concept of "action space."

Aged buildings are a naturally occurring part of an organic, urban landscape, just as trees of different vintages are natural and necessary in a healthy forest by adding temporal variety to sylvan flora (Scott, 1998). As new buildings age, other things equal, their market value tends to decline, making them more affordable in a competitive land market. Jacobs appreciated this and saw it as a natural aspect of a healthy urban process. And just as you can't plant old trees, you can't build old buildings, and Jacobs saw them as critical to economic development. How so?

Quite simply, an aged or worn-down building offers comparatively cheap space for people, often young people, with new ideas but little capital. Such a building typically has unpleasant or inconvenient aspects—its location is not ideal, the floors are uneven, the plumbing unreliable, or the roof leaks. But in this case, these things are, as they say, a feature not a bug. A building with a good location and well-functioning amenities, perhaps because it is new or newly renovated, would be too costly for most people to occupy to test out new ideas. Only the already wealthy could afford new digs and even they would tend to shun using them for risky experimentation. But an old, run-down building allows a promising-but-poor innovator to trade-off a bad location or fewer amenities for cheap space to experiment. If a living city is where economic development takes place through innovation, it needs somewhere, indeed many places, for inspired people to incubate ideas, to test them, and to survive mistakes. Old buildings in this way are ideal incubators, which is why Jacobs (1961: 188) declares, "New ideas need old buildings!"

You can find examples of abandoned factories and warehouses repurposed as homes and studios to artists all over the world.[7]

It is important to note that Jacobs is not at all referring to what today is known as the "landmarking" of historically significant buildings that lend distinction or character to a particular place.

---

[7] See for example, "Why warehouse conversions are sweeping the globe"
https://www.cnn.com/2017/10/26/world/industrial-renovation-one-square-meter/index.html (accessed 9 May 2023) and "Upcycled Space: 8 Exemplary Industrial to Residential Conversions" https://architizer.com/blog/inspiration/collections/industrial-to-residential-conversions/ (accessed 9 May 2023).

By old buildings I mean not museum-piece old buildings, not old buildings in an excellent and expensive state of rehabilitation—although these
make fine ingredients—but also a good lot of plain, ordinary, low-value old
buildings, including some rundown old buildings. (Jacobs, 1961: 187)

In other places, Jacobs does discuss landmarking of a sort, again of
particular buildings and not of entire districts, and takes her cue from
Kevin Lynch (1960) who wrote about the importance of "landmarks" to
urbanites for navigating the urban landscape (such as the Arch at
Washington Square). Often, however, these landmarks might simply be a
neighborhood diner that locals use as a point of reference. Sometimes
these landmarks are prominent historical buildings, and Jacobs was
indeed a strong supporter of using municipal authority to preserve buildings of that sort. Such landmarking typically requires the costly restora-
tion of buildings often located in high-rent areas where well-heeled
residents use political clout to do the preservation.[8] That is obviously not
what Jacobs has in mind here when she talks about the importance of
"old buildings" for promoting land-use diversity, although many misinterpret her as saying as much.

Jacobs is careful to note that old buildings should "mingle" with newer
ones. That is because when old, worn-down buildings dominate a neighborhood, it likely reflects its residents lack capital for local improvements,
and combined with an absence of primary uses the neighborhood is
probably in decline, or what she calls a "slumming slum" (Jacobs, 1961:
270–90). In a general sense, however, a "slum" is simply a neighborhood
where people on low-incomes can afford to live (or work, in the case of a
commercial or industrial slum). It may well have enough primary and
secondary uses to attract and, just as importantly, to retain people along
with their precious social connections so there is increasing density (without overcrowding), land-use diversity, and rising per-capita wealth—that
is, it is "unslumming" (Jacobs, 1961: 270). It is also the case that if there

---

[8] I have been able to find little written evidence that Jacobs would approve of the landmarking of
entire districts (West Greenwich Village being the sole exception), especially to the extent to which
it has grown in Manhattan, where today over 25% of developed real estate has been landmarked.
See this letter: https://gvshp.org/blog/2016/05/05/continuing-jane-jacobs-work/. Accessed 9 May
2023. My guess is that Jacobs might have referred to this kind of widespread, large-scale preservation as, as you might have guessed, "taxidermy" (Jacobs 1961: 373).

is a broad range of buildings of different vintages and sizes in a neighborhood, people incubating budding enterprises are likely to find many of the amenities they need nearby (Jacobs, 1969: 188), which can also boost local development.

How relevant are these four elements for explaining economic development today?

2   Re-Thinking Jacobs's Four Generators of Diversity[9]

Given the title of her most popular book, one might well argue that Jacobs's analysis is limited to American cities of the mid-twentieth century. She herself concedes that her focus is on "great" cities and not on smaller cities or towns, a "great city," a city of innovation, in her framework being *sui generis* (Jacobs 1961: 16). That it was limited specifically to "American" cities is more debatable. The examples in *Death and Life* draw mainly from the United States, but her later writings include cities in North America, Asia, and Europe.[10] Indeed, urbanists from around the globe acknowledge the relevance of her insights for their locations. As Jorge Almazán notes, for example, "Jane Jacobs's 'eyes on the street' are now referenced worldwide" (2022: 016). In any case, as I said earlier, Jacobs herself would not insist on slavish adherence to her principles. I believe she would instead insist, as an inductivist (Jacobs, 1961: 440), on changing or rejecting them if we observe patterns that consistently contradict the ones she describes in her books and we were able to provide reasonable alternative explanations to account for those patterns.

What I would like to do here then is to offer some extensions to and re-interpretations of her "four generators of diversity" to address some of

---

[9] The MIT Technology Review in 2016 reports on a study of Italian cities by a team led by Marco De Nadai that uses databases from OpenStreetMap to empirically test Jacobs's thesis, with an emphasis on the correlation between population density and urban vitality (Emerging Technology 2016). They found that this correlation largely holds up, but that in addition to Jacobs's four generators, "third places"—public spaces where people meet informally—are also an important empirical factor. Note that this relates to the concept of "Jacobs Density" presented in the next chapter.

[10] See, for example, her references to Tokyo, London, Paris, Moscow, and elsewhere in Jacobs (1969).

these criticisms and to show that her observations are sufficiently robust to explain how a great city today, American or no, achieves cohesion among its diversity and innovation from what Jacobs calls the resulting "effective economic pools of use" (Jacobs, 1961: 148): the potential or latent complementarities among people, places, and things, that nourishes economic development. As noted, we can usefully and legitimately extend her concept of diversity beyond land-use to include the knowledge, skills, and tastes as well as the backgrounds of people. Indeed, this is implicit when we talk about land-use diversity, proper, because what leads someone to open, say, a Thai grocery and someone else a bodega is precisely the backgrounds, human capital, and preferences they bring to the market. Let's dig a bit deeper.

2.1   Re-thinking "Mixed Primary Uses"

While it is important to retain the idea of a primary use as an attractor, some might interpret Jacobs as saying that primary uses must attract people on foot, not people in cars. But Jacobs doesn't seem to denigrate the automobile as such. In her chapter in *Death and Life* on "Erosion of cities or attrition of automobiles," she says (1961: 338–9), for example, "But we blame the automobile for too much" and goes on to say,

> Suppose automobiles had never been invented, or that they had been neglected and we traveled instead in efficient, convenient, speedy, comfortable, mechanized mass transit. Undoubtedly we would save immense sums which might be put to better use. But we might not. For suppose we had been rebuilding, expanding and reorganizing cities according to the project image and other anti-city ideals of conventional planning. We would have essentially the same results I blamed on automobiles a few paragraphs back.[11]

But even more important than how they get around is what people do, how they interact or don't interact with one another, once they get out of their cars, trams, etc., wherever that may be. Because no matter how

---

[11] Still, in the preface to the 1993 Modern Library Edition of *Death and Life*, Jacobs acknowledges that her analysis corroborates the intuitions of "foot people" rather than "car people."

ubiquitous the car (and now the Internet) has become, it is still the case that people interact with one another, to a greater or lesser degree, face-to-face and informally (Christakis & Fowler, 2009: 275) in essentially the way they did in the 1950s on Jane Jacobs's Hudson Street in Greenwich Village, although the physical appearance of these locations (e.g., shopping malls) may be different. The places where face-to-face interactions take place look superficially different today and one driver of that change (no pun intended) has of course been the car.

What then has been the impact on face-to-face (FTF) contact of some of the major patterns of urban evolution in the twentieth century, such as the growth of the American suburb and especially the burgeoning popularity of social media? After all, what is the point of primary uses if there is no need for people to actually go out into public space?

Joel Garreau, author of *Edge City: Life on the New Frontier*, identifies three waves in twentieth-century urban development in the United States after World War II. The "first wave" is the era of the large-scale, residential subdivisions and of mass suburbanization. Ever since Gertrude Stein lamented about her childhood home of Oakland, California, that "there's no there there," people have equated suburbia with placelessness, the absence of identity, middle-class homogeneity, and a lack of human and land-use diversity. The "second wave" begins in the 1960s as retail businesses leave downtowns and city centers and set up in newly created shopping malls in the suburbs to be closer to where people have moved to, now establishing two broad categories of primary use outside traditional downtowns: residential and commercial. The "third wave" begins in the 1990s as office parks and other "industrial" uses cluster with residential and retail centers in suburbs and the even more distant "exurbs" near airports or where interstate highways intersect their concentric beltways outside the central city.

The consequence is the emergence of what Garreau claims is a totally new urban phenomenon: The "edge city"(Garreau, 1991: 6–7) that

1. Has five million or more square feet (465,000 m^2) of leasable office space.
2. Has 600,000 square feet (56,000 m^2) or more of leasable retail space.
3. Has more jobs than bedrooms.

4. Is perceived by the population as one place.
5. Was nothing like a "city" as recently as 30 years ago. Then it was just bedrooms, if not cow pastures.

With the edge city, Garreau announces that "density is back" (Garreau, 1991: 37). I will have more to say about how an edge city addresses the need for contact a little later when re-thinking density.

But the continuing demand for physical contact is also borne out in studies of social media. For example, Nicholas Christakis and James Fowler (2009) find that while we may have many "friends" on a social media app such as Facebook, we have contact with some of them much more than others. And who are they?

> To figure out who was close and who was not, we developed a "picture friends" method based on the photographs that people post on their Facebook pages. The idea is that two people who post and "tag" pictures of each other are much more likely to be socially close than those who do not. We studied all the Facebook pages at a college (we can't say which one), and when we counted the number of picture friends that students had, we found that, on average, just 6.6 were close friends. (Christakis & Fowler, 2009: 275–6)

While these findings date to the early 2000s and Facebook may be less popular among young people today, replaced by still other online platforms, the pattern they identify is telling: that those we have the most frequent contact with online are those we regularly see face to face. Outside of family they are the ones we feel and know relatively much about through "strong ties." (I define "strong ties" and "weak ties" in Chap. 5.)

Malcolm Gladwell (2010), journalist of the social sciences and best-selling author, reports that when it comes to risky endeavors, the effectiveness of social media is limited by how well the people connected by it already know and trust one another.

> The platforms of social media are built around weak ties. Twitter is a way of following (or being followed by) people you may never have met.

Facebook is a tool for efficiently managing your acquaintances, for keeping up with the people you would not otherwise be able to stay in touch with. That's why you can have a thousand "friends" on Facebook, as you never could in real life. (Gladwell, 2010)

He goes on to say,

The drawbacks of networks scarcely matter if the network isn't interested in systemic change—if it just wants to frighten or humiliate or make a splash—or if it doesn't need to think strategically. But if you're taking on a powerful and organized establishment you have to be a hierarchy. (Ibid)

A network such as Facebook consists of *horizontal* relationships among equals; a hierarchy is a *vertical* relationship among persons of unequal authority or status. His examples of such hierarchies include the Freedom Riders in the Deep South during the 1960s civil-rights movement or more in more recent clashes between organized citizens and public authorities in the Middle East. Risky actions of this kind mean following orders and placing ourselves in harm's way or not succumbing to the passions and fears of the moment, all without close monitoring by our superiors. That in turn requires discipline and strong ties. Facebook and Twitter, on the other hand, are useful for building networks of weakly tied individuals or, as was the case in Cairo during the "Arab Spring" of 2010, as a tool for coordinating the actions of people who are already strongly tied through other means. Strong ties with family or among deep commitment to a religion or ideology bind individuals into effective hierarchical structures. Though not impossible, it is very hard to motivate people in large numbers to take enormous personal risks or make significant personal sacrifices for strangers or impersonal, abstract concepts. In other words, to be effective in high-risk situations, social media need to link together people willing to operate in a hierarchy with strong preexisting ties among its members who can trust (in a sense that I clarify in Chap. 5) those "in charge."

On the other hand, as we will see in the next chapter, weak ties are especially important for the operation of the competitive market process. For now, the takeaway is simply that for certain actions to take place, especially those involving risky or dangerous endeavors, social media alone are not enough. Rather, along with the freedom that allows people to make and break social ties, and norms that encourage informal self-monitoring, personal knowledge gained through FTF contact remains essential (Ikeda, 2011; Bailey et al., 2017).

But there is no gainsaying that online shopping and virtual communication, for example, has had a dramatic impact on how people interact and the degree to which they do so FTF. Bookstore chains that dominated the urban landscape in the 1990s have been disappearing, although specialized bookstores have remained to serve a narrow clientele (Ikeda, 2013), and the Covid pandemic dramatically changed the classroom experience. Communication-at-a-distance can of course substitute for FTF contact up to a point, but I suggest that such technical advance serves more to complement traditional human relations. Mixed primary uses in public space should continue to play a vital role in the generation and use of diversity in cities.

2.2   Re-thinking "Short Blocks"

The virtues of FTF contact go beyond the ability to get to know one another on a more personal level and to strengthen ties. In fact, as we will see in Chap. 5, making (and breaking) ties is an essential part of a successful urban process. From the point of view of the dynamics of economic development, FTF contact creates opportunities for us to make new connections, to use them if the opportunity arises, and to spread information outside our local networks, whether or not we want to. Much of this can occur deliberately or simply through casual or serendipitous contact, if social institutions and the design of public spaces allow for it. By encouraging more frequent contact, "short blocks" is, as we've seen, an important aspect of the urban design.

For decades of the twentieth century, urban-design theory was dominated by the "superblock" concept that cuts the number of intersections, with street frontage sometimes stretching hundreds of meters, putting more space between people and land-uses than has historically been the case. As we will see in Chap. 7, this is especially true of the urban approaches of the pioneers of large-scale urban design: Frank Lloyd Wright, Ebenezer Howard, and Le Corbusier. Some of this was in response to the rapidly growing urbanization and the negative externalities that took place in the West after 1800, but it was also due to modernist ideologies that became popular during the early twentieth century. But in some ways, the centuries-old yearning for walkable urban areas found expression in other ways.

Although shopping malls are partly the unintended consequence of zoning restrictions and public policy, they are also, in large measure, the demand for density and diversity reasserting itself. Indeed, the designer and "mall maker" Victor Gruen saw in the enclosed shopping mall an opportunity to recreate the vibrant street life of his native Vienna, Austria (Hardwick, 2004). Since the 1990s, even as malls grew to enormous size, they continued to develop the earlier malls' themes of walkability and intricacy. And with the advent of cheaper outdoor heating and cooling technology, malls began to shed their enclosures in the twenty-first century and are increasingly finding their way back into downtowns, in part because of reaction against mid-twentieth-century urban planning and rebuilding. To that extent, these malls supplement rather than replace the intricate short blocks of historical downtowns, even as they attempt in some degree to mimic them (Bird, 2018). In addition, today highways are being torn down and replaced by more walkable pathways and streets are finding their way back to blocks that had been sealed off decades before (Barone, 2018).

But having shorter blocks means more intersections, and more intersections, in the absence of creative traffic solutions (such as "shared space"), can increase congestion and slow car mobility, which Alain Bertaud (2018) characterizes as essentially a real-estate problem. (An important topic that I will discuss in Chap. 9.)

2.3   Re-thinking "Old, Worn-Down Buildings"

One thing Jacobs did not fully consider is that to the extent old buildings effectively serve to incubate new ideas, other things equal, demand for them will increase making them scarcer and pricier unless their supply increases. Unfortunately, this can only happen gradually over time since, as noted, you can't build old buildings. What might keep prices affordable for entrepreneurs, who are often relatively young and poor?

On the supply side, every building standing today grows older and more worn down by the moment. For some building owners and in some circumstances, the resulting economic depreciation may be less than the cost of repair and renovation, and if someone thinks the value of the refurbished building exceeds those costs then the renovation will take place. In that case, the price will probably be too high for the bright-but-poor entrepreneurs in our story. But in other circumstances it may not pay for an owner to undertake costly renovations, which will add to the supply of old, worn-down buildings. Whether on net such an increase in old buildings will outnumber top-to-bottom renovations will depend on how rapidly the demand for space-to-innovate-in rises relative to the supply, and on the rate of new construction. New construction tends at the margin to draw wealthier buyers away from renovation projects and on the supply side starts the clock on the process of adding to the supply of old buildings.

The fundamental question, however, is how do those who control scarce resources ration them among those who would like to use them? As noted, rich people will tend to shun old buildings unless they find it worthwhile to renovate or to pay someone else to do it. But who decides who gets space in a building if it goes unrenovated? In a market, it is a matter of competition among buyers: Whoever is willing and able to pay the most will get the space. People with little financial capital and a powerful vision will struggle to compete. But that is simply the way things are bought and sold in a dynamic market, where buyers and sellers are free to adjust prices, quantities, qualities, and other relevant factors. So one method of rationing is to let the competition of buyers against buyers and of sellers against sellers determine it.

Another path to cheaper space for experimenting is for someone to subsidize the experimenters. A time-honored source of subsidy is parents and friends. Other examples of private subsidy include "crowdfunding" or the way the Walentas family in the 1970s famously offered low- and zero-price rentals to artists to kickstart development in what has become the wildly successful "Dumbo" district in Brooklyn, New York (Pogrebin, 2008).

Of course, another way to cheapen space is to get taxpayers to subsidize it. But the economics of government subsidies is entirely different from that of market competition. Jacobs (2000: Loc. 1471–75) herself criticized business subsidies because she understood that they distort the feedback from money prices. It is also the case that, whether private or public, subsidies tend to be rationed according to someone's personal judgment based on something other than willingness and ability to pay. How is that different from the market method? To the extent rationing takes place based solely on ability and willingness to pay, the market process is *impersonal*: it doesn't matter whether buyer and seller know each other, belong to the same ethnic or cultural group, have the same social connections, and so on. But to the extent that the rationing process is not impersonal, those who wish to buy or rent a subsidized space have to demonstrate to whomever distributes the subsidy that they are somehow deserving "on the merits of the case"—for example, they are poor artists or an entrepreneur under 30 years old or a relative of the subsidizer or someone with the right political views—these factors are more likely to come into play. In other words, to the extent the decision is not market-based, an outcome that most would consider fair may be more difficult to achieve because the deciding criteria will tend to be arbitrarily personal.

If I may digress here slightly to note that no market is entirely driven by the principle of ability and willingness to pay (which as we will see from a market-process viewpoint is not necessarily a bad thing), and so to the extent it is not even private, subsidizers will have to make decisions based on their own preferences, constrained by opportunity costs and a hard budget constraint. As a result, the basis for determining success from the point of view of the ultimate interests involved, whoever they may be, are harder to pin down. Success and failure of any kind of subsidy is harder to determine without the profit and loss signals markets provide. But even though both private and public subsidies suffer from this weakness vis-à-vis pure market competition, public subsidies tend to have softer budget constraints that are further removed from the discipline of profit and loss. And since the taxing powers of a government not only soften constraints but also generally make available much larger sums than private subsidies, the consequences of error in such cases are, other things equal, potentially much greater and the incentive to avoid error is smaller because of the absence of a direct material interest in success. We tend to care less if our investments fail if the loss is borne mostly by somebody else. If people in government had perfect knowledge—that is, enough knowledge such that they would never regret any policy decisions they make—then they could plan perfectly *if they wanted to.*

Finally, another private option that has emerged where real-estate prices are far above the national average is for several start-up companies to share office space. "Shared office space" and "shared co-living space"[12] highlight another advantage of a private approach over public subsidy: The greater possibility, where social institutions empower us to actually innovate in the creation of new ways to innovate. Chapter 5 elaborates on the advantages of social networks for this kind of creativity and innovation. (Solutions like this, as we will see in Chaps. 8 and 9, depend on the ability of informal rules and formal regulations and regulators to appropriately adjust to changing human and natural conditions.)

2.4   Re-thinking "Population Density"

After the first wave of decentralizing, low-density urban sprawl following World War II, and the second wave of suburban commercial "malling" beginning in the 1970s, we noted that Garreau sees in edge cities a novel setting for old-fashioned population density (Garreau, 1991: 37). Their "five million plus square feet of office space," combined with "six-hundred thousand square feet of retail" and "more jobs than bedrooms" reflect an updated, car-based version of Jacobsian urbanism and means that an edge city, at least to those who inhabit it, is a unique "place" and not a placeless exurb. What once might have been sprawl has evolved into a new kind of

---

[12] For shared office space, see, for example, Alton (2017) and for co-living space, Mather (2018).

city, but still a city in Jacobs's sense of an engine of innovation and economic development (Jacobs, 1969: 262).[13]

In addition, Peter Gordon and I (Gordon & Ikeda, 2007) propose an alternative to conventional density called "Jacobs Density," which tries to capture the interdependence among proximity, population size, and diversity. We define *Jacobs Density* as "the level of potential informal contacts of the average person in a given public space at any given time" (Gordon & Ikeda, 2011: 448). It is roughly the number of possible connections within a given group of people. Jacobs is the first to introduce the term "social capital" as it is commonly used today into the literature of social theory (Jacobs, 1961: 138), and Jacobs Density is an extension of the idea of social capital. The caveat discussed earlier about the current overemphasis among some urbanists on density still holds, however. (I develop this more fully in Chap. 5.)

3   It Is the Interaction of These Factors That Generates Diversity

According to Jacobs, these four factors complement one another.

All four in combination are necessary to generate city diversity; the absence of any one of the four frustrates a district's potential. (Jacobs, 1961: 151)

All need to be present in the same neighborhood to interact over time for diversity, and ultimately cohesive complementarities, to emerge and thrive.

---

[13] But some of the data show only a weak relation between density and development.

To measure whether density is related to the kind of innovation implied in Jacobs's definition of a city, Peter Gordon and I examined the relation between population density and a proxy for innovation; namely, the percentage of the population holding a master's degree or above. We found that at the city-level, this relation appears to weakly hold, but looking closer at the micro-level (at Public Use Microdata Survey data on zip codes from the American Community Survey), the relation vanishes (Gordon & Ikeda, 2007). Even if we are mindful of the limitations I pointed out earlier of population density as a defining characteristic of a city, we need to ask what is going on here? One possibility is that there is interaction across rather than within PUMS in a city that are important for the development of human capital. Glaeser et al.'s (1992) "Jacobs spillovers" perhaps? This is an area of future study.

Without mixed primary uses to operate as a people-attractor, for example, not enough of us will have a reason to use public spaces so that even high population density will not supply "eyes on the street"; if there are mixed primary uses, but population density is too low, there will not be enough of us in public space at different times for safety and to form social networks; blocks that are overly long will discourage lively pedestrian use and FTF contact, what Jacobs calls the "small change from which a city's wealth of public life may grow" (Jacobs, 1961: 72), resulting in dull, often scary public spaces; and without enough cheap space mingling with the new, a neighborhood will lack a crucial foothold for potential experimenters to spark innovation. The interaction of all these factors generates Jacobs's effective economic pools of use.[14] The neighborhood may survive but will fail to contribute to the long-term economic development of the city.

Another point to keep in mind is that a variety of land-uses and other forms of diversity cannot emerge or sustain themselves unless social institutions—that is, shared rules, norms, conventions, networks, and organizations—are stable enough for people to rely on for making plans, especially complicated plans for the long-term. It may sound paradoxical, but Jacobs argues that one of the factors important for such institutional stability is the mobility of the population: How easy or time-consuming is it for people to move from one part of the city to another either for daily commuting or for longer-term residence (Jacobs, 1961: 139)? Similarly, Alain Bertaud points to the critical importance of the mobility of urban populations from the perspective of cities as labor markets (Bertaud, 2018: 19–49). If an area that is otherwise highly desirable to be in is difficult to enter or leave, it is unlikely to generate much diversity because people will tend to avoid it. If living in "Lonely Gardens" means having an inconvenient commute—perhaps because of long distances

---

[14] The noted urban planner Alain Bertaud offers a good example of such an effective pool of use:

For instance, a lawyer who specializes in European agriculture regulations would not be very productive if she were surrounded only by people with the same skills. To be effective, she will have to be in close contact with other specialists in taxation and import tariffs, and she will need to engage the services of workers who will fix her computer, clean her office, deliver coffee to the board room, and prepare and serve the food that she will eat at lunch. In the same way, an unskilled industrial worker is likely to work in a factory requiring a large array of workers specialized in electronics, mechanics, labor law, insurance, and so on (Bertaud 2018: 32).

from jobs and poor transport options, or because it abuts a dangerous area—this may deter us from moving there in the first place or from staying very long if we do. That is one of the problems with what Jacobs calls "slumming slums": Most people want to get out of them as soon as they can. Whereas "unslumming slums" are those low-income communities that can maintain reasonably healthy social institutions and connections because people have an incentive to live or work there long enough for social networks to take root and flourish (Jacobs, 1961: 270–90).

3.1   Diversity and Resilience

Stable, however, doesn't mean static. Social institutions need to be able to adapt to changing tastes, technologies, and resources; or to changes in demographics, lifestyles, and the natural environment (Ikeda, 2012). A diversity of land-uses within a neighborhood or district fosters an ongoing process of creativity in an economy and its culture. Jacobs points out their common foundation in urban diversity:

> [W]herever we find a city district with an exuberant variety and plenty in its commerce, we are apt to find that it contains a good many other kinds of diversity also, including variety of cultural opportunities, variety of scenes, and a great variety in its population and other users. This is more than coincidence. The same physical and economic conditions that generate diverse commerce are intimately related to the production, or the presence, of other kinds of city variety. (Jacobs, 1961: 148)

Such diversity can also promote urban resilience during an emergency. *The New York Times* architecture critic Michael Kimmelman observes, for example, that just after Hurricane Sandy in 2012 severely damaged parts of the New York–New Jersey shoreline, clubs and other public spaces quickly transitioned to serve as emergency shelters and gathering places for those threatened by or made homeless by the storm.

> Less ravaged neighborhoods were more densely populated, with vibrant commercial strips and social networks, community gardens, parks and well-tended sidewalks. They drew people out of overheated homes and into

the streets, shops, gardens, parks, and into libraries, too: places where there were things to do and friends to meet. (Kimmelman, 2013)

Not only could the same land be used differently over long periods of economic development, the same space could be used for entirely different purposes and re-tasked very quickly if the social networks in the surrounding neighborhood are sufficiently robust ("multiplex" in the language of social-network theory of the next chapter) to enable strangers to come together in a crisis. As Kimmelman suggests, that kind of rapid adaptability and resilience, a form of inter-temporal complexity discussed in the previous chapter, is most likely where land-use is diverse.

Combined within an urban setting, these four generators of diversity enable ordinary people to more effectively utilize the complex divisions of labor that result and to better explore, experiment, and adjust to unexpected change.

3.2   Safety and Diversity

Jacobs places prime importance on safety and security in a great city, calling it a "bedrock attribute" (Jacobs, 1961: 30), and it is worthwhile spending a little more time on this subject.

Feeling unsafe in a public space discourages us from seeking out the diversity and uniqueness of others for mutual gain, and it also discourages us from displaying our own diversity or developing our own uniqueness in public interactions. Other things equal, we would be less willing to look and behave differently from the prevailing norm. Differences that are complementary within a heterogeneous population might still exist, but it would not be to anyone's advantage to try to make otherwise valuable contact with people, especially strangers, very different from ourselves. Fear makes us less welcoming to strangers. Withdrawing from people we don't already know strengthens norms of exclusivity and weakens norms of inclusivity and tolerance in our social networks, so that support for immigration within and among cities wanes. The critical factor of urban mobility (and Jacobs Density) declines.

While relying heavily on professional police to maintain public safety may be one way to restore a general feeling of security in public space, a successful city is one in which safety and security arise with a minimum of conscious direction or formal policing. Jacobs points out (1961: 32) that if the only way to keep public order is to place professional security on every street corner, that city is failing in its "bedrock" function.

> The first thing to understand is that the public peace—the sidewalk and street peace—of cities is not kept primarily by the police, necessary as police are. It is kept primarily by an intricate, almost unconscious, network of voluntary controls and standards among the people themselves, and enforced by the people themselves. (Jacobs, 1961: 31–2)

How have cities historically achieved public safety informally?

Jacobs begins with the observation that we are less likely to threaten or provoke others if we know we are casually being watched by eyes on the street than if we don't think we are. In most cases, then, the more likely it is we believe someone is watching us, the more restraint we will show. Contrariwise, if we believe no one is watching then, other things equal, we tend to feel less constrained to follow norms of civility. It is probably not even necessary for someone actually to intervene were we misbehave; merely being seen is usually enough deterrence for any but the most determined offenders.

If not more police, the key then is to find a way to get more unofficial eyes on the street, people who though we may not know them at all are familiar enough with the norms of the particular area to know whether those norms encourage or discourage private intervention should a problem arise (Wilson & Kelling, 1982). Jacobs refers to this "brains behind the eyes" (Jacobs, 1961: 56). It is especially important to know whether or not someone's "got our back" if we intervene.

Using public space for parades or other special events may occasionally get people out in large numbers and contribute to community spirit, but sporadic interactions aren't likely to create the same kind of long-term relationships that ground an effective social infrastructure. And, of course, forcing us to attend public gatherings, as some governments do, may generate some benefits but also great costs and negative consequences, including the loss of personal freedom and spontaneity. So there needs to be positive incentives to encourage people to use public spaces throughout any given day.

Enter mixed primary uses. People attract people in part because there is "safety in numbers" and because we may have no particular reason to go out in public other than that we like watching other people, and perhaps like being watched by them in turn. Land-use diversity within the same neighborhood or location of the city, created by people supplying or demanding different goods and services at different times, attracts people in sufficient numbers to provide the eyes on the street. And the more diverse the uses of public space—for schools, residences, offices, museums, movie theaters, night clubs, shopping, commerce, etc.—the more likely that these attractors will operate at different times, producing Jacobs's "intricate sidewalk ballet."

But business-improvement districts or municipal centers between 6 pm and 6 am on weekdays or on weekends tend to be deserted and lacking in interest, creating an urban vacuum. This is true of any single, massive use, governmental or private. The absence of *short blocks* and the presence of such vacuums can easily drain the life out of an area.

While in *Death and Life* Jacobs's focus is on the diversity of land-use rather than on the diversity of people themselves, people will use a space, say a store front, as nail salon or a coffeehouse, if they are allowed to, in a manner that depends a great deal on their individual knowledge and skills, or what economists call "human capital." Moreover, the kind of diversity that attracts people and provides safety in a great city is not only diversity of land-use (on the supply side) but also (on the demand side) a diversity of tastes and an openness to, or at least a tolerance of, the new and the different, which can depend on a person's personal background and experience.

But how do cities and the economic processes within them find the balance between balance diversity and cohesion? Besides social networks and connections, what else enables and encourages us to voluntarily use public space, provide land-use diversity, and reach out to the socially distant? What other mechanism transforms diversity into a coherent set of complementary uses, and turn potential conflict into cooperation? Just below the surface of Jacobs's analysis, present but largely unspoken, is the force of economic incentives. Time to look at it from this angle and make it explicit.

4   How the Market Process Solves Jacobs's Problem of Diversity and Cohesion

The two apparently opposing forces of diversity and cohesion are essential to urban vitality. The four generators of diversity create a variety of land-use that set the stage for safety, peaceful contact, and dynamic social networks to emerge, all of which are necessary for large-scale, voluntary social cooperation and economic development.

As noted in Chap. 2, Jacobs appears to take it for granted that the people she is writing about operate under a regime of economic freedom: that is, private property, free association, rule of law. Also, while she doesn't draw on the standard economic analysis of markets, supply and demand and all that, at least not until *The Nature of Economies* in 2000, neither does she offer a clear alternative explanation for why people would take advantage of the institutional setting I have just described. The latent complementarities of Jacobs's "effective economic pools of use" offer the *potential* for discovering valuable complementarities, but what incentive do people have to bring these elements together?

Jacobs lacks an explicit theory of markets or entrepreneurship to pull everything together and complete her theory of economic development.

This section introduces concepts from market-process economics to fill in these important gaps in Jacobs's analytical framework, which I believe will strengthen the analytical power of Jacobs's economics. At the same time, connecting competition and entrepreneurship with the "non-market" or sociological foundations of social cooperation that Jacobs relies on—for example, social networks, social capital, norms of trust, and reciprocity—nicely complements market-process economics.

While not all diverse elements in a population are complementary, or may not be at any particular moment, it is important to note that productive complementarities cannot exist at all unless people perceive[15] them in the first place and have an incentive to act upon those perceptions. Complementarity would not be possible without heterogeneity. There would be little reason for us to associate with one another unless we perceive valuable complementary diversities among ourselves that would make associating worthwhile. (This is a version of the basic economic principle of comparative advantage.)

Beyond merely perceiving differences among diverse elements, for us to regard those elements as complementary, as fitting together in a way that is more useful to us than the individual elements by themselves, we need to see them as parts of a plan (Lachmann, 1978: 54). That is, we need to have a goal in mind that the diverse elements we perceive can in our estimation help us to achieve, as means to an end. If we want to drive from New York to Chicago, then a car and gasoline—two otherwise very heterogeneous elements—would serve as complementary inputs for getting us there. On the other hand, for a different goal, such as commuting to work, neither a car nor gasoline may in our estimation be even necessary if a train or walking is more convenient.

It is also possible that we have a plan and see potentially valuable, complementary diversities around us but the rules, norms, or conventions of our community somehow discourage us from engaging with outsiders—"We don't associate with those kinds of people!"—preventing us from exploiting those complementarities, thereby lowering the value to us of those diversities. In such cases, what differentiates a person, place, or thing from others could easily be an obstacle to cooperation and those differences easily lead to conflict. The value of diversity would fall to the extent that we are prevented or discouraged from relying on or interacting with that which is different from ourselves.

Again, the questions we have been addressing are: What are the conditions that enable complementarities and cohesiveness to emerge and to be exploited among diverse persons, places, and things? What factors determine the balance between diversity and cohesion? What are the forces that maintain or adjust that balance under changing conditions

---

[15] "Perceive" here means both (1) become aware of or (2) subjectively believe the existence of and so may be true or false (i.e., result in net gains or not).

(which Jacobs refers to as "dynamic stability" (Jacobs, 2000: 84))? How does a city and the socioeconomic processes it fosters successfully enable this? In the presence of self-interested persons with imperfect knowledge operating in a world of scarce resources, why would socially distant strangers freely choose to associate with one another at all?

4.1 Markets Turn Diversity into Complementarity

The answer lies in the incentives, institutions, and resulting choices that drive the market process. And the organizing principle of the market process as well as the living city is competition, supported by norms such as fair play, honesty, reciprocity, and trust.[16] Again, a community of people with socially distant backgrounds offers a wide range of mutually beneficial opportunities in the form of potentially complementary diversities within effective pools of use. Under the right conditions, the more diverse they are, the wider will be the range of such opportunities. There are net gains to be made not only by substituting one use for another—for example, a Shake Shack for a Burger King—but more importantly, from the standpoint of innovation, by bringing complementary heterogeneous uses together in novel ways, for example, connecting a car owner with time on her hands with someone who needs and is willing to pay for a ride with the help of an app. And in the urban process, alertness to such opportunities and the discovery of radical ignorance is the role of entrepreneurship (Kirzner, 1973). In the market process, entrepreneurial competition is one of the main cohesive forces that transforms heterogeneous elements into complementary uses.

As I pointed out in Chap. 2, it was not until Jacobs published *The Nature of Economies* in 2000 that she effectively explains the essential role of money prices as a feedback mechanism that guides decisions on the market. Even then, she doesn't present a full and detailed explanation of the competitive market process. She doesn't carefully explain what motivates people to engage in trade with those whom they don't know and the role of prices and competition in that process, perhaps because she takes

---

[16] These and other elements of what Jacobs calls the "Commercial Moral Syndrome" in Jacobs (1992) are discussed on Chap. 9.

it for granted. But she does articulate an understanding of the role of profit-seeking and loss-avoidance in a living city.

Now, some may find the word "profit" in this discussion troubling or objectionable. Jacobs does not. A quick search of my electronic version of *Death and Life* of "profit" and "profitability" shows 36 results. Of those, it is true that by my count (the reader may come up with a different number) a plurality (16) cast profit in a negative light. None of these, however, disparage profit-seeking and profitability, per se. Ten or so of these negative characterizations appear in her discussion of "the self-destruction of diversity"—an important dynamic that I will treat in Chap. 6—in which she doesn't condemn profit-seeking, but the consequences it can lead to under certain circumstances. Similarly, the remaining six or so negative results, which relate to public housing and the use of eminent domain, take aim less at profit-seeking than at gains earned by gaming public policy (which is called "rent seeking"). Sixteen results are neutral references, and only four can be considered positive characterizations of profit-seeking. Of the latter, however, it is worth highlighting the following passage because it plainly expresses the way in *Death and Life* Jacobs sees the strong connection between "profit-making enterprises" and lively, livable cities:

> Nor is the diversity that is important for city districts by any means confined to profit-making enterprises and to retail commerce, and for this reason it may seem that I put an undue emphasis on retail trade. I think not, however. Commercial diversity is, in itself, immensely important for cities, socially as well as economically. Most of the uses of diversity on which I dwelt in Part I of this book [on the significance of sidewalks, parks, and neighborhoods for successful cities] depend directly or indirectly upon the presence of plentiful, convenient, diverse city commerce. (Jacobs, 1961: 148)

Still, there are important gaps in her economic framework and filling them in makes for a powerful tool for understanding the living city as a socioeconomic phenomenon, by offering a more complete explanation of how a living city peacefully resolves the tension between diversity and cohesion. To that end, the following is a brief outline of the role of entrepreneurial competition in market-process economics.

4.2   Entrepreneurship Is a Coordinating Force in the Market Process

Market-process economics takes as its starting point the presence of radical ignorance in any really existing social order. As noted in Chap. 3, radical ignorance refers to the phenomenon of "not knowing that you don't know." For example, a property owner who would like to sell a particular parcel at a price no lower than $1 million may be unaware that the person sitting next to him at a local café would be interested in buying it, or knows someone so interested, for up to $1.3 million, but is totally unaware of it. Clearly, there are pure gains from trade to be made here from their differences in valuation. It is not that either person has *chosen* not to know about the other because it is too costly, for which economists would use the term "rational ignorance" or ignorance by choice, but that neither is even *aware* of the opportunity that awaits them, at no or very little cost, at the next table. To become aware of the profit opportunity would require an act of discovery on the part of one or the other or perhaps of a third party acting as an intermediary. The aspect of human action responsible for such acts of discovery is the *entrepreneur* (Kirzner, 1973; Ikeda, 1994).

In a mature market economy, the prices that emerge from competition among sellers and among buyers aid us in making an entrepreneurial discovery, in learning about someone or something that up to now we didn't even know we didn't know. In the example, the difference in the potential prices offered ($1 million) and bid ($1.3 million) represents a reward of pure profit (net of any selling or buying costs) that provides the incentive for each person to become aware of the other. As I indicated, any third parties also have an incentive to discover the opportunity and profit from selling the information they have uncovered. The owner, potential buyer, or anyone else stands to earn a pure profit from uncovering radical ignorance and they are all potential competitors in the process of competitive discovery. This simple example reflects the essence of the entrepreneurial-competitive process. Differences in the way we value people, places, and things represent potential profit opportunities to an entrepreneur who can discover and transform those differences into value-creating, mutually beneficial complementarities. Jacobs's insight that a great city facilitates creative experiment depends precisely on this transformation.

Also, to the extent market prices reflect the preferences of buyers and sellers, they reflect the scarcity of resources—land, labor, capital—in the market process. So, market prices serve a dual function in market-process economics: (1) if people are unaware of the preferences for tradable resources in the system, the emergence of market prices from trade, even if they are a little off and deviate from their equilibrium values, assist in the entrepreneurial discovery of those preferences; and (2) market prices, imperfect though they may be, give buyers and sellers at least some indicator of whether their plans have a chance of succeeding. Without market prices, we would be operating in the blind, utterly unable to calculate expected profits and losses. That means we wouldn't be able to know if we are using scarce resources wisely or poorly or if we are passing up profitable opportunities that we stood a much better chance of discovering if we had market prices to go on (Mises, 1981[1922]).

Even in a well-functioning market, the discovery process is never perfect. Indeed, just like living cities, when no one has perfect knowledge, we should expect mistakes, disappointment, and failed plans. The question then becomes, in the presence of imperfect knowledge, what sort of environment is best suited to help us discover and correct our mistakes? For market-process economics, the rules, norms, conventions, institutions, and organizations that minimize coercion and compulsion, that rely as much as possible on voluntary cooperation, are what enable flexible adjustment in the face of unexpected change. And if society has tolerance for the inevitable failures and disruptive successes of the competitive process, the consequence tends to be robust economic development.

It is, by the way, the same with scientific progress. When the practice of science is healthy, "expert opinion" and beliefs old and new are open to challenge and radical criticism (Polanyi, 2015). True science is never settled and neither is the market process—or a great city. But just as the residents of a living city need to be tolerant of ideas, offerings, and lifestyles that may offend them to some degree, in science, such criticism requires radical tolerance of the strange. Free science, free cities, and free societies thrive with heavy criticism and constructive conflict. But the balance between tolerance and criticism is crucial, and when that balance is right, the market process will flourish. Tolerance without criticism and criticism without tolerance lead by different routes to uncreative, social torpor.[17]

Entrepreneurship, in the form of coordinating complementary resources, takes place in both private and public spaces. People working within a private space such as in a company may discover new ways of doing something old, or a new use for an existing factor of production or procedure, or discover an innovation that cuts across existing processes and markets (Jacobs, 1969: 52, 197).

But for our purposes, it is worth emphasizing again that cultural and commercial entrepreneurship takes place in public space rather than private space. As I indicated in Chap. 2, it is in public space where the main challenge of the urban and market processes lies and where you will see most of the heavy lifting of entrepreneurially competitive coordination and cohesion. It is where ideas are tested. Economic development involves new ways of thinking that greater potential for disruption when local agents can connect despite long social distances (Ikeda, 2012). And for this, as we have seen, multiple attractors, the intricacy of short blocks, population density, and widely affordable space for experimentation, represent elements in a complex reciprocating system (Ikeda 2012a). The result of these interactions, as we saw in the last chapter, is a social order of "organized complexity."

(The next chapter applies the concepts of entrepreneurship and entrepreneurially driven competition to the realm of social networks.)

5   Concluding Thoughts

In *Death and Life of Great American Cities*, Jane Jacobs explicates four factors that together generate diversity in public space. I have shown that these four "generators of diversity" are a useful framework for helping us to understand how social cohesion emerges from diversity, but one that may be extended and reinterpreted as I have done here. Jacobs also

---

[17] I offer my thoughts on tolerance and criticism in this short essay: https://fee.org/articles/the-fruits-of-imperfection/. Accessed 26 May 2023.

explains how social networks, which are the result of as well as generators of trust, also enable all that diversity to cohere. But social networks are only one way that a living city can make heterogeneous elements of its space, as well as its people, complementary. The other way is through the competitive market process, which offers opportunities for alert entrepreneurs to profit from turning the diversity that living cities continually generate into a rich, complex, dynamic, and unpredictable mosaic that hangs together through time. Adding market-process economics to the Jacobsian analysis of the nature and significance of urban diversity reveals the strong incentives we have to take advantage of the effective economic pools of use that a living city spontaneously generates. Combining Jacobs's analysis with market-process economics effectively explains how a system capable of generating so much diversity can be equally effective in achieving cohesion.

Just as it is possible to enhance Jacobs's theory of economic development with market-process economics, it is also possible to develop her insights into social networks by applying more formal social-network concepts and theory, and that is what the next chapter is about. By so doing, it will also be showing the value of adding a social-network approach to the market-process theory of entrepreneurial discovery.

Works Cited

Alton, L. (2017, March 9). Why More Millennials Are Flocking to Shared Office Spaces. *Forbes*. Accessed 25 January 2023. https://www.forbes.com/sites/larryalton/2017/05/09/why-more-millennials-are-flocking-to-shared-office-spaces/?sh=1aa5ee6f69e8

Angel, S. (2020). *Solly Angel's Lecture on the Anatomy of Density*. Marron Institute of Urban Management. Accessed 9 May 2023 https://marroninstitute.nyu.edu/blog/solly-angels-lecture-on-the-anatomy-of-density

Bailey, M., Cao, R. (Rachel), Kuchler, T., Stroebel, J. & Wong, A. (2017, July). *Measuring Social Connectedness* (NBER Working Papers #23608). Accessed 9 May 2023. http://www.nber.org/papers/w23608

Barabasi, A.-L. (2003). *Linked: How Everything Is Connected to Everything Else and What It Means for Business, Science, and Everyday Life*. Plume.

Barone, J. (2018, May 18). How Seoul Transformed a Disused Highway Overpass into a Botanical Garden in the Sky. *Independent.* https://www.independent.co.uk/travel/asia/seoul-skygarden-location-opening-seoullo-7017-south-korea-best-parks-a8346771.html

Bertaud, A. (2018). *Order Without Design: How Markets Shape Cities.* MIT Press.

Bird, J. (2018, June 17). The Future of the Shopping Mall Is Not about Shopping. *Forbes.* https://www.forbes.com/sites/jonbird1/2018/06/17/the-future-of-the-shopping-mall-is-not-about-shopping/?sh=689e62385cf2

Bruegmann, R. (2006). *Sprawl: A Compact History.* Univ. of Chicago.

Christakis, N. A., & Fowler, J. H. (2009). *Connected: The Surprising Power of Our Social Networks and How They Shape Our Lives.* Little Brown and Co.

Desrochers, P., & Szurmak, J. (2017). Jane Jacobs as Spontaneous Economic Order Methodologist: Part 1: Intellectual Apprenticeship. *Cosmos + Taxis,* 4(2/3), 2–20.

Emerging Technology from the arXiv. (2016, March 24). Data Mining Reveals the Four Urban Conditions that Create Vibrant City Life. *MIT Technology Review.* Accessed 9 May 2023. https://www.technologyreview.com/2016/03/24/161419/data-mining-reveals-the-four-urban-conditions-that-create-vibrant-city-life/

Garreau, J. (1991). *Edge City: Life on the New Frontier.* Anchor Books.

Gladwell, M. (2010, September 27). Small Change: Why the Revolution Will Not Be Tweeted. *The New Yorker.* Accessed 25 January 2023 from http://www.newyorker.com/magazine/2010/10/04/small-change-malcolm-gladwell

Glaeser, E. L., Kallal, H. D., Scheinkman, J. A., & Shleifer, A. (1992). Growth in Cities. *Journal of Political Economy, 100*(6), 1126–1152.

Gordon, P., & Ikeda, S. (2007). *Power to the Neighborhoods: The Devolution of Authority in Post-Katrina New Orleans* (*Mercatus Policy Series*, Policy Comment No. 12). Arlington, VA.

Gordon, P., & Ikeda, S. (2011). Does Density Matter? In D. E. Andersson, Å. Andersson, & C. Mellander (Eds.), *Handbook of Creative Cities.* Edward Elgar.

Hardwick, M. J. (2004). *Mall Maker: Victor Gruen, Architect of an American Dream.* Univ. of Pennsylvania Press.

Ikeda, S. (1994). Chapter 4, Market Process. In P. J. Boettke (Ed.), *The Elgar Companion to Austrian Economics.* Edward Elgar.

Ikeda, S. (2011). "The limits of social media" in Foundation for Economic Education online, 8 February 2011. https://fee.org/articles/the-limits-of-social-media/?utm_medium=related_widget; https://fee.org/articles/facebook-and-familiar-strangers/

Ikeda, S. (2012). Economic Development from a Jacobsian Perspective. In S. Hirt (Ed.), *The Urban Wisdom of Jane Jacobs*. Routledge.

Ikeda, S. (2013). "Bookstore wars" in Foundation for Economic Education online, 16 August 2013. https://fee.org/articles/bookstore-wars/ and https://fee.org/articles/the-breezes-of-creative-destruction#axzz2biYFHgiJ

Ikeda, S. (2020). Urban Diversity and Cohesion. *Cosmos + Taxis*, 8(8&9), 28–45.

Jacobs, J. (1961). *The Death and Life of Great American Cities*. Vintage.

Jacobs, J. (1969). *The Economy of Cities*. Vintage.

Jacobs, J. (2000). *The Nature of Economies*. Vintage.

Kimmelman, M. (2013, October 2). Next Time, Libraries Could Be Our Shelters from the Storm. *The New York Times*: C1. Accessed 9 May 2023. http://www.nytimes.com/2013/10/03/arts/design/next-time-libraries-could-be-our-shelters-from-the-storm.html

Kirzner, I. (1973). *Competition and Entrepreneurship*. Univ. of Chicago Press.

Koeppel, G. (2015). *City on a Grid: How New York Became New York*. Da Capo Books.

Koolhaas, R. (1994). *Delirious New York: A Retroactive Manifesto for Manhattan*. The Monacelli Press.

Krier, L. (2007[1998]). *Architecture: Choice or Fate*. Papadakis.

Lachmann, L. (1978/1956). *Capital and Its Structure*. Sheed, Andrews and Mcmeel, Inc.

LeGates, R. T., & Stout, F. (Eds.). (2000). *The City Reader*. Routledge.

Lynch, K. (1960). The City Image and Its Elements. In R. T. LeGates & F. Stout (Eds.), *The City Reader 1996* (pp. 98–102).

Mather, L. (2018, March 9). "What It's Like to Live with 19 Complete Strangers. *Clever*. https://www.architecturaldigest.com/story/what-its-like-to-live-with-complete-strangers-common-co-living

Mises, L. von (1981[1922]). *Socialism: An Economic and Sociological Analysis*. (Trans. J. Kahane). : Liberty Classics.

Pogrebin, R. (2008, March 6). The lords of Dumbo Make Room for the Arts, at Least for the Moment. *The New York Times*. Accessed 9 May 2023. https://www.nytimes.com/2008/03/06/arts/design/06dumb.html?rref=collection%2Ftimestopic%2FWalentas%2C%20David%20C.&action=click&contentCollection=timestopics&region=stream&module=stream_unit&version=latest&contentPlacement=5&pgtype=collection

Polanyi, M. (2015[1958]). *Personal Knowledge: Toward a Post-Critical Philosophy*. Univ. of Chicago Press.

Price, A. A. (2013, November 28). Optimizing the Street Grid in *ALEXANDERANDREWPRICE*. Accessed 9 May 2023. http://andrewalexanderprice.com/blog20131128.php#.Xmp_JkN7lp8

Price, A. A. (2015, October 21). Granularity. *Strong Towns*. Accessed 9 May 2023. https://www.strongtowns.org/journal/2015/10/21/granularity

Scott, J. C. (1998). *Seeing Like a State: How Certain Schemes to Improve the Human Condition Have Failed*. Yale Univ. Press.

Szurmak, J., & Desrochers, P. (2017). Jane Jacobs as Spontaneous Economic Order Methodologist: Part 2: Metaphors and Methods. *Cosmos + Taxis, 4*(2&3), 21–48.

Vance, J. E. (1990). *The Continuing City: Urban Morphology in Western Civilization*. Johns Hopkins Univ. Press.

Whyte, W. H. (2009/1988). *Rediscovering the Center City*. Univ. of Pennsylvania Press.

Wilson, J. Q., & Kelling, G. L. (1982). Broken Windows. In Legates & Stout (Eds.) (2000): 254–63.

5

Social Networks and Action Space in Cities

We now know that social networks help bring coherence to the amazing diversity cities generate. In her biography of Jacobs's early life in Scranton, Pennsylvania, Glenna Lang quotes Jacobs on the importance of inclusivity and informality in these networks:

> The most important thing is that there are networks of people who know each other and the more inclusive they are the better.... [I]n order to have an efficient and inclusive network of people who know each other, the very basic thing about it is people knowing each other in a public and often in a very casual way." (Lang, 2021: Loc. 2469, 2471)

Jacobs in *Death and Life* is the first to use the term "social capital" in essentially the sense it is used by scholars today,[1] that is, as stable social

---

This chapter draws in part from Ikeda (2012).

---

[1] Glenn Loury (1977) is often credited with coining the term, but he himself names Jacobs as a precursor in his Neumann Lecture in Budapest, Hungary (2005). (I thank Amy Willis for the pointer.) This is the context in which Jacobs uses the term (1961, 138): "If self-government in the place is to work, underlying any float of population must be a continuity of people who have forged neighborhood networks. These networks are a city's irreplaceable social capital. Whenever the capital is lost, from whatever cause, the income from it disappears, never to return until and unless new capital is slowly and chancily accumulated."

© The Author(s) 2024
S. Ikeda, *A City Cannot Be a Work of Art*,
https://doi.org/10.1007/978-981-99-5362-2_5

networks that increase the value of its member's human capital (Coleman, 1990: 300). Sociologists and mathematicians have further refined the concept in ways that are congenial to both Jacobsian analysis and market-process economics, as we will see.

Now, social capital can be either inclusive or exclusive in nature. Both forms are important in a living city—inclusive networks contribute dynamism, exclusive networks stability—but Jacobs is not always clear which meaning she has in mind. The quotation above, for example, is characteristically ambiguous in this respect. She says social networks need to be "inclusive" but also that their members should "know each other." So, are strangers welcome to these networks or not? This is something I will try to sort out in this chapter.

I have said that Jacobs in her early work relies less explicitly on the market process per se and more on these social networks to explain how cohesion and complementarity take place among a great city's heterogeneous elements. In this chapter, I explain in some detail how entrepreneurial competition operates in both markets and social networks. This also develops the theme of Chap. 4 of how markets and cities take differences that have historically driven people apart and turn them into value-producing complementarities.

I have also noted that Jacobs seems to take for granted individual freedom of choice, mobility, and association in her analysis, and that these are implicit in her discussion of urban diversity and cohesion. How otherwise would the transformation of diversity into complementarity take place so robustly in a great city if social institutions and pressures (private or governmental) hampered the process? Without freedom of this kind we would be less able to act on gainful opportunities we discover among heterogeneous urban elements. As we have seen, we are more apt to discover these valuable connections when we can freely and safely make contact in public spaces. Jacobs makes this point using the example of city sidewalks.

> Lowly, unpurposeful and random as they may appear, sidewalk contacts are the small change from which a city's wealth of public life may grow. (Jacobs, 1961: 72)

Such informal contact might last only for a moment, as when strangers navigate around each other on a busy sidewalk. Or it may linger, as when we fawn over a stranger's pet on the street, strike up a conversation with someone in a bar, or when we nod at a "familiar stranger" in an apartment lobby (Milgram, 1972). These contacts may lead to nothing substantial, but sometimes they do. This is especially the case at gatherings, such as a party or even a formal meeting, where we get to know new people in a context in which we may be familiar. Contacts like these might involve riskier, longer-term commitments, such as starting a friendship or getting a job offer. To engage in mobility of that kind requires the freedom to make and break social connections. It also requires trust of some kind. In this chapter, then, the roles of freedom, social and economic, and trust are made explicit.

I begin by further explicating market-process economics with particular emphasis on the nature and significance of entrepreneurship. This allows me to show how adopting certain concepts from social-network theory, some of them pioneered by Jacobs herself, increases the explanatory power of market-process economics. Next, I interpret Jacobs's insights on the importance of face-to-face contact in the light of social-network theory, and link this to the concept of Jacobs Density. (This gets just a bit technical, but I trust the patient reader will see its value.) I am then better able explain how social-network theory can be easily and usefully integrated into market-process economics, providing another common bond with Jacobsian economics. The penultimate section delves further into the meaning and significance of trust, which is so central to Jacobs's analysis of urban safety and to the dynamics of social networks. The final substantive section draws some very general policy conclusions.

1   Cities and the Market Process

As I mentioned before, long before cities became a popular subject among scholars, economists had addressed the question of how cohesion in the sense of systemic order tends to emerge out of independent, individual actions. They asked, for example, how do countless buyers and sellers competing for scarce resources manage to coordinate their personal buying and selling plans without a central authority telling them what to do?

For instance, the Scottish moral philosopher and reputed father of economics Adam Smith explained in 1776 how self-interest constrained by peaceful competition drives the successful operation of markets via an "invisible hand," which his famous book *The Wealth of Nations* (Smith, 1976[1776]) helped to make more visible. As this line of thought progressed over the next 100 years, a core problem for economic science became to develop the link between individual actions and orderly social outcomes through the medium of markets. In the late nineteenth century, the French economist Léon Walras pioneered a mathematical method to specify the conditions under which individual decisions in many separate markets throughout an economy simultaneously dovetail in an economy-wide "general equilibrium" (Walras, 1977[1874]). As economics developed through the twentieth century, two fundamentally different approaches emerged: (1) the microeconomic analysis of equilibrium outcomes in which individual decisionmakers have perfect knowledge and don't make systematic mistakes and (2) the analysis of economic outcomes as primarily determined by the interaction of macroeconomic aggregates—such as aggregate demand and supply and national output—where errors in the private sector recur regularly and lead to systemic crises that require effective government interventions to correct.

The story is of course much more involved and far more interesting than I have described here. The point, though, is that, with some noteworthy exceptions, mainstream economic theory has strayed from studying the connection between individual actions and systemic outcomes, such as how markets enable individual plans to dovetail over time, even when our knowledge is imperfect. Instead, under the powerful influence of mathematical equilibrium theory and macroeconomic aggregation, the competitive process of discovery—an entrepreneurial process—all but disappeared from the literature (Kirzner, 1997). At the same time and largely under the same influences, the kind of social institutions we examine in this book—for example, public space, social networks, norms of trust and reciprocity—have also faded from economics. Unfortunately, as a result, little in mainstream economics today is particularly relevant for investigating experiment and creativity and the social setting in which they take place.

1.1   Entrepreneurship

One of the exceptions to this historical trend traces its heritage to a founder of modern economics, the Viennese economist Carl Menger, a pioneer of what is known as marginal analysis. Nearly 100 years after Adam Smith, Menger helped to reorient the economic theory of value from backward-looking labor costs, which sees the value of a good as deriving from the historical cost of producing it, toward the forward-looking, subjective perceptions of individual actors, in which a good's value depends on what we expect its usefulness to us to be in the future. Menger utilizes a "genetic-causal method" by which social order and institutions emerge unplanned from our actions based on our perceptions. That method explains the unintended emergence of a complex social institution, such as money, by tracing its logical evolution through the self-interested actions of individuals over time. Bartering a sack of grain for a goat leads to the use of goats as a medium of exchange, to the use of more-portable and divisible media, and eventually to precious metals and later to coinage, banking, and paper currency (Menger, 1981).[2]

In the same vein, a student of Menger's, Eugen von Böhm-Bawerk, developed a time-based theory of *capital*, that is, produced means of production, one of the central problems of which is how heterogeneous capital goods, spread over an entire economy, can without central direction form complex structures of diverse complementary inputs that over time eventually become goods that we directly consume (Böhm-Bawerk, 1959: 23). Or, as author Leonard Read expresses it, "How do you make a pencil?" How do you combine bits of knowhow, skill, wood, rapeseed oil, and myriad heterogeneous elements scattered around the world to create something as seemingly simple as a pencil, such that it has greater value than all of its components taken separately (Read, 1958)?

In turn, one of Böhm-Bawerk's students was Ludwig von Mises, whose contributions to economic theory, especially to the problem of economic calculation under socialism, set the stage for some of the most important debates in twentieth century economics. Mises was in his day the clearest

---

[2] The final chapter of Menger (1981) on the evolution of money is a prototype for this kind of "genetic-causal" reasoning. See also O'Driscoll and Rizzo (1985).

exponent of how money prices enable entrepreneurs to coordinate their plans via profit and loss signals, across industries and across time, without the need for deliberate, central planning. Mises's protégé Friedrich A. Hayek, winner of the Nobel Prize in Economics in 1974, develops this theme in one of the most cited articles in economics, "The use of knowledge in society" (Hayek, 1945). There, Hayek explains how market prices themselves can serve as *knowledge surrogates* that, when individuals are free to adjust their plans without excessive external constraint, tend to accurately reflect the relative scarcities of the underlying resources (Thomsen, 1992). When market prices do this accurately, they perform the feedback Jacobs describes in her book *The Nature of Economies* (written in the style of a dialog):

> "Price feedback is inherently well integrated," said Hiram. "It's not sloppy, not ambiguous. As [Adam] Smith perceived, the data carry meaningful information on imbalances of supply and demand and they do automatically trigger corrective responses. So data and its purport and responses are all of a piece." (Jacobs, 2000: 110)

The price system according to Hayek enables us to harness knowledge that we are completely unaware of because it is embedded contextually in the "knowledge of the particular circumstances of time and place" of individuals dispersed across an entire economy (Hayek, 1945: 80). Leonard Read's pencil is a simple but effective example of both this knowledge problem and its solution via the price system. (Recall that I have noted the similarity of Hayek's "local knowledge" to Jacobs's "locality knowledge.")

Israel M. Kirzner, a prominent American student of Mises and someone we also encountered in the last chapter, has gone on to develop an entrepreneurial theory of the competitive market process, which views *entrepreneurship* as alertness to profit opportunities that arise when people make mistakes owing to their radical ignorance (Kirzner, 1973). Adding another dimension to Mises's explanation of the role of money prices in economic calculation and to Hayek's explanation of the signaling role of market prices, Kirzner argues that entrepreneurial discovery relies on market prices for arbitrage opportunities (buying low, selling high) created by the misjudgments of buyers and sellers, who may be overly optimistic or pessimistic about the future. Without entrepreneurial discovery, we wouldn't be able to correct our mistakes by removing "radical ignorance," that is, relevant knowledge we don't know we don't know.

While these ideas are consistent with Jacobs's economics, much of it, including competition and entrepreneurship and what I said earlier about the underlying assumption of economic freedom, is mostly implicit in her writings. By the same token, economic theorists, perhaps under the influence of equilibrium analysis and macroeconomic aggregation, have mostly failed to appreciate the importance of social institutions and fluid social networks that are important elements in Jacobs's theory of city-centered, economic development.

1.2   Extending the Boundaries of Market-Process Economics

Thus, economists in the "mainline" Mengerian tradition[3] of economics have understood the market process as an evolutionary and dynamic phenomenon, and the causes and consequences of purposeful human action (Mises, 1963). They have, however, placed less emphasis (though more than most) on the "thick" social context in which we discover opportunities at a particular time and place. We might ask, for example, through what medium do we become aware of relevant knowledge? Action never takes place outside a particular spatial context, but is instead always undertaken by someone for something at a certain time *and at a certain place*.[4] And how do we become aware of the very "knowledge of the particular circumstances of time and place," the local, contextual knowledge, that helps us to interpret and evaluate those price signals and social institutions?

---

[3] See Peter J. Boettke's (2012) distinction between mainstream versus "mainline economics," the latter following more closely to the agenda of Adam Smith.
[4] Andersson (2012) contains a variety of relevant essays on "the spatial market process." See also Virgil Storr's (2008) discussion of the related concept of "social space."

Others have addressed the importance of the temporal dimension of action; that action necessarily takes place through time, adding an under-appreciated element of complexity into economic analysis (O'Driscoll & Rizzo, 1985). But it is at least as important to recognize that action is never placeless; that where people can and do choose to act can be equally important.

2   Action Space and Social Networks

We have noted that Kirzner (1973) characterizes entrepreneurship as alertness to pure profit opportunities and as essentially an act of arbitrage, of buying low and selling high. But his analysis takes place at a high level of abstraction and doesn't tell us how we are first exposed to the information that leads to the discovery of those opportunities. Where does that information come from and how reliable is it?

Suppose someone tells me that I can buy apples around the corner for one dollar apiece and then sell them across the street for two dollars. Does this information represent an opportunity to earn a pure arbitrage profit? I contend that it does not until we can satisfactorily answer two questions: (1) What is our relationship to the sources of the information and (2) how reliable are they? The first question is about the nature of interpersonal contacts; the second is about trust. The answer to both questions lies in social networks—the entrepreneurial-competitive process is embedded in social networks. Social networks provide the channels through which information flows to and from the entrepreneur. One never buys and sells in the abstract, whether in the market for plumbers or in the market for corporations. It is always necessary to some extent to ask, "Buy low from whom, sell high to whom?" The issues of trust, reciprocity, and trustworthiness immediately enter each side of the exchange. These issues in turn are tied to place.

Within a network or set of networks, finding a reliable source of information (which might also carry information to others) and making a discovery from information gained from that source are both creative acts. In the first case, entrepreneurs make a valuable personal connection in a way that others have not; in the second, they recognize and profitably interpret information passing through that connection in a way that others have not. An online platform or video may broadcast a vast amount of information indiscriminately across a vast number of people, but the most critical information for entrepreneurship tends to come to us through personal contacts, often from people we may not know very well.

These creative acts—of forming and dissolving social ties and of discovering profit opportunities—take place in action space.

2.1   The Nature of Action Space

What exactly is "action space"? Simply put, an action space is where we do things; it is the physio-social environment in which we can act. And by "act" I mean making a conscious decision to do something or not, to execute a plan however big or small.

Now, to put more content into the concept, I need to talk about what is required for us to act, to "do" something. The first three prerequisites for human action are (Mises, 1963: 13):

1. A felt uneasiness
2. A vision of a state of affairs in which our uneasiness is reduced
3. Means available to realize that vision

Adding a final condition makes these four conditions sufficient for taking an action:

4. Awareness of the means to realize that vision

If we feel perfectly at ease, we would have no reason to act. But suppose we feel uncomfortably thirsty; we feel ill at ease. So, do we now act? No, because we don't yet know if there is a better alternative to being thirsty. For instance, we could imagine the possibility of not feeling thirsty or of feeling less so. However, it is still not possible to act because the means to remove our thirst, perhaps a button to request a glass of water, may not be available to us. If we had access to such a button, it would satisfy the third condition. But we would not yet act if we were unaware that pressing the button (or some other action) would remove our thirst. Thus, the first three conditions are necessary to make a choice or to execute a plan, but they are not sufficient. To act requires the fourth condition: that we are aware of the button and its significance.

Imagine waking up fully conscious, but not knowing where we are. We notice we are lying down, covered in something white, surrounded by pale walls and some objects. We feel painfully thirsty (condition 1) and we can imagine not being so thirsty (condition 2). But how can we choose to act without knowing more about the space we are in? Suppose we see that next to us is a call button (condition 3). We still don't do anything unless we know the meaning and significance of that object. If suddenly we realize that we are lying in a hospital room, the thing next our bed is a call button, and pressing it connects with someone who can relieve our thirst (condition 4), we can now act. We can choose to press the button—or not. That is, under these circumstances, choosing not to press it would also be an action.

And if, say, the button doesn't work or no one responds, now that we know (or believe we know) where we are, other possible actions may present themselves. We could call out or walk (if able) to the nurses' station for help—once we understand the rules of behavior and the possible connections we might have with others in that space.

In our initial conscious but unwitting state, the space we occupy is not yet an action space for us (although it may be for the hospital staff). We don't know what to do or indeed if anything at all can be done to improve our situation. Once the first three conditions are fulfilled, however, it then becomes an action space, a hospital room, where the possibility of taking an action exists. As long as we are unaware of the means that are available to remove our uneasiness, we would not act, even though in some objective sense everything is in place for us to do so. The fourth element is missing.

What does this have to do with cities?

Remember my discussion of Kevin Lynch's "city image" back in Chap. 3? We each have a mental image or mental map that serves as shorthand for understanding the place we wish to enter and navigate. That image changes over time as our experience grows. The image of a local is different from that of a tourist. We can thus add a social dimension to Lynch's more physically based concept. Not only does our image contain physical structures and land-uses—Lynch mentions paths, edges, nodes, districts, and landmarks—it also holds social elements that we expect to find there. Who will we see and how will they (and we) behave? The social dimension makes a place more navigable.

Suppose we are considering taking a six-kilometer walk for exercise. What might our image consist of if the walk takes place in the countryside? There are certain aspects we first must consider. There is the physical aspect: weather, trees, trails, terrain, pleasing wildlife, shelter; the aspect of security: lighting, angry bears, muggers, other eyes on the "street"; and the social: who we might encounter along the way (welcome or unwelcome). Expectations such as these will determine where we choose to walk or whether to go out at all.

And, of course, this also applies to walking in urban locations. There is the physical aspect, which includes the land-uses or granularity of the city blocks we pass along; security, in terms of which streets are safe and which to avoid; and the social dimension of how crowded with strangers the public spaces will be and where we might likely meet people we know. Whether we plan to walk in a particular location depends on these kinds of expectations.

I have lived in New York City for decades. Nevertheless, there are entire districts I have never been to, some of which I do plan to explore someday, while others I do not. My city image consists not of the entire city, but of a patchwork of streets, blocks, and neighborhoods. A subset of those are my action spaces—places I am able and willing to do something in—while the rest of that city image are not my action spaces, at least for now. My action spaces need not be places I have actually been to, but where I think I know what to expect to some degree.

In short, action spaces are where we believe we may encounter certain people, places, and things. They contain our expectations about how people will behave and the kinds of contacts we might have with them. Not all action spaces are created equal, nor is a given action space potentially fruitful at all times. It depends on who and what is in that space, our expectations, and our alertness. Entrepreneurship happens in action space.

Being creative, making connections, and making discoveries are necessarily unpredictable. We cannot say with certainty where valuable ties will be made or unmade, or which action spaces will bear fruit, otherwise someone would probably have already made or unmade them. And even if we are exposed to information that contains a profit opportunity, there is no guarantee we will in fact recognize it (Ikeda, 2007). The "who, what, and how" of a discovery depends on the spatiotemporal context, that is, the "where and when."

We also cannot predict how a social tie, having been established between person A and person B for one purpose, might later serve other purposes that neither A nor B could have foreseen (i.e., multiplexity). For example, a regular customer might tell you about a new competitor who has moved into your neighborhood, a teacher might introduce you to a future business partner, your sister-in-law turns out to be an excellent tax attorney, or a colleague might offer a tip about someone working on a project related to your own (Desrochers, 2001).

Again, some sources of information, a broadcast about stock prices for example, may be impersonal, but still have a high degree of reliability. Even in that case, however, the broadcast will depend on someone making critical decisions along the way, the owner or managers of the platform, for example. Usually, the most important entrepreneurial information, information that tips the decision-making balance one way or the other, comes through personal channels, often informally. Important decisions big and small rely on information conveyed by flesh and blood people who are connected to us in ways that are not arbitrary. From choosing a stock to choosing a mechanic to choosing the site of a new business, making a decision in the "impersonal market" depends a great deal on how much we know about the people with whom we plan to work or from whom we plan to buy or sell. And we may never know those countless others who are also involved, but are far upstream or downstream from us in a production network. *Trust*—reliance on another when we may be taken advantage of—is an essential element in that process.[5]

---

[5] I have gained a great deal of insight and stimulation on the nature and meaning of trust from Seligman (1997).

We know Hayek (1945) argued long ago that the price system is a marvel at coordinating the decisions of myriad anonymous decisionmakers, while at the same time economizing on the amount of information anyone needs to know to perform successfully up and down the supply chain. What he didn't emphasize is that, nevertheless, each decisionmaker has to possess an enormous amount of contextual knowledge about the local situation, much of it gained from face-to-face contact (Ikeda, 2002). This contextual knowledge includes knowledge about personal connections and their reliability or relevance. Who we would ask for advice about potential investors for a project need not be the same person who we would ask about projects to invest in. And what we can safely say to different people is an important skill in all aspects of life. This ability to tell who we can trust and for what purpose and to what extent is vital, even though we may not be able to explain how we do it, even to ourselves. So Hayek is right about the price system economizing considerably on the technical knowledge we need to, say, build a house ("knowing that"), but we should not underestimate the amount of contextual knowledge required to decide who to ask about where to find the best house for the lowest price ("knowing how").

Now, if our information were perfect, there would be no need either to make or to break social connections, at least for the purpose of coordinating our plans, because the problem of having to acquire relevant information from others would not exist. Like price signals, social networks are a way of coping with less-than-perfect information. Like price signals, social networks enable us to utilize the tastes and human capital of others who would otherwise be inaccessible. As sociologist Ronald Burt observes: "Through relations with colleagues, friends, and clients come the opportunities to transform financial and human capital into profit" (Burt, 1995: Loc. 155). And economist Paul Seabright adds: "Just as nobody can plan an artistic revolution, nobody quite plans the networks that make them possible" (Seabright, 2004: 111).

This raises important questions about the relation between entrepreneurship and action space, which is where making and breaking connections with social networks happens. How do entrepreneurs alter social networks and why do they do it? What does it mean to trust? What is the nature of that trust? What are the unintended consequences of entrepreneurship in action space?

I believe introducing some technical concepts from social-network theory will help answer these questions and extend the Jacobsian-cum-market-process framework of analysis.

2.2   Density, Distance, and Structure

What is a social network in this context? A *social network* is a set of people (or nodes) who are connected to one another through personal ties (Degenne & Forsé, 1999: 28).

> In a very basic sense, then, a social network is an organized set of people that consists of two kinds of elements: human beings and the connections between them. (Christakis & Fowler, 2009, p. 13)

The origins of a network may be planned or unplanned, although once established, they will change in unforeseeable ways. Social networks are thus spontaneous orders. As this suggests, social networks may have vague boundaries. However, despite the claim of Degenne and Forsé that "no network has 'natural' frontiers; researchers impose them" (1999: 22), I believe it is possible in practice to identify nonarbitrary social networks— such as our immediate family, close friends, or colleagues—even though their frontiers may be fuzzy and changeable.

The ties between any two people may be relatively weak or strong. The sociologist Mark Granovetter (1973) defines the *strength of a tie* between persons as an increasing function of the following elements:

1. Its duration
2. Its emotional intensity
3. The level of intimacy
4. Frequency of exchange of services

To this list, Degenne and Forsé (1999: 109) add a fifth criterion, *multiplexity (m)*, which is the ability to transact several kinds of exchange, for different purposes, concurrently within the same tie; or for the algebraically inclined,

$$m = n / p$$

where n is the total number of different kinds of exchanges and p is the number of agent-pairs effecting at least one kind of exchange (ibid: 46), so that there may be more kinds of exchanges (n) than personal connections we have with others (p). Recall the example of your sister-in-law as your tax attorney.

It is sometimes useful to talk about an *ego network*, which is simply a social network considered from the viewpoint of a particular person (ego) in that network. If z_{jq} is a variable that indicates a relationship between agent j to agent q, and if N_i is the size or the number of agents in ego's (i's) network, then we can derive a simple measure of the *density of ego's network* by dividing the sum of all actual relationships between all of the agents in that network ($z_{jq} = 0$ if there is no relationship between j and q, $z_{jq} = 1$ if there is) by the maximum possible number of relations among all of the agents in the network, or $N_i(N_i -1)/2$.[6] In algebraic terms it looks like this.

$$Network\ Density = \left(\Sigma_j\ \Sigma_q\ z_{jq} \right) \Big/ \left[N_i \left(N_i - 1 \right) / 2 \right], j \neq q$$

Network Density is then the ratio of actual connections to all possible connections in a given network and is a percentage that varies between zero and one.[7] For example,[8] the network in Fig. 5.1 has 9 connections out of a possible maximum of 28 (e.g., agent 1 is directly connected to agents 2 and 3, but only indirectly connected, through agents 2 and 3, to agents 4 through 8).

---

[6] For the moment, I will ignore the strength of these relations. Also, I will assume that the value of all ties are equal and they are bidirectional and positive, that is, the relationships are non-hierarchical and they add rather than subtract value to the agents, although, of course, that need not be true.

[7] This is similar to Neal (2013: 112): "Thus, the network city model focuses not on the density of the area's population, but instead on the density of the network of interactions within it."

[8] Figures 5.1 and 5.2, and some of the accompanying analysis, are based on Degenne and Forsé (1999: 4).

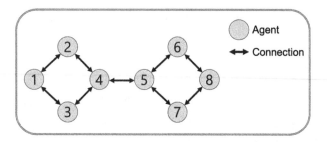

Fig. 5.1   Network A

Its density is therefore

$$D = 9 / 28 = 0.32,$$

or is 32%.

Next, the *distance* between any two agents, i and j, is the shortest path (minimum number of ties or "degrees") between them. You can calculate the *average distance* that a person would expect to travel to reach any other person in a network, as follows: For a given person, find the total distance she would have to travel to reach each and every other person in the network on separate journeys, then sum these distances over all N persons and divide that result by $N_i(N_i -1)/2$. For Network A the average distance is (64/28 =) 2.29 degrees. In other words, agent 1 (or any other agent in the network) would have to travel over an average of 2.29 ties to reach anyone else in the network. (I have shown one way to calculate the average distances for Networks A and B in the Appendix to Chap. 5.)

Now, the *structure* of a network refers to the way in which the nodes are connected (or not) to one another. Network B in Fig. 5.2 has the same number of nodes and ties as Network A, but because they are connected differently we say the structure is different.

Next, an agent i is said to be *structurally equivalent* to agent j to the extent i and j have the same contacts in the network (Burt, 1995: 276). In Network C in Fig. 5.3, for example, agents 1 and 2 are structurally equivalent.

Because agents 1 and 2 are structurally equivalent, the tie connecting them does not help either one to reach any other agent in the network

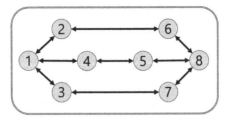

Fig. 5.2   Network B

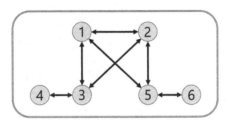

Fig. 5.3   Network C

(other than each other); that is, it does not reduce the average distance for agent 1 or 2. From that strategic point of view, such a tie is said to be *redundant*.

Burt (1995: 270) discusses another form of redundancy that is not based on structural equivalence but on cohesion. *Cohesion* here[9] means having a strong tie with another agent who has access to and possesses the same information as you do, so that knowing her gives you no strategic advantage. "Cohesion concerns direct connection; structural equivalence concerns indirect connection by mutual contact" (Ibid: 277). So, redundancy is an increasing function of both structural equivalence and cohesion.

2.3   Population Density Versus Network Density

I have noted that in the real world, we don't randomly distribute ourselves across space. Most of the time we choose to occupy locations for

---

[9] Note this is different from how we used "cohesion" in Chap. 4.

specific reasons because some places are more conducive than others for certain kinds of action. Sociologist William H. Whyte (1980), for instance, explains why we may choose to sit or stand in certain spots in a public plaza according to how comfortable, convenient, safe, and interesting it is. Larger agglomerations, such as cities, attract people for similar reasons with the added draw of economic opportunity, cultural diversity, and privacy (Jacobs, 1961: 56, 143). Of course, terrain and natural resources strongly influence the site and situation of settlements. But hills, rivers, and harbors are valuable only because we find them useful for particular purposes—trade, defense, or beauty, for example. Whether something constitutes a resource is entirely a matter of our perception of its usefulness.

In the late nineteenth century, public authorities and the modern urban-planning profession began to regard the congestion and squalor that accompanied the rapid development of cities as a major public-policy problem. Their solution, broadly speaking, was to bring open space to urban residents (e.g., Le Corbusier) or to move urbanites out to the countryside (e.g., Ebenezer Howard). They regarded population density as a source of social ills if not a vice in itself, a view which I will critique in Chap. 7. The tide began to turn in favor of density in the latter third of the twentieth century, in part because of Jane Jacobs,[10] and for better or worse, planners began to see density as a virtue.[11]

As we have seen, other things equal, in a population rich in diversity of human capital and tastes, the closer we live to one another (without overcrowding) and the greater our freedom of movement, the greater is the likelihood that formal and especially informal contacts will occur. These contacts in turn form the basis for mutually beneficial trades and other

[10] This derives from her emphasis on "high concentrations of people at different times of the day," but as I argued in the previous chapter, too many have ignored her warning that density is not an urban virtue per se, but is important only insofar as it works reciprocally with the other factors as a "generator of diversity" (Jacobs, 1961: 143).

[11] Among those today who attribute the productivity, or at least the liveliness, of cities in large measure to population density are New Urbanists and advocates of Smart Growth policies, whose arguments I will address in Chap. 8. See, for example, the emphasis on density in this website dedicated to the New Urbanism http://www.newurbanism.org/ and Leccese and McCormick (2000). Accessed 28 May 2023.

forms of voluntary contact and association that result when urbanites discover valuable complementarities.

Skeptics will point to continuing advances in communication and transport technology, which seemingly annihilate physical distances among people, as serious challenges to the raison d'être of the traditional city. Each wave of technical change—telephony, radio, television, the Internet; the railroad, car, airplane—has indeed increased the possibility and perhaps the appeal of living in greater physical isolation while remaining socially connected. Ebenezer Howard's "Garden City"or Frank Lloyd Wright's "Broadacre," each predicated on low-density and relatively autonomous residential development (the former transit based, the latter automobile based), have never been within closer reach. While in the last decades, the relative density of the traditional city center has generally been falling throughout the developed world, urbanized areas anchored to one or more central cities have at the same time grown apace and is estimated to account for 75% of the global population by the mid-twenty-first century (Burdett & Sudjic, 2008). Population gradients, the change in population density as we move away from the center, have also shifted upward (i.e., higher density for any given radius) even as they have flattened out (Bruegmann, 2006). And technical advances in communication and transport have certainly perturbed the evolution of the city, but not stopped it.

There is no denying, however, that technical change, especially the rise of cyberspace and mobile communication, has had an enormous impact on the way we interact. For instance, apps like Tinder can make first contact with strangers easier and greatly extend the range of connections beyond what is possible from face-to-face contact or word of mouth, alone. However, while advances of this kind might for some represent a partial substitute for bar hopping, etc., for most of us, it would be challenging to carry on a romance exclusively over social media or from distant locations.[12] They complement social interaction, not substitute for it. Typically, we really don't get to know another person very well until we physically meet someplace. And an FTF date arranged through an app

---

[12] Which is the plot of Helene Hanff's novel "84 Charing Cross Road" and the movies "You Got Mail" and "Her."

will mean encountering people we didn't expect, which again creates unknown networking possibilities.

Nevertheless, despite the persistent human propensity to agglomerate, it may be helpful to retool the standard concept of population density in the face of these changes with the aid of social-network theory. Therefore, in Section 3, I offer the concept of "Jacobs Density," which may be better suited to this novel environment.

2.4   The Importance of Network Structure

Economic development, by which I mean (with Jacobs) economic growth that consists of innovation and the increasing division of labor and knowledge, is driven by entrepreneurship. To address the two questions posed at the beginning of this chapter—how agents acquire and then diffuse entrepreneurially relevant information—it is important to appreciate how even small differences in network structure can dramatically influence social distance. One way to clarify this point is to compare the two networks in Figs. 5.1 and 5.2.

We already know that Network A has a density of 0.32. Network B, using the same algorithm, has the same density. However, while the average distance in Network A is 2.29, the average distance in Network B is lower at 1.93. To reach anyone else in the network, the distance any given agent has to travel would be about 15% shorter in Network B than in Network A. The networks have the same number of connections but they have different structures. If the goal is to facilitate the movement of entrepreneurially relevant knowledge, other things equal, Network B has a structural advantage over Network A, the shorter average distance among the agents within the network.

This simple example suggests that a change in network structure that reduces the average distance between agents can shorten the "social distance" between them. And by closing this distance, structural changes—by which I mean here adding or subtracting ties to different agents—can increase the flow of entrepreneurially relevant knowledge and thereby increase the likelihood of profitable discoveries and development. It also suggests that we can do this without a net increase in the number of ties (i.e., people we know), or by adding ties indiscriminately, which is costly.

2.5   Social Distance, Strength of a Tie, and Diversity

What exactly is *social distance*? I have been treating social distance as the minimum number of ties or "degrees of separation" between two agents. In Fig. 5.2, for example, agent 7 is the most socially distant from agent 1 (at three degrees of separation) compared with anyone else. The maximum social distance between any two agents in Network B is three degrees and the minimum is one degree. Earlier I calculated "average distance" by taking the weighted average of those distances.

But social distance seems to have at least two other meanings in the literature. The first has to do with the level and kind of interaction between two agents. This is essentially Granovetter's concept of a weak versus a strong tie. The weaker the tie between two agents—that is, the shorter the duration and the less intimate, emotionally intense, frequently used, and multiplex the contact—the more socially distant they are said to be. Therefore, I will subsume this aspect of social distance into the concept of "strength of the tie."

The second meaning of social distance relates to what are called "affective" and "normative" social distances. *Affective social distance* varies inversely with the level of sympathy one feels for another (Bogardus, 1947). While important, this concept of social distance is for the moment not relevant. More relevant is *normative social distance*, which pertains to whether an agent is regarded as an insider or outsider to the group or social network (Karakayali, 2009).[13] This includes cultural differences—for example, Christian versus Muslim, urbanite versus ruralite, American versus Japanese. Related to the concept of normative social distance are differences in an agent's knowledge and skills (which together constitute her *human capital*) and differences in tastes, since we can infer from Granovetter that someone very different from us in respect of these factors are more likely to be outside than inside our social networks. While differences in knowledge, skills, and tastes may not always be normative differences, it will be convenient to treat them as if they were. I will therefore fold "normative social distance" into the concept of "human diversity."

---

[13] The latter seems to underlie Robert Putnam's distinction between *bonding social capital* and *bridging social capital*, see Putnam (2000: 22–23).

In sum, I treat the level and kind of personal interaction between agents as factors in the strength of a tie, and normative social distance as factors in their diversity. Doing so will help me to distinguish social distance, *qua* "degrees of separation," from both the "strength" of a particular tie and how "diverse" two agents are from each other.

While conceptually separate, these factors do interact. Most importantly, closing social distance can (though it need not) result over time in the strengthening of ties which can, because of more frequent and intimate contact, reduce the diversity among more strongly tied agents. This is a matter of the dynamics of action space, to which I will return later. For now, let us return to the concept of density and how we might most usefully interpret it, especially in the context of modern technology.

3   "Jacobs Density"

Recall that the simple definitions of population density and network density are, respectively, the number of individuals per unit area and the ratio of actual to potential ties within a given network. In some respects, in terms of promoting entrepreneurial discoveries, network density is less important than the diversity of the agents in a network, similar to the way population density is secondary to the diversity of land-use. That is, population density alone fails to do the heavy lifting some urbanists expect it to do. Following Jacobs, population density interacts reciprocally with mixed primary uses, street intricacy, and "old buildings" to generate valuable land-use diversity. For example, Smart Growth policies impose "green belts" and other interventions to increase population density hoping it will produce a host of benefits, from community building to environmental sustainability to reducing income inequality and suburban sprawl (Leccese & McCormick, 2000: v–vi). And in the case of social networks, I have shown that sometimes network density has little to do with closing social distance because, there, "average distance" may be the more relevant concept. Moreover, the correlation between measured population density and economic vitality is tenuous at best (Gordon & Ikeda, 2011). Instead, diversity—in land-use and human capital—rather than density per se is a principal condition for economic development.

For Jacobs "high concentrations of people at different times during the day" are mostly needed to supply a steady stream of eyes on the street in public space around the clock (Jacobs, 1961: 37) and to feel safe and comfortable using public space (as a result of the interaction of all four generators of diversity). Personal proximity is also valuable when it increases the likelihood that we will have informal contact with others who are socially distant but complementary to us.[14]

So, I think the intuition that density is in some way an important factor in fostering greater contact is a strong one. After all, other things equal, it makes sense that the more people in an area, the more contacts there will be. The following is my attempt to align that intuition with a view of economic development, as an entrepreneurial competitive process, by means of a concept of density that is applicable to both abstract social networks and to actual urban environments.

I mentioned in Chapter 4 an alternative to conventional density called "Jacobs Density," defined as "the level of potential informal contacts of the average person in a given public space at any given time" (Gordon & Ikeda, 2011: 448). It is possible to conceptualize Jacobs Density in terms of action space and social network theory.

The *Jacobs Density* of an action space is the total number of potential contacts Ego can access through direct contacts divided by the actual number of direct contacts Ego has. Jacobs Density differs then from the measure of network density, which is the ratio of actual to all possible connections in a *given* network. Jacobs Density is related to network density, but places greater emphasis on potential rather than actual network contacts. Here is a simple illustration of increasing Jacobs Density.

In Fig. 5.4, Ego in the first case forms a triad with John and Mary in one of her action spaces, which indirectly connects her to Juan, Jamal, Marcie, and Mariko, who may be outside that particular action space.

If Marcie later creates a new link with Morticia, with whom Ego had previously no or only very distant social contact, Ego's Jacobs Density increases by 0.5, as is shown in Fig. 5.5.

Morticia was previously entirely outside Ego's network and socially distant from Ego, but Marcie now constitutes a "bridge" that shortens

---

[14] Desrochers (2001: 34) illustrates how such contacts often result in unexpected benefits.

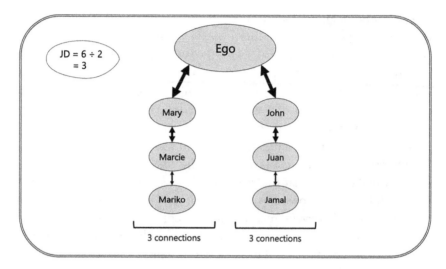

Fig. 5.4 Example of Jacobs Density (JD)

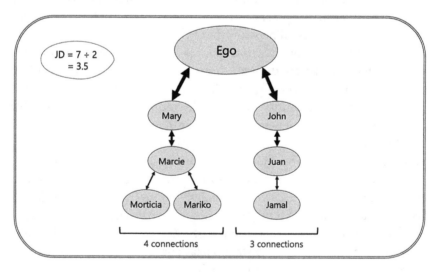

Fig. 5.5 Example of increasing Jacobs Density

the distance between them, but at the same time increases the degree of human (normative) diversity in the network by including Morticia.

Ego can also herself strategically choose to break an old tie and form a new one if she discovers the opportunity to do so and the expected net benefit is positive. In the third case, Ego believes that although cutting ties with John would lose her three connections, she can by so doing expect to increase her Jacobs Density by forming a new tie directly with Frank in her action space and indirectly link with Fergie, Fernando, Alice, Alina, and Kalim (Fig. 5.6). Perhaps Ego believes her connections with John, Juan, and Jamal are unlikely to serve as a conduit to diverse and socially distant people.

Once again, it is possible to make changes in the structure of a social network that leave standard network density unchanged (in this case, by keeping the number of Ego's direct connections constant at two), but reduce average social distance, and thereby create new sources of potentially novel information for entrepreneurial discovery.

Note that in each of these three cases, I have limited the distance between Ego and the farthest contact to three degrees, following the finding of Christakis and Fowler (2009: 485) that influence and information

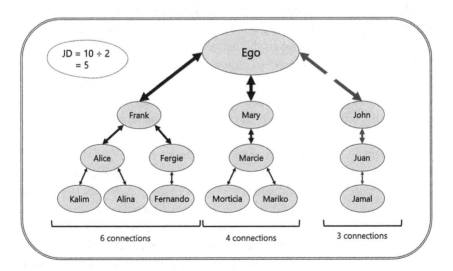

Fig. 5.6 Example of strategic ties to increase Jacobs Density

typically degrade significantly beyond three degrees of separation. If influence and information did not degrade in this way, and if it is true that any two people on earth are separated by around six degrees, as mathematician Albert-László Barabasi (2003: 25–40) reports, then everyone's Jacobs Density would be nearly the same extremely large number, or approximately $JD = 53,000,000$: that is, the current population of the world of just under 8,000,000,000 divided by the maximum number of contacts a person can have at any time, which according to experimental psychologist Robin Dunbar (1992) is around 150 persons. Since each of us is a member of several, perhaps partially overlapping, social networks—family, friends, school, work, club, and so on—our potential contacts might indeed comprise a significant percentage of the world population. But in this case, if Christakis and Fowler's 3-degrees rule holds, our Jacobs Density in any given action space would be a great deal lower.

We have thus far discussed two independent factors that can promote entrepreneurial discovery. The first is an increase in Jacobs Density, which potentially expands the amount and diversity of information that we can access through our contacts. The second is a reduction in average social distance, which because of the 3-degrees rule means less information would be lost among people in a particular network. If Ego were to link directly to Marcie, or indeed anyone in the network beyond John and Mary, the average distance in the network would fall.

What is the relation between action space and Jacobs Density? Action space consists of a physical and social dimension, and Jacobs Density relates to the social. Action space, then, is more than mere physical extension. Within a given area, there may be at any time higher or lower Jacobs Density. For instance, we can expect, other things equal, that potential Jacobs Density increases as the concentration of people and the granularity of land-uses in that area increases, because the possibility of connecting with more diverse and socially distant persons increases. In a small town of, say, 10,000 residents the low concentration of people and courser granularity of land-uses will result in fewer encounters with strangers (as friendly as locals may be to those they meet). Whereas, in a great city, within that same space, higher concentration and finer granularity increases Jacobs Density. (This is also true when comparing two cities with equal populations, with one livelier than the other.) It is quite possible for the same Jacobs Density to occur in a great city in a fraction of the action space of a town. The more "things to do" in an action space, the greater the Jacobs Density will tend to be.

In its present, purely conceptual form, Jacobs Density, like the more conventional average social distance, is not easily operationalizable.[15] Nevertheless, I believe the concepts of Jacobs Density and of average social distance help us to see behind the intuition that density is somehow related to entrepreneurship and economic development. Density in this sense still depends partially on physical proximity, but Jacobs Density goes beyond that to consider the diversity and social distance among the people to whom we are indirectly linked via mutual connections.[16] And it is now possible to say more.

4   Connected or Trapped?

At a given time, action space both constrains what we can know and liberates our creative powers. The number and strength of ties that at any moment connect us also limit what we might become aware of. For example, doctors who spend most of their time among patients and professional colleagues are unlikely to discover a profit opportunity in, say, the construction business. But those very limits may prevent the information generated in a dynamic economy from overwhelming them, allowing them to focus on recognizing meaningful patterns that may lead to valuable discoveries in their specialties. As Ronald Burt observes, "Given a limit to the volume of information that anyone can process, the network becomes an important screening device" (Burt, 1995: Loc. 212). Indeed, in a dynamic economy, the areas on which we focus may be changing all the time, and cognitive limits keep the number we can be

---

[15] However, Alain Bertaud's observation that "The frequency of face-to-face contact among the millions of people living in large cities depends entirely on the efficiency of a motorized urban transport system" (Bertaud, 2018: Loc. 1027) may suggest how to use the concept to rationalize certain transport policies, as a means to increase Jacobs Density.

[16] In Chaps. 9 and 10, I will address what impact the emergence of the so-called "multiverse" may have on the need for face-to-face contact and the applicability of Jacobs Density to this phenomenon.

aware of at a fairly manageable level. At the same time, however, making direct and indirect connections with socially distant networks increases the Jacobs Density of our action spaces and shortens average distances in our networks, effectively increasing within those limits the number of areas from which we might draw new and useful information, enabling us in a sense to be smarter and more creative. A doctor might notice that a technique used to brace delicate walls in a building renovation could be applied to the setting of bones in the human body.[17]

Besides Jacobs Density and shorter average social distances, there are two other factors to consider in evaluating the entrepreneurial effectiveness of an action space: prevailing norms and levels of trust.

4.1   Norms

Beyond those in our networks and our relationships to them (i.e., Jacobs Density and social distance), which we have just covered, there are also the norms and conventions prevailing in them and our action spaces. In some cultures, for example, a restaurant on a weekday is a more socially acceptable time and place to conduct business than, say, a funeral; elsewhere it may be the opposite. More importantly, the greater the freedom with which we can observe or mingle with others, the better the chances that we will encounter diverse and perhaps novel information that we might then interpret in profitable ways. As Burt observes:

> Everything else constant, a large, diverse network is the best guarantee of having a contact present where useful information is aired. This is not only to say that benefits must increase linearly with size and diversity…but only that, other things held constant, the information benefits of a large, diverse network are more than the information benefits of a small, homogenous network. (Burt, 1995: Loc. 247)

Here norms of inclusion are crucial. What makes a social network inclusive or exclusive? What is it that enables us to form a new tie with

---

[17] This example comes from a conversation I had with a well-known New York orthopedic surgeon.

someone we don't already know or break a tie with an old acquaintance? The answer depends on trust.

But I contend that we attach two fundamentally different meanings to the word "trust" and that by differentiating between them, we can learn something essential and interesting about the dynamics of social networks in living cities.

4.2   Trust

If we understand trust as purely a function of how well we already know someone, how well person A knows person B, then we might say the stronger the tie,[18] the more likely A will trust B, if B is trustworthy. Political scientist Russell Hardin (2002: 58) refers to this kind of trust as *cognitive trust*, or trust based on how much we know about someone. Again, in the context of a static network structure, in which ties are neither forming nor dissolving, stronger ties correlate with greater cognitive trust. The downside of this is that over time, strong ties are likely to grow redundant—everyone in the network knows all the same people. In a completely static world, novelty and diversity would eventually disappear owing to what we earlier called "redundancy by cohesion" (Burt, 1995: Loc. 18).

There is, however, another phenomenon that also goes by the name of "trust" that, while relevant for static social networks, is even more important for dynamic social networks.

4.3   The Dynamics of Action Space

As we saw earlier, simply multiplying weak ties willy-nilly may raise simple network density and shorten average distance, but it is costly and does not necessarily increase Jacobs Density. A person would do better to focus on nonredundant ties. Burt, again:

---

[18] Christakis and Fowler (2009) report on other factors such as homophily that also increase the level of this kind of trust.

But increasing network size without considering diversity can cripple a network in significant ways. What matters is the number of nonredundant contacts. (Burt, 1995: Loc 255)

Back in Fig. 5.1, for example, the tie between agents 4 and 5 is nonredundant. It is also a *bridge*, which Degenne & Forsé define as follows:

An edge is a bridge between two parts in a graph when it is the only link that spans the two parts, that is, every node in one part can only reach a node in another part via that link…. An edge can be considered a local bridge if it is the shortest path between two parts of a graph, that is, where all other chain lengths are 2". (Degenne & Forsé, 1999: 110)

The entrepreneurial discovery of a new nonredundant tie will be profitable if it yields greater benefits than the cost of establishing the new tie. (Which also includes the expected costs of breaking an old tie, because Dunbar's Number places a limit on the number of ties we can have at any one time.) According to Burt (1995), ties with lower redundancy, perhaps even bridges, can be found in what he calls "structural holes," which are the social network analog to Kirzner's entrepreneurial arbitrage opportunities.

Structural holes "are disconnections or nonequivalencies between players in the arena" (Burt, 1995: Loc. 47), but as such they are also unexploited "entrepreneurial opportunities for information access, timing, referrals, and control" (Ibid). In the context of social networks, therefore, entrepreneurship manifests itself in the discovery of strategically valuable ties that span structural holes. Structural holes shorten average distances but, crucially, there is no certain indicator that a structural hole is present. The hole itself is an "invisible scam of nonredundancy waiting to be discovered by the able entrepreneur" (Ibid: Loc. 648). In other words, a structural hole is veiled in radical ignorance.

Note the close similarity to market-process theory and specifically to Kirzner (1973). As it is for Kirzner and market-process economics, for Burt, "competition is a process, not just a result," whereas "most theories of competition concern what is left when competition is over" (Burt, 1995: Loc. 102). Moreover, Burt states "the structural hole argument is a theory of competition made imperfect by the freedom of individuals to be entrepreneurs" (Ibid: Loc. 111). These imperfections represent profit opportunities to alert entrepreneurs, who can establish the weak ties that span structural holes, shorten social distances, and increase Jacobs Density.[19] Entrepreneurship is thus critical in forming these weak ties. Over time, competitive rivalry helps entrepreneurs to identify structural holes *qua* profit opportunities, just as in market-process theory.

Where social-network analysis goes beyond the Kirznerian analysis is the recognition that when an entrepreneur E buys from A and sells to B, this is not only an act of arbitrage, it also establishes a triangular relationship among E, A, and B. That relationship may not last beyond the single exchange, but it represents a weak tie if the agents have had little or no contact before. All three agents form a *transitive* relation (Christakis & Fowler, 2009: 339). If the relation persists, it can later transmit novel information from more distant networks, with A or B or E acting entrepreneurially with another agent D. Or in time, it can serve multiplex uses beyond the original trade function (e.g., A and B might become friends as well as business partners).

Although structural holes may exist in one's existing networks, they are, as we have seen, most likely to be found between people in different networks or cliques. That is because, owing to *homophily*, that is, the tendency to form stronger ties with those with whom you share more characteristics (Christakis & Fowler, 2009: Loc. 308), strong ties tend to bind people into a network that is relatively homogenous with low average distances from other network members, so that any new ties will tend to be with persons from other, likely more diverse, social networks.

In terms of the complementarities and cohesiveness discussed in the previous chapter, weak ties are crucial: "weak ties are essential to the flow of information that integrates otherwise disconnected social clusters into a broader society" (Burt, 1995: Loc. 364). And the new nonredundant tie

---

[19] This shortening has been essential historically for urban development through long-distance trade. Pierenne (1952) is the authority on the social impact of trade in the Late Middle Ages; Algaze (2008: Loc. 166) has found evidence of the role of long-distance trade in the southern Mesopotamian delta in the late Uruk period, circa 3400 to 3100 BC.

or bridge must initially be a weak tie because "no strong tie is a bridge" (Granovetter, 1973: 1364).[20]

Now, Christakis and Fowler argue that

> [p]eople with high transitivity live in densely clustered cliques where everyone knows everyone else. People with low transitivity, in contrast, tend to have friends in several different groups. Such people often act as bridges between completely different groups of people (Christakis & Fowler, 2009: Loc. 3694).

In a social network that has been around for a very long time, it may be extraordinarily difficult to discover structural holes because so many ties would already have been formed among its members (Granovetter, 1973), approaching maximal (non-Jacobs) network density. Because of structural equivalence or cohesion, over time, ties will become more and more redundant. So, in long-established and static networks, we should expect transitivity to be very high, but there will also be few opportunities for the entrepreneurial discovery of either new bridges or new complementarities within existing pools of economic use. Strong ties would dominate. We are more likely to find low transitivity and structural holes among socially distant and more diverse networks. As Burt observes,

> As you expand your inventory from your closest, most frequent contacts to your more distant, contacts tend to be people like yourself before you reach a sufficiently low level of relationship to include people from completely separate social worlds. (Burt, 1995: Loc. 387)

This was illustrated earlier in Figs. 5.5 and 5.6. But this raises a paradox. If by "trust" we mean "cognitive trust"—agent A's propensity to rely on another agent because she knows him well via a strong tie (Hardin, 2002; Ikeda, 2007)—and if agents in diverse and socially distant networks are most likely to be strangers, how can weak ties form in the first place?

---

[20] Granovetter cites Jacobs's discussion of "public characters" as an example of a bridge or network hub (Granovetter 1973: 1375). "A public character is anyone who is in frequent contact with a wide circle of people and who is sufficiently interested to make himself a public character" (Jacobs 1961: 68).

From whence comes the trust that would enable her to connect to another agent, about whom she knows little or nothing? Cognitive trust is the basis of the strong ties with agents in networks closer to A's own. Now, it is true that an agent C, who may be acquainted with both A and B, can serve as a bridge between them. This, however, simply pushes the question one step back: If only cognitive trust exists, how did the tie between C and A and B first form? (This is the ambiguity I pointed to in the Jacobs quote at the beginning of this chapter.) Indeed, it stands to reason that at some time in the past, C was not strongly tied to both—perhaps to neither.

I believe the paradox can be resolved by identifying a fundamentally different phenomenon which we also call "trust."

4.4   Behavioral Trust

That concept is *behavioral trust*, which I have defined elsewhere as "an act of choice that overcomes uncertainty or a lack of knowledge" (Ikeda, 2007: 219). Let me try to be more precise.

In a probabilistic sense, we can define "complete knowledge" of another agent's trustworthiness as 100% certainty, and "complete ignorance" as 0% certainty. Suppose then that A thinks she needs to feel more than 75% certainty before cognitively trusting B enough to trade with him. Following the sociologist James Coleman (1990: 99), in simple algebraic terms we can describe this as the point at which

$$Gain\, x\,(0.76) > Loss\, x\,(1-0.76),$$

That is, where the expected gain is greater than the expected loss. At a level higher than 75%, A will then cognitively trust B. For example, if Gain = \$100 and Loss = \$300, and her certainty level is 75%, A would be exactly indifferent between trusting or not trusting B if her level of certainty were exactly 75% and definitely trust B even if it were higher.

Suppose, however, that A can only trust B up to 60%, but that to engage in trade with B she still needs to feel at least 76% certain. Here we can say that A does not cognitively trust B and will not trade because the expected value of the Gain, E(G), would be less than the expected value of a Loss, E(L). Now, A would trust B if, say, Gain > \$200 and Loss < \$100 because then E(G) > E(L). Indeed, with the cognitive-trust approach, A would have no choice but to trust B, that is, not to do so would be "irrational" according to standard economic theory. But if neither A nor B can alter the gains and losses then, given the initial gain, loss, and certainty level, behavioral trust is what could enable A to trade with B and overcome the 16 percentage point gap if that is what A *chooses* to do. Behavioral trust, then, gives A the possibility of taking a kind of "leap of faith."

In other words, while cognitive trust is a psychological propensity (Hardin, 2002: 58)—that is, you either have it or you don't—behavioral trust is teleogical, an act of choice taken in the presence of "radical uncertainty" or uncertainty not subject to an ordinary probability calculus, in contrast to Coleman's notion of trust based on what economists call "calculable risk" (Coleman, 1990: 97–108).[21]

An agent who cognitively trusts says: "I can trust you because I know you very well." An agent who behaviorally trusts says: "I don't know you very well, so I'm going to have to trust you."

Cognitive trust, based on our familiarity with another person, is thus the strong fiber that binds a network together.

Behavioral trust, on the other hand, is what enables the formation of a new tie. Because, by definition, we form a weak tie with someone we don't know very well or at all, especially a socially distant person with a very different background from ourselves, the level of cognitive trust will

---

[21] The difference between cognitive and behavioral trust appears to be closely related to Paul Seabright's (2004) distinction between "calculators" who only trust when expected benefits exceed expected costs and "reciprocators," who return harms or favors without such calculation "no matter what." Coleman's trustors are explicitly calculators in Seabright's sense, which leaves no room for the kind of reciprocity that Seabright argues is the basis for trustworthiness and serves to ensure the keeping of the kind of promises that are indispensable for flourishing markets and social orders generally.

be close to zero. To form a tie, to have contact, and establish a relation with a stranger requires a degree of faith.[22]

Breaking a tie may involve both kinds of trust.[23] Should we leave our hometown, family, and childhood friends for the strange, big city, or not? Letting go of a relationship or a familiar clique or network may be based purely on calculation of given estimated benefits and costs, and when the former exceeds the latter, a rational agent automatically severs the tie. Typically, however, we lack the information to make such a fully informed decision and we then have to choose based at least in part on behavioral trust. The choice to seek some unspecified opportunity, perhaps in a different country, can again involve a lot of faith. Which way we choose is indeterminate, making such decisions sometimes very hard.

A few caveats here. Strengthening a tie doesn't necessarily mean that A will automatically place greater reliance on B. After all, A's repeated contact with B may simply confirm her opinion that he is a scoundrel. There may be members of our family with whom we have very strong ties that we have learned are untrustworthy, and so forth. In fact, under these circumstances, relying on someone we are strongly tied to would require behavioral trust! Nevertheless, with more knowledge, we, like A, can place greater reliance on our evaluations of another's trustworthiness or lack thereof. Nor is it the case that a social network consisting of relatively strong ties need be *ipso facto* an exclusive one since familiarity is one thing and norms of exclusivity are another. In practice, however, we can infer from Granovetter that members of a strongly tied group will tend to be quite similar, especially over time, with respect to the things that draw them together—for example, kinship, status, ideology, race, religion, age, language, musical interests—which can act as a thick filter for

---

[22] Some might still argue that behavioral trust simply amounts to a "risk-loving" propensity, which, in this case, would mean you might rationally take a chance even if the net expected values were somewhat against you. I deal with this objection elsewhere (Ikeda, 2006) and can't address it fully here, but the essential point is that even a rational, risk-loving person, when faced with two gambles involving identical risk, would never choose the one about which she is less informed than the other simply based on calculation. Behavioral trust, however, would at least open the possibility that she might indeed choose a gamble about which she is ill-informed.

[23] Adding new ties may indeed necessitate the cutting of old ones, when we take into account Dunbar's Number, especially when the ties are strong, because of the limited number of personal relations we are able to maintain (Christakis & Fowler 2009: Loc. 3914).

membership. Finally, even a relatively inclusive social network will have some members who are tied strongly to one another through cognitive trust, otherwise the network would not last, and weak ties do strengthen over time. What makes a social network relatively inclusive are the norms within the group governing its decision to admit members via weak ties and the rate at which those ties are allowed to strengthen.

4.5   Freedom and Competition

As mentioned, the ability to form weak ties and to dissolve strong ties also depends on the norms held by people across society that influence the level of individual freedom to move among the various networks. Again, Jacobs seems to take this for granted. I am speaking here specifically of the freedom to enter or exit any social network we choose to, assuming that network is willing and able to allow us to do so, and our tolerance to let others do the same. "Freedom" in this sense includes the legal-rights triumvirate of private property, freedom of contract, and the rule of law that we typically associate with *economic freedom*.[24] Of course, "social pressure" might issue from traditional norms and conventions that, despite the presence of formal grants of freedom, stifle the movement of persons across either geographic or social distance. The law may give same-sex couples the right to marry, for example, but strong disapprobation from family and community members may discourage those who might wish to.

When either social pressure or legal coercion prevents contact with outsiders, at least some will feel trapped as the thickness of ties encroaches ever further into their personal autonomy. You could say that in the extreme case, all private space becomes public space. But from the point of view of entrepreneurial competition and economic development, it may be closer to the truth to say that in these stifling circumstances, all public space becomes private space in which no strangers are permitted. Ties would be interchangeable and redundant through both cohesion

---

[24] See, for example, Gwartney et al., (2022)

and structural equivalence—that is, everybody knows everybody else really, really well[25]—and structural holes disappear.

Improving our situation as we see it, entails not only forming new ties (that may turn out to be no better than the old ones) but also, crucially, letting go of old ones; adding new friends, colleagues, suppliers, customers, and competitors and leaving familiar ones behind. Adding new ties may indeed necessitate cutting or loosening old ones, when we take into account Dunbar's Number, especially when the ties are strong, because of the limited number of personal relations we are able to maintain (Christakis & Fowler, 2009: Loc. 3914). Norms of tolerance are obviously key to free entry and exit. But equally important is the freedom to criticize and to do so passionately, short of violence. Radical tolerance and radical criticism are complements. To paraphrase something from the previous chapter, tolerance without criticism is insipid; criticism without tolerance is intolerable.

Freedom of that kind, which we might call "social freedom," creates both the opportunity and the necessity to enter and exit. That it creates the opportunity is clear enough. It is competition, however, that makes it necessary. The fact that entry and exit into social networks is free (although actually forming or dissolving ties may involve costs) makes the process of discovering structural holes in action space a competitive one. The agent who fails to effectively and profitably make and break ties is at a competitive disadvantage.

Recall that competition takes place along two different dimensions. Entrepreneurial agents compete over already-established networks, and they also compete to form and dissolve connections. Competition thus refers not only to the activities of rivals who are using already-established networks through which they acquire information about, say, prices and quantities, but it also refers to their attempts to profitably change the very structure of their networks, by filling structural holes or increasing Jacobs Density.

---

[25] I pointed out earlier in this chapter that the so-called "three-degree of influence rule" and "Dunbar's number" will ensure that the actual size of ego's local network is relatively small (see Christakis & Fowler (2009: Loc. 3914).

To summarize: Social networks are a way of coping with imperfect knowledge. Free entry and exit into and out of the networks that occupy our action spaces enable us to discover opportunities and to gainfully alter the structure of our networks. Behavioral trust is essential in that dynamic, and without it we would be unwilling to either form new weak ties or cut old strong ones. Trade is typically the catalyst here, with personal contacts as the main source of the information about trades—for example, price signals, tips, assurances, and so on. Once aware of this information, we evaluate it and its sources and may then choose to form a relationship with a new contact. We can, of course, make valuable connections by means other than trade. Nevertheless, a casual or informal non-market contact often opens the door for important, multiplex trading opportunities in the future, even if that is not why we make the contact in the first place.

(The next chapter applies these concepts to the process of economic development, and in so doing may help the reader to get a firmer grasp of them.)

But because of our cognitive limits, changing the structure of our networks will have some unpredictable consequences. These are some of them.

4.6   Unintended Consequences

As we have seen, a new tie may become multiplex, or others may later use a tie in ways we may or may not like.

Also, the same connections that bring information to us often help to diffuse the knowledge we generate back out to our networks and beyond. Sometimes we don't mind this happening (even if we don't intend it), as when we earn a reputation for trustworthiness. Other times we may, as when we get a reputation for untrustworthiness, or when we wish to keep rivals in the dark about a discovery we have made.

Another important unintended consequence arising from competitively restructuring a social network occurs when ties grow stronger over time.[26] As trade increases, the frequency and intimacy of contact increases between A, who reflects the values and norms of her network, and B, who reflects the values and norms of his. Then, following Granovetter (1973), over time differences between their respective networks may lessen as they learn more about one another. So, while a higher degree of homogeneity and homophily may reduce some kinds of conflict, the downside is that overall diversity—which can inspire novelty and innovation in commerce and culture—will also tend to decline over time. Relations become more redundant and therefore less complementary. Sufficiently high social freedom may counteract this homogenizing tendency to some extent, by spurring mobility and experimentation, both within an existing network community and across the greater global network. In this way, it may be possible to maintain high levels of cultural and economic development while maintaining a relatively stable system of social networks. Freedom to experiment and innovate means diversities will likely re-emerge so that the development can continue.

Also, making and breaking ties have third-party or "external" effects. As Paul Seabright notes:

> They [social networks] are the outcome of the various affinities that move ordinary people in their choices of where to live and work. Every time someone moves, she changes the environment she leaves and gives a new character to the environment she joins, without intending or necessarily even being aware of it. And the most innovative people have always been footloose, restlessly seeking out opportunities over time and space. (Seabright, 2004: 111)

Moreover, if someone severs an old tie by leaving a network, it may thereby create a kind of external benefit for those "left behind," as they become marginally less redundant than they were before the old network structure changed. If A severs ties with B, and the shortest way for C to reach B had been through A, it opens a structural hole between C and B

---

[26] Weak ties don't always grow into strong ties. Indeed, as Jacobs (1961: 62–5) points out, there are good reasons for an agent not to let too much personal information become public. Great cities enable anonymity and privacy, and if sacrificing those precious assets is the price of making public contacts, people may simply avoid doing so, resulting in more insularity and population homogeneity, and action spaces that are less interesting.

that someone—B, C, or some other agent D—might profitably fill. At the same time, if A connects to a new network by bridging a structural hole, this raises to some degree the level of redundancy in the new network and lowers the value of making a new connection to it, which is a kind of external cost.

Finally, when A connects with a nonredundant agent N, she increases both the Jacobs Density for her own network and the Jacobs Density of anyone connected to her. If N then forms a connection with a diverse, socially distant agent with a different set of connections, that would further increase A's Jacobs Density. This corresponds to Fig. 5.5. Of course, N could also sever a tie that would reduce A's Jacobs Density. Other things equal, however, A would find it in her interest to support freedom of mobility in general to maximize her own average Jacobs Density, which down the road could unintentionally promote economic development.

How does this relate to urban design?

5   Implications for Urban Design: Fostering Social Capital in Action Space

We noted in Chap. 4 that the specific form of social network called social capital is one of the key factors in Jacobs's analysis of how the design of public space can profoundly influence economic development. According to Burt (1992: Loc. 194): "Social capital is at once the resources contacts hold and the structure of contacts in a network." Recall for Jacobs "social capital" contributes to a city's cohesion in the face of an inflow of outsiders (Jacobs, 1961: 138), which is particularly relevant to economic development and the market process.[27] Granovetter (1973) elaborates on the concept in his work on social networks, and mathematicians such as Barabasi (2003) then formalize aspects of Granovetter's work. Finally, as we have seen, Burt (1995) applies social-network theory to the study of

---

[27] I have written elsewhere that, from the perspective of the market process, social capital consists of "norms of generalized reciprocity and networks of trust that emerge unplanned over time, that operate in public space among members of an open-ended community, and that help to promote entrepreneurial discovery" (Ikeda, 2008: 181). For a collection of relevant articles on social capital, see Lewis and Chamlee-Wright (2008).

entrepreneurship in the context of imperfect competition. Here we may bring the circle back to Jacobs.

The difference between weak and strong ties is the basis for the difference between what political scientist Robert Putnam (2000) calls "bridging social capital" that is inclusive toward outsiders, and "bonding social capital" that is exclusive. The terminological parallel between bridging social capital and a network "bridge" seems more than coincidental. The same norms of tolerance and criticism that foster free entry and exit across social networks also underlie bridging social capital. Bridging social capital, as the name suggests, promotes weak ties between socially distant and diverse agents. It rests on norms and beliefs that value inclusivity as well as change. On the contrary, bonding social capital and the norms that sustain it serve to increase homogeneity, homophily, and strong ties among agents in a network. It promotes exclusivity, stability, and stasis. As a result, bonding social capital, while a stabilizing element in social orders, tends to dominate in less dynamic and less socially free orders. In creative market processes, then, bridging social capital is at least as important as bonding social capital (Ikeda, 2007, 2008).

5.1   The Design of Public Spaces and Social Capital

Jacobs describes some of the mechanisms by which social capital is either nurtured or undermined by the physical environment. As we know, Jacobs, influenced by William H. Whyte (Flint, 2009: 26), pioneered the analysis of the way the design of public spaces affects economic development. Whyte (1980) offers specific recommendations at the micro level based on his classic time-lapse studies of public spaces, after recording the effects of location, seating, light, accessibility, and other factors on how people use public plazas in New York City. His research emphasizes the importance of safety, location, comfort, and seating in the design of those spaces, and it has been applied by city planners—perhaps nowhere more successfully than in Bryant Park in Midtown Manhattan (Gratz, 2010: 123).

In addition, we know from the previous chapter that Jacobs's analytical framework explains how, given the proper conditions, safety, trust, and land-use diversity emerge spontaneously in successful urban environments. These are the fruits of strong social capital. Recall that she recommends minimizing visual dullness (short blocks), buildings of different ages (old buildings) that lower the cost of experimentation, multiple attractors to bring people into public areas (mixed primary uses), and a local population high enough to supply a flow of people throughout the day and year (population density). These measures help to make public space relatively safe and secure, a prerequisite for the formation of social capital (Jacobs, 1961: 30, 143–221).

5.2   Border Vacuums, Cataclysmic Money, and Visual Homogeneity Again

Although mindful that those conditions would manifest themselves differently depending on time and place, Jacobs argues that they would encourage the prime ingredient for economic development: informal contact in public space, the "small change from which city's wealth of public life may grow" (Jacobs, 1961: 72). On the other hand, for Jacobs border vacuums, cataclysmic money, and visual homogeneity undermine social capital in the same way that the erosion of social freedom would do so. These run counter to spontaneous economic development because they undermine granular land-use diversity and produce what Jacobs aptly calls a "great blight of dullness" (Ibid: 41). People generally avoid dullness, unless they wish to be unseen, and fewer people means fewer "eyes on the street" and higher levels of perceived, and eventually actual, danger (Ibid: 257–317). Jacobs Densities fall and action spaces shrink or disappear altogether.

Norms that discourage informal contact with strangers, and thus the formation of bridging social capital would, like a border vacuum, block free interactions that promote the discovery of serendipitous complementarities among socially distant persons. Indeed, cataclysmic money, border vacuums, and visual homogeneity—by discouraging the kind of informal contact that breeds social capital—might themselves over time engender norms and beliefs that are more exclusive than inclusive, more intolerant than tolerant of strangers. Again, the result is a downward spiral that Jacobs calls a "dynamic of decline," in which the lack of interest in a public space results in fewer eyes on the street, which reduces the perception of safety, which discourages people from sharing the public space, which in turn means fewer eyes on the street, and so on.[28]

In general policy terms, the design of public spaces should advance the diversity of people, places, and things—ideally creating the sort of safe, trust-promoting environments in which network-rich action spaces can emerge. This is obviously a challenge, given the typical mindset of divisive urban politics. Left to its own resources, however, local politics may be more responsive to genuine local needs or at least do less harm than policies financed, initiated, and directed from higher levels of governmental administration, where the knowledge problem is even more intractable. This is an issue that we will explore in some depth in Chaps. 8 and 9.

6   Concluding Thoughts

Social networks furnish conduits through which we send and receive information. By discovering structural holes, we alter our networks, unaware of all the consequences, in a way that can increase Jacobs Density, shorten average social distance, and facilitate the flow of information. So while market prices serve as guides to entrepreneurial discovery and social cooperation, they are not the only guides. When knowledge is imperfect, social networks also convey relevant information to decisionmakers. In that sense, social networks, and changes in their structure enabled, by freedom of mobility and norms of tolerance and trust, are as important to the market process as prices.

Our action spaces enable us to plug into those networks. What is their conceptual status?

The concepts of purposeful action and entrepreneurship may be more fundamental to market-process economics than action space. But while we can grasp the nature of entrepreneurship without invoking action space, I believe the concept of action space is essential for understanding how entrepreneurship operates in real markets. Trying to understand what promotes or suppresses entrepreneurship without considering action space is like trying to understand how well a car performs without

---

[28] In Ikeda (2021), I elaborate on the relation between "urban values" such as tolerance and inclusivity and urban planning interventions.

considering roads. Thinking seriously about how we actually acquire and convey information in the market process reveals the importance of the spatial environment, in particular the spatial environment in a city.

In this chapter, I have presented a way of employing social networks to integrate Jacobs's analysis of urban processes with market-process economics. In this way, social-network theory may also serve as a useful link between Jacobsian-cum-market-process economics and their common social theory. In the next chapter, I will use this integrated socioeconomic framework to present and interpret the mechanics of Jacobs's theory of economic development.

Works Cited

Algaze, G. (2008). *Ancient Mesopotamia at the Dawn of Civilization: The Evolution of an Urban Landscape*. University of Chicago Press. (Kindle Edition location indicators "Loc." rather than page numbers).

Andersson, D. E. (2005). The Spatial Nature of Entrepreneurship. *Quarterly Journal of Austrian Economics, 8*(2), 21–34.

Andersson, D. E. (Ed.). (2012). *The Spatial Market Process. Special Issue of Advances in Austrian Economics* (Vol. 16). Emerald Group Publishing.

Andersson, D. E., Andersson, A. E., & Mellander, C. (Eds.). (2011). *Handbook of Creative Cities*. Edward Elgar.

Barabasi, A.-L. (2003). *Linked: How Everything Is Connected to Everything Else and What It Means for Business, Science, and Everyday Life*. Plume.

Bertaud, A. (2018). *Order Without Design: How Markets Shape Cities*. MIT Press.

Boettke, P. J. (2012). *Living Economics: Yesterday, Today, and Tomorrow*. Independent Institute.

Böhm-Bawerk, E. von (1959[1884]). *Capital and Interest: Volume II, Positive Theory of Capital* (Trans. George D. Huncke & Hans F. Sennholz). Libertarian Press.

Bogardus, E. S. (1947). Measurement of Personal-Group Relations. *Sociometry, 10*(4), 306–311.

Bruegmann, R. (2006). *Sprawl: A Compact History*. University of Chicago.

Burdett, R., & Sudjic, D. (2008). *The Endless City: The Urban Age Project*. Phaidon Press.

Burt, R. (1995). *Structural Holes: The Social Structure of Competition*. Harvard 5 University Press. (Kindle Edition location "Loc." indicators rather than page numbers).

Christakis, N. A., & Fowler, J. H. (2009). *Connected: The Surprising Power of Our Social Networks and How They Shape Our Lives*. Little, Brown. (Kindle Edition location indicators "Loc." rather than page numbers).

Coleman, J. S. (1990). *Foundations of Social Theory*. Belknap Harvard.

Degenne, A., & Forsé, M. (1999). *Introducing Social Networks*. Sage.

Desrochers, P. (2001). Geographical Proximity and the Transmission of Tacit Knowledge. *Review of Austrian Economics, 14*(1), 25–46.

Dunbar, R. I. M. (1992). Neocortex Size as a Constraint on Group Size in Primates. *Journal of Human Evolution, 22*(6), 469–493.

Flint, A. (2009). *Wrestling with Moses: How Jane Jacobs Took on New York's Master Builder and Transformed the American City*. Random House.

Gordon, P., & Ikeda, S. (2011). Does Density Matter? In D. E. Andersson & A. E. A. C. Mellander (Eds.), *Handbook of Creative Cities*. Edward Elgar.

Granovetter, M. S. (1973). The Strength of Weak Ties. *American Journal of Sociology, 78*(6), 1360–1380.

Gratz, R. B. (2010). *The Battle for Gotham: New York in the Shadow of Robert Moses*. Nation Books.

Gwartney, J. D., Lawson, R. A., Hall, J. C., Murphy, R., Djankov, S., & McMahon, F. (2022). *Economic Freedom of the World*. Cato Institute. https://www.cato.org/search/category/economic-freedom-world. Accessed 29 May 2023.

Hardin, R. (2002). *Trust and Trustworthiness*. Russell Sage Foundation.

Hayek, F. A. (1945). The Use of Knowledge in Society. In *Individualism and Economic Order*. Gateway.

Ikeda, S. (2002). The Role of 'Social Capital' in the Market Process. *Journal des Economistes et des Etudes Humaines, 12*(2/3), 229–240.

Ikeda, S. (2006). Is It Rational to Trust? (Unpublished working paper).

Ikeda, S. (2007). Urbanizing Economics. *Review of Austrian Economics, 20*(4), 213–220.

Ikeda, S. (2008). The Meaning of 'Social Capital' as It Relates to the Market Process. *Review of Austrian Economics, 21*, 167–182.

Ikeda, S. (2012). Entrepreneurship in action Space. *Advances in Austrian Economics: The Spatial Market Process, 16*, 105–139.

Ikeda, S. (2021). Urban Planning and Urban Values. *Social Philosophy and Policy, 38*(2), 191–209.

Jacobs, J. (1961). *The Death and Life of Great American Cities*. Vintage.

Jacobs, J. (1969). *The Economy of Cities*. Vintage.

Jacobs, J. (2000). *The nature of economies*. Modern Library.

Karakayali, N. (2009). Social Distance and Affective Orientations. *Sociological Forum, 23*(3), 538–562.

Kirzner, I. M. (1973). *Competition and Entrepreneurship*. University of Chicago Press.

Kirzner, I. M. (1997). Entrepreneurial Discovery and the Competitive Market Process: An Austrian Approach. *Journal of Economic Literature, 35*(1), 60–85.

Lang, G. (2021). *Jane Jacobs's First City: Learning from Scranton Pennsylvania*. New Village Press.

Leal, Z. P. (2013). *The Connected City: How Networks Are Shaping the Modern Metropolis*. Routledge.

Leccese, M., & McCormick, K. (Eds.). (2000). *Charter of the New Urbanism*. McGraw Hill.

Lewis, P. & Chamlee-Wright, E. (Eds.) (2008). Special Issue on Austrian Economics, Economic Sociology and Social Capital, *Review of Austrian Economics* 21(2/3). https://www.academia.edu/37191438/Social_embedded ness_social_capital_and_the_market_process_An_introduction_to_the_ special_issue_on_Austrian_economics_economic_sociology_and_social_ capital?email_work_card=view-paper,107

Loury, G. (1977). A Dynamic Theory of Racial Differences. In P. A. Wallace & A. Le Mund (Eds.), *Women, Minorities, and Employment Discrimination*. Lexington Books.

Menger, C. (1981[1871]). *Principles of economics*. NYU Press.

Miles, M., Hall, T., & Ian Borden, I. (2000). *The Urban Cultures Reader*. Routledge.

Milgram, S. (1972). The Familiar Stranger: An Aspect of Urban Anonymity. In *The Division 8 Newsletter, Division of Personality and Social Psychology*. American Psychological Association.

von Mises, L. (1963[1949]). *Human Action: A Treatise on Economics* (3rd ed.). Regnery.

Neal, Z. P. (2013). *The Connected City: How Networks Are Shaping the Modern Metropolis*. Routledge.

O'Driscoll, G. P., & Rizzo, M. J. (1985). *The Economics of Time and Ignorance*. Blackwell.

Pirenne, H. (1952). *Medieval Cities: Their Origin and the Rival of Trade*. Princeton University Press.

Putnam, R. D. (2000). *Bowling Alone: The Collapse and Revival of American Community*. Simon & Schuster.

Read, L. E. (1958). *I, Pencil: My Family Tree*. Foundation for Economic Education. https://oll.libertyfund.org/title/read-i-pencil-my-family-tree-as-told-to-leonard-e-read-dec-1958

Sasaki, K.-I. (1998). For Whom Is City Design? Tactility Versus Visuality. In M. Miles, T. Hall, & I. Borden (Eds.), *The Urban Cultures Reader*. Routledge.

Seabright, P. (2004). *The Company of Strangers: The Natural History of Economic Life*. Princeton Univ. Press.

Seligman, A. B. (1997). *The Problem of Trust*. Princeton University Press.

Smith, A. (1976[1776]). In R. H. Campbell & A. S. Skinner (Eds.), *An Inquiry into the Nature and Causes of the Wealth of Nations*. Liberty Classics.

Storr, V. H. (2008). The Market as a Social Space: On the Meaningful Extra Economic Conversations that Can Occur in Markets. *Review of Austrian Economics, 21*(2/3), 135–150.

Thomsen, E. F. (1992). *Prices and Knowledge: A Market-Process Perspective*. Routledge.

Walras, L. (1977[1874]). *Elements of Pure Economics, or the Theory of Social Wealth (Éléments d'économie politique pure)* (Trans. William Jaffé). Augustus M. Kelley.

Whyte, W. H. (1980). Small Urban Spaces. In A. LaFarge (Ed.), *(2000), The Essential William Whyte*. Fordham University Press.

6

The Life and Death of Cities

For Jacobs, cities spearhead innovation, and innovation drives economic development. In a living city, stasis is not an option. If it doesn't constantly innovate and increase its diversity, a city will begin to die. As we saw in Chap. 2, it is this urban-centered approach to economic development that Nobel Laureate, Robert Lucas, found so suggestive in Jacobs's work (Lucas 1988).

This chapter explores in detail the mechanics of Jacobs's theory of economic development, as presented in her 1969 book *The Economy of Cities*. We see how the generation of diversity serves to increase the scope and complexity of a city's division of labor and knowledge. Entrepreneurial forces draw upon the expansion of potential complementarities— "effective pools of economic use"—to discover new kinds of work and novel outputs. She argues that forces internal to the urban process may sometimes retard this development and initiate a "dynamics of decline."

This chapter draws in part from Ikeda (2020).

© The Author(s) 2024
S. Ikeda, *A City Cannot Be a Work of Art*,
https://doi.org/10.1007/978-981-99-5362-2_6

1   Cities and Economic Development

In a living city, under the right rules of the game, both population and per capita Gross Domestic Product (GDP)—the value of all final goods and services produced in a region in one year—tend to grow. But for Jacobs, this kind of growth alone does not constitute economic development. Similarly, falling per capita GDP and a shrinking population are only symptoms of a failure to diversify and innovate, much as a rising body temperature or loss of weight are the symptoms of illness and not the underlying cause. The causes of both development and decay are more fine-grained than standard macro-measures indicate.

Economic development implies not simply change, but in some sense "change for the better." Now, there is a long tradition in economics that takes our preferences as given and not open to question, and so regards what constitutes "better" as purely subjective. In this subjectivist view, "better" may bear no relation to anything objectively measurable at all. That said, to the extent that subjective betterment is related to material well-being, which is in turn related to the output available for us to consume, per-capita GDP or something similar could approximate subjective well-being. But as I mentioned, for Jacobs, such macro-measures are too crude to reveal the important underlying factors. More relevant would be a measure of the degree of diversity of its urban space (Chap. 4) and the extent of the division of labor, or what she calls "new work," because these provide the effective pools of use to draw on for experiment that are the precondition for creativity and innovation of all kinds.

Measured economic growth such as GDP has two sources. One is the production and consumption of "more of the same things," while the other is the production and consumption of "more different things." Both can increase material well-being. Economic development for Jacobs refers to improvements to our material well-being because we do things differently from before or because we broaden our consumption of novel goods and services. I argue, along with Jacobs, that this kind of development, in both its consumption and production aspects, has a deeper and more lasting impact on socioeconomic progress than simply making and consuming more of the same things. Therefore, our focus is on the causes and conditions that promote or retard change of this kind.

I begin, as Jacobs does in *The Economy of Cities*, with an analysis of how cities first emerged in the Neolithic period, circa 10,000–4500 BCE. It may seem odd to frame a discussion of economic development relevant for today in terms of events some 12,000 years ago, especially since material welfare rises significantly only after 1800 CE.[1] But in its own way, the Neolithic period was one of rapid social change and innovation compared to the previous 300,000 years or so of Homo sapiens' existence. It saw the emergence of agriculture and animal husbandry as well as the beginnings of writing, numbering systems, precision calendars, regular long-distance trade, large-scale engineering, institutionalized government (Childe, 1951). Most importantly, it was in the Neolithic period that the first large settlements and proto-cities emerged in the Near East (Childe, 1951; Bairoch, 1988). By some estimates, the population of the world in the period between 10,000 BCE and 5000 BCE rose four- to tenfold, from around 1–5 million to 10–20 million.[2] For these reasons, studying the Neolithic age can shine a revealing light on the nature of the city and its significance for modern economic development.

That economic progress is tied to urbanization is uncontroversial. As Edward Glaeser observes, "There is a near perfect correlation between urbanization and prosperity across nations" (Glaeser, 2012: 7). To gauge the level of material prosperity, look for cities. But this leaves unanswered the question of whether cities are the cause or the consequence of early cultural and economic development. Here, Jacobs's conclusion is sharply at odds with the conventional view of her day.

The belief that cities are historically the consequence and not the cause of substantial accumulation of capital and increasing material wealth has led to the conventional belief that cities must have been preceded by smaller villages that were in turn preceded by even smaller, isolated

---

[1] As Deirdre McCloskey illustrates with her "hockey stick" of per-capita income (2010: 6–8).
[2] See U.S. Census "Historical Estimates of World Population" https://www.census.gov/data/tables/time-series/demo/international-programs/historical-est-worldpop.html. Accessed 10 May 2023.

settlements originally founded by bands of hunter-gatherers.[3] According to this view, Homo sapiens scratched out a nomadic existence for tens of thousands of years, living on wild food until they eventually established small, permanent settlements about 12,000 years ago and gradually learned how to practice farming and to domesticate animals. In time, they turned that knowledge into surpluses of agricultural products until they had accumulated enough to support a nonagricultural labor force that could build the physical infrastructure and to establish the basic social infrastructure that are the necessary preconditions for larger, more complex settlements. These larger settlements then became convenient places to trade surplus goods to outsiders, and the greater wealth accumulated in this way could be used, by sometime in the fourth millennium BCE, to construct the first real cities with walls, streets, monumental buildings, and irrigation systems, as well as codified laws, a permanent government, and a priestly class (Childe, 1951).

According to this conventional view, a city is essentially the same social phenomenon as a small village, only on a larger scale and with many more people and buildings—what economists call a "luxury good," collectively affordable only after a settlement's real income has become high enough. This is in line with the "more of the same" version of economic growth. In that narrative, cities enter the picture long after we had begun the practice of agriculture and animal husbandry, corresponding roughly to the Chalcolithic era and the early Mesopotamian city-states of the late fourth to the third millennium BCE. Significant economic development must therefore precede the appearance of cities, which are the epiphenomena of agriculture.

We should note here that it is also widely accepted, even among those who adhere to this conventional view, that one of the most important functions of a city is to serve as a market, even if it may have originated as a non-commercial site, such as a shrine or fortress (Weber, 1958;

---

[3] This view dates back to at least Adam Smith (1776). Among others, the geographer James E. Vance questions this view: "...the traditional concept of classical geography that the village grows to the town and the town in turn to the city is little supported by either history or logic" (Vance, 1990: 102). See also (Ibid: 298).

Mumford, 1961). The assumption here being, however, that the construction of those sites necessarily rests on a solid base of developed agriculture and husbandry.

Jacobs's alternative thesis sees cities as an originating *cause* of economic development, including agriculture. But it must resolve a paradox: How can a city be both an *originating* cause of and the product of robust economic development.[4] How can a city, a large, diverse, economically and socially vibrant settlement that presupposes a very high level of social cooperation, itself be the source of those very things?

2   The Problems of Discovery and Diffusion

I think it is useful to frame her argument in terms of the concepts of discovery and diffusion. That is, economic development, creating new things or making existing things in a different way, requires us to overcome two problems. The first is how to acquire information from a variety of perspectives and to see it in a novel and useful way. This is the problem of *discovery*.

This can take a lot of work or a lot of luck or both. But it doesn't have to. Why not?

To begin with, in a dynamic world where our knowledge is imperfect, we encounter a stream of opportunities large and small, often appearing as problems, not all of which we notice. But if we are placed in an environment in which new opportunities are regularly presented in a clear or obvious way, other things equal, it would be easier to discover and find ways to solve or use them. Ordinary people under these dynamic circumstances can, by choice or necessity, make more discoveries or become better able to foster their creativity. These opportunities emerge with frequent contact with many people with diverse knowledge, skills, and tastes. It is also important that these contacts take place in relative peace and safety because, as we know, proximity of many diverse people offers

---

[4] Again, here I am speaking of the historical emergence of the first cities. What I term "living cities" are indeed both a cause and consequence of continuing economic development.

occasions for violent conflict, which can obscure gains from trade and association. What robust discovery requires is a "clash of culture" in which the clashers resolve their differences without violence, constructively, and ideally to their mutual advantage. As we have seen, economic freedom, the ability to associate without compulsion, is vital here because then following our self-interest means we are more apt to learn to tolerate differences with others and to practice (behavioral) trust and follow norms of fairness (Henrich, 2015).

The second problem we have to solve, or our social environment has to enable us to solve, for ongoing economic development is to maximize the likelihood that the useful knowledge we actually discover can spread easily to those for whom such knowledge—for example, of new goods, markets, techniques, concepts—would be valuable. This is the problem of *diffusion*.

Such diffusion can happen either because of or despite the existence of rules, norms, or conventions regarding intellectual property. That is, preventing others from profiting without permission from our discoveries is usually necessary to encourage us to make those discoveries in the first place. So it would be good if there was some way to capture enough benefit at reasonably low transactions costs to make it worth our while to do so.[5] At the same time, however, a lot of economic development is the result of word of mouth, imitation, and various kinds of behavior that might be called "free riding." Competition that results from copying someone who exploits a net gain from trade has well-known benefits for material prosperity. It is precisely the practical impossibility of a fully specified, clearly defined, and enforceable system of property rights that leaves room for this kind of beneficial competitive free riding. (This could get us into a very complicated discussion regarding the optimal framework of property rights that I need not engage in here.)

Neither the problem of discovery nor the problem of diffusion is likely to be easily solved by nomads or farmers in small, isolated settlements. A

---

[5] Whether these property rights are formal or informal I will not discuss here, except to note that formal property rights would seem to be needed most when people live and work close together and have frequent contact with strangers, rather than living dispersed across smaller settlements. Glaeser (2012: 22): "The commercial cities developed the legal rules regarding private property and commerce that still guide us today."

person in those circumstances would have little to innovate with and few sources of new information with which to make a discovery. Hints, clues, and new ways of looking at the world would be relatively rare. Innovation and invention would take a level of creativity and independence far beyond the norm of the community, especially in places where dealing exclusively with familiar persons and ideas almost always trumps dealing with the new and unfamiliar. And even if extraordinarily creative and independent-minded individuals were to make an important discovery that their kinsmen were willing to adopt (e.g., three-field crop rotation or a new way to organize production), in the absence of regular, peaceful dealings with distant settlements, whose inhabitants are likely also quite resistant to change, how would that discovery be diffused? Who, with limited contact with outsiders, would be able to take on the highly risky task of spreading the good news, and why would they want to?

In this light, the conventional assumption that rural growth must historically precede cities can itself seem paradoxical. Cities don't foster economic development only in its later stages. According to Jacobs's reasoning, economic development beyond a rudimentary level cannot proceed unless reasonably large, diversely populated settlements appear much closer to the beginning of the Holocene era (i.e., about 11,500 years ago). This implies hunter-gatherers must have become urban dwellers before developing agriculture as we know it.[6] An assessment that anthropologists David Graeber and archeologist David Wengrow appear to share:

> Our world as it existed just before the dawn of agriculture was anything but a world of roving hunter-gatherer bands. It was marked, in many places, by sedentary villages and towns, some by then already ancient, as well as monumental sanctuaries and stockpiled wealth, much of it the work of ritual specialists, highly skilled artisans and architects. (Graeber & Wengrow, 2021: 164)

---

[6] Although this may have taken several intermediate steps. In fact, Graeber and Wengrow argue that many early human societies were neither entirely nomadic nor sedentary but both, depending on the season, for quite a long time. Moreover, they report on the construction of monumental structures at Göbekli Tepe as early as 10,000 BCE (Graeber & Wengrow, 2021: 89), which may lend some support for Jacobs's "cities first" thesis.

Jacobs's counterintuitive hypothesis becomes more plausible if we imagine the urbanization of hunter-gatherers as the product of trade. Some archaeological evidence indeed indicates that hunter-gatherer groups in the Middle East during Neolithic times traded with one another in large settlements.[7] People in the Neolithic period are no different from Mark Zuckerberg or Oprah Winfrey in that all strive to improve their situation, as they see it, through mutually beneficial exchange. In the early Neolithic period, before the emergence of true cities, the potential gains from trade must have been enormous, but the uncertainty and danger of coming face-to-face with strangers outside one's own thick social network must have been very great as well. Other things equal, under these circumstances, just as important as with whom or what one trades is *where* one trades. As with real-estate markets, the most important factors would seem to be location, location, and location.

Jacobs's contribution to this line of thought is significant, and she presents it as a hypothetical history of a settlement called "New Obsidian." First, an ideal trading location is accessible to members of multiple hunter-gatherer groups (Jacobs, 1969a: 19). Places like these usually have certain physical characteristics, such as proximity to waterways or well-traveled overland routes with low transport costs, and they must be perceived as relatively safe. Next, she discusses how persons from hunter-gatherer (HG) groups begin to trade. To do so, two hunter-gatherer groups, HG1 and HG2, may initially use an intermediary from another group, HG3, with whom some members of HG1 and HG2 may already be familiar and whom they both (cognitively) trust[8] and who arranges the trade. If trade among these groups proves successful and regular, other hunter-gatherer groups with weak ties to HG1, HG2, or HG3 might then test the new trading area to see if it is an attractive

---

[7] Archaeological evidence at Çatal Hüyük also lends some support for this hypothesis. See Mellaart and Wheeler (1967) and the website: http://www.catalhoyuk.com/ (accessed 10 May 2023). Also, Algaze (2008, chapter 6) provides evidence on 'import replacement' (in which Jacobs's analysis plays a central role in the urban development process) in the economic growth in Lower Mesopotamia in the middle to late Uruk period (4000–3100 BC), particularly with respect to flint, wool, metals, and other products not indigenous to that area.

[8] In terms of Chap. 5, this pushes the problem of trust back to the question of how HG1 and HG2 came to trust HG3 in the first place. At some point, logically, some persons from each of two or more diverse HG groups must have exercised behavioral trust to form an initial weak tie.

option. As traders from these groups return for more frequent and extended visits, ties strengthen and they may then build structures and dwellings that become more permanent with time. In this way, the trading area evolves unplanned into a settlement with an ever-growing population of socially distant people from diverse, strongly tied hunter-gatherer groups gradually connecting with one another via weak ties. These proto-cities are "market cities" in the sense of the sociologist Max Weber (1958), with their genesis in trade.

A settlement may also evolve into a market city after having originally been established for other (e.g., ceremonial or defensive) reasons. So what later becomes a living city need not have originated in trade, but to become a living city, trade and eventually innovation must be the essential elements.

> [C]ities are places where adding new work to older work proceeds vigorously. Indeed, any settlement where this happens becomes a city. (Jacobs, 1969a: 50)

Thus, it is no contradiction to point out that ancient Romans planted or imposed settlements across Europe as outposts (e.g., Milan, Paris, London) that later developed into living cities.

As noted in Chap. 2, Jacobs defines a (living) city as "a settlement that consistently generates its economic growth from its own local economy" (1969a: 262). In her sense, then, these early settlements were proto-cities, but not only because they contained historically large numbers of people living fairly close together.[9] What the trading settlement did have that hunter-gatherer groups lacked, in addition to a large population, was an enormous and increasing diversity of knowledge and skills on the supply side, and expanding tastes and expectations on the demand side, that diverse, socially distant traders and their families brought with them. Here was an unprecedented opportunity to make new connections and utilize existing connections in unforeseen ways ("multiplexity"). Here

---

[9] Large agglomerations of people such as the latter are sometimes, of course, referred to metaphorically as cities, but they are not cities in almost anyone's sense. Thus, Edward Glaeser's remark that "cities are the absence of physical space between people and companies" (Glaeser, 2012, Loc131) is not useful in this regard.

emerged action spaces, where a wide diversity of social networks could arise and intersect. Some social ties might weaken and dissolve, or sometimes become a source of disadvantage, but overall, the rate at which advantageous new ties and new networks formed among strangers would have been much higher, resulting in growing and increasingly complex networks and complementary relations.[10]

James Coleman (1990) points out that through such "relations of trust," useful complementarities among diverse human capital are formed, as we saw in the previous chapter. Typical urban dwellers under these circumstances encounter more people in a year than they likely would in an entire lifetime as a nomad or villager. They will also encounter more opportunities to buy and sell, make friends or enemies, trust or distrust, than they could have elsewhere; and in the process, their knowledge, attitudes, beliefs, skills, expectations, and tastes will likely change faster and more dramatically than they would have thought possible (and perhaps desirable). In this environment, things don't stay the same, inside the minds of the individuals or in their environment. There are several dimensions along which that change can take place—psychological, moral, and of course cultural—but Jacobs focuses primarily on the economic (although she does later develop the moral dimension in her *Systems of Survival* (Jacobs 1992)).

For example, people will find new uses for already-existing goods. Jacobs suggests that leather pouches used to carry precious volcanic stones to be sold in New Obsidian make, with some local modifications, fine purses that could then be exported, adding value to pouch production. Thus, the "new work" of pouch-making for local products creates opportunities for local innovations, such as decorative pouches for export: "Some of the new local work must also be a precursor of new exports" (Jacobs 1969a). People will discover new ways of doing old tasks as well

---

[10] A good discussion of the pros and cons of social networks is Christakis and Fowler (2009). Also, in research sponsored by the Netherlands Organization for Scientific Research, Gerald Mollenhorst reported (2009): "Over a period of seven years the average size of personal networks was found to be strikingly stable. However, during the course of seven years we replace many members of our network with other people. Only thirty percent of the discussion partners and practical helpers still held the same position seven years later. Only 48 percent were still part of the network." Reported in ScienceDaily 27 May 2009, https://www.sciencedaily.com/releases/2009/05/090527111907. htm (Accessed 3 September 2023.)

as new tasks altogether, new kinds of work, based on their exposure to the diversity they see daily around them. Crucially, this tends to raise the value of their own labors even as it devalues lines of work that are replaced by the new. But the expectation of increasing value productivity through greater contact with a diverse range of people, etc., is what has attracted and continues to attract many to urban life, although things may not always happen in the way we expect them to. In Jacobs's view, it is when the settlement is able consistently to generate net increases in wealth in this fashion that the settlement becomes a great or living city. This is, again, the starting point of all major economic progress and social change. As Jacobs puts it: "Opportunity, not necessity, is the mother of invention" (Jacobs 2000: 90).

3   Solving the Problems of Discovery and Diffusion

A living city with its high population density,[11] diversity of knowledge and tastes, and dynamic social networks and markets that give coherence to these disparate elements solves the problem of discovery and diffusion. In this urban context, innovation depends much less on the lone creative genius working against astronomical odds.

It is sometimes said that markets economize on altruism by harnessing the power of self-interest. Creative genius, like altruism, is also rare and markets economize on it, too. Richard Florida (2005) argues that if cities today wish to rejuvenate, they need to pursue policies that attract creative people. I believe he is partly right. But the marvel of the living city is that it makes people extraordinary, by locating them daily within a matrix of

---

[11] We saw in Chap. 4 how the role of population density has been the subject of much debate among urbanists. Particularly since the invention of the car and high-speed communication, the demand for living and working in proximity has fallen. But this is not the same thing as saying that the need for personal or face-to-face contact has been reduced. Quite the contrary, I think. Density, in the sense of being able to interact easily with large numbers of persons outside one's own strongly tied network, is still as important as it ever was for economic development. Recall from Chap. 5 that the term "Jacobs Density" relates to this idea. I address this topic again in Chap. 10.

networks and action spaces in which information and opportunities, conducted by weak social ties, come at them from many different and often unexpected directions. Decreasing average social distance and increasing Jacobs Density make it more likely that useful novelty diffuses to those who value it, even if they don't know the innovator personally (and whether or not they pay for it). A developing economy means more work and a greater variety of work, increasing the options of city dwellers and lowering the cost of trying new things. As Glaeser (2012: 25) notes: "An abundance of local employers also provides implicit insurance against the failure of any particular start-up." City dwellers experience these things at lower expected cost than their rural cousins.

Jacobs demonstrates this by suggesting how agriculture and animal husbandry likely historically emerged unplanned within the boundaries of a city.[12] She first explains how a large trading settlement might be established by hunter-gatherers, which then grows and develops spontaneously, as I sketched earlier in this chapter. I also mentioned that one of the locational advantages of the city is that it lowers the cost of transport, so goods can be traded there from other locations more conveniently than before. But location does a great deal more than simply lower transport costs.

Jacobs (1969a) uses the example of seed from distant areas, perhaps with significant variations in size, nutrition, or heartiness, which are brought together in unprecedented proximity in a large trading settlement. The chances of deliberate, or more likely, accidental mixing of different varieties of seeds are thus much greater there than in a smaller, less

---

[12] To clarify, it is not my contention that cities must be either exclusively a cause or a consequence of development. The object here is to use the logic of Jacobs's analysis, of how historically agriculture and animal husbandry may have first arisen in cities, as a framework for understanding how other essential elements of culture—writing, numeracy, etc.—could also have had their genesis in cities. Fernand Braudel (1979: 484) endorses this view of cities. Peter Taylor (2014) has almost single-handedly taken on the archeologists critical of Jacobs's "cities first" thesis, in particular Smith et al. (2014). My own take on this debate, given along the lines presented here, can be found in Ikeda (2018). As noted, the recent research reported by Graeber and Wengrow (2021) casts doubt on the very idea of a sudden switch from hunting-gathering to permanent farming settlements. And while the economic historian Paul Bairoch disputes Jacobs's cities-first thesis he doesn't dismiss it out of hand, saying "the margin of uncertainty around that period is such that the hypothesis cannot be rejected outright" (Bairoch, 1988: 17).

"cosmopolitan" settlements. Also, those responsible for storing wild seed grain, itself new work invented in the proto-city, are, out of self-interest, much more likely than isolated farmers to have the opportunity to notice the different characteristics of the seed varieties. Moreover, unlike farmers in rural settlements, experimentation becomes more practicable since failure need not lead to starvation. Indeed, seed-stewards only need to notice differences that appear in the normal course of business, and they have profit motive to do so. They become experts in a new specialization of seed stewardship; an expertise they pass along, intentionally or not, to rival seed-stewards, whose economic interest is, among other things, to keep a sharp eye out for new developments.

The important lesson here is that little of this need be done deliberately. The seed-stewards-turned-hybridists were not aware that they were advancing agriculture, but that is what they did. New businesses, new work, and systematic hybridization becomes in this way an unintended consequence of urban life.

Jacobs tells essentially the same story about animal husbandry. Some former hunter-gatherers specialize in feeding and minding, say, wild goats and keeping them for their owners until they want them. Again, a new business and new work is thereby created. In a small village, whoever tends goats would rarely, if ever, see so many varieties of goats at one place and time. In the large, dense, and diverse settlement, they could not help but notice differences in quality, size, and temperament. In time they might, out of sheer convenience to themselves and their clients, add the work of slaughtering to their business. When this happens, some wild-goat owners who leave their animals with the goat-keeper for care themselves transition from customers to suppliers of wild goats for the keeper's breeding and slaughtering business. With so many goats at their disposal, the keepers find themselves in a position to pick and choose which goats to slaughter and which they will retain for breeding. (They will also likely need specialized tools and labor to engage in the new endeavor, again necessitating new goods and new work.) As in the case of seed-stewards, purely out of self-interest, goat-keepers will probably choose the most difficult-to-manage goats first and retain the more docile and easier-to-care-for goats for breeding. After a few generations of goats, a breed of domesticated goat emerges. Again, in the milieu of urban diversity and density, accidental breeders and their competitors advance animal husbandry without intending to.

The knowledge of and benefits from these discoveries spread rapidly through dense social networks of the city. In this way, social networks and market incentives make discovery and diffusion closely bound processes. Without the lines of contact that bring new opportunities to urban entrepreneurs, far fewer discoveries would take place. And knowledge quickly diffuses over dense social networks because people are entrepreneurially alert to profit opportunities that can accrue through them.[13]

Agriculture and animal husbandry emerge as spontaneous orders within a living city, which, as we have seen, is itself a spontaneous order. The new knowledge and skills that seed-stewardship and the goat-keeping create would have been far more difficult or even impossible to discover or, if discovered, more slowly spread or easily lost, in a region of smaller, non-commercial villages. The urban processes described here simply cannot be replicated consistently in a less complex, less dynamic rural setting. A city is, indeed, not simply a scaled-up hamlet, village, or town. It is a fundamentally different social phenomenon.

Although perhaps historically interesting in themselves, these provocative theories of the spontaneous origins of the city and of the unplanned innovations that happen within it tell us something about the nature of all living cities, including those of today. For instance, to be incubators of ideas and generators of innovation, cities require an ever-changing variety of knowledge on the supply side and of a broadening of tastes and expectations on the demand side. And to accommodate diversity, it is critical to have flexibility in land-use to provide space for and adjustments in the actions that constitute that diversity. Action spaces expand, and along with them so do dynamic social networks and rising Jacobs density.

All this presupposes the existence of substantial economic freedom.

---

[13] Again, the standard reference for the role of entrepreneurship is Kirzner (1973).

4   Economic Freedom¹⁴ and Social Networks

Economic freedom promotes market formation by lowering the costs of trading, but it does far more. First of all, not much diversity-generating discovery and development happens unless people feel secure in their person and belongings, and feel free to pursue gains from trade where and when they see them. Indeed, the original market areas, the proto-cities, cannot get off the ground unless members of socially distant groups trust, are trustworthy, and are permitted to trade with one another. By enabling extensive trade, economic freedom also enables the formation of norms of behavioral trust and reciprocity that promote weak ties and bridging social capital, which in turn promotes dynamic, robust, and long-term economic development. And to the extent that trusting produces net gains for both trusters and trustees, it bolsters the willingness of people to trade and trust even more.

Trade between strangers, where there may have been a history of hostility between their respective groups, may not result in friendship or strong ties, even if they have been trading for a long time. But that they are trading at all instead of shunning or fighting each other means their desire to improve their situations through peaceful association has overcome to some extent their mutual aversion. And while their levels of behavioral trust may be barely high enough to overcome their uncertainties, that they have reached an agreement at all indicates a mutual understanding of what constitutes a fair trade and perhaps a recognition of other common values. Over time, their tie may strengthen and their cognitive trust may grow, possibly leading to multiplex interactions and

---

¹⁴ I am using the term "economic freedom" in the sense used by the authors of the *Economic Freedom of the World Annual Reports* at http://www.freetheworld.com/index.html. The four cornerstones of economic freedom are:

- Personal choice
- Voluntary exchange coordinated by markets
- Freedom to enter and compete in markets
- Protection of persons and their property from aggression by others

more and diverse socially distant partners.[15] But to get this virtuous spiral going means someone has to make the first move, an act of behavioral trust, a leap of faith. And to keep it going requires traders to keep being trustworthy once it does.

There is, of course, no guarantee this will happen, and it's not hard to find examples where it has not. But in modern times they are far outweighed by instances where it has, for otherwise how could the historic levels of wealth creation and global trade over the last several centuries have taken place? In the modern world, economic freedom, limited as it is by political power, has been essential for economic development and the discovery and diffusion of knowledge that characterize the process of innovation.

With this understood, what are the mechanics of innovation according to Jacobs?

5   The Process of Innovation: Parent Work and New Work

Those mechanics rely in part of the concept of the "division of labor."

The principle of the division of labor is most famously articulated by Adam Smith, the titular "father of economics," in his book published in 1776, *An Inquiry into the Nature and Causes of the Wealth of Nations*, a.k.a. *The Wealth of Nations*. Smith describes how the daily output of a group of workers working independently—pin-making in Smith's example—can increase astronomically if they divide production into several parts with each worker specializing in one or two tasks. Smith observes that the division of labor increases the daily output of ten workers from

---

[15] As you might imagine there is a large literature on the relation between trust and trade, notably by Heinrich et al. (2001), some of which I cited in Chap. 5 under "Connected or Trapped." Another good place to look may be Jonathan Anomaly (2017) and the references therein.

perhaps 200 pins to 48,000 pins—a factor of 240 times![16] Jacobs takes Smith's concept and puts a more dynamic spin on it.

Jacobs sees innovation and the creation of new work as growing out of existing "parent work" in the division of labor (DOL). Innovations appear at the margins of the current DOL as offshoots of existing specializations. Characterizing it, Jacobs says: "To be sure this process is full of surprises and hard to predict – possibly it is unpredictable – before it has happened…" (1969a: 59). Being essentially creative, innovation is inherently unpredictable.

New work represents a dramatic departure from parent work. That is because, while an innovation may depend on the intelligence, awareness, and connections of those working within an established business, the new product or service they create tends to serve the demands of a very different clientele from that of the parent business or perhaps even of the industry in which the parent operates. Henry Ford went from working on ships to selling automobiles. Amazon.com went from being an online bookseller to now serving as a platform for a multitude of products with home delivery, as well as a producer of original movies and television series, none of which anyone, including founder Jeff Bezos, could have foreseen. So if you are trying to understand the salient aspect of this essentially dynamic process, narrow categories such as "local services" or "light manufacturing" are not helpful (1969a: 61).

For this reason, while the new work may originate within an established firm, it is more likely to break away or spinoff from the parent if there is economic freedom to do so. Ford, for example, was a young mechanic for a Detroit firm that made marine engines before breaking away to design and produce his first working automobile, with local carriage makers providing his auto-body frames (Glaeser, 2012: 46). Some exceptional businesses do reinvent themselves repeatedly over time to supply a shifting customer base or to enter new markets (Google, now

---

[16] Oddly, while modern mainstream economics pays tribute to Smith's division of labor, to explain how productivity increases, it relies exclusively on what is known as a "production function," in which homogeneous units of labor are combined formulaically with homogeneous units of capital, with no mention of division of labor. Why this is the case is a story too long to tell here, but it does reflect the tendency of mainstream economics, noted in earlier chapters, to prize mathematical elegance. See Ikeda (2012).

Alphabet Inc., and Apple Inc. being well-known current examples). But radical innovations are also the initiative of marginal individuals or small groups short on capital. Indeed, while there is a tendency to equate entrepreneurship too narrowly with start-up companies, it does reflect a common perception that supports the spin-off model.[17]

Without a wide diversity of people, places, and things readily at hand—that is, "effective economic pools of use" or "co-development"—that will serve to complement and support new start-ups, new projects may never get off the ground. Other things equal, diversity inspires and enables innovation. As we will see, diversity generates knock-on effects in the local economy as employment and investment rise in the new local businesses, and in the suppliers of inputs for those businesses, even as they decline in other established businesses (locally or abroad).[18]

We have seen that the freedom to move into and out of existing spaces or to convert existing spaces to new uses is crucial. Flexibility of land-use means businesses have the freedom to easily repurpose space with expected changes in demand- and supply-side conditions, and it allows for a greater accommodation of differences in human capital and tastes. Contrariwise, land-use rigidity retards adjustment, innovation, and creative urban development. If the innovation that drives economic development consists chiefly of new organizations that spring up among the old, where both the old and new might prosper or die, then the legal-institutional framework must be flexible enough to let this happen; if, that is, economic development rather than preserving privilege or mere redistribution is an aim of public policy (Cozzolino 2018). And beyond the regulatory environment, the customs, norms, and social networks operating within this environment should also welcome, or at least tolerate, new ways of doing things, new products, and new services. Just as importantly, they should accommodate new consumption behaviors and lifestyle choices of those whose diverse interests and tastes drive the dynamic demand side of economic development. We need to be allowed, and to

---

[17] And here we might recall the role of "old buildings" in incubating such start-ups. Also, while start-ups may grow into large concerns themselves, the successful ones typically sell out to larger, well-established companies.

[18] Recall that these effective pools of use are among the diversities generated by the four conditions discussed in Chap. 4.

allow ourselves, to experiment with and adopt new tastes and attitudes, and to welcome diverse outsiders into our community networks. The urban environment should, as I emphasized in Chap. 3, tolerate, even encourage, trial and error, success and failure, and the messiness that comes with it.

Tolerance in each of the aspects of social change described here can help keep the inevitable clashes of ideas and cultures between new and old that arise in a dynamic environment from bursting into violent conflict. In fact, shunning force, collaborating with strangers, and being (peacefully) competitive are three values of the "commercial syndrome" Jacobs develops in *Systems of Survival* (2002), which investigates the differences in the ethics that should guide behavior in the market and government.[19]

6   Economic Development via Import Replacement and Import Shifting[20]

Central to Jacobs's development theory is the combination of "import replacement" on the supply side of the market and "import shifting" on the demand side. In the story of the origin and evolution of New Obsidian, they are the dual engines of the economic expansion in a city's DOL.

6.1   The Division of Labor as a Spontaneous Order

Before looking into those details, however, it is important to keep in mind that the DOL of a city is a spontaneous order. To quote Adam Smith:

---

[19] See also Ikeda (2002, 2008, 2021) and Mises (1978).

[20] For a more detailed but succinct description of this process, see Ikeda (2020) or the appendix to Jacobs (1969a, 1969b), which contains some helpful diagrams. Readers seeking a concise summary of Jacobs's theory of economic development should also see Charles-Albert Ramsay's *Cities Matter* (2022).

This division of labour, from which so many advantages are derived, is not originally the effect of any human wisdom, which foresees and intends that general opulence to which it gives occasion. It is the necessary, though very slow and gradual, consequence of a certain propensity in human nature, which has in view no such extensive utility; the propensity to truck, barter, and exchange one thing for another. (Smith, 1981: 25)

As defined in Chap. 2, a spontaneous order is an unplanned, largely self-regulating set of complex social relations that effectively adjust to changing conditions over time (Hayek, 1967). Recall that like the individual, the household, or a business firm, the city is a natural unit of economic analysis, unlike the political construction of the nation-state. The process of economic development for Jacobs takes place in a living city in relation to other cities.

We have seen that for Jacobs, economic development occurs by "adding new kinds of work to other kinds of older work" (1961: 51). "Break away" or spin-off activity adds new work that begins as part of a specialization within the DOL of an existing firm. Someone thinks of a new way of doing an old task or discovers a way of taking the skills and resources used in that task and doing something different with them, perhaps something very different, that takes production in a new direction.

Examples Jacobs uses include the way 3M Company, originally a Minnesota-based supplier of industrial sand, gradually adjusted to market demand via trial and error to manufacture vastly different products, ranging from adhesive tape to reflective sheeting, all of which were logically (but unpredictably) derived from some aspect of the production of industrial sand; or the way bicycles were first manufactured in Japan by local entrepreneurs who discovered they could assemble all the necessary inputs from local suppliers of replacement parts for bicycles imported from abroad (a good example of exploiting an effective economic pool of use) (Jacobs, 1969b). Thus, expanding complementarities of production in some areas of a local economy increases the extent and complexity of the DOL and creates sources of potential new products some of which may be exported.

6.2   Innovation as a Process of Import Replacement and Shifting

Delving into this more deeply, an urban economy expands when the rate at which new DOLs emerge exceeds the rate at which old divisions and specializations recede. While in retrospect the new goods and services created at some margins of production are logically traceable to the older parent work, these new goods and services and their location in the increasingly complex and extended DOL are, as Jacobs observes, unpredictable. We can see in retrospect the logical steps by which adhesive tape evolved from the process of producing industrial sand, but we can't predict beforehand that it would happen. Existing parts of the DOL, *qua* effective economic pools of use, inspire new extensions such as texting apps or the creation of online content, while other parts wither away, such as manufacturing CRT monitors or teaching handwriting. And the more extended and complex the DOL, the more opportunities there will be to stimulate new work and new divisions and specializations. Paraphrasing Adam Smith, the scope and complexity of the DOL is limited by the extent of the market (Smith, 1981: 31).

Routine, non-innovative growth occurs when businesses make, and their customers consume, more and more of the same kinds of goods and services. Development through innovation is different. At the level of the individual firm, innovation tends typically to build gradually on old work. At the level of the city, however, economic development happens in discontinuous, sometimes explosive leaps, as alert copycats rapidly diffuse successful discoveries over urban networks. This is as true of the modern city as it was for the Neolithic city. Economic development through innovation takes place as the result of diversification and differentiation by producers and consumers. This is where imports and exports play key roles.

Recall that in Jacobs's story of the New Obsidian, wild food is at first imported by hunter-gatherers who bring wild goats with them to the settlement. Caring for them requires, in addition to the goats, other inputs such as someone to tend them, water and feed, and a sturdy pen to hold them all. When the goat-keeper adds domesticating and

butchering to the business, this adds new work and new and more complex divisions of labor to the existing system. It also means that less of the
same wild food needs to be imported into the city—some imports will be
replaced by local production. The new product, say butchered meat or a
new breed of goat, is added to the shopping list of locals. Since the new
product is likely an improvement over the original, having been vetted to
better suit local demand, it may then turn out to be attractive to consumers in other cities who do not yet have access to the new breed. In this way
diversity of tastes shape the demand side of the process. Along with the
extended DOL, the export of new products brings added wealth into
the city.

Part of the new wealth, according to Jacobs, will increase the demand
for consumable goods and services produced both locally and abroad. An
increase in local production means a greater demand for inputs including
labor, which in a regime of economic freedom will be met from both
local and foreign suppliers, and an extension of the local DOL. Jacobs
well understood that exports (i.e., the value of what a city's inhabitants
sell abroad) must ultimately equal imports (the value of what they buy
from abroad). So, with exports growing and consumption of cheaper
local products replacing some imports, locals will use the difference in
those values to import more goods, including some they had not imported
before. This is a process Jacobs calls "import shifting" and it is a natural
and important complement to import replacing:

> [T]his process of replacing present imports, *and buying others instead*, is
> probably the chief means by which economic life expands, and by which
> national economies increase their total volumes of goods and services.
> (Jacobs, 1969a, 1969b: 148; emphasis added)

In summary, the stages of economic expansion are: (1) exporting local
products and resources to buy imports, (2) using local pools of diversity
to entrepreneurially replace some imports with locally produced goods,
thereby (3) increasing the extent and complexity of the DOL, generating
additional income and more potential complementarities, (4) exporting
more local production, (5) increasing imports and shifting to new kinds

of imports, (6) so that in time, some of these imports are themselves replaced, beginning the process anew.[21]

Jacobs uses a simple schematic to express the basic relations (Jacobs, 1961):

$$D + A \rightarrow nD$$

That is, to the existing DOL in an economy (D), is added a new activity (A) engaged in new exports or replacing some imports with local production, which generates new work in some new part of the DOL (nD) forming what she terms a "new generality" from which a larger more complex DOL emerges. (There is a much more detailed schematic explanation in the appendix to Jacobs (1961).)

As noted, many of the new imports that residents shift over to will be goods and services they will not have purchased before. On the demand side, then, a significant consequence of import shifting to novel goods is that locals will be further exposed to foreign cultures, customs, and perhaps ways of thinking that could expand their tastes to products they might previously have eschewed or overlooked. Also, the new kinds of work added to the existing DOL may require certain tools, materials, and know-how not available locally, and so locals will have to import those too (until they can be replaced locally) and learn the skills to use them. Moreover, some of these "imports" will arrive embodied in the human capital of immigrants to the city. The importation of novel goods and services in all forms, again, sets the stage for further rounds of input

---

[21] In *The Nature of Economies*, Jacobs (2000: 39–64) summarizes economic development in three points this way:

1. Differentiation emerges from generality.
2. Differentiations become generalities from which further differentiations emerge.
3. Development depends on co-development.

The first two points refer to the process by which new work arises from parts of old work, and to new work over time becoming the old work from which even newer work will emerge. The third point on development and co-development refers to cities with diverse ecosystems of dynamic, complementary uses of space fostering innovation by providing sources of ideas, inputs, and customers, as well as a kind of safety net (i.e., alternative jobs and customers) when the economic environment unexpectedly shifts.

replacement and shifting, greater complexity of the local DOL, rising exports, and growing local wealth, and so on. (These interrelated processes are another example of "reciprocating systems" mentioned in Chap. 4 in reference to the four generators of diversity.)

When local entrepreneurs imitate successful innovators, it also expands local output, employment, wealth, and consumption, but this does not directly contribute to local innovation.

In living cities, the import-replacing and shifting process repeats again and again. There is no upper bound to this process, no limit to the size, wealth, and complexity of the living city,[22] as long as we are able to utilize our resources and resourcefulness to stay ahead of the problems we create. Once again, the ever-growing complexity of the local DOL lays the groundwork, the effective economic pools of use, for future innovation. These pools of use accumulate, and beyond some threshold become rich hunting grounds of entrepreneurial discovery that sets off import replacement and the export of new products.

Of course, cities can also decline—the title of Jacobs's most famous book is after all *The Death and Life of Great American Cities*—owing either to forces within the urban process itself (i.e., endogenous factors), which I discuss a little later in this chapter, or to policy interventions (i.e., exogenous factors), which is covered in Chap. 8.

6.3   A Digression on Tariffs[23]

Jacobs is careful to distinguish what she calls "import replacement" from the familiar-sounding but very different policy of "import substitution," which she describes as "a short-lived fiasco of the 1970s" (Jacobs, 2000: Loc. 1198). Import substitution is a policy of erecting legal import barriers and protections to shield local, usually politically connected, businesses or industries from foreign competition. While Jacobs cautiously supports tariffs to protect distressed regions, she does so because she believes this offers them limited, imperfect shelter against changes in the

---

[22] In particular, the size of cities follows a "power-law distribution." See Krugman (1996: 39–46).
[23] I present a more extensive exposition and critique of Jacobs's argument in the Appendix to this chapter.

exchange rate of a national currency. I will say something more about this because it has led to misunderstanding; it will also allow me to introduce her reasons for recommending the breaking up of nation-states into city-states.

Jacobs believes that tariffs can stimulate the process of economic development in regions of a nation-state that are subject to "false feedback" from the rate at which that country's currency exchanges with the currency of another country. If a nation-state consists of regions with industries that are in significantly different stages of economic development or states of health (e.g., agriculture, manufacturing, finance), and if some of those regions are dominant in the sense that their exports are a plurality of the country's total exports compared to exports from the other regions, then the dominant regions will largely determine the exchange rate between that nation-state's currency and those of the countries with whom it trades. That is bad for the less developed, less healthy regions according to Jacobs.

If a country, say the United States, has a "strengthening dollar" (e.g., the number of Euros it takes to buy a dollar is increasing) then that means foreigners have to spend more Euros for any American product priced in dollars, which effectively adds to the prices foreigners have to pay for all American goods, including those goods sellers are struggling to sell in poorer regions. It also means, other things equal, that buyers in those poorer regions are more likely to import more, including goods that might have otherwise been sold in their region, because the prices of foreign goods are now effectively cheaper because a dollar will now buy more Euros than before.

In the absence of a devolution of nation-states into smaller, more economically relevant regional- or city-states with their own currencies, Jacobs recommends governments in less-developed regions be permitted to impose protective import tariffs when the dollar becomes stronger (and presumably lower them when the dollar becomes weaker). This is currently forbidden under the United States Constitution. As I explain in the Appendix to Chap. 6, there are good economic reasons to doubt that protective tariffs of this nature will achieve the objectives Jacobs set forth, reasons that have to do with ignoring knowledge limitations and the political-incentive effects set into motion by protectionist policies. In other areas, Jacobs is keenly aware of knowledge problems (see Chap. 7), but she often overlooks perverse incentive effects of policy interventions (see Chap. 8).

But even for Jacobs, erecting a protective tariff is really a second-best policy. Her best recommendation is to devolve nation-states, as orderly and early as possible, into autonomous regional- or city-states which could then issue their own local currencies, thus removing any false feedback from a national currency because there would be no national currency (Jacobs, 1984: 168). Still, Jacobs seems to ignore another perfectly good solution to the false-feedback problem, one that may be more realistic than dissolving nation-states, as attractive as that may be. That is to enable or even encourage the natural evolution toward a global currency, whether the dollar, the Euro, a cryptocurrency, or whatever. With a truly global currency, used in every city and region of the world, the need to exchange one currency for another would disappear altogether and along with it the false-feedback problems Jacobs complains of. Instead, changes in the relative prices of regional goods would make the necessary adjustments as they normally do, falling when demand decreases relative to supply, rising when demand increases relative to supply.

Jacobs does recognize that economic development cannot take place unless locals are reasonably free to import and export as they see fit, which is something tariffs interfere with (Jacobs, 1984: 168).[24] And to reiterate, for Jacobs, far from being a problem to be removed, imports and the ever-diversifying tastes they stimulate and the opportunities they offer for entrepreneurial replacement help to drive the process of economic development.

6.4   The Inefficiency of Economic Development

A final thing to bear in mind, mentioned in Chap. 3, is that, because the essence of economic development is a creative and radically unpredictable process, the standard categories of efficiency and inefficiency are not really relevant. Moreover, greater static efficiency via what economists call

---

[24] I discuss this further in the Appendix to this chapter. Recall from Chap. 2 that this is an area where I particularly differ with Jacobs.

"economies of scale and of scope," or a more extensive division of labor within an already existing production process, will produce "more of the same" and contribute to measured gross domestic product. This is not especially helpful for economic development based on discovery and innovation. And while the DOL by itself is a useful device for achieving operating efficiency under a given set of tastes, technology, and resources, its power to promote ongoing economic development is limited. All further increases in efficiency, once existing work has been suitably divided into specialized tasks, will depend upon the addition of new activities, new work, and the increasing organized complexity of the DOL (Jacobs, 1969a, 1969b: 82–83).

For Jacobs, a better measure of the development of an economic system would be the ratio of new work to total work. She would therefore replace the norm of economic efficiency with the norm of new work,[25] which is measured by how much the DOL multiplies and becomes more complex over time (Jacobs, 1969a: 57). Jacobs suggests using the ratio of the "value of new products" to the value of all projects produced in a city over time as a proxy (Jacobs, 1969a: 94). This deserves further consideration, although to my knowledge it has not been tested.

7   The Self-Destruction of Diversity

A living city contains powerful forces for expansion, but what might lead to its decline? The next two chapters look at how certain attempts to consciously direct overall urban development can have negative unintended consequences for urban life, and Chap. 9 investigates whether some projects to rebuild or revitalize a city could be successful. Here, however, we outline Jacobs's claim that forces internal to the very process of economic expansion can lead to a dynamics of decline; in particular, that a neighborhood or district may become a victim of its own success. It goes like this....

A lively location filled with successful innovators tends to attract imitators. Other businesses and residents will want to move into spaces

---

[25] Jacobs (2000) adds what is perhaps another evaluative norm, that of "dynamic stability."

currently occupied by established users. Investors and developers will want to follow the same "formula for success" by building or retrofitting spaces there to accommodate uses already proven to be successful. The demand for space will increase and, other things equal, raise the average cost of real estate in the area. As a result, "cheap space in old buildings" begins to disappear as they are expensively renovated, removing one of the four generators of diversity. The rising cost of space particularly discourages younger people with new ideas and lots of energy but little capital, the very ingredient that probably sparked the initial experimentation and creativity, from moving to or staying in that location.

> The first of these powerful forces is the tendency for outstanding success in cities to destroy itself – purely as a result of being successful. In this chapter I shall discuss the self-destruction of diversity, a force which, among its other effects, causes our downtowns continually to shift their centers and move. This is a force that creates has-been districts, and is responsible for much inner-city stagnation and decay. (Jacobs, 1961: 242)

This tendency homogenizes land-use. Large, well-established firms that are less likely to innovate with new concepts will be better able to afford the area and so displace smaller, independently owned establishments.

> Whichever one or few uses have emerged as the most profitable in the locality will be repeated and repeated, crowding out and overwhelming less profitable forms of use. (Jacobs, 1961: 243)

Smaller "start-ups" that merely copy successful uses will also contribute to the homogenization. The result is an endogenous self-destruction of diversity, reducing potential complementarities and local pools of economic use. Less imaginative, copycat competition homogenizes the land-use diversity that initially enabled risky trial and error. While some independent proprietors may remain, fewer new ones will appear.

In their introduction to a collection of Jacobs's shorter works, Zipp and Storring describe this process at work in Jacobs's own West Village neighborhood:

> So the Village endures, but as a bright and blurry clone of a past self. With astronomic rents came chain stores, fashion boutiques, luxury condo

conversions in glass and steel. They have crowded out hardware stores, bodegas, diners, bookstores, small manufacturing shops, the unpredictable and the odd. Real estate speculation, long a New York obsession, has finally chased out most everything else but rarefied shopping and eating and looking. The diverse mixture of people with plans both humble and grand that Jacobs celebrated can find little purchase in this meager city soil. (Zipp & Storring, 2016: xvii)

Ironically, it is the very entrepreneurial competitive process that helped create the original liveliness of an area that can drive this result.

This process represents what some might call a "market failure." This is a term I resist using here because what economists mean by market failure—that is, a market equilibrium that is inefficient—is entirely different from what Jacobs is describing—that is, an endogenous process that results in a decline of innovation, not efficiency, in a particular location. Thus, a district or city may have a growing per-capita GDP, at least for a while, and be full of expensive residences and high-end stores, and yet be "declining" in terms of creativity and innovation, as public and private spaces become increasingly monocultural. Other examples in New York would be the now posh district of Soho, which, in the 1970s, was the home of artists and serious art galleries but today, especially along the main thoroughfare of West Broadway, has taken on all the glitz (though not the glamour) of Madison Avenue. What to do?

The key policy response, according to Jacobs, is to ensure there are other locations in the city where the conditions for generating diversity obtain, so entrepreneurial energies stifled by homogeneity and high real-estate prices can take root elsewhere in the city (Jacobs, 1961: 255). If all that energy and resourcefulness can find other, congenial locations—neighborhoods or districts that have adequate generators of diversity—the city as a whole might avert the self-destruction of innovation. In the longer term, perhaps expanding areas of potential development to include so-called "suburban sprawl" may be a practical way to nurture innovation and creativity. After all, the basements and garages where some legendary rock bands and tech geniuses got their start were in the 'burbs. In any case, without local outlets like these, entrepreneurial innovators will look elsewhere for cheaper, more workable places, stunting local innovation and draining life from the city.

Finally, one of the most important endogenous causes of urban decline is over-specialization in a particular industry, giving rise to a city's heavy dependence on a single, dominating use or industry. When demand or supply conditions change, this heavy dependence, along with stakeholders with a vested interest in resisting change, makes adjustment extraordinarily difficult. Wealth and imports decline and declining with them are import replacement, import shifting, new exports, and so on, generating a spiraling dynamics of decline that takes a very long time to reverse, if ever. Detroit's decline in beginning in the 1950s might be a good example (Glaeser, 2012: 49). (But despite its severe challenges, Detroit lately may be slowly reviving, evidently largely through the efforts of devoted locals—billionaires, small businesses, and ordinary citizens—using their local knowledge to strategically invest in plentiful cheap space (Agar, 2015).) Dynamics of decline can also occur as the result of public policy—for instance, when protectionist tariffs and quotas on imports favor local industries and stifle innovation and development, when rent regulations stifle residential construction, and of course when urban planning is insensitive to, as Jacobs phrases it, "the kind of problem a city is."

8   Concluding Thoughts

As we have seen in these last two chapters, Jacobs takes an alternative perspective that includes the essential roles of cities, of entrepreneurial discovery, of the non-market foundations of economic development (e.g., trust and social networks), and of demand- and supply-side diversity. Hers is a vision of a dynamic process in which diversity and density give rise to discovery and development, enabled by economic freedom and tolerance. In this process, innovations emerging from parent work depend crucially on co-development within a process of entrepreneurial import-replacement, taste-broadening import-shifting, and expanding exports. Discovery and innovation are rooted in an ever-growing range of complementarities in the division of labor, and their diffusion is reliant on dense and complex social networks that emerge and adapt dynamically. Measured increases in GDP are a result.

Regarding policy, because of problems of knowledge and political incentives, public authorities should beware of interventions that discourage new and valuable uses of space that hinder people from adjusting locally to changes in tastes, technologies, and resources, and adjusting in the longer term to changes in demographics, environment, and geography. The inherently unpredictable and evolutionary character of economic development cautions against large-scale projects, especially when ill-informed and politically motivated public authorities are making the big decisions and when the need for creative adjustments will inevitably arise. Chapters 7 and 8 explore these themes.

Works Cited

Agar, S. (2015, May). Tough, Cheap, and Real, Detroit Is Cool Again. *National Geographic.*

Algaze, G. (2008). *Ancient Mesopotamia at the Dawn of Civilization: The Evolution of an Urban Landscape.* Univ. of Chicago Press. (Kindle Edition Location Indicators "Loc." Rather Than Page Numbers).

Anomaly, J. (2017). Trust, Trade, and Moral Progress: How Market Exchange Promotes Trustworthiness. *Social Philosophy and Policy, 34*(2), 89–107.

Bairoch, Paul (1988). *Cities and Economic Development: From the Dawn of History to the Present.* (Trans. C. Braider). Chicago: Univ. of Chicago Press.

Braudel, F. (1979). *The Structures of Everyday Life: Civilization & Capitalism, 15th–18th Century* (Trans. S. Reynolds) (Vol. I). Harper & Row.

Childe, V. G. (1951). The Urban Revolution. In R. T. Legates & F. Stout (Eds.), *The City Reader 1ˢᵗ (ed) 1996.* Routledge.

Coleman, J. S. (1990). *Foundations of Social Theory.* Belknap Harvard.

Cozzolino, S. (2018). Reconsidering Spontaneity and Flexibility after Jane Jacobs. How Do They Work Under Different Kind of Planning Conditions? *Cosmos+Taxis, 5*(3/4), 14–24.

Florida, R. (2005). *The Rise of the Creative Class, and How It's Transforming Work, Leisure, Community, and Daily Life.* Basic Books.

Glaeser, E. L. (2012). *Triumph of the City: How Our Greatest Invention Makes Us Richer, Smarter, Greener, Healthier, and Happier.* Penguin.

Graeber, D., & Wengrow, D. (2021). *The Dawn of Everything: A New History of Humanity.* Farrar, Straus and Giroux.

Hayek, F. A. (1967). The Results of Human Action but Not of Human Design. In *Essays in Philosophy, Politics, and Economics*. Univ. of Chicago Press.

Henrich, J. (2015). Culture and Social Behavior. *Current Opinion in Behavioral Sciences, 3*, 84–89.

Henrich, J., Boyd, R., Bowles, S., Camerer, C., Fehr, E., Gintis, H., & McElreath, R. (2001). In Search of Homo Economicus: Behavioral experiments in 15 Small-Scale Societies. *American Economic Review, 91*(2), 73–78.

Ikeda, S. (2002). The Role of 'Social Capital' in the Market Process. *Journal des Economistes et des Etudes Humaines, 12*(2/3), 229–240.

Ikeda, S. (2008). The Meaning of 'Social Capital' as It Relates to the Market Process. *Review of Austrian Economics, 21*, 167–182.

Ikeda, S. (2012, August 7). *Whatever Happened to the Division of Labor?* Foundation for Economic Education. https://fee.org/articles/whatever-happened-to-the-division-of-labor

Ikeda, S. (2016, July 22). Tolerance, Criticism, and Humility Are Core Principles of Freedom. In *Foundation for Economic Education*. https://fee.org/articles/tolerance-criticism-and-humility-are-core-principles-of-freedom/

Ikeda, S. (2018). Cities, Agriculture, and Economic Development: The Debate Over Jane Jacobs's 'Cities-first Thesis'. *Cosmos + Taxis, 5*(3/4), 25–31.

Ikeda, S. (2020). *The Economy of Cities*: Jane Jacobs's Overlooked Economic Classic. *The Independent Review, 24*(4), 605–618.

Ikeda, S. (2021). Urban Planning and Urban Planning. *Social Philosophy and Policy, 38*(2), 191–209.

Jacobs, J. (1961). *The Death and Life of Great American Cities*. Vintage.

Jacobs, J. (1969a). *The Economy of Cities*. Vintage.

Jacobs, J. (1969b). Strategies for Helping Cities. *American Economic Review, American Economic Association, 59*(4, Part I), 652–656.

Jacobs, J. (1984). *Cities and the Wealth of Nations*. Vintage.

Jacobs, J. (1992). *Systems of Survival: A Dialogue on the Moral Foundations of Commerce and Politics*. Vintage.

Jacobs, J. (2000). *The Nature of Economies*. Modern Library.

Kirzner, I. M. (1973). *Competition and Entrepreneurship*. Univ. of Chicago Press.

Krugman, P. (1996). *The Self-Organizing Economy*. Wiley-Blackwell.

Lucas, R. E., Jr. (1988). On the Mechanics of Economic Development. *Journal of Monetary Economics, 22*, 3–42.

McCloskey, D. (2010). *Bourgeois Dignity: Why Economics Can't Explain the Modern World*. Univ. of Chicago Press.

Mellaart, J., & Wheeler, M. (1967). *Catal Huyuk: A Neolithic Town in Anatolia*. McGraw-Hill.

Menger, C. (1981[1871]). *Principles of Economics*. (Trans. J. Dingwall & B. F. Hoselitz). NYU Press.

Mises, L. von (1978[1962]). *Liberalism: A Socio-Economic Exposition*. Sheed Andrews and McMeel.

Mumford, L. (1961). *The City in History: its Origins, Its Transformations and Its Prospects*. Harcourt Brace.

Olson, M. (1982). *The Rise and Decline of Nations: Economic Growth, Stagflation and Social Rigidities*. Yale Univ. Press.

Ramsay, C.-A. (2022). *Cities Matter: A Montrealer's Ode of Jane Jacobs, Economist*. Baraka Books.

Smith, A. (1981[1776]). *An Inquiry into the Nature and Causes of the Wealth of Nations* (Vol. 1). Liberty Fund.

Smith, M. E., Ur, J., & Feinman, G. M. (2014). Jane Jacobs' 'Cities First' Model and Archeological Reality. *International Journal of Urban and Regional Research, 38*(4), 1525–1535.

Taylor, P. J. (2014). Post-Childe, post-Wirth: Response to Smith, Ur and Feinman. *International Journal of Urban and Regional Research Debates and Developments, 39*(1), 168–171.

Vance, J. E. (1990). *The Continuing City: Urban Morphology in Western Civilization*. The Johns Hopkins Univ. Press.

Weber, M. (1958). *The City* (Trans. & Ed. D. Martindale & G. Neuwirth). The Free Press.

Zipp, S., & Storring, N. (Eds.). (2016). *Vital Little Plans: The Short Works of Jane Jacobs*. Random House.

Part III

Planning and Revitalization (and a Coda)

7

A Living City Is Messy (and What Not to Do About It)

If we were transported from the present day to any large city of two centuries ago, London perhaps, what would we notice first? The strange way people dress or the primitive technology they use for communication and transport (pre-telegraph, those two activities not yet being distinct) or the odd way they speak? Maybe. But I bet what would strike us right away is the smell—that being bad—of all kinds in the street. The world reeked of unwashed bodies, animal waste, sewage, smoke, slaughterhouses, and piles of rotting garbage—truly, the wretched refuse of their teeming shore!

We have seen why a living city is an incubator of ideas and a principal locus of entrepreneurial discovery, innovation, and economic development. But creativity is the result of experiment, experiment involves trial and error, and trial and error entails, well, error with its accompanying failures, conflicts, and disappointments. As wonderfully creative as they are, there is no denying that great cities, like flesh-and-blood people, can be unpleasant, annoying, and sometimes dangerous. Any city that aspires to greatness will have something to offend everyone.

Viewed up close, the process of economic development via import replacement and shifting is not pretty. There are fits and starts at every stage and along the relevant margins of the division of labor. Replacing

© The Author(s) 2024
S. Ikeda, *A City Cannot Be a Work of Art*,
https://doi.org/10.1007/978-981-99-5362-2_7

an import with a locally created substitute is the tip of an iceberg, the end of a long chain of events, and Jacobs doesn't make all of them explicit. When local entrepreneurs find ways to profitably compete with producers in other cities, it means two things. First, a successful (for the time being) import replacement is what we see; what we don't see is the disappointment of those who tried and failed or the travails of those who eventually do succeed. Second, we don't see the people who lose their businesses and jobs owing to the local import-replacer and now have to scramble for new occupations. True, when the import-replacement process is working well, there is a greater volume and higher value of imports (including both familiar and new inputs and consumer goods), but the people who benefit may not be the same ones who lose. While the outcome of economic development is expanding trade, higher real per capita incomes, and greater comfort and convenience overall, it often takes time to adjust to the constantly changing reality and the messiness of it all, and not everyone experiences the benefits equally. To paraphrase Rem Koolhaas, in a living city the forces of order do manage to stay ahead of the forces of chaos but sometimes just barely (Koolhaas, 1994: 59). Which is to say that a living city is never a finished product but an ongoing process of becoming, a nexus of processes—social, economic, cultural—that interact complexly and unpredictably over time.

Someone we trust in one of our social networks gets us in touch with a person whom she trusts in a different network who offers an attractive opportunity in a distant city, and so we take it, to the distress and inconvenience of family, friends, and colleagues. Large and small, such events, as suggested in Chap. 5, could have enormous benefits socially, economically, and culturally. Even when working well, however, some of these social dynamics have wider, negative by-products such as conflict, congestion, pollution, inequality, epidemics, depravity, and crime.[1]

---

[1] Except for mass murders of four or more victims evidently, which in America takes place mostly in rural and low-density areas. For example, as reported in *USA Today* (18 August 2022): "Homicides with fewer than four victims are more common in larger cities, but mass killings with higher death tolls often take place in smaller towns or rural settings." Accessed 28 August 2022. https://www.usatoday.com/in-depth/graphics/2022/08/18/mass-killings-database-us-events-since-2006/9705311002/

I have been drawing some deep connections between Jacobs's thought and that of F.A. Hayek. It shouldn't be a surprise, then, that Hayek's comments on urbanity sound quite Jacobsian.

> Civilization as we know it is inseparable from urban life. Almost all that distinguishes civilized from primitive society is intimately connected with the large agglomerations of population that we call "cities," and when we speak of "urbanity," "civility," or "politeness," we refer to the manner of life in cities. Even most of the differences between the life of the present rural population and that of primitive people are due to what the cities provide. It is also the possibility of enjoying the products of the city in the country that in advanced civilizations often makes a leisured life in the country appear the ideal of a cultured life. (Hayek, 1959: 340)

His next observation, hinting at Koolhaas's forces of disorder, is sobering.

> Yet the advantages of city life, particularly the enormous increases in productivity made possible by its industry, which equips a small part of the population remaining in the country to feed all the rest, are bought a great cost. City life is not only more productive than rural life; it is also much more costly. Only those whose productivity is much increased by life in the city will reap a net advantage over and above the extra cost of this kind of life. Both the costs and the kinds of amenities which come with city life are such that the minimum income at which a decent life is possible is much higher than in the country. Life at a level of poverty which is still bearable in the country not only is scarcely tolerable in the city but produces outward signs of squalor which are shocking to fellow men. Thus the city, which is the source of nearly all that gives civilization its value and art as well as of material comfort, is at the same time responsible for the darkest blotches on this civilization. (Hayek, 1959: 340-1)

I begin this chapter by discussing in general terms the sources of those unpleasant by-products and then review some of the ambitious visions modern urban designers promoted and policies governments implemented to address them. I then examine their consequences, especially their unintended consequences, owing to incentive and knowledge problems.

1   Urbanization and Its Problems

Paul Seabright (2004) quotes writer Patrick Susskind (1988), who vividly describes the "atmosphere" of early Paris:

> In the period of which we speak [eighteenth-century Paris], there reigned in the cities a stench barely conceivable to us modern men and women. The streets stank of manure, the courtyards of urine, the stairwells stank of moldering wood and rat droppings, the kitchens of spoiled cabbage and mutton fat; the unaired parlors stank of stale dust, the bedrooms of greasy sheets, damp featherbeds, and the pungently sweet aroma of chamber pots...People stank of sweat and unwashed clothes; from mouths came the stench of rotting teeth...The rivers stank, the market places stank, the churches stank, it stank beneath the bridges and in the palaces. The peasant stank as did the priest, the apprentice stank as did the master's wife, the whole of the aristocracy stank, even the king himself stank, stank as a rank lion, and the queen like an old goat, summer and winter.

You get the picture. Perhaps a little exaggerated; or perhaps not.

The same population density that contributes to the diversity of land-uses and attracts people to a city also produces congestion. But as Koolhaas pointed out, culture arises from congestion, from people in close contact and communication with one another (Koolhaas, 1994). Recall that Jacobs carefully distinguishes between congestion and population density on the one hand and overcrowding on the other, where density refers to the number of persons or housing units per acre, while overcrowding means too many people per room (Jacobs, 1961: 205). Overcrowding is usually bad, while density is one of the four generators of diversity. As wealth per person increases, overcrowding tends to decrease.

Still, the problems identified with industrialization in the late nineteenth and early twentieth centuries appeared to many, rightly or wrongly, to stem from capitalism, urbanization, and the resulting density and congestion of cities. Contemporary critics of the living conditions of the urban poor in the mid- and late-nineteenth century paint a bleak picture.

For instance, Friedrich Engels, collaborator and friend of the father of "scientific socialism," Karl Marx, writes graphically and passionately about the deplorable living conditions of the working poor of Manchester, England (Engels, 1845). He recounts walking through the narrow streets of squalid neighborhoods with courtyards of ramshackle dwellings where there is "a filth and disgusting grime the equal of which is not to be found"; to public outhouses whose overflow generates "foul pools of stagnant urine and excrement." In short, he describes this district as "…a planless, knotted chaos of houses, more or less on the verge of uninhabitableness, whose unclean interiors fully correspond with their filthy external surroundings" (1845: 52). Likewise, in London he found "the very turmoil of the streets has something repulsive, something against which human nature rebels" (1845: 47), a place where, echoing philosopher Thomas Hobbes, there is "the social war, the war of each against all" (1845: 48), and where "all the disadvantages of such a state must fall upon the poor" (Ibid). Engels believed he had found a visceral illustration of the "chaos of the unplanned market."

Speaking of London, the historian of urban planning Peter Hall cites the Reverend Andrew Mearns reporting on the quarters of the working poor, particularly after dark, and the human tragedies inside the shabby, teeming dwellings:

> Every room in these rotten and reeking tenements houses a family, often two. In one cellar a sanitary inspector reports a father, mother, and three children, and four pigs! In another a missionary found a man ill with small pox, a wife just recovering from her eighth confinement, and the children running about half naked and covered with filth. Here are seven people living in one underground kitchen, and a little child lying dead in the same room. Elsewhere is a poor widow, her three children, and a child who has been dead thirteen days. Her husband, who was a cab driver, had shortly before committed suicide. (Hall, 1996: 17)

For the Reverend Mearns, perhaps the worst consequence of the poverty and physical depravation he witnessed was moral depravity. "Ask if men and women living together in these rookeries are married, and your simplicity will cause a smile" (Hall, 1996: 17). Families share their cramped domiciles with strangers, who rent their beds (and what else?) for the night and send their children into the dark, where robbery, prostitution, and incest are common. Compared to these descriptions, the dingy atmosphere of working-class London painted by Charles Dickens might seem tame. Likewise, as historian Gertrude Himmelfarb notes, "Whatever the differences…among those of all parties and classes who addressed themselves to the subject of poverty, there was a strong consensus that the primary objective of any enterprise or reform was that it contribute to the moral improvement of the poor…" (1991: 7). Although poverty and the related problems of poor housing, health, and nutrition among the working class had been diminishing in many parts of the world since 1800 (McCloskey, 2010), the rising expectations of the time made the plight of the poor more visible and far less tolerable (Ashton, 1963).

Before the late-nineteenth century, it was not widely seen as the responsibility of national governments to address such problems. These were left to the parishes or to the Church. Indeed, as historian T.S. Ashton reminds us, before literacy became common and living standards significantly improved in the mid-nineteenth century, grinding poverty and depravation were the norm and taken for granted—a common feature, not a bug (Ashton, 1963). That changed as cities generated unprecedented wealth as the young, the ambitious, and the desperate flooded into them. Largely because of that migration, despite these transitional problems in the growing industrial cities, living standards and average incomes rose to historical levels, especially after 1800 (McCloskey, 2010; World Bank).[2]

This increase in measured living standards, however, typically does not include the downsides of urbanization, of the sort listed at the beginning of this chapter. It was not until the mid-twentieth century that the life expectancy of urbanites in the United States finally surpassed that of rural inhabitants. In rapidly developing Western Europe and America, the first large-scale governmental reaction in modern times can be seen in and around London and in New York City. What were these policy responses and the reasons for them?

---

[2] Ashton (1963) also argues that Engels and other critics of the urbanization of England significantly overstate the plight of the working poor in terms of real wages and general living conditions.

2   The Constructivist Response: Large-Scale Approaches

Chapter 3 identified the trade-off between complexity and spontaneous order on the one hand and the scope and level of design on the other. The greater role of planning (scale and design), the less space for spontaneous complexity. To understand the role and limits of urban planning and urban interventionism, we need once again to understand the underlying reasons behind those trade-offs, reasons that center on the "knowledge problem" and the way that problem might be solved. This is a cornerstone of the social theory of both market-process and Jacobsian economics. Effective solutions to urban problems hinge crucially on the extent to which we appreciate the nature and significance of the knowledge problem and that, in fact, the failure of planning and interventionism in general is a direct consequence of the failure to appreciate or even acknowledge the existence of that problem (Ikeda, 1998).

2.1   Constructivism and "Cartesian Rationalism"

Jacobs attacks mid-twentieth-century urban planning for ignoring street-level human interactions and the influence the built environment exerts in encouraging or discouraging them. These interactions are the building blocks that form an invisible social infrastructure that is not the result of any person's or group's deliberate design but rather the outcome of myriad unpredictable contacts that take place in public space. To reiterate, Jacobs sees the living city as a spontaneous order (Jacobs, 1969: 3–48) and a problem of organized complexity (Jacobs, 1961: 429). A city thrives when the individual plans of its inhabitants collectively contribute to the unplanned emergence of complex and dynamic social networks. Once again, it is in this sense that as she says, "Cities have the capability of providing something for everybody, only because, and only when, they are created by everybody" (Jacobs, 1961: 238).[3]

Jacobs argued that under the proper institutional conditions, the living city has a tremendous capacity to be largely self-generating, self-sustaining, and self-regulating. In other words, we create, discover, and then solve a host of social problems typically from the ground (or sidewalk) up. This is essentially the same perspective market-process economics adopts toward social orders in general. We have seen that markets and cities are complex orders that can emerge and evolve from countless individuals pursuing their own plans without central direction. Living cities and free markets both depend on property rights, norms of tolerance, and freedom of association. Both depend on inclusive social capital and trust. Where Jacobs's analysis and market-process analysis differ, they tend to complement rather than conflict, since they both issue from the same underlying social theory.

Moreover, both Jacobs's critique of urban planning and the economic critique of collectivist economic planning attack planners who ignore Hayek's "knowledge of the particular circumstances of time and place" (Hayek, 1948: 80) or Jacobs's "locality knowledge" that city-dwellers gain in their daily experience (Jacobs, 1961: 418). They each draw on an appreciation of the epistemic and cognitive limits of the human mind.

As Jacobs says in her last book, *Dark Age Ahead*:

> Central planning, whether by leftists or conservatives, draws too little on local knowledge and creativity, stifles innovations, and is inefficient and costly because it is circuitous. It bypasses intimate and varied knowledge directly fed back into the system. (Jacobs, 2004: 113)

In Jacobs's critique of local central planning, it is the failure of planning authorities to understand how the design of public spaces impacts

---

[3] As I noted in Chap. 4, those who try to locate Jacobs's intellectual contribution mainly in the area of political theory (e.g., social democracy), for which there is relatively little documentary support, often cite this passage, but they do so out of context. In context, in *Death and Life*, p. 238, Jacobs's point is to praise great cities for their tolerance of strangeness and diversity, which contributes to their greatness. Tolerance is a characteristic of democracy, of course, but not only of democracy.

the fine-grained and intricate interactions among people who, for the most part, are strangers to one another.

> Among those responsible for cities, at the top, there is much ignorance. This is inescapable, because big cities are just too big and too complex to be comprehended in detail from any vantage point—even if this vantage point is at the top—or to be comprehended by any human; yet detail is of the essence. (Jacobs, 1961: 121–2)

The economic critique of central planning of the early twentieth century covered in Chap. 3 is therefore robust in that it applies *mutatis mutandis* to the urban planning problems Jacobs identifies in the mid-twentieth century.

Recall from that chapter Jacobs's account of a living city as a "problem of organized complexity." Here is how Gene Callahan and I summarize Weaver's three categories of scientific problems:

> The first are *problems of simplicity*, which deal with situations involving a very few independent variables, in which the rules of ordinary algebra are appropriate. The second level are *problems of disorganized complexity*, which concern situations involving so many independent variables that their interactions produce random variations. Here formal statistical analysis is appropriate. Finally, there are *problems of organized complexity* that lie between the first two kinds of problems. This is the realm of social orders in which the movement of individual elements are not predictable but overall, non-statistical patterns are discernable. Jacobs's and Weaver's warning is that the methods appropriate to solving one problem should not be used for the solution of the others. (Callahan & Ikeda, 2004: 17; emphasis added)

The problem, according to Jacobs, is that "the theorists of conventional modern city planning [circa 1961] have consistently mistaken cities as problems of simplicity and of disorganized complexity, and have tried to analyze and treat them thus" (Jacobs, 1961: 435). Which boils down to treating a living city as a machine comprehensible to the human mind, much as an experienced architect might design an efficient apartment building, or as one might approach the purely formal problem of calculating the optimal amount of light and air necessary to maintain the health of an "average person."

Unlike problems of either simplicity or disorganized complexity, a city as a problem of organized complexity is predictable only in its general patterns and not in its specific outcomes. Just as in economics where it is not possible to make accurate point predictions about the exact rate of inflation a year from now, in urbanology it is not possible to predict precisely what a "Jacobsian neighborhood" will look like. The four conditions for diversity (i.e., mixed primary uses, short blocks, high concentrations of people, and old buildings) interact over time such that we cannot say exactly what form organized complexity will take, save that the outcome will be land-use diversity. A lot of that diversity will not be what we expect or even what we like. There is in fact no assurance that any exact pattern will emerge, no matter how much we plan for it, only that over time it will promote a sense of safety and trust that will encourage peaceful interaction in public space. But what that process generates no one can say with complete accuracy. Indeed, if we could say, it would not be a truly complex order; it would not be a living city.

The concept of organized complexity, along with spontaneous order, is a core principle of Jacobs's social theory.

The French philosopher René Descartes—he of "I think therefore I am" fame—represents a line of thought that F.A. Hayek calls "rationalist constructivism" or "Cartesian rationalism," which affirms "the belief in the superiority of deliberate design and planning over the spontaneous forces of society" (Hayek, 1967: 96). In a constructivist framework the world is divided into two mutually exclusive and exhaustive categories: the "natural" (e.g., a cloud) over which human reason has no direct control and the "artificial" (e.g., a clock) which human reason can design or remake at will. The category of "spontaneous order" as the result of human action but not of human design, an unplanned emergent order, does not exist. In that case, a living city, since it is clearly not natural in the sense that a cloud is natural, must be artificial or "man-made" like a clock and is therefore, despite its (man-made) complexity, in principle completely comprehensible and subject to control by human reason.

Rationalist constructivism is the social theory that came to dominate policy-making globally in the twentieth century at all levels of government, in particular at the national level in economic policy and in urban planning at the local level.

So, to treat a city as if it were a clock would be an instance of rationalist constructivism. But to view a city as anything other than a problem of unplanned organized complexity is to risk missing an essential quality of urban life and indeed all genuinely social life. Moreover, policies that follow a Cartesian-rationalist approach will have little hope of attaining their stated goals, except perhaps by sheer luck, because they will become entangled in the spontaneous complexity of a living social order—the very phenomenon they ignore—as it adjusts unpredictably to attempt to consciously direct it. The greater the scope or detail of such policy interventions, the more unpredictably entangled they become. Indeed, the consequences of constructivist policy-making can result, and have indeed resulted, in unfortunate unintended outcomes, as we will see.

2.2 Kindred Spirits

Jacobs was not alone among urbanists in characterizing a living city as a spontaneous order. Indeed, she acquired much of her understanding of cities from researchers such as urbanist and organizational analyst William Whyte (1988), whose careful studies of the various and subtle ways ordinary people use public spaces, such as plazas, led to practical conclusions for the design and placement of public plazas.

Christopher Alexander, an architect and urban theorist whom Jacobs admires, deciphers the "pattern language" shared by successful spaces in general, private and public.

> A building or a town will only be alive to the extent that it is governed by the timeless way. *It is a process which brings order out of nothing but ourselves; it cannot be attained, but it will happen of its own accord, if we will only let it in.* (Alexande,r 1979: ix; emphasis original)

Elsewhere Alexander describes this quality as "self-maintaining" (Alexander, 1979: x), which is a feature of a spontaneous social order.

Ken-ichi Sasaki's discussion of the "urban tactility" we experience at street level (see Chap. 3) highlights a crucial dimension of the urban experience. Recall that as we become familiar with a place, what we feel through our entire body becomes more important than just what we see.

> The most important factor in the aesthetics of the city is not visuality but tactility. I consider visuality as the viewpoint of the visitor to a city, and tactility as that of its inhabitants. (Sasaki, 1998: 36)

"Tactile knowledge" is what we feel in the presence of an object: the smells of a street, the texture of a building, the grade of a hill. It is the knowledge we gain through contact or direct experience with an event or environment and is an example of Jacobs's locality knowledge and F.A. Hayek's local knowledge. While Sasaki focuses on our perception of physical objects, rather than the social relations with which Jacobs and especially Hayek are concerned, the significance he attaches to these perceptions is a part of Hayek's "knowledge of the particular circumstances of time and place."

The bias in twentieth-century urban planning and policy toward the car and away from the pedestrian (see the discussion of Robert Moses, below) reduces our experience of the city to the visual, insulates us from the tactile, and takes away a vital dimension of the urban environment. This in turn discourages the formation of social capital, which as we have seen is crucial for utilizing local knowledge, because there will be less meaningful contact as we tend to shun dull places.

Sasaki concludes:

> City design should take the view point [sic] not of the visitor but of the inhabitant, and should not pursue a "good" form on the planning sheet, but a good feeling of tactility recognized by inhabitants, and even visitors. (Sasaki, 1998)

Similarly, recall how Kevin Lynch describes the way we spontaneously come to a common understanding of our image of a city (and its action spaces), one that is useful for navigating the complex urban environment. Once again:

There seems to be a public image of any given city which is the overlap of many individual images. Or perhaps there is a series of public images each held by some significant number of citizens. Such group images are necessary if an individual is to operate successfully within his environment and to cooperate with his fellows. Each individual picture is unique, with some content that is rarely or never communicated, yet it approximates the public image, which in different environments is more or less compelling, more or less embracing. (Lynch, 1960)

The shared images of a city among its inhabitants (and their action spaces) emerge without anyone intending it. And we have seen that while a newcomer to a city may plan a rendezvous by giving a precise street address (e.g., 1 Washington Place at 1 pm), a long-time resident might simply mention a customary spatiotemporal landmark (e.g., by the Arch at lunchtime).

What these approaches have in common—Jacobs, Whyte, Alexander, Sasaki, and Lynch—is an understanding that for planners to successfully plan they need to observe and appreciate the intricate ways in which people see and interact with the urban environment, something that completely escapes planners who treat a city as a problem of simplicity or of disorganized complexity.

2.3   The Consequences for Urban Design

In *Death and Life* Jacobs identifies a number of consequences of using a constructivist approach and failing to see a city as a problem of organized complexity. But I believe three are especially important for our analysis of urban planning and design, two of which I introduced in Chap. 4 but bear repeating here.

Border Vacuums Jacobs learned her craft from several notable urbanist thinkers including Kevin Lynch. Her concept of a border vacuum parallels Lynch's concept of an "edge" but with an important difference. First, Lynch (1960) defines an edge as

The linear elements not considered as paths: they are usually, but not quite always, the boundaries between two kinds of areas. They act as lateral references. [...] Those edges seem strongest which are not only visually prominent, but also continuous in form and impenetrable to cross movement. (Lynch, 1960)

For Lynch an edge is part of what helps make a city's image legible and its streets navigable to its inhabitants. It is likely that Jacobs adopted and expanded Lynch's concept into what she calls a "border vacuum."

> Massive single uses in cities have a quality in common with each other. They form borders, and borders in cities usually make destructive neighbors. A border — the perimeter of a single massive or stretched-out use of territory — forms the edge of an area of "ordinary" city. Often borders are thought of as passive objects, or matter-of-factly just as edges. However, a border exerts an active influence. (Jacobs, 1961: 257)

That active influence for Jacobs is largely negative. A single, massive use in a neighborhood or district—e.g., a river, a park, an enormous residential or office complex, a sports stadium, a sprawling parking lot, a walled university campus—means people crowd into that area mainly or only during certain times of the day or days of the week. Secondary diversities (e.g., restaurants, dry cleaners, banks) cater mainly to those who use it during those times. When not used, however, it becomes a vacuum mostly devoid of people, making it less interesting, less populated with fewer eyes on the street, and therefore potentially dangerous. Without land-use diversity or granularity in the area, the influence of the border vacuum can radiate from the original "great blight of dullness" into the surrounding streets and public spaces, making these adjacent spaces in turn duller and less attractive. It may take some distance before the influence of livelier streets can offset these forces of dullness.[4] Although critical of private endeavors as well, Jacobs took particular aim at the massive

---

[4] This may be the place to mention my hypothesis that the farther away from a border vacuum you go, the better the quality of the restaurants becomes. That is because the high concentration of persons using a border vacuum, say a municipal center, the majority of its users will have only a short time for lunch, so that restaurants will tend to cater to higher-volume, low-priced, quickly prepared meals. The differences in capital requirements, especially human capital, are generally too great for such establishments to also offer a lower volume of diners a better-quality menu. Farther from a border vacuum, these lunchtime pressures weaken and, other things equal, the quality of restaurants become higher. My casual empiricism supports this hypothesis over a range of locations and for different kinds of border vacuums. What's your experience?

projects of her time that were funded by taxation of one kind or another, such as urban renewal, monumental government buildings, and public housing projects: "Extraordinary governmental financial incentives have been required to achieve this degree of monotony, sterility and vulgarity" (Jacobs, 1961: 7).

This brings us to the next consequence of rationalist constructivism. **Cataclysmic Money** Jacobs writes:

> Cataclysmic money pours into an area in concentrated form, producing drastic changes. As an obverse of this behavior, cataclysmic money sends relatively few trickles into localities not treated to cataclysm. Putting it figuratively, insofar as their effects on most city streets and districts are concerned, … [cataclysmic money behaves] like manifestations of malevolent climates beyond the control of man— affording either searing droughts or torrential, eroding floods. (Jacobs, 1961: 293)

As a practical matter, cataclysmic money that floods into an area often produces border vacuums. That is because public projects and public-private partnerships supported by taxation or eminent domain tend to be much larger in scale than purely private, market-based projects. And as argued in Chap. 3, other things equal, as the scale and designed complexity of a project increase, the mind of the planner increasingly substitutes for, rather than complements, the spontaneous complexity of the market process. How might revitalization occur without cataclysmic money?

Gentrification, despite its sometimes deserved bad reputation, is a way of developing or reviving a neighborhood non-cataclysmically. Indeed, gentrification—which the Merriam-Webster online dictionary[5] defines as "a process in which a poor area (as of a city) experiences an influx of middle-class or wealthy people who renovate and rebuild homes and businesses and which often results in an increase in property values and the displacement of earlier, usually poorer residents"—is a comparatively gradual process. While the pain of disruption in the civic life of low-income residents is real, it seems to be a natural pattern in the evolution of a thriving city (Morrone, 2017). In any living city, the physical and

---

[5] See https://www.merriam-webster.com/dictionary/gentrification. Accessed on 3 September 2022.

social structures in it today, including those that are seen as historically valuable, must have displaced what was there before. It is only in static societies that institutions remain unchanged generation after generation. What compounds the hardship of gentrification, however, rather than the gentrification itself, is the lack of affordable housing in other parts of the city to which residents of gentrifying neighborhoods could move, if necessary. (In the next chapter I will discuss the regulatory constraints on residential construction that bears much of the responsibility for this state of affairs.)

Superficial Visual Order The way an area looks, particularly from a distance or on a PowerPoint slide, is less important than the way people perceive it and, as Sasaki might say, feel it up close and personal. A city should be legible, first and foremost, to those living in it and not the planner or designer. This is about why "a city cannot be a work of art" and Jacobs's observation that "there is a basic esthetic limitation on what can be done with cities" (Jacobs, 1961: 372). So a conscientious planner is aware that the beauty of a living city is in the eyes of its inhabitants who behold it on the street, not the planner or designer who wants to shape the city according to a preconceived image.

Which is not to say of course that Jacobs sees no role for active urban planning, or even for an ideal of visual order, as long as planners respect the nature of a living city and the limits of their esthetic visions. More precisely,

In seeking visual order, cities are able to choose among three broad alternatives, two of which are hopeless and one of which is hopeful. They can aim for areas of homogeneity which look homogeneous, and get results depressing and disorienting. They can aim for areas of homogeneity which try not to look homogeneous, and get results of vulgarity and dishonesty. Or they can aim for areas of great diversity and, because real differences are thereby expressed, can get results which, at worst, are merely interesting, and at best can be delightful. (Jacobs, 1961: 229)

The first kind of visual order arises when planners impose a visual uniformity such as we find in the work of the great urban designer Le Corbusier. The second kind of visual order is what we find in Disney

World. Both tend to be constructed at the same time by the same architects, designers, or planners—or by people who have grown up under the same cultural, technological, and educational influences of a particular era. Consequently, their constructions strongly reflect the temporal and stylistic tendencies of their time. The harder they try to design diversity or impose a particular order, the more fake it will feel. As Jacobs declares,

> There is a quality even meaner than outright ugliness or disorder, and this meaner quality is the dishonest mask of pretended order, achieved by ignoring or suppressing the real order that is struggling to exist and to be served. (Jacobs, 1961: 15)

The third "hopeful" kind of visual order evolves spontaneously over decades if not generations and from a wider variety of designers and investors, inspired by different influences. Again, like heterogeneous capital in the structure of production, the elements of the city need to fit together without an overall planner. Visual diversity can then generate order by enabling a city's inhabitants to read and navigate, à la Lynch, its public spaces. Without that visual diversity, navigating public space would be like trying to find your way through a snowstorm. In such areas, it's easy to get lost (and not enjoy it) and it's hard to find your way back.

I was once trying to navigate the gray, monumental government buildings and enormous city blocks just off the mall in Washington, D.C. Visual homogeneity made the area difficult to read—this was before smart phones with GPS—largely because individual buildings were massive and hard to distinguish, so I got lost and walked several minutes before I realized I was going the wrong way. Then the only way to correct my mistake was to spend several more minutes tediously retracing my steps through the same boring, impermeable landscape, an experience shorter blocks and greater land-use granularity would have spared me.

Superficial visual order is typically the result of constructing enormous projects funded by cataclysmic money. Planners achieve visual order in this way by imposing their designs onto a large area over a short time.[6]

---

[6] See the Appendix to Chap. 9 for why time is such a constraint in megaprojects.

The profound sameness is not only the result of the planners' common generational outlook but also the result of cost constraints that make architectural distinctiveness and individual creativity prohibitively expensive.

The fundamental error is one of hubris. Humility in the face of the spontaneous complexity of the city being a rare quality among ambitious urban designers and flashy "starchitects" seeking wow factors. As a result, some combination of border vacuum, cataclysmic money, and pretended visual order, as well as a certain inflexibility in design, accompanies and often undermines the approaches of legendary urban planners and designers.

3   Constructivist Theories of Urban Planning and Design

According to Jacobs, the urban planners of her day hated cities (Jacobs, 1961: 17). Or at least they hated the messiness and seeming disorder of cities, the congestion and smoke, noise and crime, and disease and poverty they saw in them. This is an understandable and forgivable, even laudable, reaction, unless you cannot also see beyond these negatives, which accompany economic development in any city that aspires to be great. The following are four sketches of major planning theorists. All in their own way reflect the emerging constructivist-rationalist ethos of their time and who have had a profound influence on their profession.

Frederick Law Olmsted (1822–1903) We begin with Fredrick Law Olmstead. Although a landscape architect and not an urban planner in the sense of Ebenezer Howard, Frank Lloyd Wright, or Le Corbusier, Olmstead's response to the "chaotic" industrial city was, like the others', based on a firm belief in the power of "modern science" and the therapeutic powers of sunlight, fresh air, and open space. Olmstead is an example of an inchoate Cartesian rationalism that ruled much of twentieth-century planning in both the city and the economy.

A giant in landscape architecture, Olmstead famously partnered with Calvert Vaux to design New York's two great parks: Central Park in Manhattan and Prospect Park in Brooklyn. Contrary to the trend among many of the urban and regional planners who followed, Olmstead sought not to relocate inhabitants of the modern city to the countryside but to bring nature into the city to promote physical and mental well-being.

> Air is disinfected by sunlight and foliage. Foliage also acts mechanically to purify the air by screening it. Opportunity and inducement to escape at frequent intervals from the confined and vitiated air of the commercial quarter, and to supply the lungs with air screened and purified by trees, recently acted upon by sunlight, together with the opportunity and inducement to escape from conditions requiring vigilance, wariness, and activity toward other men, - if these could be supplied economically, our problem would be solved. (Olmstead, 1970: 339)

Reflecting the sensibilities of the emerging modernist social science, with its emphasis on "statistical people" as Jacobs puts it (Jacobs, 1961: 136), Olmstead relied on estimates of how much sunshine and cubic feet of fresh air the average urbanite requires and the square-footage of outdoor space they need to avoid the mental stress that comes simply from walking from place to place on crowded city streets.

> We may understand these better if we consider that whenever we walk through the denser part of a town, to merely avoid collision with those we meet and pass upon the sidewalks, we have to constantly watch, to foresee, and to guard against their movements. This involves a consideration of their intentions, a calculation of their strength and weakness, which is not so much for their benefit as our own. Our minds are thus brought into close dealings with other minds without any friendly flowing toward them, but rather a drawing from them. (1970: 338)

Olmstead clearly means these astute observations to critique what he thinks is an unnecessary and unhealthy aspect of urban life, which can be removed (at least for the upper classes of society) with carefully designed and located parks. Yet, I would point out that what he highlights in this passage is in fact an example of the complexity of urban life, both on the sidewalk and in each individual human mind, which urbanites have successfully coped with for generations. No doubt most of us need occasional respite from this kind of activity. And what Olmstead means to do is to ease this hustle and bustle so that city life doesn't scar the human body and psyche, much as sociologist Georg Simmel diagnoses the mental impact of the market economy with its exacting demands and time schedules in his famous "Metropolis and Urban Life" (Simmel,, 1903).

But it looks like the street activity that requires this kind of local skill and alertness has little value to Olmstead. Evidently not for him is Jacobs's "eyes on the street" or the way sidewalks "assimilate children." Instead, he speaks disparagingly of neighborhoods where there are people "a half a dozen sitting together on the door-steps or, all in a row, on the curb-stones, with their feet in the gutter; driven out of doors by the closeness within; mothers among them anxiously regarding their children who are dodging about at their play, among the noisy wheels on the pavement" (Olmstead 1970: 342). Olmstead observes the same activities as Jacobs but makes the opposite diagnosis. Where Jacobs sees healthy street life, Olmstead sees something pathological. Parks and trees are the desperately needed cure. "Air is disinfected by sunlight and foliage" (Ibid.: 339) and parks offer space for much-needed recreation "strongly counteractive to the special, enervating conditions of the town" (Ibid.: 340).

Jacobs not only appreciates, as Olmstead does not, the "street ballet," but she also warns that "parks are volatile places" (Jacobs, 1961: 89) that can easily become border vacuums with their anti-social consequences. You cannot count on a park of any size to automatically complement the character of the neighborhood or district in which it is placed. Unless you take great care in its design and especially its location, a park can drain the life out of an area.[7] Located almost anywhere other than in Midtown Manhattan with its vibrant street life and its perimeter of primary uses, Central Park's 840 acres would overwhelm its surroundings with its vast emptiness. In the 1960s and 1970s Central Park did indeed notoriously decline, giving the Park and the City of New York a reputation for danger and dereliction that it still has to many, mostly non-New Yorkers, despite being far less deserved today. With the greater economic vitality and

---

[7] Jacobs devotes her entire Chap. 5 in *Death and Life* to parks and the threat to urban vitality they can pose.

growing population of New York, Central Park is today as safe as it has ever been, but it is just as potentially volatile.

Ebenezer Howard (1850–1928) Jacobs's harsh characterization of Ebenezer Howard, an early and influential utopian urban planner, is typical of her view of the great urban planners of her day. Howard looked at the living conditions of the poor in late-nineteenth-century London, and justifiably did not like what he smelled or saw or heard. He not only hated the wrongs and mistakes of the city, he hated the city and thought it an outright evil and an affront to nature that so many people should get themselves into an agglomeration. His prescription for saving the people was to do the city in. (Jacobs, 1961: 17)

Howard, who developed and popularized the concept of the "Garden City," evidently found inspiration in the writings of the American economist Henry George (of land value tax fame), who, following William Cobbett, finds little to appreciate in a great city like London, comparing it to a tumor.

This life of great cities is not the natural life of man. He must, under such conditions, deteriorate, physically, mentally, morally. Yet the evil does not end here. This is only one side of it. This unnatural life of the great cities means an equally unnatural life in the country. Just as the wen or tumor, drawing the wholesome juices of the body into its poisonous vortex, impoverishes all other parts of the frame, so does the crowding of human beings into great cities impoverish human life in the country. (George, 1879: Loc 21655-21659)

Rural life fares no better. For Howard the town and country of his time, particularly of his English homeland, were each a mixed blessing. People are drawn to the two "magnates" of town and country for different reasons. The city being rich with opportunity and liveliness but overcrowded and polluted, while the country is full of healthful, natural beauty, but where life is dull, isolated, and poor. His solution is the "town-country magnate" which, no great surprise here, captures the best of town and country and sheds the worst aspects of each.

There are in reality not only, as is so constantly assumed, two alternatives—town life and country life—but a third alternative, in which all the advantages of the most energetic and active town life, withal the beauty and delight of the country, may be secured in perfect combination; and the certainty of being able to live this life will be the magnet which will produce the effect for which we are all string [sic]—the spontaneous movement of the people from our crowded cities to the bosom of our kindly mother earth, at once the source of life, of happiness, of wealth, and of power. (Howard, 1898: 247)

His carefully designed, utopian Garden City consists of 6000 acres, divided by function into zones, etched with enormous roadways forming concentric circles, and linked to similar settlements by highways and high-speed rail lines. His ambition is evidently to empty the great cities that had formed under industrial capitalism and disperse their populations across these interconnected pinwheels, each limited to a population of about 30,000 persons, which in the aggregate represents a grand, integrated Garden City. Residents live and work within a carefully planned and subdivided matrix of lots averaging 20 feet by 130 feet with plenty of open space, today we might call them "green belts," for parks, nature, and farmland, which confine the de-densified population within predetermined districts (Howard, 1898: 315).

Garden City is a highly rationalist in concept, and looks like it, but Howard is no socialist. Private investment, not government taxation, would finance the project, and he worked out a scheme involving a sinking fund out of which the collective expenses of the Garden City would be paid (Howard, 1898: 349). This is not unlike a modern cooperative apartment arrangement of the kind found in New York City, in which residents own shares in the building as stockholders but do not own their individual apartments, instead renting their units from the building corporation.

Nevertheless, according to Jacobs, Howard's concept of the market, consistent with the static approaches to utopias of the day, is hardly dynamic and entrepreneurial in the manner of market-process or Jacobsian economics:

He conceived of commerce in terms of routine, standardized supply of goods, and as serving a self-limited market. He conceived of good planning as a series of static acts; in each case the plan must anticipate all that is needed and be protected, after it is built, against any but the most minor subsequent changes. (Jacobs, 1961: 19)

Even so, Howard also believes that private companies should be able to compete with the city in the provision of infrastructure and city services.

Even in regard to such matters as water, lighting, and telephonic communication—which a municipality, if efficient and honest, is certainly the best and most natural body to supply—no rigid or absolute monopoly is sought; and if any private corporation or any body of individuals proved itself capable of supplying on more advantageous terms, either the whole town or a section of it, with these or any commodities the supply of which was taken up by the corporation, this would be allowed. (Howard, 1898: 352)

It is also possible (so I have been told) that Howard, in detailing the many particular structures and activities in his "sales pitch," is merely imaging a possible development and not one that he expected would actually come about. Nevertheless, the appeal of the Garden City is that of the modern planned community, with none of the grittiness and incessant change of an innovative city, and it has had a powerful and continuing influence on urban planning.

Frank Lloyd Wright (1867–1959) The decentralization idea takes a different form in Wright's "Broadacre City," though in essentials it remains the same. Like Howard, Wright proposes to employ new and emerging technologies in his plan, including telecommunication and even aviation in the design of his ideal quasi-city, which makes it possible for him to decentralize urban life and spread populations out over undeveloped land. Think well-planned suburbia. Where Howard dreams of creating a "town-country magnate," Wright envisions a kind of techno-suburban magnate founded on "three major innovations": the "motor car," "electrical inter-communication," and "standardized—machine-shop—production"

(Wright, 1935: 377–8). Wright's is an "organic architecture" in which "form and function are one" and "every Broadacre citizen has his own car" (Ibid: 380). With this formula and with the right sort of planner, Wright audaciously claims Broadacre City would somehow "automatically end unemployment and all its evils forever" (Ibid: 379).

While he would devolve government down to the level of the county (foreshadowing in governance if not in form what author Joel Garreau calls "edge city"), Wright is no advocate of laissez-faire. Despite talk of devolution of authority, he is highly authoritarian in the way Broadacre is created and operated: "In the hands of the state, but by way of the county, is all redistribution of land—a minimum of one acre going to the childless family and more to the larger family by the state" (Wright, 1935: 378). This is somewhat reminiscent of urbanist Peter Hall's description of the ancient Greek polis as "minimal state socialism" (Hall, 1996: 43).

On their one-acre plots and liberated from the constraints of density by distance-annihilating transport and communication technology, residents would build single-level, low-cost "Usonia" houses out of cinder block. This technique seems to have morphed into the cement-slab, ranch-style home, complete with car port, which today sprawls across the western United States. Wright might be called, unfairly perhaps but understandably, the patron saint of low-density American suburbia, against which the New Urbanist movement would later rail. All of is this to be administered by the wise (and very visible) hand of the "agent of the state," echoing a familiar theme:

> The agent of the state in all matters of land allotment or improvement, or in matters affecting the harmony of the whole, is the architect. All building is subject to his sense of the whole as organic architecture. (Wright, 1935: 378)

Change is carefully, artfully controlled by the master architect, someone like, well, Frank Lloyd Wright.

Charles-Edouard Jeanneret a.k.a. Le Corbusier (1887–1969) Olmstead wants to bring the country into the city, Howard to decentralize and de-

densify the city, and Wright to transform the city into a techno-suburb. Le Corbusier, like Olmstead, seeks the greening and opening up (and tidying up) of the city, not by decentralizing it but by hyper-densification. Among our quartet of constructivist visionaries, Le Corbusier appears to be the most forthrightly Cartesian in his rationalism.

Nevertheless, in high modernist fashion Le Corbusier claims to construct "a theoretically water-tight formula to arrive at the fundamental principles of modern town planning" (Le Corbusier, 1929: 368–9). Those principles include what he refers to as site, population, density, lungs/green open spaces, the street, and traffic. Drawing on Howard and Olmstead, Le Corbusier intends to make cities both greener, more spacious, and denser, especially "where business affairs are carried on" (Ibid: 370). Yes, somewhat like Jacobs, he sees density as a necessary characteristic in his design of the modern city. For Le Corbusier, the problem of urban design can be boiled down to: How do you decongest a city center while increasing its density? His resolution to these seemingly contradictory goals is to construct "machines for living": high-rise offices—his famous "towers in a park"—and multi-story residences that populate his "Radiant City." Le Corbusier wants to save the city by modernizing and mechanizing it, but unlike Howard and Wright, he does so by packing a lot of us into specific areas. The result is a population density of 1200 persons per acre with two-thirds fewer streets and where streets are separated by an astonishing 400 yards, creating his famous "superblocks" (Ibid.: 371)! By comparison, the Upper East Side of Manhattan, one of the densest districts in New York City, has about 185 persons per acre, and the average distance between avenues is around 300 yards.

As for street legibility, Le Corbusier takes the perspective of the planner rather than the inhabitant, i.e., a highly visual perspective. He achieves visual order by homogenizing the cityscape and smoothing out the unplanned irregularities of the traditional city. As Jacobs describes it:

> Furthermore, his conception, as an architectural work, had a dazzling clarity, simplicity and harmony. It was so orderly, so visible, so easy to understand. It said everything in a flash, like a good advertisement. (Jacobs, 1961: 23)

It is largely the result of accommodating the latest in transport technology: the car. This is a city made for covering macro-distances quickly at very high speed. Indeed, Corbusier states explicitly that his design perspective at ground level is that of passengers in a "fast car" speeding down a superhighway as row after row of carefully spaced, symmetrical skyscrapers whizz past (Le Corbusier 1929: 374). The problem, of course, is how people will travel the micro-distances between these widely spaced and segregated primary uses. It is unclear whether micro-distances are relevant at all in Radiant City, having been especially designed for fast, contained transport. And as some have noted, where to park all those cars and how to address the resulting congestion bottlenecks were evidently details that didn't warrant his attention (Hall, 1996: 209).

Ken-ichi Sasaki's exploration of urban tactility is again relevant here, what we feel in the presence of an object: the smells of a street, the texture of a building, the grade of a hill. It is the knowledge we gain from contact or direct experience with an event or environment, the "knowledge of the particular circumstances of time and place" or "locality knowledge." In contrast, Radiant City is almost purely visual and starkly so. We experience little urban tactility from inside a car, no perspective from the street except speeding along a freeway, because the meaning of the urban environment, its legibility and detail, comes from the bird's-eye perspective of the designing architect, of a first-time visitor and not an inhabitant of the city.

How do you attract people to the resulting mega-neighborhoods at different hours of the day and days of the week in different seasons? What would we find visually and tactilely interesting in the broad, homogenous superblock grids of what Le Corbusier calls a "City of Three Million," to tempt us to linger in public spaces and to make informal contacts? How do Le Corbusier's super-high densities, without short navigable blocks and nearby mixed primary uses, prompt people to serve as the eyes on the street? In their absence, how do spontaneous social networks and webs of communication form to foster the trust in public spaces that historically have done the heavy lifting of providing safety and security on the street? Without cheap, worn-down buildings, how can poor young people with fresh ideas get their start near all that brand-new density? Will we be so content in our high modernist residences, separated by great, unwalkable distances from our jobs and recreation (their Adam Smithian "necessaries, conveniences, and amusements") that we would simply and inexplicably behave in a trusting, civil manner toward one another? Is formal policing and electronic surveillance supposed to substitute completely for the social capital that great cities have relied upon for security throughout history? Or does he assume that the inhabitants of Radiant City are just going to be nice people, that civil society will spring up *ex niholo*? While as we have noted, Christopher Alexander's city is a "semi-lattice," for Le Corbusier a city is indeed a "tree."

His high modernist architecture ignores the essential human networks and purposes described in previous chapters and that Jacobs rightly identifies as the backbone of a living and spontaneous city. In practice, high modernist design à la Le Corbusier and those he inspires seems to have failed almost as spectacularly and tragically as the application of Cartesian rationalism in collectivist economic planning in the Soviet Union.[8] In Le Corbusier's Radiant City, there is no space for anything as unpredictable, seemingly chaotic, and messy as a living city to emerge. Certainly no semi-lattice intermixing of primary uses. Not surprisingly then, Le Corbusier left little wiggle room for spontaneous order or unplanned, disruptive development. And so "he came to believe in the virtue of centralized planning, which would cover not merely city-building but every aspect of life" (Hall, 1996: 210). As James C. Scott observes, while Le Corbusier's "own political affiliations in France were firmly anchored on the right, he would clearly have settled for any state authority that would give him a free hand" (Scott, 1998: 113).

For Le Corbusier, border vacuums, cataclysmic money, and pretended visual order are essential ingredients in his urban designs and combine in spectacular ways. It is perhaps fortunate, as Peter Hall remarks, that unlike Olmstead or Wright, whose plans and theories have been applied at least on some scale in structures actually built somewhere, "the remarkable fact about Le Corbusier is just how phenomenally unsuccessful he was in practice" (Hall, 1996: 211). Nevertheless, according to Hall, "the evil that Le Corbusier did lives after him...."

---

[8] Some might point to Islamabad, the modern capital of Pakistan, as an exception.

Ideas forged in the Parisian intelligentsia of the 1920s, came to be applied to the planning of working-class housing in Sheffield and St. Louis, and hundreds of other cities too, in the 1950s and 1960s; the results were at best questionable, at worst catastrophic. (Hall, 1996: 204)

These failings lie not with Le Corbusier alone. All the schemes for urban design outlined here combine those same three features on a huge scale. But Jacobs's problem with their visions is not so much that they are grandiose. Her problem is that their grandiosity is the result of failing to grasp the nature of living cities or their significance as incubators of ideas and social change. Rather than closely observing how people in cities actually live and use public spaces, they treat the city as a problem of simplicity or of disorganized complexity that will passively accommodate their ambitions, instead of a complex spontaneous order. They leave no significant room for improvisation. The planners alone, not countless ordinary people, have the freedom to experiment. "As in all Utopias, the right to have plans of any significance belonged only to the planners in charge" (Jacobs, 1961: 17).

Instead, planners impose their contrived image of a city, sweeping away and tidying up the messiness, in place of the largely invisible (to them at least) social infrastructure and the action spaces that occupy our city images. What we get is Jacobs's "dishonest mask of pretended order, achieved by ignoring or suppressing the real order that is struggling to exist and to be served" (Jacobs, 1961: 15).

4   Classic Examples of Cartesian Planning in Practice

How have these constructivist approaches worked in practice? Here are sketches and critiques of prominent attempts to implement the kind of large-scale constructivist visions we have been discussing, some celebrated and some notorious. (In Chap. 9 we look at some recent attempts to rebuild cities.) For more thorough treatments of these historical episodes, I recommend reading the books cited in this section.

Baron Eugène Haussmann (1809–1891) in Paris Baron Haussmann's major rebuilding projects took place in the mid-nineteenth century, and so he is a precursor rather than a follower of Olmstead, Howard, Wright, and Le Corbusier. I begin with him because he is a good example of the modernist urge to rebuild on an enormous scale within an already existing and highly developed modern city. Indeed, roughly between 1853 and 1870, Haussmann, Prefect of the Seine under Emperor Napoleon III, conducted one of the most massive urban renewal projects since Nero set fire to Rome.

The project was massive indeed, working among a population of similar to Nero's Rome of over one million. To get a sense of the scale of the undertaking, according to historians Michael Carmona and Patrick Camiller (2002: Loc. 5991–2) between 1852 and 1869, Haussmann demolished 117,553 dwellings in order to construct 273,311 new ones. The principles guiding the renewal, as set forth in Napoleon III's vision, "were intended to meet the requirements of movement, public hygiene, and elegance" (Carmona & Camiller, 2002: Loc. 77). Essentially, their objective, like the planners we have discussed, was to make Paris appear cleaner and less chaotic, more beautiful to outsiders, and controllable by public authorities.[9]

In the years after the economic and sociopolitical upheaval of the French Revolution, Paris, which had shrunk to around 500,000 inhabitants (Hussey, 2006: 217), experienced a rebound in both prosperity and population (although a large part of this was Napoleon III's annexation of communes, forming eight additional *arrondissements*), which coincided with the crowning of King Louis-Philippe in 1830. Paris had also become a city of innovation and creativity. As Andrew Hussey observes, "It was one of the paradoxes of the era that, in spite of the continuous political and social upheavals, Paris produced a remarkable number of writers, artists and thinkers during this period" (Hussey, 2006: 230). And Carmona and Camiller:

---

[9] Interestingly, before he became Napoleon III, Louis-Napoleon is reported to have been impressed by London's wide streets and parks, which suggests that John Nash's accomplishments (see below), at least indirectly, had an influence across the Channel.

Together with the neighboring communes of the Seine department, it was the country's leading area for novelty and experiment. Paris was the birthplace of the artificial soda industry, gas lighting, commercial fertilizer, starch production, and the clothing industry. (Carmona & Camiller, 2002: Loc. 1715–1716)

Of course, "If there were brilliant and not so brilliant successes, there were also failures, social stagnation, and downfalls" (Carmona & Camiller, 2002: Loc. 1766–1767). Moreover,

The wildly increasing density in the city center left neither the time nor the space for the necessary amenities to be introduced there. Sewers were too few and their capacity insufficient; sanitation in the blocks was rudimentary, with courtyards serving as garbage dumps and latrines; the water supply system was notoriously faulty, the dirtiness of the blocks revolting. (Carmona & Camiller, 2002: Loc 1914–1916)

And "the streets of any Parisian *quartier* at night were an excellent place to be robbed and killed" (Hussey, 2006: 229). Moreover, "The center of Paris, which for so many centuries had symbolized its economic, human, and intellectual wealth, was growing so impoverished that owners of rental buildings were seriously worried" (Carmona & Camiller, 2002: Loc. 1894–1895).

One of Haussmann's priorities then was the installation of streetlamps, some 20,000 in all, which helped to establish the reputation of Paris as "The City of Light." Echoing the Reverend Mearns and other urban reformers, Carmona and Camiller report that one of the particular ideas of Napoleon III "was that well-organized urban life had a positive effect on morals; the gutting of the unhealthy old districts would help in spiritually uplifting the popular classes" (Carmona & Camiller, 2002: Loc. 2034–2035). But having experienced two revolutions and several popular insurrections in the decades before coming to power, according to James C. Scott: "At the center of Louis Napoleon's [Napoleon III's] and Haussmann's plans for Paris lay the military security of the state. The redesigned city was, above all, to be made safe against popular insurrections" (Scott, 1998: Loc. 867–868).

As Scott further observes, "such an undertaking could have been accomplished only by a single executive authority not directly accountable to the electorate" (Scott, 1998: Loc. 855–856). Napoleon III thus granted Haussmann enormous discretionary power.

> To tackle a program of this scale, it was first of all necessary to have the administrative means. Haussmann was at one and the same time head of central state functions in the Seine department (excluding those that came under the chief of police), chief executive for the local Seine community in relation to the departmental council, and mayor of Paris. (Carmona & Camiller, 2002: Loc 5472–5474)

Recall from Chap. 2 that in his study of the New York City street grid, author Gerard Koeppel quotes Danish-born Niels Gron:

> The kind of beauty that makes Paris charming can only exist where private rights and personal liberty are or have been trampled on. Only where the mob rules, or where kings rule, so that there is at one time absolutely no respect for the property of the rich and at another time for the rights of the poor can the beauties of Paris be realized. (Koeppel, 2015: Loc 3542–3544)

However, Haussmann's top-down style evidently focused on the form of public spaces and did not extend to how people should use the vast private spaces he was constructing. According to Carmona and Camiller:

> Haussmann was interested only in public space; the inside of buildings (unless they were in official use), the private space of Parisians, was not his concern (Carmona & Camiller, 2002: Loc. 5505-5507). […] Similarly, Haussmann-style city planning never concerned itself with the functions of buildings but only with the provision of "salubrious" streets as the precondition for "healthy" blocks (or rather "houses," as they were significantly called in this context) to be built along the way. The actual manner in which lodging, productive labor, or trade was organized inside these structures did not concern the city of Paris. (2002: Loc. 5516–5518)

In terms of the design-spontaneity trade-off, this may have left enough breathing space for that other vital dimension, *time*, to allow sufficient adjustment to changing conditions over the ensuing decades and a greater level of complexity to emerge than American-style functional or "Euclidean" zoning, with its rigid restrictions on land-use, would have permitted. This perhaps enabled the organic, urban processes to heal the Parisian fine structure more rapidly than otherwise.[10]

John Nash in London (1752–1835) Several decades before Haussmann, English architect John Nash was able to accomplish something in London that no one had been able to do in a dense modern city, namely, build extensive arterial roads, plazas, and boulevards without relying on the heavy-handedness or political clout of an agent such as the Prefect of the Seine. Laboriously negotiating with private entities for private purchase, Nash successfully constructed one of the first major thoroughfares in a metropolis, Regent Street. According to the *Regent Street Conservation Area Directory*, "Regent Street is one of the earliest and most important examples of town planning in this county" (RSD: 6). Author Peter Ackroyd reports that, presumably for the time, it was "The only successful and permanent attempt to bring uniformity and order to London's chaos…" (Ackroyd, 2001: 513).

But as Great Britain was then a constitutional monarchy operating within a strong tradition of individual liberty, "It was not possible for Nash to create a straight boulevard in the French style due to land ownership issues" (Regent Street Directory: 6). Nash apparently had painstakingly to navigate and negotiate with the quasi-autonomous townships of which London at the time consisted, outside the City of London proper. He was not always successful. For example:

> When Regent Street and Portland Street meet, before the straight run up to the Park [Regent's Park], there is a kink in the road, caused by the refusal of the landowner to sell. (Flanders, 2015: 265)

---

[10] This sort of land-use flexibility that enables at least limited unplanned order is analyzed in Cozzolino (2018) in which he argues that "In brief, from a planning perspective, flexibility and spontaneity can be welcomed in two ways: (i) building spaces that are adaptable and easily reinterpretable, and (ii) providing rules that enable spontaneity, unpredictable changes and innovation."

Without the political power of the Crown or of eminent domain to draw on, Nash was left to rely mainly on his negotiating skills and the purse of his patron, the Prince Regent. Even when backed by such great wealth, planning on a grand scale is much harder without authoritarian muscle, but evidently not impossible. Unlike Haussmann (or as we will see, Robert Moses and Lúcio Costa), Nash completed a large and important public project without trampling on personal liberty.

Robert Moses in New York (1888–1981)   Haussmann's efforts in mid-nineteenth-century Paris inspired twentieth-century urban planners in the United States. Ed Bacon in Philadelphia and Robert Moses in New York City come to mind. Moses, in particular, "The Master Builder" as he has been called, seems cast from the same mold as Haussmann in the grandness of his vision and the copious use of political power. He was a man, according to his biographer Robert Caro, who could "get things done." Intellectually, Moses was an attentive student of Le Corbusier, especially in his efforts to retool New York City to accommodate the automobile rather than investing in mass transit. Like Haussmann, the object of Moses's vision was the biggest metropolis in the nation, this one with a population of over eight million.

Robert Moses has been the subject of much discussion among modernist intellectuals,[11] admiring in the beginning of his career but largely disapproving toward the end, most famously by Jane Jacobs. (Although Jacobs mentions Moses by name only once or twice in her attacks on urban planning in *Death and Life*.)

Like Haussmann, Moses was no small thinker. His vision extended beyond the limits of the largest city in the United States to the surrounding region. He has been described as a reforming idealist as a young man, and in a sense he remained an idealist as he employed corruption while brutally wielding power in pursuit of the ideal city. Caro describes him as, "an idealist possessed, moreover, of a vision of such breadth that he was soon dreaming dreams of public works on a scale that would dwarf any yet built in the cities of America" (Caro, 1974: 4).

---

[11] Moses is also the subject of a major theatrical production, "Straight Line Crazy."

Like Le Corbusier, front and center in that vision is the automobile or, more specifically, widened streets and new highways to accommodate the automobile. Moses saw, rightly, the growing importance of travel by car to the wealthy and independent American lifestyle emerging in the twentieth century and transferred enormous resources to direct New York City away from its pedestrian and transit orientation to a car-based one. Moses inspired planners from Los Angeles, which had just begun to construct its now iconic tangle of freeways. He found clever and often heavy-handed ways to finance new roads, miles and miles of them, through existing neighborhoods in the city and the vast estates of the superrich on Long Island.

In addition, he exploited powers of eminent domain to take private property for highways, parks, and other public infrastructure. Architecture critic Paul Goldberger observes:

> Before Mr. Moses, New York State had a modest amount of parkland; when he left his position as chief of the state park system, the state had 2,567,256 acres. He built 658 playgrounds in New York City, 416 miles of parkways and 13 bridges. (Goldberger, 1981)

Moses exemplifies as well anyone discussed so far the "expert mentality" and its flaws (Kopple, 2020). Even from his early days as an idealistic reformer, and throughout the rest of his life as a pragmatic politico, he was annoyed by "the human" element that was "constantly interfering with the mathematical perfection of his system" and determined that "it must be suppressed" (Caro, 1974: 76). As Caro notes of his early scheme to reform New York's civil service:

> Shining through all of Moses' statements was confidence, a faith that his system would work, a belief that the personalities of tens of thousands of human beings could be reduced to mathematical grades, that promotions and raises could be determined by a science precise enough to give every one of those human beings the exact rewards he deserved. (Caro, 1974: 76)

Curiously, I have observed some activists for various causes today— advocates of sweeping policy measures to solve problems of climate change, sustainability, racial and class inequality, the opioid crisis, urban sprawl, and so on—who sneer at the very mention of Robert Moses's name, betray an ambivalence toward Moses's authoritarianism. On the one hand, they abhor his particular vision of a car-centered city and the insensitive, heavy-handed way he pushed his massive projects upon a largely defenseless citizenry and weak administrations. But some of them grudgingly admit his bullying, top-down approach may in fact be an effective way to implement their own idealistic visions. Cartesian rationalism in the pursuit of a worthy cause is no vice? The hard reality is that resources are scarce and not all such causes can be the government's "top" priority (Campanella, 2011). Apparently, while Moses's heart and head were in the wrong place, in the hands of the right kind of people with the right kind of vision, his odious methods may be necessary to reach a more progressive future. Or as Moses himself liked to say, you got to break some eggs to make an omelet.

Lúcio Costa (1902–1998) and Oscar Niemeyer (1907–2012) in Brasilia   In Brasilia, a fully planned and rapidly constructed capital, the City Beautiful and the City Monumental are realized on a near ideal Corbusian "open plain" in the central highlands of Brazil. Its construction was the result of a political decision and a deliberate effort to break with the nation's colonial and coastal past. Unlike another Corbusian-inspired city—Chandigarh in Punjab, India—Brasilia was not designed by Le Corbusier, although the communal apartment blocks were based on Le Corbusier's *Ville Radieuse* of 1935 and the superblocks on the North American Radburn layout from 1929. That responsibility fell to the Brazilians Lùcio Costa as overall designer and his former intern Oscar Niemeyer as architect. "Even so," says James C. Scott, "Brasilia is about the closest thing we have to a high modernist city, having been built more or less along the lines set out by Le Corbusier and CIAM" (Scott, 1998: 118).[12]

Each of the individual superblocks was to have a distinct style and a uniform color scheme that set it apart from the surrounding superblocks.

---

[12] CIAM being *Congrès Internationaux d'Architecture Moderne* or International Congresses for Modern Architecture, founded by a group of European architects headed by Le Corbusier.

Costa's goal for the superblocks was to create neighborhoods and communities that were small, self-contained, and self-sufficient. (This "tree-form" of local self-sufficiency continues to be a hallmark of urban design of such figures as Léon Krier, whom we will discuss in Chap. 9, and the more-recent "15-minute city" of Carlos Moreno.) Jacobs's insights about the design of public spaces promoting the informal mingling of strangers evidently played no part in Costa's conception. The distances are so vast; travel by foot is out of the question, unless you happen to be marathon sprinter. Indeed, the whole is legible not from the ground but from high above, from a distance. As described by Peter Hall:

> The plan was variously described as an airplane, bird or dragonfly: the body, or fuselage, was a monumental axis for the principal public buildings and offices, the wings were the residential and other areas. In the first, uniform office blocks were to line a wide central mall leading to the complex of governmental buildings. In the second, uniform apartments were to be built in Corbusian superblocks fronting a huge central traffic spine; precisely following the prescription of *La Ville radieuse*, everyone, from Permanent Secretary to janitor, was to live in the same blocks in the same kind of apartment. (Hall, 1996: 216)

Despite having a nearly level plain on which to arrange this ambitious construction, compromises owing to finance and politics had to be made. According to Hall (1996: 219):

> Niemeyer himself, by this time, was saying that the plan had been distorted and reduced; only a Socialist regime, he felt, could have implemented it. Corbusier suffered from the same feelings much of his life: it is hard to build a City Beautiful amidst the confusion of democracy and the market.

This is reminiscent of like the great twentieth-century macroeconomist John Maynard Keynes's comment (in the Preface to the German edition of his path-breaking *General Theory* of 1936) that his large-scale, top-down macroeconomic interventions into the market economy would be best suited to a totalitarian regime:

[M]uch of the following book is illustrated and expounded mainly with reference to the conditions existing in the Anglo-Saxon countries. Nevertheless the theory of output as a whole, which is what the following book purports to provide, is more easily adapted to the conditions of a totalitarian state, than is the theory of the production and distribution of a given output under conditions of free competition and a large measure of laissez-faire. (Keynes, 1973)

The comparison is of course unfair, for the Brazil of the 1950s was not a totalitarian state in this sense. The point, however, is that constructing a capital city in such a short time—41 months!—from a unified plan is certainly not the bottom-up, spontaneous result of a people pursuing their own interests and plans. As Scott comments:

Although it was surely a rational, healthy, rather egalitarian, state-created city, its plans made not the slightest concession to the desires, history, and practices of its residents. (Scott, 1998:125)

The Brazilian government flooded the Brazilian Highlands with cataclysmic money to establish a monumental capital for a proud nation-state. The man-made "city" of Brasilia is, perhaps more than any other in modern history, "a work of art"—a immense tribute to pretended order—something Jacobs argued a great city could not and should never strive to be.[13]

5   Concluding Thoughts

Urbanization causes serious problems that are unknown in nonurban settings and sometimes hard to imagine in today's wealthy and highly developed cities (which have peculiar problems of their own). A great city's problems, its messiness, are an unavoidable by-product of ordinary people who are free to try to better their situation as they see it, under conditions of scarcity, human and natural diversity, and imperfect knowledge.

---

[13] A more recent report indicates that while somewhat changed, time has not yet filled in all of Brasilia's initial shortcoming (Banerji, 2012).

This entails ongoing trial and error, real disappointments, and apparent (and sometimes real) chaos. Indeed, a living city is creative not only because it is able to successfully address these problems but because it actually *creates* most of the very problems it solves. Novel problems, novel opportunities, novel solutions. An organism that is not continually facing fresh problems of this kind is no longer alive.

This chapter has focused on large-scale rational-constructivist responses to the problems that many believe are caused by urbanization. It analyzed and evaluated those responses using the Jacobsian concepts of border vacuum, cataclysmic money, and pretended visual order, combined with insights from market-process economics. In the context of Jacobs's social theory, the worst errors of urban planning and policy-making stem from treating complex, dynamic social orders as a problem of simplicity or disorganized complexity rather than of spontaneously organized complexity. The results are not living cities but, as Jacobs put it, taxidermy.

The designs of Howard, Le Corbusier, and Wright (and to a lesser extent Olmstead) reflect a rationalist-constructivist mindset in which planners impose their visions onto the living flesh of a city or attempt to create new social orders out of whole cloth. Their approaches entail border vacuums, cataclysmic money, and artificial visual orders that generate deep disorder. They fail to account for the microfoundations—the norms and social institutions—that enable us to discover, solve, and cope with the inevitable problems that come with the astonishing benefits of city life. The same holds true for the practitioners of urban planning and design: Haussmann, Moses, Costa, and others we will encounter in Chap. 9. While their intent may be to bring order (as they see it) to the messiness of dynamic urban environments, their plans and policies typically fail to account for realities of imperfect knowledge, unpredictable change, and the entrepreneurial resourcefulness and frequent unruliness of ordinary people who are just trying to better their situation. In short, they do not appreciate the nature of a living city as a complex, spontaneous order.

Moreover, as Hayek (1959: 523) observes, their attitude—neglect of property rights, social networks, and markets—can be characterized as "anti-economic." The consequence is to stifle the creativity unique to a great city.

In the next chapter I will address urban interventions that also tend to be anti-economic and anti-Jacobsian, though on a smaller scale. Among other issues, I will examine why housing affordability appears to be an ever-growing problem and what might effectively be done about it. It is of course reasonable and necessary to ask what we can do to make a living city more livable and affordable and to examine various interventions in which governments may play a greater or lesser role. But seeking to effectively improve today's cities still demands that we appreciate their nature and significance and to try as best as we can to understand how they work and so might work better.

Works Cited

Ackroyd, P. (2001). *London: The Biography*. Anchor Books.

Alexander, C. (1979). *The Timeless Way of Building*. Oxford Univ. Press.

Ashton, T. S. (1963). The Treatment of Capitalism by Historians. In Hayek (Ed.).

Banerji, R. (2012, December 7). Niemeyer's Brasilia: Does It Work as a City? *BBC News* online. https://www.bbc.com/news/magazine-20632277 Accessed 10 May 2023.

Callahan, G., & Ikeda, S. (2004). The career of Robert Moses: City Planning as a Microcosm of Socialism. *Independent Review, 9*(2), 253–261. Also, Kindle Edition, Location Given in the Text.

Campanella, T. J. (2011). Jane Jacobs and the Death and Life of American Planning. In M. Page & T. Mennel (Eds.), *Reconsidering Jane Jacobs*. Taylor and Francis.

Carmona, M., & Camiller, P. (2002). *Haussmann: His Life and Times, and the Making of modern Paris*. Kindle Edition. (Kindle Locations 5506-5507).

Caro, R. (1974). *The Power Broker: Robert Moses and the Fall of New York*. Vintage.

Cozzolino, S. (2018). Reconsidering Urban Spontaneity and Flexibility After Jane Jacobs: How Do They Work Under Different Kinds of Planning Conditions? *Cosmos + Taxis, 5*(3/4).

Engels, F. (1845). The Great Towns. In LeGates & Stout (1996).

Flanders, J. (2015). *The Victorian City: Everyday Life in Dickens' London*. Macmillan.

Garreau, J. (1991). *Edge City: Life on the new frontier*. Anchor Books.

George, Henry (1879). Progress and Poverty. Page References to Locations in the Kindle Edition.

Glaeser, E. (2011). Triumph of the City: How Our Greatest Invention Makes Us Richer, Healthier, and Happier. Penguin Books.

Goldberger, Paul (1981, July 30). Robert Moses Dead at 92. The New York Times. https://archive.nytimes.com/www.nytimes.com/learning/general/onthisday/bday/1218.html?mcubz=3. Accessed 10 May 2023.

Hall, P. (1996). Cities of Tomorrow. Blackwell.

Hayek, F. A. (1948). The Use of Knowledge in Society. In F. A. Hayek (Ed.), Individualism and Economic Order. University of Chicago Press.

Hayek, F. A. (1959). The Constitution of Liberty. Regnery.

Hayek, F. A. (1963). Capitalism and the Historians. University of Chicago Press.

Hayek, F. A. (1967). The Results of Human Action but not of Human Design. In Studies in Philosophy, Politics and Economics. University of Chicago Press.

Himmelfarb, G. (1991). Poverty and Compassion: The Moral Imagination of the Late Victorians. Knopf.

Howard, E. (1898). "Author's Introduction" and "the Town-country Magnate". In Legates & Stout (Eds.), (1996).

Hussey, A. (2006). Paris: The secret history. Bloomsbury.

Ikeda, S. (1998). Dynamics of the Mixed Economy: Toward a Theory of Interventionism. Routledge.

Jacobs, J. (1961). The Death and Life of Great American cities. Vintage.

Jacobs, J. (1969). The Economy of Cities. Vintage.

Jacobs, J. (2004). Dark Age Ahead. Random House.

Keynes, J. M. (1973). In E. Johnson & D. Moggridge (Eds.), The General Theory of Employment, Interest, and Money, Vol. 7 of the Collected Writings. Macmillan, Cambridge University Press, and St. Martin's Press for the Royal Economic Society.

Koeppel, G. (2015). City on a Grid: How New York Became New York. Da Capo Books.

Koolhaas, R. (1994). Delirious New York: A Retroactive Manifesto for Manhattan. The Monacelli Press.

Koppl, R. (2020). Expert Failure. Cambridge University Press.

Le Corbusier (1929). A Contemporary City. In: LeGates & Stout (1996).

LeGates, R. T., & Stout, F. (Eds.). (1996). The City Reader. Routledge.

Lynch, K. (1960). The city image and its elements. In R. T. LeGates & F. Stout (Eds.), The City Reader 1996 (pp. 98–102).

McCloskey, D. (2010). *Bourgeois Dignity: Why Economics Can't Explain the Modern World*. University of Chicago Press.

Morrone, F. (2017). The Kind of Problem Gentrification Is: The Case of New York. *Cosmos + Taxis, 4*(2/3).

*Nash in London (*1752–1835*)* https://www.britannica.com/biography/John-Nash-British-architect. Accessed 10 May 2023.

Olmtead, F. L. (1970). Public Parks and the Enlargement of Towns. In LeGates & Stout (1996).

Page, M., & Mennel, T. (Eds.). (2011). *Reconsidering Jane Jacobs*. Routledge.

Sasaki, K.-I. (1998). For Whom Is City Design? Tacility Versus Visuality. In M. Miles, T. Hall, & I. Borden (Eds.), *The City Cultures Reader*. Routledge.

Scott, J. C. (1998). *Seeing Like a State: How Certain Schemes to Improve the Human Condition Have Failed*. Yale Univ. Press.

Seabright, P. (2004). *The Company of Strangers: A Natural History of Economic Life*. Princeton Univ. Press.

Simmel, G. (1903[1971]). In D. Levine (Ed.), *The Metropolis of Modern Life*. Chicago Univ. Press.

Susskind, P. (1988). *Perfume* (Trans. J. Woods). Knopf.

Whyte, W. (1988). The Design of Spaces. In LeGates & Stout (1996).

World Bank. (Updated). Poverty Overview. https://www.worldbank.org/en/topic/poverty/overview. Accessed 10 May 2023.

Wright, F. L. (1935). Broadacre City: A New Community Plan. In LeGates & Stout (1996).

8

Fixing Cities

Jacobs opens *Death and Life* with the bold statement that "This book is an attack on current city planning and rebuilding," but in the next breath announces that "It is also, and mostly, an attempt to introduce new principles of city planning and rebuilding" (Jacobs, 1961: 3). While strongly opposed to the remaking of cities or attempts to construct cities, Jacobs does offer positive recommendations for fixing and improving existing cities. This chapter looks beyond the ambitious, large-scale, utopian visions of twentieth-century urban designers to smaller-scale plans to rebuild and their consequences.

Jacobs attacks the wholesale reconstruction of cities à la Howard, Le Corbusier, and Wright because projects of such scale and scope create border vacuums, release cataclysms of money, and impose pretended orders that undermine the vibrant complexity at the heart of a living city. And market-process economists criticize sweeping economic planning because it inhibits the ability of markets to cope with scarcity, diversity, and imperfect knowledge. Thus, from the point of view of Jacobsian and market-process approaches, when top-down planning shrinks the domain of individual initiative, it substitutes at the margin the limited mind of a planner for a multitude of resourceful minds of limitless complexity,

© The Author(s) 2024
S. Ikeda, *A City Cannot Be a Work of Art*,
https://doi.org/10.1007/978-981-99-5362-2_8

thereby hampering the spontaneous creativity that can most effectively solve social problems.

Top-down urban planning works best when the imposed designs are limited to interventions that complement rather than replace private (individual or collective) initiative, improve plan coordination, and, in the case of land-use, permit ordinary people to adjust to changes in the demand for and supply of floor space. Ideally, the consequences of these limited interventions should be predictable, so that we can design and execute our plans with a reasonable expectation of success. This can happen the more modest, general, and stable are the aims of central planning. Jacobs argues that planning should take place at the level of effective governance closest to the actual users of an urban space. This is often the neighborhood or district, where motivated and resourceful people with locality knowledge live and work, the ones most directly affected and sometimes best equipped to do the job (Jacobs, 1961: 418), even if some solutions require the cooperation of or assistance from higher levels of governance.

In part because of Jacobs, there is much less emphasis today in the United States on comprehensive urban design and planning in the manner of Le Corbusier et al. Still, urban planners are as active as ever,[1] as local planning authorities have moved to micromanage specific uses of space. Moreover, as I will discuss in the next chapter, recent movements have to some extent revived the ambitions of an earlier generation of planners and envision a scale and degree of urban design that, while differing in architectural style and apparent sensitivity to public concerns (Pennington, 2004), retain much of their hubris (Grant, 2011).

Local governments' interventions into spontaneous social and economic forces may be more limited than the constructivist planning of Moses and Haussmann, but they also encounter unintended consequences, which raises the question of whether and to what extent the criticisms Jacobs and market-process economics level at large-scale central planning also apply to smaller-scale or more piecemeal urban interventions.

---

[1] Although far more modest in scale, much to the regret of some urban planners who lament: "For who, if not the planner, will advocate on behalf of society at large?" (Campanella, 2011: 147).

The answer lies in acknowledging that even at the local level the fundamental problems of knowledge and incentives remain. Like the extreme forms of Cartesian constructivism, proponents of local interventions also tend to ignore the spontaneous complexity of the neighborhoods and districts they seek to regulate (Ikeda, 1998, 2004). Even limited forms of intervention are prone to serious, unintended consequences that policymakers cannot adequately foresee or want, owing to knowledge and incentive problems (Ikeda, 2015). What those unintended consequences are depend, as they always do, on the details of the case. But there are general conclusions or *pattern predictions* that Jacobsian social theory and market-process economics can help us to reach concerning public housing policies, rent ceilings, and building and zoning regulations. These, too, have been proposed to combat the messiness and hardships that accompany urban dynamics described in previous chapters. I will analyze these policies and their possible consequences here.

I first tackle policies Jacobs herself explicitly criticizes. I then assess other common urban interventions from a market-process perspective and consider whether and the extent to which Jacobs might agree or disagree with that assessment. In the final section I address post-Moses policies that Jacobs does not commented on but do so from the Jacobsian-cum-market-process framework—what I will refer to as "Market Urbanism"—developed so far.

1 Urban Interventions That Jacobs Criticizes

I begin with zoning ordinances. Strictly speaking, zoning and the specification of private land-uses, at least in the United States, are distinct from urban planning per se, which deals mainly with physical infrastructure and the separation of private land from public land. But zoning regulations are "urban interventions" and thus subject to a critique of urban planning broadly considered. It certainly does for Jane Jacobs.

1.1   Functional Zoning

Alain Bertaud points out that Le Corbusier's lasting practical impact on urban planning has been at a smaller scale than his Radiant City.

> Le Corbusier's influence was felt less through the design of new cities and more through land use regulations and the design of public housing. Practically all housing projects built in the Soviet Union and in China before 1980 were based on norms with foundations in Le Corbusier's concepts. (Bertaud, 2018: 75)

So while the grand utopian plans of Le Corbusier et al. have fallen out of favor (i.e., outside the Middle East and Asia), elements of those plans on a smaller scale continue to influence planners in Europe and North America. Chief among them is functional zoning, sometimes referred to in the United States as "Euclidean" zoning, in which municipal authorities physically separate land-uses by functions they deem incompatible, such as residential, commercial, and industrial uses. This is a common form of zoning practiced in many countries, although according to planning expert Sonia Hirt (2015) nowhere as rigidly as in the United States with its fixation with detached, single-family housing.

Functional zoning is partly a response to the environmental problems that arise from the congestion and messiness of urban life we have discussed. The purely economic rationale for functional zoning is in terms of limiting "external costs" or costs imposed involuntarily on third parties. These include various forms of pollution and conflicts of (often unclear or unspecified) property rights that occur at close quarters.[2]

Germany adopted functional zoning in its modern form[3] around 1870, according to urban economist William Fischel (2004), while New York City and San Francisco were among the first American

---

[2] Any popular microeconomics text such as Landsburg (2014) would give a rigorous explanation of the problem of externalities.

[3] Sonia Hirt makes the case that zoning in some form dates from ancient times (Hirt 2015). Hers is currently the best source covering the history of zoning in the United States in relation to the rest of the developed world, while the best, most thorough critique of zoning in the United States is by Nolan Gray (2022).

municipalities to adopt city-wide zoning measures early in the twentieth century (Dunlap, 2016). One of the purported benefits of zoning by function and various subcategories thereof is that it frees municipal governments from having to deal with nuisances on a time-consuming, case-by-case basis and gives developers and residents a measure of certainty and security via "as of right" development, which could potentially boost the value of their property (Fischel, 2002: 12). At the same time, however, this means that combinations of diverse land-uses—such as mixtures of commercial, residential, and industrial uses—are separated and prevented from complementing one another in a manner that would help generate land-use diversity and granularity. And if such valuable complementarities were desired by the community but contrary to zoning code, they would need to be accommodated by piecemeal, case-by-case exceptions. As these exceptions accumulate over time and zoning regulations become more specific to ever smaller locations, the resulting complications can render development increasingly costly and confusing and compromise the meaning of "as of right."[4] Indeed, according to a report in *The New York Times* zoning has become so restrictive in New York City that "40 percent of buildings in Manhattan could not be built today" (Bui et al. 2016).

But as urban historians have observed, zoning regulations have often been used as a way to exclude what locals regard as "undesirable elements" (Fischel 2004), especially lower-income families and minorities, who may be unable to reside in a particular neighborhood because they are associated with an excluded business (e.g., laundries, bodegas, poultry shops) or because lower-cost, multifamily construction is banned. Opposition to these uses goes under the banner of "Not In My Backyard" (NIMBY). Although explicitly exclusionary zoning of this kind may be

---

[4] In New York City the watershed may have been the "1961 Zoning Code" which according to Salins and Mildner (1992: 71) "not only encouraged developers to clone the Seagram building but created a system of protective or 'exclusive' zoning in which each parcel was restricted to one and only one use." They go on to say, "The amended zoning plan has proven to be so restrictive that over half of all new construction in the city [circa 1992] and virtually all of it in Manhattan now requires some new kind of exception to the established as-of-right land-use rule and has essentially prohibited the residential redevelopment of large areas of the city."

outlawed, NIMBYism can and does often achieve the same end.[5] In fact, preventing developers, large and small, from building multifamily dwellings in residential areas rigidly zoned for single-family homes (as is the case in most American municipalities) deprives low-income households of one of the most effective ways they have to outbid the rich for the right to live in a particularly desirable location: dividing a single plot of real estate into multiple units each selling at a lower price than a single-family home (Gray 2018).

Recall that it is precisely this sort of zoning by function that Jacobs strongly objects to and not only for its discriminatory impact. Forcibly separating diverse land-uses means that, in the case of business districts, fewer of us will use public spaces there outside business hours, or during business hours in the case of residential districts, both of which result in fewer "eyes on the street." This in turn makes us feel less secure in public space and discourages mingling at different times of the day. Jacobs's unequivocal opposition to functional zoning is one of the centerpieces of her critique of the urban policies of her day.

Jacobs experienced the organic, "semi-lattice" dynamics of a healthy community growing up in her hometown. In her biography of Jacobs's early years in Scranton, Pennsylvania, Glenna Lang gives us a superb description of spontaneous urban development without zoning:

> Scranton's outer city developed without large-scale plans or zoning restrictions. Like all the city's neighborhoods, Green Ridge grew organically over time. Even the earliest developers of Green Ridge, as they laid the groundwork for the kind of neighborhood they envisioned, varied the size of the lots they plotted and the restrictions they placed in the deeds. In an unplanned process, the many other individuals seeking opportunity in Scranton – like the Olvers and the Judickis – who bought the lots and put up houses, spontaneously fabricated a neighborhood by enlarging the city's grid with adaptive anomalies as they saw fit to encompass a lively mix of land-uses, buildings, and people. (Lang, 2021: Loc. 1045)

---

[5] In terms of its economic consequences, exclusionary zoning tends to raise the cost of housing and doing business because it constrains the mobility of urban dwellers and prevents sellers and buyers of land from using floor space as they value it the most.

Jacobs argues that the segregation of people and land-uses undermines one of the four principal generators of diversity, namely, having "mixed primary uses" in a neighborhood, which ultimately dampens the social and economic vitality of a city. The valuable synergies, the effective pools of economic use, are less likely to form with sufficient quantity, variety, and proximity to promote successful experimentation. This is obvious in the bland residential suburbs of our cities (Kunstler, 1996). (Exceptions to this may perhaps be found in the legendary Jobs-Wozniak collaboration in a suburban garage that gave birth to Apple Computer.)

Jacobs does, however, advocate other forms of zoning. For example, she believes zoning is needed to limit the scale or dominance of a street by a single land-use to forestall the creation of border vacuums, a version of what we today call "form-based zoning" (Jacobs, 1961: 37)[6]; to prevent the excessive repetition of particular land-uses in a given location in order to promote land-use diversity and visual intricacy (Jacobs, 1961: 252); and some form of what we call today "performance zoning" (Kendig, 1980) that is mainly aimed, as in traditional "good neighbor" regulations, at minimizing dangerous spillovers. As Jacobs argues in her last book, *Dark Age Ahead*:

> Zoning rules and tools neglect performances that outrage people. What are actually needed are prohibitions of destructive performances (Jacobs, 2004: 153).... Any enforceable code depends upon specific standards; an effective performance code must, too. Obnoxious levels of mechanical or amplified sound can be specified as decibels from a building or its outdoor property. (Ibid: 154)[7]

At the same time,

---

[6] Chapter 9 examines versions of form-based zoning that are taken much further and to which Jacobs would and did in fact object (e.g., some versions of the "New Urbanism").

[7] Jacobs lists the following as the kinds of nuisances such a code might cover:

"1. Noise from mechanical sources 2. Bad smells and other forms of air pollution; also water pollution and toxic pollution of soil 3. Heavy automotive through-traffic and heavy local truck traffic 4. Destruction of parks, loved buildings, views, wood-lands, and access to sun and sky 5. Blighting signs and illumination 6. Transgressions against harmonious street scales" (Jacobs 2004: 154).

The object of a good performance code should be to combine the greatest degree of flexibility and adaptability possible with the most germane and direct protections needed in the close-up view. (Jacobs, 2004: 157)

Importantly, Jacobs does say: "How an enterprise confines sounds within its premises would be no concern of the code" (Jacobs, 2004: 154), so the policy should avoid mandating specific remedies but instead respect our autonomy and resourcefulness.

Unfortunately, some municipalities have expanded the meaning of "performance" to cover building appearance, minimum setbacks, floor area limits, etc., that don't aim at hazardous performances. Thus, the same criticisms of functional zoning would apply to performance zoning (Kendig, 1980). Performance zoning ought best stick to limiting clearly dangerous practices.

1.2   Rent Regulation and Inclusionary Zoning

In the United States, regulations to cap residential rents below market levels, "rent control," are rare today outside of California, Oregon, New Jersey, Minnesota, and New York, although individual municipalities may still practice it. While the immediate goal of rent regulation is to keep residential rents below market levels, they range from hard caps to controlled increases over time. Like zoning, most developed countries practice some form of rent regulation.

To fully appreciate the consequences of rent regulation requires a good grasp of how market prices provide feedback to buyers and sellers and reflect the relative scarcities of resources, which we covered in Chap. 2. As we have noted, at least by the time she published *The Nature of Economies* in 2000, Jacobs's understanding of the incentive and feedback roles of prices in a market economy is quite evident. For example:

Common sense tells us that if a town's truck factory expands its workforce to five thousand jobs from a previous three thousand, the town will enjoy expanded sales of clothing and groceries; more schoolteachers are needed, and another half dozen doctors. Maybe rents and house prices rise, stimulating residential construction. (Jacobs, 2000: Loc. 740)

Also evident is her understanding of the consequences of fiddling with market prices in an attempt to achieve particular outcomes through direct intervention. This fictional dialogue from her *The Nature of Economies* on the distortionary effect of subsidies applies equally to direct price manipulation:

"Price feedback is inherently well integrated," said Hiram. "It's not sloppy, not ambiguous. As [Adam] Smith perceived, the data carry meaningful information on imbalances of supply and demand and they do automatically trigger corrective responses. So data and its purport and responses are all of a piece. But – and this is a very big but – the data themselves, prices, can be false, and of course that makes the inherent integrity count for nothing – go haywire." "Costs are a major ingredient of prices," Murray put in. "Costs can be falsified, and if so, then prices will be falsified too." "Yes, subsidies falsify both costs and prices," said Hiram. "And as I indicated in passing earlier, lies of that sort warp development." (Jacobs, 2000: Loc. 1628–1635)

And this passage about the former Soviet Union:

"But the successor economy in post-Soviet Russia is as cavalier about costs and prices for quite different reasons," said Murray. "Change in the political system there hasn't restored price feedback controls. Russian enterprises still ignore cost accounting. Their people don't know how to do it, and they don't seem to learn, because they evidently don't understand its importance as guidance to what they're doing well and what they're doing badly." (Jacobs, 2000: Loc. 1649–1652)

Although she admitted that in the special circumstances of World War II rent control might have been tolerable, she clearly recognized the impact it had on the supply of floor space: "New York City failed to abandon rent controls instituted after civilian construction was halted during the Second World War; then, as anachronisms, ironically, rent controls depressed construction" (Jacobs, 2000: Loc. 1728–1729).

And from her last book:

Rent controls helped check the avarice of profiteering landlords. Evictions for inability to meet rent increases diminished or halted. But otherwise, on balance, rent control was counterproductive, because *it did nothing to correct the core problem, the lack of new or decently maintained affordable housing*, the missing supply that was a legacy of fifteen years of depression and war. (Jacobs, 2004: 142; emphasis added)

Echoing this sentiment, journalist Matt Iglesias argues:

Rent control is, at its best, a regulatory policy that aims to manage scarcity. Many US cities developed housing scarcity during World War II as part of the legacy of the Depression-era collapse in homebuilding paired with wartime restrictions on civilian construction. A giant global war was a perfectly good reason to implement anti-building regulations, and rent control was a perfectly good response to the regulation-induced scarcity. But modern-day scarcity-inducing regulations are not defeating Hitler. They are, at best, maintaining people's privileged access to in-demand public schools. (Iglesias, 2018)

This is also consistent with her views on the basic limits of urban planning, for example, beyond the indirect influence on urban vitality of the siting of public buildings.

In city downtowns, public policy cannot inject directly the entirely private enterprises that serve people after work and enliven and help invigorate the place. Nor can public policy, by any sort of fiat, hold these uses in a downtown. But indirectly, public policy can encourage their growth by using its own chessmen, and those susceptible to public pressure, in the right places as primers. (Jacobs, 1961: 167)

And the following seems to express her attitude toward public policy in general:

Public policy can do relatively little that is positive to get working uses woven in where they are absent and needed in cities, other than to permit and indirectly encourage them. (Jacobs, 1961: 175)

Her view of public policy beyond these enabling interventions is correspondingly guarded:

> Given enough federal funds and enough power, planners can easily destroy city primary mixtures faster than these can grow in unplanned districts, so that there is a net loss of basic primary mixture. (Jacobs, 1961: 177)

This attitude would also apply to the more recent attempts to impose rent regulation via so-called inclusionary zoning, which Jacobs does not directly discuss. While traditional rent regulation targets existing dwellings city- or district-wide, inclusionary zoning typically applies to a subset of new housing construction in a specific location. While it appears different, inclusionary zoning has many of the same consequences as traditional rent regulation, especially if it is mandatory.

1.2.1 Mandatory Inclusionary Zoning

The term "inclusionary zoning" may be somewhat misleading since it doesn't refer to zoning in the traditional sense of separating land-uses according to function, but instead to ordinances aimed at achieving greater socioeconomic diversity in a particular location through a form of price regulation. It is called inclusionary zoning because the intent is to include historically excluded groups in areas where high-income households tend to predominate.

More specifically, inclusionary zoning (IZ) entails setting aside a percentage of new housing, typically between 10% and 30%, to be offered at below-market rates, usually between 80% and 120% of median house prices, depending on the market in that location. Because abiding by IZ practices, other things equal, means developers earn lower revenues on those units, private developers tend not to provide them voluntarily. Therefore, authorities will either make IZ mandatory or offer developers incentives, typically by relaxing density or floor-area-ratio (FAR) restrictions, to make up some of the lost revenue. The former is "mandatory inclusionary zoning"; the latter is "voluntary inclusionary zoning."

Under mandatory inclusionary zoning (MIZ) a developer cannot build new housing unless a certain percentage of units are offered at below-market rates. Sometimes MIZ policies may offer to offset the resulting loss in revenue from the lower prices by relaxing maximum-density limits. Alternatively, in some cities developers who do not comply must pay into a fund. Like traditional rent regulation, however, MIZ mandates buyers and sellers of housing to trade at rates below what they would otherwise have agreed upon, i.e., it is a legal maximum price above which it is illegal to trade. And like traditional rent regulation either the quantity of subsidized units people demand will be greater than the quantity supplied, or the expected loss of revenue to developers will discourage them from building the new housing. Therefore, in practice, only a fraction of eligible applicants willing and able to pay the below-market rates will benefit.[8]

The winners are the lucky applicants who get the subsidized units (typically via a lottery), while the losers are the far greater number of people able and willing to buy at the regulated price but who cannot because there aren't enough units at that price. Whether the losers' loss is greater or less than the winners' gain depends in part on the relative sensitivity of demanders and suppliers to changes in price. (According to basic economic theory, other things equal, the less price-sensitive demand is relative to supply, the greater the likelihood that losing buyers will lose more than the winning buyers gain.) Moreover, because the overall supply of new construction will be lower than it would have been because of developers' lower revenues, the market price of the unregulated portion of new construction will also tend to be somewhat higher, or the units will be of cheaper quality, or both.

The consequences of MIZ and price regulation are economically the same, although because the mandate falls on new, rather than existing

---

[8] As Bertaud points out, "The mismatch between the limited supply and the large potential demand from eligible households is embedded in the concept itself of inclusionary zoning" (Bertaud, 2018: Loc. 6524–6526).

construction, they don't apply city-wide, and so their effects are less widespread.[9]

1.2.2   Voluntary Inclusionary Zoning

Rather than a mandate, municipalities may extend incentives to developers to induce them offer below-market set-asides in new construction voluntarily. This is so-called voluntary inclusionary zoning (VIZ). In addition to loosening maximum-density requirements, incentives might also include relaxing building and zoning regulations or even offering monetary bonuses.

Suppose, for example, that easing local restrictions on maximum density and permitting a developer to increase the floor area ratio (FAR) of a new housing construction adds $1 million to its annual revenue if it, say, adds another story and charges market rates for these extra units. There are, however, at least two major costs that offset that revenue in part or in whole. First there is the annualized cost of constructing and maintaining the additional floor, and second there is the lost annual revenue from the units that have to be sold or rented at the lower, regulated price. If these two costs are less than the added revenue of $1 million, then it might participate in VIZ, but if those costs exceed $1 million, then participating would not be worthwhile for the developer, which means no below-market units.

While the goals of VIZ may be laudable, VIZ doesn't induce developers to build more units in total than it would have, although it could increase the amount of below-market housing. Because VIZ is optional and not mandatory, it should be no surprise that fewer below-market units have actually been supplied under VIZ than under MIZ.[10]

---

[9] Ironically, if MIZ is applied to all new residential construction across the city, under the same demand-sensitivity assumptions, MIZ could transform a relatively competitive residential market into one that mimics a cartel that is able to get developers to restrict supply collectively in a way they could not on their own. The resulting higher rents or prices sellers receive on the unregulated units might then more than make up for the losses they suffer because fewer units are rented or sold. In such a case, developers might have an incentive to lobby for city-wide MIZ!

[10] In Portland, Oregon, for example, VIZ is likely at least partly responsible for an absolute decrease in the number of new constructions shortly after it was implemented (Renn, 2018).

1.2.3   Other Problems with Inclusionary Zoning

Inclusionary zoning, mandatory or voluntary, is often justified by the goal of guaranteeing "affordable housing for all." This goal could be more easily approached if housing authorities didn't at the same time set high minimums for the quality of housing, parking space, setbacks, or FAR. Other things equal, this works against housing affordability since higher standards and more amenities mean higher costs of construction and fewer units built on a given construction budget.

Also, like rent regulation, the lower-income households that do obtain subsidized units will be less inclined to move should, for instance, a better job opportunity arise in a distant location, since that would mean abandoning their subsidized dwellings if commuting costs (and income taxes) increase too much (Bertaud, 2018). Thus, like rent regulation, IZ can perversely limit the mobility of IZ beneficiaries and tie them to a specific location.

The problem is compounded by the fact that advocates for IZ commonly demand that low-income households have "equal access" to the same kind of housing units in high-demand, high-value locations, where typically only the relatively wealthy can afford to live or work. There are at least two unfortunate consequences of this policy.

First, where land is expensive and construction costs are high, MIZ means fewer units of all income-levels will be built. Indeed, empirically even VIZ has generated only a small amount of affordable housing compared to what public authorities claim is needed.[11] This may induce authorities to replace VIZ with MIZ, with the unfortunate result that some projects become unprofitable to build.

Second, because poorer households must make their smaller incomes stretch farther than wealthier ones, they may prefer to live in smaller units of lower quality at a different location than those with higher incomes. The subsidy represented by IZ may be a boon to the lucky few who obtain the subsidized units, but the "equal access" policy means that

---

[11] See, for example, this report on "Inclusionary Zoning" from The World Bank: https://urban-regeneration.worldbank.org/node/46. Accessed 1 June 2023.

they probably end up consuming more house than they would otherwise have chosen with a cash equivalent. If instead of a gift of subsidized housing equal to, say, $2000 per month, they could receive a cash subsidy of $2000 per month, or if they were allowed to sell or sublet their units to anyone else, they would have the freedom to spend (or not spend) the proceeds on housing, education, or whatever they want. But under a standard "IZ lottery" system, someone decides that for them.

1.3   Housing for Low-Income Households

In Chap. 7 we saw that housing for the poor became a policy issue in late-nineteenth-century London and in the United States especially after World War II (Jackson, 1985: 227–8). Initially a matter of morality and sanitation, by the mid-twentieth century affordable housing became more a matter of rising expectations that accompanied an overall rise in prosperity, and today it is increasingly framed as an issue of social justice in the face of "market failure."

It is easy to assume that throughout history the majority of those in the poorest segment of society were unable to afford newly built housing that they didn't build themselves. That, however, has not always been true, and it is not the case even today in some places. The poor can still find affordable dwellings, for example, in trailer parks and long-stay hotels and motels, at least where they haven't been banned. These are typically very basic and sometimes unpleasant but on the whole better than living on the street or in even worse public shelters. In New York City and elsewhere, however, traditional single-room occupancy (SRO) hotels have been practically regulated out of existence (Groth, 1994). Before then, SROs offered the otherwise homeless the possibility of a relatively secure place to sleep and to store their belongings, as well as an address to use for job applications, despite also offering venues for prostitution and other questionable activities. But basic economics doesn't say entrepreneurs can't profitably build cheap, dense, multifamily residences in areas where, other things equal, construction costs are low relative to real-estate costs (Barr, 2016: 142; Bertaud, 2018: 122–6).

SROs are certainly not the safest or most pleasant places for people and their families to live, in the same way that a $14,595 Chevrolet Spark[12] or an old, used car is probably less comfortable or safe to ride in than a $77,000 Lexus LS.[13] Relatively cheap, low-quality housing serves an important and increasingly unmet demand. Such dwellings play a similar role as old, worn-down buildings (á la Jacobs) in the long-term vitality of a city by giving low-income households a permanent place to live. Or at least it would were it not hampered by legislators and local stakeholders or "homevoters" (Fischel, 2002).

It is curious that we make this special assumption about the housing market, when for most other products there is usually a segment devoted to low-income consumers, including essential categories. Why are there brand-new, inexpensive cars and smart phones and so little brand-new, inexpensive housing? Why is there a chronic lack of affordable housing in New York City and San Francisco and far less so in crowded Tokyo where the prices have risen at a fraction of the rate (Harding, 2016)?

Later in this chapter we look at some reasons.

1.3.1   Jacobs's "Guaranteed Rent" Method for Subsidizing Housing

Earlier, I mentioned an approach Jacobs offers to the problem of affordable housing. In it Jacobs begins from a different premise from most housing advocates:

> What is the reason for subsidizing dwellings in cities? The answer we long ago accepted went like this: The reason we need dwelling subsidies is to provide for that part of the population which cannot be housed by private enterprise.... This is a terrible answer, with terrible consequences. A twist

---

[12] The "cheapest new car in 2022" according to *Car and Driver* (2022). https://www.caranddriver.com/features/g39175084/10-cheapest-new-cars-in-2022/?utm_source=google&utm_medium=cpc&utm_campaign=arb_dda_ga_cd_md_bm_prog_org_us_g39175084&gclid=CjwK CAiA9NGfBhBvEiwAq5vSy34QScPjnbfp6Y0tJHh3GfLjRjz_H6oXKBcM-xXO8yKSMLEASv9xJxoCoJsQAvD_BwE. Accessed 13 May 2023.

[13] According to "Lexus LS 2022" *Car and Driver* (2022) at https://www.caranddriver.com/lexus/ls-2022. Accessed 13 May 2023.

of semantics suddenly presents us with people who cannot be housed by private enterprise, and hence must presumably be housed by someone else. Yet in real life, these are people whose housing needs are not in themselves peculiar and thus outside the ordinary province and capability of private enterprise, like the housing needs of prisoners, sailors at sea or the insane. *Perfectly ordinary housing needs can be provided for almost anybody by private enterprise. What is peculiar about these people is merely that they cannot pay for it.* (Jacobs, 1961: 323–4; emphasis added)

Jacobs was not being ironic here. Where people cannot afford housing, there is a way to subsidize housing that doesn't make the government a landlord or create a class of persons excluded from markets or create the problems of mobility, etc., I described earlier.

The housing problem is a large and complex topic, and Jacobs's solution offers only one of a number of possible approaches. What is significant about her solution, however, is the implicit social theory behind it. The dominant approach to housing in her day was to gather poor families together in one place, segregated in public housing projects, after bulldozing neighborhoods to make room for them. In this way, housing authorities believed, the problems of the poor could be handled most efficiently. Once "helped out of poverty," they would vacate their subsidized units to make room for others more needy.

Jacobs proposed instead to subsidize private developers, getting government out of the landlord business and allowing greater scope for "private enterprise" by first guaranteeing below-market mortgage rates for construction (1961: 321–37). The catch is that, while landlords could charge market rates for the residential units, they would have to accept tenants from a specific list of candidates who qualify for the program based on income and whether they already reside in that neighborhood in order to maintain neighborhood networks and limit the size of waiting lists. Taxpayers would make up the difference between the market rental rate and what the government determines the tenants could actually pay, based on their reported taxable income. Once their ability to pay matches the market price, the subsidy falls to zero. Tenants would lose the subsidy but could choose to stay, continuing to pay the full market rate out of their own pockets.

There are many presumptions here, but Jacobs's approach attempts to minimize the kinds of disruption to communities and economic development that large-scale housing projects create.

> In particular, it is a means of introducing new construction gradually instead of cataclysmically, of introducing new construction as an ingredient of neighborhood diversity instead of as a form of standardization, of getting new private construction into blacklisted districts, and of helping to unslum slums more rapidly. (Jacobs, 1961: 326)

Because her proposal lowers the subsidy as the tenant's income rises then if, say, a better job opportunity arises that is beyond practical commuting distance, the sacrificed subsidy is minimized. Her proposal creates less of a barrier to mobility than rent regulation or means-tested housing projects, even if it is not a purely market solution.

Jane Jacobs's approach is both practical and sensitive to the stigma of poverty, although like most such proposals it would probably have a hard time withstanding the privileging and cronyism that tend to infect all political solutions, even hers.

1.3.2 The Need for "Substandard" Housing

As suggested earlier, a living city should in a sense permit "substandard housing" for anyone who wants it. Dwellings such as SROs and trailer parks may not please middle-class sensibilities, but they enable low-income households get off the streets. Today these sensibilities backed by political clout mandate costly minimum-unit sizes and other restrictions that put housing out of reach of many of the poor. As urban historian Robert B. Fairbanks observes, in the early twentieth century "the new emphasis on good housing as a package of neighborhood amenities actually made it more expensive to produce housing for the poor in the 1920s" (Bauman et al., 2000: 39). That is even truer today.

"Section 8" housing vouchers are in some places offered as an alternative to public housing.[14] These vouchers provide "assistance to eligible low- and moderate-income families to rent housing in the private market" where "eligibility for this program is based on a family's gross annual income and family size." Like Jacobs's solution, vouchers tend to take the government mostly out of the landlord business and offer subsidies directly to renters rather than to developers and landlords. Unlike Jacobs's approach, however, offering vouchers to tenants would tend to increase the demand for housing in general and so drive up housing prices. This, of course, disadvantages tenants who don't qualify for the subsidy and who then may have to pay higher prices for housing than before.

1.4 The Housing Problem Is Historically a Poverty Problem but Has Lately Become a Policy Problem

Probably as long as there have been cities, city dwellers have complained about the cost and quality of housing. Part of that is only natural because there will always be a "nicer" house beyond our price range. For nearly all of us, that means that while we could conceivably afford to pay $1000 a month for an apartment, we would rather spend only, say, $750 and use the other $250 for things we deem more important at the margin. Even the richest persons in the world would find some price for a house (or anything else for that matter) too high because there are other things at the margin that they would rather spend the extra money on.

But the inability to find any housing at a price we are able and willing to pay, i.e., a genuine housing shortage, is a different matter. Economists recognize that long-term, chronic shortages of any resource, whether gasoline or housing, are usually due to the failure of prices to adjust owing to regulations that cap prices below the level at which the market would tend to clear. We saw this earlier with rent regulation and inclusionary zoning. Even if there is no shortage in the strict sense, constraints that artificially limit the supply of that resource (e.g., minimum lot sizes and parking requirements and maximum-density regulations) can drive

---

[14] See, for example, in New York City, https://www1.nyc.gov/site/nycha/section-8/about-section-8. page. Accessed 13 May 2023.

market prices sky high. In communities in North America and Europe, serious problems of housing affordability have become more widespread with each passing year. This is unusual, since throughout history all but the most destitute have been able to afford some permanent dwelling, usually in slums of one kind or another, at a price they are able and willing to pay, although under conditions likely considered deficient by the standards of the middle class in the twenty-first century. Recall the hovels of the working poor in Manchester that Friedrich Engels described.

Instead, the problem of "affordable housing" has been couched in terms of the affordability of "decent" housing at a norm set by planning authorities. Naturally, as real per capita income has risen almost everywhere over the last century, the expectations of what constitutes decent living conditions have risen in tandem, and regulations that impose such standards, whatever the benefits they produce, tend to raise housing costs. But the utter unavailability of livable housing *at any price* for large numbers of "homeless" persons[15] or the exodus of middle-class populations out of expensive cities into more affordable areas appears to be largely a modern phenomenon: "The percentage of the population that can afford a typical home today has been shrinking as the average home size increases—trends that have been continuing for decades… (Bivins, 2019).[16]

Of course, as a city becomes more prosperous through innovative economic development, the rising demand to live there will put upward pressure on housing prices. But for most of human history, supply, sometimes leading sometimes lagging, tends to offset that rising demand over time. Why should the real price of housing persistently rise over time, while the real price of almost everything has fallen? The explanation again lies mostly on the supply side.

---

[15] For example, "In recent years, homelessness in New York City has reached the highest levels [in absolute numbers] since the Great Depression of the 1930s." Coalition for the Homeless (3 December 2019).

[16] See the website of the National Association of Home Builders for the latest data on housing affordability based on their "Housing Opportunity Index," which shows a secular downward trend in affordability in the United States. https://www.nahb.org/news-and-economics/housing-economics/indices/housing-opportunity-index. Accessed 13 May 2023.

Understandably, those who are better off today tend to feel that someone worse off ought to live in what they regard as "safe and decent" dwellings, but they have resorted to legislation to that end. Again, high regulatory standards especially regarding minimum FAR, building setbacks, and lot sizes increase the cost of housing construction and lower the supply. A literature survey by urban economist Emily Hamilton and myself details research showing that housing unaffordability for low-income families in America today is due primarily to overly restrictive land-use regulation (Ikeda & Hamilton, 2015).

What might the more market-based approaches entail?

We might begin by recognizing that the problem of "substandard" housing can be traced directly to the problem of poverty. For instance, Hayek observes:

> The housing problem is not an independent problem which can be solved in isolation: it is part of the general problem of poverty and can be solved by a general rise in incomes. (Hayek, 1963: 348)

It is fascinating to relate this to Jacobs's attitude toward the phenomenon of poverty in general. She quite boldly states that "poverty has no causes. Only prosperity has causes" (Jacobs, 1969: 1751–2). Just as evil is sometimes defined as the absence of good, for Jacobs poverty is essentially the absence of economic development, with no explanation necessary except in this negative sense. Rather than seek the causes of poverty, it is more to the point to discover the causes of prosperity.

As economic historians T.S. Ashton (1963) and Dierdre McCloskey (2010) document, poverty has been the default condition of the mass of humanity throughout history. But today, the incidence of extreme poverty has never been lower. From the World Bank (2022):

> According to the most recent estimates, in 2015, 10 percent of the world's population lived on less than US$1.90 a day, compared to 11 percent in 2013. That's down from nearly 36 percent in 1990. Nearly 1.1 billion fewer people are living in extreme poverty than in 1990. In 2015, 736 million people lived on less than $1.90 a day, down from 1.85 billion in 1990.

In fact, what changed historically and gave rise since the mid-eighteenth century to an accelerating growth in per person real income is the growth of great cities in the West. The spectacular increase in prosperity and decline in poverty parallel the rise in urbanity around the world, and our discussion thus far should help to persuade us that this is not a coincidence.

While living cities and free markets continue to be wrongly blamed for generating or exacerbating poverty, the opposite is true. The relatively poor who arrive in a city seeking opportunities for a better life, and those who lose their livelihood and connections because of those same urban processes, adds to the visible poverty in a city.[17] But if urban economist Edward Glaeser is right, poverty in a living city can in some sense an indicator that it is functioning well:

> Cities aren't full of poor people because cities make people poor, but because cities attract poor people with the prospect of improving their lot in life. (Glaeser, 2012: Loc. 1241–3)

Under the right "rules of the game," including bridging social capital and norms of inclusiveness and tolerance, cities can be places where the poor may effectively strive to better their lives and the lives of their children. In this sense, a kind of dynamic inequality, which includes the relative poverty of such strivers as well as those who have succeeded spectacularly, is characteristic of any living city.

So if the process of urban economic development is working well, if people are free to use their resources and resourcefulness in an environment of tolerance and competition, poverty and poor housing need not be permanent for the vast majority of low-income households. While some of the policies we have covered may be more effective than others for improving the conditions of the least well-off in society, historically, there has been no anti-poverty program more effective than the rise of free, innovative cities. Certainly, some of us benefit from economic development sooner or to a greater degree than others, and some yet lag far

---

[17] Recall from Chap. 7 that T.S. Ashton (1963) points out how the descriptions of the working poor by Engels and Mearns, amplified by the greater literacy of a better-informed public, failed to take into account the even more dismal living conditions many were leaving behind in the countryside.

behind. But nothing has enabled the poor to rise out of poverty and to live in better material conditions by almost anyone's standard more effectively than spontaneous urban development.

2   Market Urbanist Critiques from a Jacobsian Perspective

The term "Market Urbanism" is relatively new. I will describe it here as an approach that offers market-based policy solutions to the socioeconomic problems facing cities, such as the ones we have been considering. Market Urbanism will be the label I will apply to the Jacobs-cum-market-process framework presented in this book.[18] The following are policies about which Jacobs writes relatively little, but I maintain that the Market Urbanist perspective I use to analyze them is consistent with her own.

2.1   Building Codes

Although I am not aware that Jacobs published very much about building codes, I think it is safe to assume that she strongly favored them for the conventional reasons, especially when they serve to protect residents from hazards "behind the walls and beneath the floors." (This is why I placed scare-quotes around "substandard" earlier—dwellings should have this baseline standard of safety, however enforced.) Still, given her firm understanding of economics, I believe she would appreciate the trade-off between increasing quality and decreasing affordability I have underlined and that ignoring this trade-off is itself dangerous.

Among the first building codes in the modern era were those instituted in London after the Great Fire of 1666 and the Chicago fire of 1871, the latter resulting in mandated fire walls between adjacent buildings, as well as improvements in light, ventilation, and sanitation. Other cities followed suit, including New York where "during the first two centuries of

---

[18] As we will see in the next chapter, there are differences in emphasis among the proponents of Market Urbanism, and not all of their approaches have an explicitly market-process economics or even Jacobsian foundation, as I am giving it.

New York City's history, building law was concerned primarily with the prevention of fire and disease" (Plunz, 1990: 1), and with limiting the hazards of poor construction and from congested, urban living. Unlike the modern zoning ordinances discussed earlier, these "good neighbor" policies focused mainly on negative externalities and clearly hazardous practices.

Responding to concerns over the living conditions of the working poor, the influential trade journal *Plumber and Sanitary Engineer* held a contest to design an efficient, low-cost, multifamily dwelling that would meet the standards of New York State's Tenement House Act of 1867. The winner was the New York architect, James E. Ware, for what has since become known as the notorious "dumbbell tenement," a design now synonymous with overcrowding, poor ventilation, and inadequate sanitation! While these consequences were surely unintended, nevertheless "such dwellings...promoted both physical and social pathology" (Fairbanks & Robert ,2000: 24) and were finally outlawed by the Tenement Law of 1901 (Fairbanks & Robert, 2000: 26).

Along with the Commissioners' street plan for New York City of 1811, the dumbbell tenement created significant health problems.

> By 1865 a total of 15,309 tenements existed in New York City, and the city's population approaching 1,000,000. The new development at tenement densities was beginning to expose some generic problems with the Manhattan gridiron...adopted in 1811.... (Plunz, 1990: 11)

Those problems, which have been decried since the Plan's inception, had mostly to do with the exclusively north- or south orientation of the long Manhattan avenues. Not only did this impede traffic flows along the narrow length of the Island, which would become chronic with the growing number of and accommodation for the automobile, but it also meant that north-facing dwellings would lie in freezing shadows during the winter, while the south-facing would suffer sweltering summers.

This is not to say of course that any plan implemented by a governmental authority is bound to fail; a street plan as ambitious as the Commissioners' will have its problems. But historian Gerard Koeppel painstakingly documents how private plans offered at the time—some designed and partially implemented by owners of large estates located on what is now Lower Manhattan—would have been superior to the plan eventually adopted and adopted in haste with little serious thought by the Commissioners (Koeppel, 2015). But we shouldn't be surprised: the economic analysis of politics teaches us that inertia and perverse incentives are a feature not a bug when it comes to most political decision-making.

2.2   Mobility

If the supply of housing within reasonable commuting distance to where most jobs are significantly lags behind increases in demand, housing costs will rise there and induce us to reside farther away. This becomes a problem when the commuting cost, especially the increased time cost, increases significantly. This is how housing affordability and mobility are strongly linked. Or, as Alain Bertaud puts it, "transport is a real estate issue" (Bertaud, 2018: 143).

A finite stock of buildable land area doesn't necessarily place a finite limit on living space. For instance, Singapore, a city with geographic conditions similar though not quite as extreme as Hong Kong, has adopted the moto, "limited land, unlimited space" (Hamilton, 2020). As long as development is relatively free, the supply of and demand for land will determine whether housing construction takes place upward, when land costs exceed building costs at the margin, or outward when the reverse is true. In Singapore and Hong Kong, it's been upward; on the other hand in Phoenix, it's mostly outward.

Mobility will not be a serious problem if local authorities carefully monitor the use of roads, bridges, transit, and other transport infrastructure that connect us to our workplaces at low time cost and use appropriate methods (e.g., construction, closures, or congestion pricing) to adjust to demand. But this kind of monitoring and adjustment is typically problematic. Costs of commuting will also rise if means of transport (e.g., cars, buses, jitneys, scooters, bicycles, or shared services) are legally restricted because of pressure from entrenched private and city interests in bus services, licensed taxis, and public transport, all of which have a financial interest in quelling spontaneous competition. As Jacobs notes, for example:

> Jitneys were systematically put out of business by municipalities, with the cooperation – to their shame – of electric transit systems, to protect their own monopolistic franchises. (Jacobs, 2004: 187)

Costs of mobility will also rise if the high cost of floor space induces us to move farther away from the centers of economic activity. And this relates to our earlier discussion of how zoning and building codes can raise the cost of floor space and thereby reduce urban mobility. Thus, is mobility tied to land values.

The availability of cheap land on the periphery of a city combined with rising average incomes and common human aspirations has in the twentieth century, especially in North America, led to the phenomenon of so-called urban sprawl. Sprawl is often conceived in a purely geographical aspect, evoking flat landscapes spreading from horizon to horizon. But from an economic point of view, sprawl is not something properly measured in strictly geographic or demographic terms—i.e. the average population density of a given area or the average physical distance needed to travel from place to place. More relevant is the average time cost needed to get from one place to another. For example, compared to Manhattan, Los Angeles is at least half-again as spread out geographically and with a much lower average population density. (However, 20 miles from the center of Los Angeles, we find much denser development than the same distance from Manhattan.) But the economically relevant question is "on average how long does the average trip take door-to-door in Manhattan compared to Los Angeles, car or no car?" Mobility in the living city is critical and should be evaluated in these terms.

This leads us to the next topic for discussion from the point of view of Market Urbanism.

2.3   Urban Sprawl

Architectural historian Robert Bruegmann defines sprawl as "low density, scattered, urban development without systematic large-scale or regional public land-use planning" (Bruegmann, 2006: 2). He observes, however, that contemporary urbanists' negative judgments about sprawl "were still based on assumptions codified in the late 1960s when American suburbs were booming and city centers seemed to be in grave danger of collapsing" (Ibid: 7–8). Economist William T. Bogart's *Don't Call It Sprawl* (2006) makes the similar point that the classic period of "there's no there there" urban sprawl is best understood as a time of transition from monocentric to polycentric metropolitan development between the early and late twentieth century. Nevertheless, urban sprawl has provoked one of the more serious urban-policy responses in modern times, exemplified best by the attempt to deliberately re-densify urban areas by means of establishing "green belts" to confine economic development nearer to the center of a city.

At first blush Jacobs's attitude toward sprawl may appear less sympathetic than Bruegmann's or Bogart's and more aligned with the conventional wisdom when she says: "One advantage possessed by measures to repair sprawl is that sprawl is so clearly wasteful and inefficient" (Jacobs, 2004: 157). This strikes me as a curious way for her to criticize sprawl, given her positive and I think pragmatic attitude, noted in previous chapters, on the virtue and necessity of urban inefficiency. In any case, in a letter she wrote to me dated March 2004, written at almost the same time as the book from which I drew that quote was published—and I am quoting slightly out of context (see footnote)—Jacobs seems to be agreeing with Bruegmann and Bogart, or perhaps demonstrating her characteristic caution, when she writes:

> In the meantime, I hope you'll have a chance to read in *Dark Age Ahead* (chapter 7, I think) my view of suburban sprawl as an awkward interim stage between less and more intensive land use – if interventionism doesn't prevent natural, self-organized corrections to some interventions of the past. I wish that [Ludwig von] Mises and [F.A.] Hayek had said more about privately initiated and operated interventions, such as those by General Motors and oil refiners which have been and still are, more effective directly,

and influential indirectly than public policy decisions; but, of course, such private interventions would have no force or standing without public policy—and hence citizens' approval.[19]

(The "interventionism" of which Jacobs speaks in this passage refers to a dynamic in which a particular intervention creates problems that public authorities then seek to solve by subsequent interventions. The dynamics of interventionism are fueled by a combination of imperfect knowledge and perverse incentives set up by the attempt to blend two incompatible aims: to harness the power of spontaneous orders (e.g., markets and cities) and to consciously direct them toward a particular end (Ikeda, 1998, 2004, 2015).)[20]

As historian Kenneth T. Jackson in his 1985 classic *Crabgrass Frontier* has astutely observed:

The stereotype [of the suburb] is real, embodying uniformity, bicycles, station wagons, and patios. It has been sustained because it conforms to the wishes of people on both ends of the political spectrum. For those on the right, it affirms that there is an "American way of life" to which all citizens can aspire. To the left, the myth of suburbia has been a convenient way of attacking a wide variety of national problems, from excessive conformity to ecological destruction. (Jackson, 1985: 4)

---

[19] The quoted passage is part of a private correspondence from Jacobs to the author and not from a currently published document or one that Jacobs probably intended to be published. I have largely confined myself to published works to avoid becoming embroiled in controversies arising from informal or off-hand statements Jacobs may have made on different occasions on various issues. I feel justified in including it here because she was responding to a professional inquiry relating to specific articles I had given her to read and to which she is here directly responding. In the paragraph prior to the one from which I drew this quote, Jacobs writes, in part:

Thank you so much for your letter of March 19 [2004] and especially for the two articles you had given me. I found them so interesting and helpful to my own thinking. I see the perils of interventionism much as Hayek and Mises do, and, like Mises, consider that the instability at the end of that road, is ultimately fatal.

[20] I have applied the interventionist dynamic to the case of Robert Moses's planning in Brooklyn, New York in Ikeda (2017).

The other narrative about the rise of sprawl, one that I believe Jacobs is sympathetic to, focuses on large-scale federal government interventions that shortly preceded and accompanied the rise of sprawl. Jackson documents the dramatic impact of these interventions in *Crabgrass Frontier*:

> I seek to determine whether the results of such policies were foreseen by a government anxious to use its power and resources for the social control of ethnic and racial minorities. Has the government been as benevolent – or at least as neutral – as its defenders have claimed? (Jackson, 1985: 191)

He answers in the negative and singles out the Federal Highway Acts of 1916 and 1956, which "moved the government toward a transportation policy emphasizing and benefiting the road, the truck, and the private motorcar" (Jackson, 1985: 191); the Home Owners' Loan Corporation Act of 1933, which "initiated the practice of 'redlining'" (Ibid: 197); and the Federal Housing Act (FHA) of 1934, which "favored the construction of single-family projects and discouraged construction of multi-family projects through unpopular terms" (Ibid: 206). The FHA, in particular, like the early exclusionary zoning policies of individual cities, "helped to turn the building industry against the minority and inner-city housing market, and its policies supported the income and racial segregation of suburbia" (Ibid.: 213).

Operating together, these interventions and direct federal funding for infrastructure boosted private suburban development and enabled a greater number of middle-class households to realize their residential aspirations, but not without sprawling unintended consequences.

2.3.1 Sprawl, Historically Considered

Bruegmann finds that the phenomenon of sprawl has been around for a very long time — "a feature of urban life since time immemorial" — and that it is a result of wealth and the personal aspirations (Bruegmann, 2006). From Babylon and Ur to Paris and Phoenix, urban dwellers have sought to escape the noise and messiness of city life to the quieter urban fringe, while staying within easy reach of its delights. Only recently, however, have we had the wealth, gained through rapid economic development, to realize this dream, especially in the United States. In the mid-twentieth century, suburban tract homes and vast housing developments—associated with the likes of John F. Long and William Levitt—sprouted up around urban centers across the country but especially in the American West. America experienced large-scale sprawl sooner than Europe and got richer and multiplied faster than that war-torn and earnestly socializing continent, whose governments spent a great deal of their countries' remaining resources on projects to repair and rebuild burned and bombed-out cities.

Bruegmann emphasizes the more positive side of sprawl in an effort to counterbalance the overwhelmingly negative opinion of sprawl that he finds in the literature.

> Because the vast majority of what has been written about sprawl dwells at great length on the problems of sprawl and the benefits of stopping it, I am stressing instead the other side of the coin, that is to say the benefits of sprawl and the problems caused by reform efforts. (Bruegmann, 2006: 11–12)

Like Bruegmann and Bogart (and Jacobs), I think that much of the rationale behind so-called smart growth or more recently "sustainable urbanism," as well as the New Urbanism that I will discuss shortly, was and largely still is a reaction against a state of affairs that has long since evolved into new urban forms. Indeed, Bruegmann finds that

> Whatever validity these generalizations might have had in the late 1960s – and even then they were far from adequate – they were completely inadequate to describe metropolitan areas by the 1990s. [...] Many of the city centers were roaring back. Densities were rising in subdivisions at the urban periphery, many of which were being swelled by working class and minority families. (Bruegmann, 2006: 8)

An example of this trend is the "edge city" of Joel Garreau (1991) that we discussed earlier in the book and which, while it doesn't look much like a traditional downtown (largely because it is new, it tends to lie outside the legal limits of cities), it nevertheless shares the density, diversity, and economic dynamism that has always characterized living cities.

2.3.2   Andrés Duany and Elizabeth Plater-Zyberk: "New Urbanism" as a Response to Sprawl

One response to the sprawling state of affairs is an urban-design movement that may be partly inspired by Jane Jacobs called "New Urbanism."[21] Two of the movement's prominent leaders are Andrés Duany and Elizabeth Plater-Zyberk, perhaps best known for designing the planned community of Seaside on the Gulf Coast of Florida.[22] It is more accurate to say that they are "Jacobs-inspired" in some aspects of architecture and walkability but with a Cartesian rationalist spin.

Jacobs's warning about pretended order and antiquarianism should be heeded!

My idea, however, is not that we should therefore try to reproduce, routinely and in a surface way, the streets and districts that do display strength and success as fragments of city life. This would be impossible, and sometimes would be an exercise in architectural antiquarianism. (Jacobs, 1961: 140)

Compare to Duany et al.:

Sprawl repair should be pursued using a comprehensive method based on urban design, regulation, and strategies for funding and incentives – the same instruments that made sprawl the prevalent form of development. Repair should be addressed at all urban scales, from the region down to the community and the building – from identifying potential transportation networks and creating transit-connected urban cores to transforming dead malls into town centers, reconfiguring conventional suburban blocks into walkable fabric, down to the adaptation and expansion of single structures. And rather than the instant and total overhaul of communities, as pro-

---

[21] Jill L. Grant argues that New Urbanism "reiterates many of Jacobs's principles of good community design" (Grant, 2011: 91). However, "a close reading of Duany's work finds relatively few explicit connections to Jane Jacobs" (Ibid: 95). Grant's reservations about New Urbanism are also largely my own.

[22] In Chap. 9 I will discuss and critique another pioneer of the New Urbanist movement, Léon Krier, his design philosophy, and his project in Guatemala City.

moted so destructively in American cities half a century ago, this should be a strategy for incremental and opportunistic improvement. (Duany et al., 2010: 219)

Whew! Top-down planning from the regional level right down to single structures. Indeed, these New Urbanists plan at the scale of Le Corbusier et al., despite the final sentence describing their approach as "incremental" improvement. A better description would be "sweeping incrementalism." They are skeptical of the market and rely instead on local and regional governments to shape the communities they envision.

The Congress for the New Urbanism, which Duany and Plater-Zyberk helped to found, lays out its basic philosophy in the preamble of its Charter (Talen, 2013):

> The Congress for the New Urbanism views disinvestment in central cities, the spread of placeless sprawl, increasing separation by race and income, environmental deterioration, loss of agricultural lands and wilderness, and the erosion of society's built heritage as one interrelated community-building challenge.

And like most late-twentieth-century planners, New Urbanists abhor sprawl, which the Congress for the New Urbanism offers general principles and specific design principles to combat.

This is a prime example of the constructivist mentality reinterpreting certain Jacobsian insights on urban design without appreciating the underlying social theory, based on the concept of spontaneous order, from which those insights emerge. You cannot build real communities, such as Jacobs's childhood Scranton neighborhood, at least not in the dirigiste manner of the founders of New Urbanism, with a specific set of outcomes in mind. Duany and Plater-Zyberk, along with Jeff Speck (2010), are quite explicit in their interventionist approach to public policy.

> We need sprawl repair because change will not happen on its own. Sprawl is extremely inflexible in its physical form, and will not naturally mature into walkable environments. Without precise design and policy interven-

tions, sprawl might morph somewhat but it is unlikely to produce diverse, sustainable urbanism. *It is imperative that we repair sprawl consciously and methodically, through design, policy, and incentives.* (Duany et al., 2010: 218; emphasis added)

Moreover, what the human mind has done, reasonable government can undo.

From local zoning codes to federal automobile subsidies, there is a long list of regulatory forces that have proved destructive to communities in unexpected ways. Because government policy has played a major role in getting us where we are today, it can also help us to recover. (Duany et al., 2010: 218)

According to the logic of interventionism I cited earlier (Ikeda, 1998), the problems (social, economic, environmental) that comprehensive planning á la Le Corbusier or Robert Moses has wrought, new interventions can undo using a "better" comprehensive, New Urbanist design principles. F.A. Hayek characterizes this attitude as a "pretense of knowledge" (Hayek, 1974), and Jacobs might have agreed with that characterization. Rather than removing the various interventions that have promoted sprawl—e.g., the sort of policies we earlier saw Jackson (1985) identify—New Urbanism proposes adding layers to the regulatory thicket, further entangling market and governmental forces (Wagner, 2009). As professor planning Jill L. Grant cogently observes:

New urbanism projects emblematize the monopolistic control of the master planner who designs projects scaled not for appropriate social or political action but because of serendipitous land-assembly factors, and built not to accommodate time but to freeze it in place with codes and covenants. Jacobs's vision of the city as adaptive space within which citizens construct their identities and shape their own prospects in a sometimes messy urban context gets lost in the picture-perfect images of new urbanism. (Grant, 2011: 100–1)

Curiously, although New Urbanism is usually tied to a progressive political ideology, which one might associate with a greater willingness to part with the past and to embrace uncertainty and change, New Urbanists rely heavily on verbs such as "sustain," "restore," "preserve," "protect," and "conserve." This, again, is reflected in the preamble to the New Urbanist Charter, which stresses the virtues of communities of the past that have been presumably undermined by "markets."

Indeed, New Urbanism seems to be quite congenial to the ideals of modern conservatism, especially as articulated by the conservative philosopher and traditionalist Roger V. Scruton, who champions the New Urbanist design philosophy and its devotion to the virtues of the traditional community. Journalist Jeff Turrentine notes how "A new generation of conservative pundits is cheerfully blurring the line between red and blue—by embracing smart growth and New Urbanism" where "left and right amicably agree"(Turrentine, 2015).

And so in 2018 Scruton was appointed the New Urbanism Fellow at The American Conservative (McCrary 2018). While acknowledging Jane Jacobs as a comrade in pointing out the vice of Euclidean (functional) 1 zoning and the virtue of getting back into city center, Scruton goes on to suggest that the decline of city centers is fundamentally a matter of design and aesthetics. In other words, there is a sense in which a city can be, in contrast to the spirit of Jacobs's social theory, indeed must be, a work of art. Planners and architects collectively create a cohesive social order, much as one might design a comfortable home.

> A city becomes a settlement when it is treated not as a means but as an end in itself, and the sign of this is the attempt by residents, planners, and architects to fit things together, as you fit things together in your home or your room, to offer welcome vistas and a friendly patina. (Scruton,, 2012)

But Jacobs's living city is fundamentally a means, not an end; a becoming or process, not an outcome.

New Urbanism, while in some superficial ways echoing Jane Jacobs, entirely misses her more fundamental point, identified earlier by Jill L. Grant, that a living city depends on social orders emerging spontaneously, with the government first and foremost providing a basic framework in which individuals have the right to pursue their own plans, so long as they don't infringe on the equal rights of others. And that means the rights of developers, unassisted by government privileges, and their clients are free to decide what kinds of "necessaries, conveniences, and amusements" to trade, including residential, commercial, industrial, and public uses.

For Jacobs, however, this doesn't mean government interventions are unnecessary. For her, certain kinds of limited government interventions—we have seen, for example, subsidies for housing, zoning to limit size and single functions, and regulations to contain negative externalities—can promote economic, cultural, and social development if they don't crowd out individual initiatives that can do a more effective job. As noted at the beginning of this chapter, *The Death and Life of Great American Cities* is "*mostly*, an attempt to introduce new principles of city planning and rebuilding, different and even opposite from those now taught in everything from schools of architecture and planning to the Sunday supplements and women's magazines" (Jacobs 1961: 3, emphasis added). Her goal is not to jettison city planning but to overhaul it, albeit largely by limiting or eliminating most top-down and large-scale visionary designs and radically reorienting the perspective of policy-makers' urban microfoundations. But the kind of large-scale planning that advocates of New Urbanism argue for, like those of Le Corbusier and Robert Moses, is fundamentally inconsistent with Jacobs's understanding of how a successful city actually works. Despite his association with Cartesian New Urbanism, Scruton himself sensibly writes: "To try to impose a comprehensive vision against the instincts and the plans of ordinary people is simply to repeat the error of the modernists" (Scruton, 2008).

New Urbanists and most other contemporary approaches to urban design and planning do try to give the public a larger say in planning via community meetings and charettes. But from a Market Urbanist perspective, that too confronts serious problems (cognitive and epistemic), which we turn to next.

3 Policies Critiqued from a Purely Market Urbanist Perspective

Jacobs doesn't address any of the following topics in her writings, so far as I know. Yet, each is currently an important aspect of urban planning, zoning, and development in the post-Moses era. In this section I discuss these developments from a market-process-cum-Jacobsian perspective.

3.1 Government-Sponsored Community Participation

In the aftermath of the controversial "master builders" like Robert Moses, municipalities began to institute various formal hearings, citizens' boards, and public-review sessions in which citizens are supposed to freely express their opinions on proposed projects. In New York City, for example, this is the Uniform Land Use Review Procedure (ULURP).

> The new process was a rebuke to the era of urban planning czar Robert Moses, who for decades had unchecked power to transform New York City through sweeping infrastructure and housing projects. ULURP represented a move away from the Moses-era model of ramming projects through with little oversight, and gave community boards an official say in local changes. (Dunlap, 2016)

The stated intent is to make the planning process more transparent and democratic. Unfortunately, most of the affected public don't actually get to voice their views at these gatherings.[23] Attendees tend to be older and wealthier than the local demographic—a small subset of the relevant public—and don't necessarily reflect the average view of the community.

Given the costs of time and resources, only locals with material interests in such decisions have the knowledge or incentive to attend hearings

---

[23] There are many accounts of how in practice "public engagement" tends to be less than helpful or at least not what they appear to be. See, for example, Ruben Anderson at https://www.strongtowns.org/journal/most-public-engagement-is-worse-than-worthless. Accessed 13 May 2023.

and oppose or support development interests. Urban historian Thomas J. Campanella correctly identifies the general weakness of this approach:

> The fatal flaw of such populism is that no single group of local citizens—mainstream or marginalized, affluent or impoverished—can be trusted to have the best interests of society or the environment in mind when they evaluate a planning proposal. The literature on grassroots planning tends to assume a citizenry of Gandhian humanists. In fact, most people are not motivated by altruism or yearning for a better world but by self-interest, pure and simple. (Campanella, 2011: 146)

Indeed, even if they were entirely civic minded, the effectiveness of this process would still be problematic, since, given their lack of incentive and knowledge, they would be unable to accurately account for the values of those on all sides of the issue. That, of course, doesn't mean the despotic approach of a Robert Moses is better but that "community participation" of this kind is far more limited and its value far more problematic than its advocates seem to realize.

Moreover, absent serious consideration of the market prices for the resources involved, such as floor space, that emerge from the trial and error of the market process, making rational decisions about land-use is at best hit or miss. This is the same calculation problem, outlined in Chaps. 3 and 7, that plagues central planning of an economy under socialism but applied to local planning. As economist Mark Pennington points out:

> Whilst offering some improvement on technocratic forms of decision-making such models are neglectful of the co-ordination problems generated by the absence of market prices and the inability of majoritarian procedures to generate the necessary experiments in urban living…The principal difficulty with this particular view of citizen participation, however, is its failure to explain adequately *how* the relevant process of adjustment is to take place *in the absence of market generated relative prices*. (Pennington, 2004: 220; emphasis original)

Any decision concerning a scarce resource entails trade-offs, and trading off land-uses—e.g., for a hotel versus a hospital, a school versus an apartment building, a scenic view versus higher density dwellings, or greater congestion for more jobs, which ignores market prices, e.g., for land, construction, and transport—would be entirely arbitrary. If you want more green space instead of development, then what's the value of the jobs and housing units are you willing to give up for it?

Pennington takes direct aim at the intellectual foundations of the citizen participation movement, characterizing it as a clumsy and highly inaccurate mechanism to express the genuine preferences of the people who buy and sell floor space and its uses. He identifies the philosophical basis for this the community participation approach in the arguments of the philosopher Jürgen Habermas and political scientist Charles Lindblom. I think this is worth quoting at some length.

> The analysis suggests that whilst offering an improvement on technocratic modes of urban governance, participatory planning models are neglectful of the communication and co-ordination functions of market generated prices. Habermasian stakeholder models continue to be driven by a "synoptic delusion" that conceives of social co-ordination as the product of conscious organisation. As such, these models fail to grasp that the inherent complexity and inter-relatedness of many land use issues means that they are beyond the scope of conscious social control. Lindblom's appreciation of "spontaneous order" on the other hand fails to explain how an equivalent to the mutual adjustment facilitated by changing relative prices and the continuous experimentation and substitution between alternatives in competitive markets can be replicated via pluralist political processes. In light of these deficiencies attention should turn to the potential of market processes to generate the necessary competitive experimentation in urban living. Contractual forms of private land use planning based on the estate development model would seem to offer a promising alternative in this regard. (Pennington, 2004: 229)

What he calls the "synoptic delusion" seeks to substitute guesswork and opinion for the complex interplay of market demand and supply. I concur with Pennington's assessment, particularly on the need for planning to rely more heavily on the discovery features of the market process, which may take the form of local covenants and housing associations, and have offered workable if imperfect (but improvable) alternatives. In the following passage, he clearly recognizes how the imperfect knowledge of the participants, which as we know is a fundamental insight of market-process economics, calls for an institutional framework that facilitates entrepreneurial discovery:

> The best way of dealing with the relevant uncertainties, therefore, may not be to deliberately plan for an "optimal" urban form, but to permit a wider variety of experiments in urban living. The latter may allow a discovery process to reveal which particular ways of organising urban areas work best from the subjective view of their inhabitants as signalled by the relative willingness to pay for different types of development scheme. (Pennington, 2004: 220)

This is consistent with a Jacobsian appreciation of cities as effective platforms for trial and error and at odds with attempts to impose efficient or ideal urban outcomes. And because different parties weigh priorities differently or may even hold contradictory designs for land-uses, a rigid "majority rules" approach fails to offer much leeway for experiment and novelty in community problem-solving. From this perspective, markets offer a fairer and more workable solution.

> The institution of private property, by contrast, allows multiple minorities the space to try out ideas the merits/demerits of which may not be readily discerned by the majority but from which the latter may then learn. It is only when such projects are put into practice that the relevant information is revealed. A learning process may then be set in motion as previously indiscernible successes are imitated and previously indiscernible errors can be avoided. (Pennington, 2004: 225)

3.2   Surveillance City

Can cameras replace eyes?

Facial recognition technology can scan and identify the faces of thousands of city dwellers. The People's Republic of China, for instance, plans to enhance their "social credit system"—a system "to monitor, assess, and shape the behavior of all citizens and enterprises" (Cho, 2020)—by using this data-driven technology (Canales & Mok, 2022). Private concerns also use such devices. A recent news item reported that the owners of Madison Square Garden, the famous sports arena in New York City, employed facial recognition to prevent members of a law firm representing a party suing them from entering (Hill & Kilgannon, 2023).

This is an exceptionally complex subject with broad legal, political, and ethical dimensions. My concern here, however, is the narrow question of whether electronic surveillance in cities can do the same job as Jacobs's "eyes on the street" with respect to promoting a feeling of safety in public space, the "bedrock attribute" of a lively city neighborhood.

To briefly outline Jacobs's observation which we covered in Chap. 4, if we find a public space sufficiently attractive to overcome any significant fears we might have of using it then, in addition to whatever originally attracts us into that space, our very presence there will encourage others to overcome an aversion to use it. People attract people; the more eyes, the safer we feel even if no one is paying particular attention to what anyone else is doing. That is because of the human tendency not to want to be seen doing something wrong, whatever that may be, by other people, even if they are strangers.

What gets the ball rolling in this is narrative is something in public space—a job, a residence, a store, a bar, a friend in a bar—that brings us out into it. In a healthy community, formal policing, of which electronic surveillance and policing are instances, tends to work best only if informal monitoring via eyes on the street does the heavy lifting. If instead, community security relies primarily on formal policing, it indicates informal eyes are inadequate to the task and that the community, *qua* community, is not doing its job. And once formal policing becomes the principal enforcer of norms of proper public behavior, we are on a slippery slope. Less reliance on what I have called the "invisible social infrastructure" and greater reliance on formal surveillance (electronic or human) weakens internalized norms of good behavior, and so formal policing becomes more important and so on.

My sense then is that electronic surveillance is inferior to eyes on the street, but why?

First, unlike formal policing by flesh-and-blood people, electronic surveillance is impersonal and delayed (unless, I suppose, the monitor is a mobile android). Delayed enforcement is less effective than someone firmly telling me to keep off the grass. The impersonality of electronic monitoring means less or no real-time feedback, such as a warning look.[24] Surveillance cameras are often hidden or hard to see, designed to catch the unwary rather than to warn the unwise.

Second, with respect to electronic surveillance, in particular, there is a lack of contextual knowledge—the sounds, expressions, peripheral sights and movement, and circumstances of an action. Knowing an area is heavily monitored—Westminster in London comes to mind—may make us feel safe but not in the same way as (sometimes annoying) passersby with human eyes do. The absence of people can dehumanize the experience of being in public space.

Third, electronic surveillance and formal policing in general treat the symptom and not the cause of insecurity in public, which is the absence of norms of civility and community. In successful cities, electronic surveillance might complement but not substitute for lots of eyes on the street.

Fourth, to be watched by different sets of eyes belonging to strangers at different times and places is a fundamentally different experience from being watched by the same cold set of electronic eyes everywhere all the time.

> The safety of the street works best, most casually, and with least frequent taint of hostility or suspicion precisely where people are using and most enjoying the city streets voluntarily and are least conscious, normally, that they are policing. The basic requisite for such surveillance is a substantial quantity of stores and other public places sprinkled along the sidewalks of a district; enterprises and public places that are used by evening and night must be among them especially. (Jacobs, 1961: 36)

Real eyes don't record what they see with perfect, two-dimensional recall, while electronic eyes typically do, for possible compilation later

---

[24] This may actually be something in favor of impersonal surveillance when the personal element contains societal biases prejudices and predispositions.

into big data bases.[25] Informal eyes aren't always on the lookout for trouble, quite the opposite usually, which again humanizes that form of monitoring.

Formal surveillance is at best a stopgap. At worst, it can lead to the sort of abuses we see in the People's Republic of China, where government authorities can easily use it to precisely track the activities of its citizens to control their behavior by denying or granting rights and privileges.

Apparently, electronic surveillance has met with some success in reducing crime in the PRC and Hong Kong. (Fictional crime dramas would lead us to believe that it is nearly infallible in identifying or clearing suspects.) But as historian Warren Breckman has written:

> The god's-eye perspective is the ultimate expression of the human desire to make the city visible, to see it at a glance, to read it as an intelligible and unified object of human making [...] Rulers of cities have always had an interest in visibility, both in representing their power and in controlling people by *seeing* them. (Breckman (2010)

I am reminded of what Benjamin Franklin is alleged to have said, "They who can give up essential liberty to obtain a little temporary safety, deserve neither liberty nor safety."

3.3   Public-Private Partnerships in the United States

In the wake of the massive government-funded projects of the mid- and late-twentieth century, the preferred method of financing mega- and giga-projects popular today in the United States is the so-called public-private partnership (PPP). The Word Bank describes PPP as

---

[25] Time has told against it the now-defunct project, but on its website Sidewalk Labs (a subsidiary of Google) says that "Waterfront Toronto [the Toronto municipal agency overseeing the project] will lead all privacy and digital governance matters related to the project and will act as the lead in discussions with the City, the Province, the Federal government and Privacy Commissioners. We are committed to complying with all existing policies, and are prepared to comply with any future policies" (from December 3, 2020, update of Sidewalk Toronto). For more on this failed project see D'Onofro (2019).

a mechanism for government to procure and implement public infrastructure and/or services using the resources and expertise of the private sector. Where governments are facing ageing or lack of infrastructure and require more efficient services, a partnership with the private sector can help foster new solutions and bring finance.[26]

Echoing a common desire on the part of public policy advocates generally, PPPs attempt to combine the incentives and efficiency of the private sector with the borrowing powers of municipal governments in large-scale projects—e.g., housing developments, sports stadiums, and shopping complexes—presumably constructed in the public interest. PPPs have access to funding sources beyond the reach of purely private enterprises such as tax-free municipal bonds and eminent domain—i.e., the use of the government's police powers to take private property without the owner's consent with "just compensation" for "public use." Both municipal bond issues and eminent domain give developers a "soft budget constraint" that allows them to fund projects that private investors find too risky or unremunerative to finance or that stretch the limits of the meaning of "public use."[27] This can lead easily to overspending on a scale beyond the reach of purely private undertakings and methods of borrowing and to projects that favor special interests, i.e., "cronyism." Finding a "middle way" between market efficiency and public equity can thus be elusive, especially when post-Moses restraints on government abuse, such as government-sponsored community participation, don't work as they were designed.

I have pointed out that Jacobsian strictures against unnecessarily imposing border vacuums, visual homogeneity, and cataclysmic money into the urban process apply equally to purely private as well as governmental developments. But the use of public funds and eminent domain means that governmental projects and PPPs tend to be more ambitious in design and much greater in scale than projects that are exclusively funded through ordinary private investment. That is why PPPs are far

---

[26] See the World Bank's explanation at https://ppp.worldbank.org/public-private-partnership/about-public-private-partnerships Accessed 13 May 2023.

[27] As, for example, in the case of "Kelo v. City of New London, 545 U.S. 469 (2005)." https://supreme.justia.com/cases/federal/us/545/469/. Accessed 13 May 2023.

more likely to encounter the kinds of problems discussed in Chap. 3 of trading off too much complexity and spontaneity for greater scale and more detailed design and in Chap. 4 of border vacuums, catastrophic money, and the accompanying vices of visual homogeneity and a lack of granular land-use diversity.

3.4   Landmarking and Historic Preservation

Landmarks preservation is the final example of a popular urban policy that I critique from a market urbanist perspective issuing from a Jacobsian social theory. Landmarks preservation is the American version of what elsewhere is called "heritage site" designation. According to the website of the Landmarks Preservation Commission of New York City,[28]

> the purpose of safeguarding the buildings and places that represent New York City's cultural, social, economic, political, and architectural history is to:

- Stabilize and improve property values
- Foster civic pride
- Protect and enhance the City's attractions to tourists
- Strengthen the economy of the City
- Promote the use of historic districts, landmarks, interior landmarks, and scenic landmarks for the education, pleasure and welfare of the people of the City

While few would deny there is merit in preserving for future generations buildings and sites that have great meaning and historical significance, the pernicious effect of landmarking has been to promote property values (identified as purpose number one, above) which has contributed to the problem of unaffordable housing. In New York City, landmarking has been extended to entire neighborhoods and large districts. According to research conducted by the Furman Center at New York University:

---

[28] See the website of the NYC Landmarks Preservation Commission: https://www.nyc.gov/site/lpc/designations/landmark-types-criteria.page. Accessed 13 May 2023.

By 2014, 3.4 percent of the city's lots and 4.4 percent of the city's land area were either located inside a historic district or were protected as an individual landmark. However, the coverage across boroughs ranges widely. In Manhattan, 27 percent of lots were designated either as a historic district, individual landmark or interior landmark, and these lots comprised just one fifth of the lot area in Manhattan.[29]

The percentage of landmarked areas has been growing so that as of this writing (2023), according to the Real Estate Board of New York, it now approaches one-third of Manhattan (REBNY).

Although Jacobs is often invoked to justify the landmarking of entire neighborhoods or districts in this manner, there is little published documentation of her support for it. The best written evidence I have been able to find for her support of landmarking on this scale is in a letter[30] in which Jacobs argues for the landmarking of the West Village in Manhattan. On the whole, however, I believe her reference to "taxidermy" in *Death and Life* is relevant here—in this case, large-scale taxidermy for the relatively well-off at the expense of middle- and lower-income families.

Brooklyn Heights in the borough of Brooklyn, New York, might be the birthplace of the landmarks preservation movement in the United States. In an odd way, this movement has Robert Moses to thank, if not for its birth then for its accelerated emergence. That is, landmarks preservation as it applies to entire neighborhoods and districts received impetus as a response to Moses's efforts to construct a freeway, the Brooklyn-Queens Expressway, through the heart of what some call "New York's First Suburb." And that story exemplifies "interventionist dynamics" applied to urban planning, where the negative consequences of one intervention (Moses's BQE plans) call forth further interventions (landmarking) to address those problems that then create even more problems of their own (less affordable housing) and so on. I should note that in the

[29] See research by the Furman Center at New York University, summarized here: https://furman-center.org/thestoop/entry/fifty-years-of-historic-preservation-in-new-york-city. Accessed 13 May 2023. There is more data and details on the landmarking process at the NYC Landmarks Preservation Commission website: https://www1.nyc.gov/site/lpc/about/about-lpc.page. Accessed 13 May 2023.
[30] You can find a transcript of that letter at the website of the Greenwich Village Society for Historic Preservation: https://gvshp.org/blog/2016/05/05/continuing-jane-jacobs-work/

case of Brooklyn Heights, the higher real-estate prices generated in part by landmarking then resulted in a call for housing subsidies for middle-income households there.[31]

Landmarking typically freezes the heights of buildings (and usually the associated floor-area ratios) at existing levels, limiting supply and increasing housing prices when the demand for floor area increases. It also adds to the cost of construction and to building renovations of historically significant public exteriors by adding layer of bureaucracy and attendant delays. Landmarking may have laudable intentions, but one of its consequences has been to make real estate more expensive for the less well-off. It does by freezing FAR but also by shifting the demand of better-off buyers who can't afford housing in landmarked neighborhoods to other neighborhoods where housing is cheaper. In turn, other things equal, prices in the latter will rise, making them less affordable to lower-income buyers, who then shift their demand to even poorer neighborhoods and so on. This latter stage contributes to the much-complained-of gentrification of those communities. The public officials and local residents who lobby for landmarking don't seem to see or care about these costs and consequences, and so too much landmarking takes place. Where successfully implemented, landmarking and heritage designation mean stasis replaces dynamism in land-use and in meaningful diversity and vitality in that location.

To paraphrase urbanist Joe McReynolds: Historic preservation may preserve the look of a neighborhood but not its life.

4   Concluding Thoughts

If planners hope to avoid the negative unintended consequences of interventionist dynamics, they need to be aware of the knowledge and incentive problems that grow as the scope and design of their projects become more ambitious. It is the trade-off introduced in Chap. 3 and is the

---

[31] See my short essay on the landmarking of Brooklyn Heights as an example of this dynamic in Ikeda (2017).

common thread that runs through the Market Urbanist analyses in this chapter. Here is a (perhaps overly terse) summary.

Strict functional zoning tends to reduce housing affordability and urban mobility and hampers the creation of effective pools of use that fuel economic development.

Both Hayek and Jacobs recognize that housing problems stem largely from poverty and flawed institutions rather than some fundamental defect in human nature or of free enterprise and that top-down public housing is not an effective solution. Building codes and inspections should address hazards that are hard to detect, but mandates to keep raising housing quality reduce housing affordability. Banning various forms of cheap housing offers low-income households fewer, not more, options. And while Jacobs doesn't reject rent regulation outright, she recognizes that it distorts price feedback and worsens housing affordability in the long term. Bertaud links housing affordability to mobility.

Jacobs finds urban sprawl problematic but takes a dynamic perspective similar to Bruegemann and Bogart and agrees with Jackson that interventionism in transport and housing greatly accelerated and exacerbated those problems. The New Urbanist response to sprawl is essentially a return to the Cartesian rationalism of Le Corbusier, which could explain why Jacobs voiced faint support for the movement.

Government-sponsored community participation in private development gives special interests a disproportionate voice in community forums and suffers from a lack of feedback from market prices. Developments organized as private-public partnerships typically produce mega- and giga-projects that produce the problems associated with cataclysmic money, border vacuums, and visual homogeneity. And landmarking, sometimes an interventionist response to prior urban interventions, makes the cost of floor space prohibitive for the not so rich and turns older neighborhoods into museum pieces with pricey restaurants.

In the next chapter, we ask what room all this leaves for imaginative planning and design.

Works Cited

Ashton, T.S. (1963). The Treatment of Capitalism by Historians. In: Hayek.

Bertaud, A. (2018). *Order Without Design: How Markets Shape Cities*. MIT Press.

Bui, Q., Chaban, M. A. B., & White, J. (2016, May 20). 40 percent of Buildings in Manhattan Could Not Be Built Today. *The New York Times*.

Fairbanks, R. B., & Robert, B. (2000). From Better Dwellings to Better Neighborhoods: The Rise and Fall of the First National Housing Movement. In B. Bauman & Szylvian (Eds.), (Vol. 2000, pp. 21–42).

Barr, J. M. (2016). *Building the Skyline*. Oxford Univ. Press.

Bauman, J. F., Biles, R., & Szylvian, K. M. (2000). From Tenements to the Taylor Homes. In *Search of an Urban Housing Policy in twentieth-Century America*. The Pennsylvania State University Press.

Bivins, R. (2019, September 19). Solutions to the Attainable and Affordable Housing Crisis Are Varied, but Promising. *Urban Land Magazine*.

Bogart, W. T. (2006). *Don't Call It Sprawl: Metropolitan Structure in the 21st Century*. Cambridge Univ. Press.

Breckman, W. (2010). A Matter of Optics. *Lapham's Quarterly, III*(4) https://www.laphamsquarterly.org/city/matter-optics

Bruegmann, R. (2006). *Sprawl: A Compact History*. Univ. of Chicago.

Campanella, T. J. (2011). Jane Jacobs and the Death and Life of American Planning. In M. Page & T. Mennel (Eds.), *Reconsidering Jane Jacobs*. Taylor and Francis.

Canales, K., & Mok, A. (2022, November 28). China's 'Social Credit' System Ranks Citizens and Punishes Them with Throttled Internet Speeds and Flight Bans If the Communist Party Deems them Untrustworthy. *Business Insider*. https://www.businessinsider.com/china-social-credit-system-punishments-and-rewards-explained-2018-4. Accessed 13 May 2023.

Cho, E. (2020, May 1). The Social Credit System: Not Just Another Chinese Idiosyncrasy. *Journal of Public and International Affairs*. https://jpia.princeton.edu/news/social-credit-system-not-just-another-chinese-idiosyncrasy. Accessed 13 May 2023.

Coalition for the Homeless. (2019, December 3). Basic Facts About Homelessness: New York City. https://www.coalitionforthehomeless.org/basic-facts-about-homelessness-new-york-city/. Accessed 13 May 2023.

D'Onofro, J. (2019, June 24). Google Sibling Sidewalk Labs Unveils 'Smart City' Plans for Toronto Waterfront. *Forbes*. https://www.forbes.com/sites/jilliandonfro/2019/06/24/alphabet-google-sidewalk-labs-smart-city-plans-for-toronto-waterfront/#4ae4ce793ca7. Accessed 13 May 2023.

Duany, A., Zyberk, E. P., & Speck, J. (2010). *Suburban Nation: The Rise of Suburban Sprawl* (10th Anniversary Edition). North Point Press.

Dunlap, D. W. (2016, July 25). Zoning Arrived 100 Years Ago. It Changed New York City Forever. *The New York Times.* https://www.nytimes.com/2016/07/26/nyregion/new-yorks-first-zoning-resolution-which-brought-order-to-a-chaotic-building-boom-turns-100.html. Accessed 13 May 2023.

Fischel, W. A. (2004). An Economic History of Zoning and a Cure for Its Exclusionary Effects. *Urban Studies, 41*(2), 317–340.

Fischel, W. A. (2002). The Homevoter Hypothesis: How Home Values Influence Local Government Taxation, School Finance, and Land-use Policies. *Land Economics, 78*(4), 627–630.

Furman Center. (2016). *Fifty Years of Historic Preservation in New York City.* NYU Furman Center, Wagner School of Public Service.

Garreau, J. (1991). *Edge city: Life on the New Frontier.* Anchor Books.

Glaeser, E. L. (2012). *Triumph of the City: How Our Greatest Invention Makes Us Richer, Smarter, Greener, Healthier, and Happier.* Penguin.

Grant, J. L. (2011). Time, Scale, and Control: How New Urbanism Mis(uses) [sic] Jane Jacobs. In M. Page & T. Mennel (Eds.), *Reconsidering Jane Jacobs.* Taylor and Francis.

Gray, N. (2022). *Arbitrary Lines: How Zoning Broke the American City and How to Fix It.* Island Press.

Gray, N. (2018, February 5). Density Is How the Working Poor Outbid the Rich for Urban Land. *Market Urbanism,* https://marketurbanism.com/2018/02/05/density-working-poor-outbid-rich-urban-land/. Accessed 13 May 2023.

Groth, P. (1994). *Living Downtown: The History of Residential Hotels in the United States.* Univ. of California Press.

Hamilton, E. (2020, August 5). The Limits of the Singapore Housing Model. At MarketUrbanism.org. https://marketurbanism.com/2020/08/05/the-limits-of-the-singapore-housing-model/. Accessed 13 May 2023.

Harding, R. (2016, August 3). Why Tokyo Is the Land of Rising Home Construction but Not Prices. *Financial Times.* https://www.ft.com/content/023562e2-54a6-11e6-befd-2fc0c26b3c60. Accessed 13 May 2023.

Hayek, F. A. (1978). *New Studies in Philosophy, Politics, Economics and the History of Ideas.* Univ. of Chicago Press.

Hayek, F. A. (1974). The Pretense of Knowledge. In Hayek (1978).

Hayek, F. A. (1963). *Capitalism and the Historians*. Univ. of Chicago Press.

Hill, K., & Kilgannon, C. (2023, January 3). Madison Square Garden Uses Facial Recognition to Ban Its Owner's Enemies. *The New York Times*. https://www.nytimes.com/2022/12/22/nyregion/madison-square-garden-facial-recognition.html. Accessed 13 May 2023.

Hirt, S. A. (2015). *Zoned in the U.S.A.: The Origins and Implications of Land-Use Regulation*. Cornell Univ. Press.

Iglesias, M. (2018, October 22). California's Proposition 10, Explained. *Vox*. https://www.vox.com/policy-and-politics/2018/10/22/18009478/californias-proposition-10-explained. Accessed 13 May 2023.

Ikeda, S. (2017, March 17). How Urban Planners Broke Brooklyn. *Learn Liberty*. https://www.learnliberty.org/blog/how-urban-planners-broke-brooklyn/?utm_medium=web&utm_campaign=misclinks&utm_source=article_body&utm_content=intra

Ikeda, S. (2015). Dynamics of Interventionism. In *The Oxford Handbook of Austrian Economics*. Oxford University Press.

Ikeda, S. (2004). Urban Interventionism and Local Knowledge. *Review of Austrian Economics, 17*(2/3), 247–64.

Ikeda, S. (1998). *Dynamics of the Mixed Economy: Toward a Theory of Interventionism*. Routledge.

Ikeda, S., & Hamilton, E. (2015, November 4). How Land-Use regulation Undermines Affordable Housing. *Research Papers*. Mercatus Center.

Jackson, K. T. (1985). *Crabgrass Frontier: The Suburbanization of the United States*. Oxford Univ. Press.

Jacobs, J. (2004). *Dark Age Ahead*. Random House.

Jacobs, J. (2000). *The Nature of Economies*. Modern Library.

Jacobs, J. (1969). *The Economy of Cities*. Vintage.

Jacobs, J. (1961). *The Death and Life of Great American Cities*. Vintage.

Kendig, L. (1980). *Performance Zoning, with Susan Connor, Cranston Byrd, and Judy Heyman*. Planners Press.

Koeppel, G. (2015). *City on a Grid: How New York became New York*. Da Capo Press.

Kunstler, J. H. (1996, September). Home from Nowhere. *The Atlantic*. https://www.theatlantic.com/magazine/archive/1996/09/home-from-nowhere/376664/. Accessed 13 May 2023.

Landsburg, S. E. (2014). *Price Theory and Applications* (13th ed.). Cengage Learning.

Lang, G. (2021). *Jane Jacobs's First City* (Kindle Edition). New Village Press.

McCloskey, D. (2010). *Bourgeois Dignity: Why Economics Can't Explain the Modern World*. Univ. of Chicago Press.

McCrary, L. (2018). Roger Scruton Appointed New Urbanism Fellow at TAC. *The American Conservative*. http://www.theamericanconservative.com/urbs/roger-scruton-appointed-new-urbanism-fellow-at-tac/

National Association of Home Builders. (2019, September 10). Vast Majority of Americans Cite Growing Housing Affordability Problem as a Crisis. https://www.nahb.org/blog/2019/09/Vast-Majority-of-Americans-Cite-Growing-Housing-Affordability-Problem-As-a-Crisis. Accessed 13 May 2023.

Page, M., & Mennel, T. (Eds.). (2011). *Reconsidering Jane Jacobs* (Kindle Edition). Taylor and Francis.

Pennington, M. (2004). Citizen Participation, the 'Knowledge Problem' and Urban land use Planning: An Austrian Perspective on Institutional Choice. *The Review of Austrian Economics, 17*(2&3), 213–231.

Plunz, R. (1990). *A History of Housing in New York City*. Columbia Univ. Press.

Real Estate Board of New York. Landmarking, Housing Production and Demographics in NYC. Accessed 29 September 2022. https://prodweb1.rebny.com/content/dam/rebny/Documents/PDF/News/Research/Policy%20Reports/REBNY_SAH_Paper.pdf

Renn, A. M. (2018, February 15). Inclusionary Zoning Flops in Portland. *New Geography*. http://www.newgeography.com/content/005884-inclusionary-zoning-flops-portland

Salins, P. D., & Mildner, G. C. S. (1992). *Scarcity by Design: The Legacy of New York City's Housing Policies*. Harvard Univ. Press.

Scruton, R. (2012). A Plea for Beauty: a Manifesto for a New Urbanism. In *Society and Culture Outlook No. 1*. American Enterprise Institute for Public Policy Research, March 29. http://www.aei.org/publication/a-plea-for-beauty-a-manifesto-for-a-new-urbanism/. Accessed 13 May 2023.

Scruton, R. (2008). Cities for Living: Antimodernist Léon Krier Designs Urban Environments to Human Scale. *City Journal*, Spring.

Sidewalk Toronto (2019, December 3). Toronto Tomorrow: A New Approach for *inclusive* growth. https://www.sidewalktoronto.ca/. Accessed 13 May 2023.

Sidewalk Labs (2019, December 3). https://www.sidewalklabs.com/. Accessed 13 May 2023.

Talen, E. (Ed.). (2013). *Congress for the New Urbanism*. McGraw-Hill.

Turrentine, J. (2015, July 7). Painting the Town Purple. *NRDC*. https://www.nrdc.org/onearth/painting-town-purple. Accessed 13 May 2023.

Wagner, R. E. (2009). Property, State, and Entangled Political Economy. In W. Schäfer, A. Schneider, & T. Thomas (Eds.), *Markets and Politics: Insights from a Political Economy Perspective* (pp. 37–49). Metropolis.

World Bank. (2022, November 30). *Poverty: Overview.* The World Bank. https://www.worldbank.org/en/topic/poverty/overview. Accessed 13 May 2023.

9

Cities of the Future

Jacobs's critique of urban planning and her suggestions for improving cities flow from an analytical framework based on a set of coherent socio-economic insights. These are, namely, that a city is an institution indispensable for peacefully coordinating the plans of myriad, self-interested strangers with imperfect knowledge; that a city is a natural unit of economic analysis, the principal locus of innovation, a system of organized complexity, and a spontaneous order; that locals tend to know better than outsiders about the problems and opportunities, large and small, in their own urban *milieu*; and that with limited outside guidance ordinary people can cooperatively and effectively address them with intelligence, resourcefulness, and creativity.

In the last chapter we examined the limits of urban micro-interventions from this framework. Here I would like to address a different but related set of questions: To what extent is it feasible to consciously plan for "urban vitality," i.e., to promote or foster the experimentation and creativity essential for a real, living city? How much political authority do we need to accomplish this? How workable are some of the recent, imaginative proposals for city planning and rebuilding when we view it through a Jacobs-cum-market-process or Market Urbanist lens?

© The Author(s) 2024
S. Ikeda, *A City Cannot Be a Work of Art*,
https://doi.org/10.1007/978-981-99-5362-2_9

To critically examine these proposals it would be best first more carefully to distinguish "governance" from "government." Because some proposals may give the false impression that, because they suggest formal rules and explicit commands should be minimized or even eliminated altogether, this means minimizing or eliminating rules of any kind. To avoid this misunderstanding I will need to talk about the nature of different kinds of rules and how those differences relate to the distinction between governance and government. To lay the groundwork for all that, I will also take a closer look at some of the other concepts I have been using throughout this book.

1   Broader Conceptual Lessons and Necessary Elaborations

Again, I don't presume to speak for Jacobs on the issues and proposals that I raise here, except where she has herself written about them, but I do draw inferences from my understanding of her economics and social theory. Toward that end, there are several conceptual lessons we might distill from earlier chapters.

1.1   Planning for Vitality

In Chap. 4 we saw how, by promoting the four conditions for generating urban diversity (multiple attractors, population density, street intricacy, and cheap space), Jacobs argues that "planning can induce city vitality" (Jacobs, 1961: 14).

> Planning for vitality must stimulate and catalyze the greatest possible range and quantity of diversity among uses and among people throughout each district of a big city; this is the underlying foundation of city economic strength, social vitality and magnetism. To do this, planners must diagnose, in specific places, specifically what is lacking to generate diversity, and then aim at helping to supply the lacks as best they can be supplied. (Jacobs, 1961: 408–9)

For Jacobs some form of government planning is indispensable for urban vitality. Cities need

> ...a most intricate and close-grained diversity of uses that give each other constant mutual support, both economically and socially...the science of city planning and the art of city design, in real life for real cities, must become the science and art of catalyzing and nourishing these close-grained working relationships. (Jacobs, 1961: 14)

But this comes more in the form cultivating the inherent creative forces of a living city—"catalyzing and nourishing" through zoning for diversity, for example—than through wholesale rebuilding.

Jacobs argues, however, that the urban planner lacks the "locality knowledge" to effectively plan on the scale and at the level of detail Le Corbusier or Moses aspired to:

> To know whether it is done well or ill – to know what should be done at all – it is more important to know that specific locality than it is to know how many bits in the same category of bits are going into other localities and what is being done with them there. No other expertise can substitute for locality knowledge in planning, whether the planning is creative, coordinating or predictive. (Jacobs, 1961: 418)

She concludes that the government of a great city can effectively foster urban vitality, with an appropriate administrative structure that respects locality knowledge and a proper understanding of the nature and significance of living cities. The problem is that the vertical governance structure appropriate for a town or small city, in which governmental functions are mostly centrally directed, break down in a city of millions of people and dozens of distinct districts and neighborhoods. A centralized, vertical structure of administration cannot effectively transmit locality knowledge up through the chains of the municipal bureaucracy. Instead, a great city requires a different structure of government administration.

> In short, great cities must be divided into administrative districts. These would be horizontal divisions of city government but, unlike random horizontality, they would be common to the municipal government as a whole.

The administrative districts would represent the primary, basic subdivisions made within most city agencies. (Jacobs, 1961: 418)

Jacobs argues that a horizontal administrative structure, for which she invokes the concept of "subsidiarity,"[1] would need to be more complex than a vertical one. Each district would have officials responsible for overseeing the provision of most public services and collective goods in that particular district including traffic, welfare, schools, police, parks, code enforcement, public health, housing subsidies, fire, zoning, and planning (Jacobs, 1961: 419) for effective governance. "City administration needs to be more complex in its fundamental structure so it can work more simply. The present structures, paradoxically, are fundamentally too simple" (Jacobs, 1961: 421). Not all municipal functions could be administered horizontally, however; Jacobs mentions "water supply, air pollution control, labor mediation, management of museums, zoos and prisons" (Jacobs, 1961: 421) to which we could add intracity roadways.

Jacobs argues that subsidiarity, along with greater patience and openness, would place planners in a better position to learn how locals use public space and that neighborhoods, districts, and cities are neither simple nor inherently disorganized. In short, they could obtain some of that locality knowledge. But Jacobs does not expand on why planners have a hard time making that adjustment. Why don't central planners make the effort to learn about and appreciate locality knowledge? In *Death and Life* Jacobs blames their training based on the intellectual trends in the early twentieth century (Jacobs, 1961: 436).[2] This may be part of the explanation why, apart from sheer arrogance, this disconnect should persist.

---

[1] "Subsidiarity is the principle that government works best— most responsibly and responsively— when it is closest to the people it serves and the needs it addresses" (Jacobs, 2004: 103).

[2] Her observations here are consistent with F.A. Hayek's on the rise of what he calls "scientism" or the inappropriate application of the methods of the physical sciences to the social sciences (Hayek, 1942). This is the Cartesian rationalism or rationalist constructivism that we discussed in Chap. 7.

It is from F.A. Hayek and Israel Kirzner, however, that we are able to fill this gap. (No surprise since a core argument of this book is that the bulk of Jacobs's insights are highly compatible with and indeed essentially the same as Hayek's and Kirzner's social theory.) In this case, given the complex and changing nature of social reality and the inherent cognitive and epistemic limitations of the human mind, conditioned by the dispersed and contextual nature of knowledge relevant for planning by flesh-and-blood people (Hayek, 1948; Kirzner, 1992), central planners cannot *in principle* close the distance between their conception of orderliness and the facts relevant to those for whom they plan. Of course, in more general terms I have noted before that Jacobs partially recognizes this, too:

> Central planning, whether by leftists or conservatives, draws too little on local knowledge and creativity, stifles innovations, and is inefficient and costly because it is circuitous. It bypasses intimate and varied knowledge directly fed back into the system. (Jacobs, 2004: 117)

With horizontal and polycentric governance, combined with a more modest scale and detail of plans, Jacobs believes urban planners may contribute to the life of a city. As Hayek et al. explain, the fundamental challenge for the planner is to recognize and respect the knowledge problem. So why don't they? Ideology and training may explain some of it, but there may also be a psychological factor involved, working in conjunction with the epistemic and incentives.

1.2   O-Judgments Versus S-Judgments

The fundamental error that planners make stems from treating a complex, spontaneous order as as though it were subject to extensive human design and direction. In other words, as a work of art.

Our concern, of course, is with urban planning and design, but as we have discussed, planners have historically made the same mistake in the areas of macroeconomic policy and system-wide economic planning: the pretense that a comprehensive, rationally designed outcome can be realized by forcing it on a dynamically emergent system (von Mises, 1922; Lavoie, 1985; Boettke, 1990). All such approaches assume that planners possess sufficient knowledge and incentives to successfully adjust their plans to actual and changing conditions in the absence of coordinating institutions such as market prices or horizontal social networks.

But, again, why is it that urban planners typically fail to appreciate the underlying order of a city and the nature of its complexity? The political philosopher Bertrand de Jouvenel suggests an answer:

> Thinking in general terms, let us consider an arrangement of factors that serves some purpose and is instrumental to some process. Let us call it an operational arrangement. A mind concerned with this purpose, well aware of the process, dwells upon the operational arrangement and finds that it might be made more effective by certain alterations. We shall call a judgment passed from this angle an O-judgment to denote that the arrangement is appreciated from the operational standpoint. O-judgments are the principle of all technical progress made by mankind. Quite different in kind is the judgment passed upon the same arrangement of factors by a mind that regards it without any intensive interest in or awareness of the process. Such a judgment is then passed as it were from an external, extra-processive standpoint. We shall call it an S-judgment. (de Jouvenel, 1956: 46)

According to de Jouvenel, we have a tendency to seek "tidiness" and "seemliness" in the world, a desire to have a satisfyingly complete explanation for the important forces and phenomena we encounter in our daily lives. Where we have intensive and critical dealings, e.g., in our jobs or in raising our own families, we are usually able to render O-judgments because we have devoted time and effort in seeing beneath appearances to the deeper order and, I might add, to appreciate the complexity of a problem and the epistemic limits of any solution we might try to come up with rationally. We become familiar with the relevant local knowledge. Think of Jacobs's distinction between slumming slums and unslumming slums, for example (Jacobs, 1961: 270), discussed in Chap. 6. We need to spend time at street level, the tactile level, in each community to gather enough relevant local knowledge to see this distinction and to grasp what sorts of actions might work or not work to improve the well-being of their residents.

But O-judgments are difficult and costly "in terms of attention and time" they take to form (de Jouvenel, 1956: 46), and we cannot afford to gain such depth of understanding and expertise in the vast majority of situations we confront in our daily lives. Indeed, given the limits of our minds and our resources, trying to do so would not be in our best interests even if it were possible in principle. So in our quest for tidiness and expediency, we tend to resort to superficial S-judgments, in which we ignore relevant factors (at the street level). And here is the key: As the scope and complexity of the activities on which we are required to pass judgment increase, especially those outside our primary areas of direct experience and concern, the proportion of S-judgments will grow relative to O-judgments.

> Therefore the larger the number of arrangements upon which I venture to pass judgments, the higher the proportion of the arrangements examined which I shall pronounce unseemly, and the more the world will seem to me to be made up of "bad" and "wrong" arrangements. (de Jouvenel, 1956: 47)

This tendency for passing superficial judgments when confronted by the "unseemly" and apparently chaotic (such as in messy living cities) is inherent in even the most superior, rational intellects. Like Louis Wirth, we tend to rely on models or "statistical people" that abstract unhelpfully from untidy reality.

> It is a relief to turn to problems of which we are ignorant and to which we therefore may apply our models. Be it noted that the greatest scientists who have mastered prodigious complexities are apt to come out with the most naïve views on social problems, for example. (de Jouvenel, 1956: 48)

Hence, we may surmise that planners lack the cognitive and epistemic capacity to develop proper O-judgments on all matters that could be subject to urban planning. And this is why they should limit what they try to do—which relates to what I have referred to as "scope" and "designed complexity." But why don't more social scientists and urban planners acknowledge the complexity and emergent nature of urban phenomena and thus turn attention to the more-relevant locality knowledge?

This brings us back to Jacobs's discussion of organized complexity, and the tendency under the influence of twentieth-century intellectual trends to resort to explanations in terms of simplicity or disorganized complexity: "The theories of conventional modern city planning have consistently mistaken cities as problems of simplicity and of disorganized complexity" (Jacobs, 1961: 435). This in turn is closely related to Hayek's discussion (Hayek, 1942) of the "scientistic" turn in social theory in which the methods of the physical sciences are naively and inappropriately applied to social phenomena. As we have seen, when this is the basis and justification for overly ambitious urban projects, the consequences can be destructive.

Once they recognize the nature of the problem they are grappling with and acknowledge their cognitive limits in influencing the shape and direction of living cities, urban planners could then rely on emergent market prices or spontaneously formed social networks and institutions to assist them in coping with their ignorance (Hayek, 1974; Bertaud, 2018). The effectiveness of their plans therefore depends on how well these market prices, social networks, and institutions are allowed to function. The burden of Chap. 3 was to explain why beyond some point a trade-off arises between designed complexity and spontaneous complexity. When the level of intervention is low, the plans of the designers tend to complement the plans of those of us for whom they are planning; as the level of intervention rises, beyond some point their interventions begin to crowd out more than they complement. We have seen that for Jacobs and market-process economists, that turning point lies at a fairly low level of intervention (i.e., planning for basic infrastructure, removing negative externalities, and certain basic design elements that encourage safety and diversity). Increasing the scope of a project and its designed elements leaves less scope for markets and social networks to guide individual planning and foster personal autonomy and emergent order. In this way the hubris of planners obstructs the aspirations of ordinary people to cope with their imperfect knowledge.

Subsidiarity may be a step in the right direction, but by itself it cannot offset the debilitating effects of large-scale planning, particularly by governments, and administratively it is also subject to the knowledge and incentive problems, even with "government sponsored community participation" we assessed in the previous chapter. The following sections then focus on how best to make collective decisions that significantly affect an entire community. I argue that it is possible to separate the case for decentralized governance from the question of whether such governance requires extensive use of political authority.

1.3   Governance Versus Government

Recall that the spontaneity of a social system, its emergent properties, happens beyond or above the level of a particular plan. That is, you can design the layout of a piazza but except for certain negative rules (e.g., no disruptive behavior as defined by local norms) not how the people in it will use the piazza over time. To use an economic example, the capital structure of a competitive market (i.e., the way investment in capital goods of myriad people fit together) is unplanned, even if the decisions of individual businesses, households, or non-profit organizations to invest in particular capital goods are each carefully and minutely planned (Lachmann, 1978), just as a business can meticulously design a plant but not the way it fits with others businesses upstream, downstream, and horizontally. In a Jacobsian context, the decisions of our neighbors to pay attention to what is going on in front of their houses contribute in unplanned and unanticipated ways to the formation of social capital and dynamic social networks, which in turn results in the safety and security of our neighborhood and the reinforcement of social norms. While it is possible that we may know that our thoughtfully considered choices contribute to such outcomes, we likely don't know how it does so, nor do we really need to know.

As members of a community we may deliberately create the infrastructure necessary for our comfort through some form of collective decision-making—e.g., to provide roads, sewers, power, water, etc.—that then results in unintended patterns of usage. Does this imply anything about whether government authority is necessary to create and implement those designs? I suggest that although governments may provide collective or public goods (in the strict economic sense of goods that are non-rival and non-excludable), it is not always necessary for governments to do so. Governance, i.e., the making, administration, and enforcement of rules to promote social order, may be something governments typically do, but *governance is not coextensive with government.* Purely private entities also govern but must do so through non-violent persuasion rather than coercion. As Peter Hall has noted, "collective action can and often does consist in giving wider powers to private agents" (Hall, 1998: 6).

The necessity of government intervention for effective governance is hard to deny when nary an acre of land in the developed world has not been claimed by at least one nation-state or another. It is especially hard to deny if we frame the question of providing collective goods in the form of "What is the most efficient way to construct city-wide sewers, set up a network of aqueducts, and lay miles of rail lines for mass transit?" But it may widen the set of feasible solutions if we reframe the question as "What is the most efficient way to provide waste disposal, get clean water to households, and improve urban mobility?" In other words, we might think less in terms of physical assets and more in terms of capabilities.[3]

The remainder of this section deals further with the nature of government and governance in the context of the kinds of rules found in them. This provides a starting point for elaborating the Market Urbanist approach introduced in the last chapter. That then leads to an analysis and critique of some current proposals for urban revitalization and rebuilding.

1.4   Kinds of Rules and Their Enforcement

The distinction between planned and unplanned orders and between governance and government lies in the rules on which each of these phenomena is based. The rules that government authority mainly rests on tend to be of a very different nature from the rules that support voluntary governance.

---

[3] I would like to credit Professor Lynn Kiesling for this way of framing the collective goods problem for me. The usual caveat applies.

Of course all planners, whether public and private, must issue and enforce rules as commands to achieve a specific objective.[4] But the problem facing an architect who designs a single building, even a massive one, is not only quantitatively different but different in kind from the problems that arise from trying to design a city or even a single neighborhood. The knowledge requirement is impossibly large. S-judgments quickly displace O-judgements to harmful effect.

1.4.1 Rule of Law and Negative Rules

In contrast to rules as commands are rules aimed at generating a general pattern rather than a particular outcome, rules that are stable and predictable and apply to all under its jurisdiction (Hayek, 1944). An example would be a speed limit on a road, which may benefit or harm some drivers depending on the situation (e.g., leisure drivers versus those late for work) but is not intended to achieve an end other than to promote safe and orderly travel. In contrast is a rule that allows only certain individuals to use a road or that privileges them to ignore the speed limit. A rule that is general, universal, and stable may be quite wide in its scope (e.g., a national speed limit), but its content and level of design, and what it mandates or prohibits, are much more limited than a rule aimed at a specific objective, which may require extensive details, especially in its application (Moroni et al., 2018).

Other things equal, the less general, universal, and stable a rule is the more difficult and costlier it is to enforce. In the previous example, compare a rule that allows only certain privileged drivers to use a road versus a simple speed limit applied to all. Of course, a rule that is general, universal, and stable—characteristics of what is sometimes referred to as the *Rule of Law*—may be oppressive or difficult to enforce, such as a rule that says all persons 18–26 years of age must serve in the military. But this suggests that the content of the rule needs to be carefully considered.

A related concept is that of a *convention*, which we might define as a rule that has been so widely accepted that it is largely self-enforcing, such

---

[4] In the process of construction, of course, some of these rules may require adjustment, yet not without the approval of a chief architect or master planner.

as "drive on the right" (on pain of causing serious harm to oneself). And then there are *norms*, which we might think of as ethical rules that we have internalized or that are enforced through non-governmental means such as social pressure and disapprobation: I should obey the speed limit because it is morally the right thing to do (or that as a rule we should follow rules and conventions) (Greif, 2006).

People in all societies, including authoritarian societies, abide by norms, conventions, and governmentally enforced rules.[5] The difference is the degree to which governmentally mandated and enforced rules predominate. Other things equal, the greater the degree that central planning and government intervention consciously direct individual activity, the greater the reliance on rules that depend on government authority for their enforcement and less the reliance on self-enforcement, social pressure, or voluntary acceptance. Turning this around, when planners use rules to achieve concrete rather than "abstract" outcomes (i.e., outcomes not aimed at a particular goal) for particular persons or groups, the result is a planned and not a spontaneous order.

While governments sometimes abide by the Rule of Law, voluntary governance that generates robust unplanned social orders, as when buyers and sellers in competitive markets conform to abstract rules of property and exchange, cannot deviate far from it and still retain that robustness.

1.4.2   Nomos and Thesis[6]

To further clarify the distinction between government and governance, we can look at rules from another angle, one that derives from Hayek's essay, "The Errors of Constructivism," in which he distinguishes three kinds of rules:

> (1) rules that are merely observed in fact but have never been stated in words... (2) rules that, though they have been stated in words, still merely express approximately what has long before been generally observed in

---

[5] The same rule may fall under all three of these definitions, but not for the same person at a given moment in time.

[6] *Nomos*, the law of liberty; *thesis*, the law of legislation (Hayek, 1973: 126).

action; and (3) rules that have been deliberately introduced and therefore necessarily exist as words set out in sentences. (Hayek,1978: 8–9)

I will characterize these three kinds of rules, respectively, as "tacit," "contextual," and "formal." So the tendency for Cartesian or "high modernist" thinkers (Scott, 1998: 4) in urban planning, and social theory generally, is to treat social phenomena as if they were guided solely by rules of the formal type: simple enough that their meaning can be effectively expressed in words or symbols. Such rules will appeal to those prone to making S-judgments rather than O-judgments.

Drawing on our earlier discussion, we can see that the concept of rules as formal commands also fits more closely to phenomena of "simplicity" and "disorganized complexity" than to phenomena of "organized complexity" because the relationships among elements in the first two phenomena are relatively simple, either in terms of the small number of variables involved or of the applicability of simple statistical relationships. Planners who don't know better would assume they could direct complex living cities using explicit rules or commands. The urban designs of Le Corbusier, for example, entail rules that designate in detail the placement and uses of all the major structures in a "radiant city," much as detailed land-use zoning codes do in a more limited way, while ignoring the contextual and tacit rules that align more with Jacobs's "locality knowledge" that underlie the spontaneous, harder-to-see patterns that form in the interstices of the designed environment. That is why when Le Corbusier-designed or -inspired projects such as Chandigarh and Brasilia were constructed, they looked beautiful and orderly from a great distance but lifeless and chaotic (i.e., disorderly in the strict sense) at ground level. The consequence for residents is empty, unsafe, and sometimes dangerous public spaces, which even the passage of time may not fully counteract.

The emergent outcomes of social networks and living cities entail more contextual, tacit, and informal rules. Such rules are harder to articulate and conform to *nomos* or the Rule of Law, which tends more to forbid than to mandate, rather than to *thesis*, which aims for specific or more concrete outcomes. The trade-off between the scale of conscious design and the degree of spontaneous complexity reflects this distinction, because the idea that central planning should complement rather than substitute for our plans implies that in making our O-judgments, we rely on rules the central planner does not (and perhaps cannot) know.

Governance mainly by "rules as positive commands" discounts the vital role of contextual and tacit rules and can lead to deep disorder and confusion. If planners appreciate their limitations, however, their governance can harness and complement, rather than stifle and substitute.

In addition, understanding the differences among rules, norms, and conventions and among explicit, contextual, and tacit rules can help to show that governance is possible without government. This understanding becomes relevant when we later examine proposals to build new cities or to revitalize existing ones, while the distinctions among explicit, contextual, and tacit rules help us to understand why the claim that complex social orders must be centrally planned is wrong.

2   Jacobs and Market Urbanism

I have stressed throughout this book that Jane Jacobs was careful to avoid aligning herself with any ideology, left, right, or other, and that includes the so-called free market.[7] That is why I have been careful not to claim more for Jacobs regarding her political beliefs and policy prescriptions than can be documented in her books, articles, and published speeches and essays, and I have been careful to point out, as in the last chapter, where I am extrapolating into territory she did not herself tread. What I have tried to do is show how the fundamentals of her approach, and most if not all of those policy prescriptions align well, if not precisely, with market-process economics. At the same time, market-process economics, itself, as I have also stressed, is not a political ideology but rather an approach to understanding how market and non-market systems work or

---

[7] Glenna Lang (2021: Loc 285) rightly observes: "Although pundits positioning themselves at varying points on the political spectrum have tried to claim Jane as one of theirs, she was adamantly nonideological, a freethinker who refused to ally herself with a political party or doctrine of any sort." At the same time, Lang (Ibid: Loc 4287) reports that Jacobs as a high-school student favored small government: "The two Central schoolmates of vastly different backgrounds shared similar views (Jacobs and Carl Marzani), preferring the least amount of government and abhorring the brutality of the coal company police and state troopers protecting the nonunion 'scabs' during coal strikes."

don't work and interact over time, although it is often associated with policies characterized as "free market" (e.g., free trade, monetary neutrality, and minimal government intervention) and classical liberalism (e.g., open immigration, concern with individual autonomy and well-being, especially for the least well-off in society, radical tolerance, and vigorous but civil criticism).

Although urban economics is a well-established field within the discipline of economics, for market-process economics, urbanism broadly considered is a relatively new territory, and this book is among the first extensive forays into this area from a market-process perspective.[8] A growing number of market-friendly urbanists from a variety of backgrounds have (spontaneously) formed a movement dedicated to systematically applying market-based policy solutions to solve socioeconomic problems facing cities. Many have adopted the term "Market Urbanism" to describe their approach.

Adam Hengels, who coined the term, defines it succinctly as follows:

"Market Urbanism" refers to the synthesis of classical liberal economics and ethics *(market)*, with an appreciation of the urban way of life and its benefits to society *(urbanism)*. We advocate for the emergence of bottom up solutions to urban issues, as opposed to ones imposed from the top down.[9]

And the journalist and urbanist-blogger Scott Beyer defines it this way:

Market Urbanism is the cross between free-market policy and urban issues. Rooted from the classical liberal economic tradition, the theory calls for private-sector actions that create organic growth and voluntary exchange within cities, rather than ones enforced by government bureaucracy. Market Urbanists believe that were this model tried in cities, it would produce cheaper housing, faster transport, improved public services and better quality of life.[10]

---

[8] Other notable predecessors can be found in Beito et al. (2002).
[9] See the Market Urbanism website, https://marketurbanism.com/ (accessed 5 October 2022).
[10] See the Market Urbanism Report website, https://marketurbanismreport.com/ (accessed 5 October 2022) and Beyer (2022).

In the context of this book, Market Urbanism (1) is an approach to understanding living cities as complex, spontaneous orders that drive economic development and material well-being, (2) uses this understanding to identify and analyze urban problems, and (3) to recommend solutions to those problems that rely as much as possible on voluntary, local, and market-based efforts.

Would Jacobs fully endorse any of these conceptions of Market Urbanism? Probably not, although I couldn't say precisely why except for her general aversion, noted above, to identify too closely with an ideological position, in this case classical liberalism.[11] Would she, however, endorse relying principally on market-based solutions and the Rule of Law, rather than arbitrary commands, and being wary of top-down governmental authority? Yes, I think she would. What is the basis for my belief?

First is her conception of a city and the important institutions within it as complex orders that emerge within partially designed frameworks. Second is her scathing critique of large-scale urban planning at the local level (with its Cartesian "scientistic" outlook) that ignores the importance of local knowledge and spontaneously organized complexity, as in the final chapter of *Death and Life* and the first chapter of *The Economy of Cities*. Third is her hostility toward functional zoning with its forced and artificial separation of uses, again as in Part II of *Death and Life*. Fourth, her proposals that do involve governmental authority tend to be far less interventionist than conventional approaches, such as her desire to get the government out of the landlord business and instead complement "private enterprise" by making it profitable for private landlords to rent to low-income families, as in chapter 17 in *Death and Life*. Fifth is her cautious attitude toward the rent regulation because it doesn't get at the "core problem" of building new housing, as she argues in *The Economy of Cities* and *Dark Age Ahead*, which also reflects her understanding of the feedback role of market prices. Sixth, as we saw in Chap. 8 and the previous section, her support for regulations is mainly confined to addressing economic externalities, safety issues, and limited urban revitalization

---

[11] Appendix 1 to this chapter offers further evidence for Jane Jacobs as a classical liberal.

based on performance and form-based zoning, which eschew dictating how individuals should use their property à la functional zoning.

We have seen that Jacobs advocates subsidiarity in government administration, which is more complex than the more common vertical structures of administration. But this polycentric[12] solution doesn't entail increasing the political power of local officials. Rather, keeping the level of political power constant, subsidiarity's complex horizontal structure minimizes the lines of communication between the people who live and work in an area and those who govern it, empowering ordinary individuals to help discover their solutions. Far from advocating an overall increase in the scope of government authority, Jacobs argues instead for a way to minimize the negative impact of government administration on the complexity of the urban order and to maximize the effectiveness of that governance. And in a political context, again, subsidiarity works best when authority is strictly limited. Indeed, Jacobs's subsidiarity could just as well promote effective governance in voluntary, private organizations. The lesson from market-process economics is that if authorities at any level are tasked to do too much, no amount of decentralization, horizontality, or subsidiarity will improve the situation (Ikeda, 1997). As she said in an interview with journalist David Warren:

> The really important, vital government monopoly is over the use of force. [...] But to extend monopoly powers to things like railways or the mail service, which are basically commercial, is pretty ridiculous. (Zipp & Storring, 2016: 317)

As I say, Jane Jacobs probably wouldn't endorse Market Urbanism outright. But her understanding of markets and cities as complex and emergent social orders, and her limited support for government intervention, places her comfortably within the Market Urbanist camp, which ranges from an anarchist wing to the more pragmatic views of prominent urban planner Alain Bertaud (2018), who combines a Jacobsian belief in the

---

[12] On polycentricity see also V. Ostrom et al. (1961).

necessity of limited government planning with a deep, equally Jacobsian respect for the ordering capabilities of the market.[13]

I hope this offers a useful context for the proposals I now examine.

3   Cities of the Future

Experts say that by 2050 about 70% of the world's population will be urbanized.[14] But what kind of cities will they be? If I take seriously what I have said about the unpredictable nature of living cities, then the only honest answer to this question is, "No one knows…and that's probably a good thing." Still, we can use our framework to examine what is possible and to critique some of the current proposals for future cities.

---

[13] I believe Jacobs would find a great deal of common ground with Bertaud's outlook. Perhaps I should elaborate on this connection.

Bertaud's (2018) attitude is apparently highly unusual for an urban planner, especially one of his international stature. His thesis is straightforward: Urban planners need to understand basic economics—in which demand curves slope down and supply curves (usually) slope up—and apply that understanding to their work. For Bertaud, a city is first and foremost a labor market, and as such, an urban planner (as he himself has been for over five decades) needs to be aware of land values, the costs of mobility and of construction, and the trade-offs that exist among them. The job of the planner is to continuously monitor these magnitudes and to adjust infrastructure and regulations to promote the labor-enhancing mobility of urban residents, especially to ever-changing productive work, and to enable economic development.

When city governments competently provide major roads and infrastructure and deal effectively with negative externalities, people can then rely on market-determined values for land, construction, and transport to decide where to build, live, and work. When planners attempt to go beyond these critical but limited functions, as I put it in Chap. 3, they substitute the conscious design of the urban planner for the far more complex, robust, and responsive orders that emerge when ordinary people, operating in and through well-functioning markets, make their own plans and decisions. In this view, measures such as population density or floor-area ratios should be seen as dependent variables, not policy targets.

Bertaud's understanding of the city as a complex, dynamic, and emergent order and his awareness of the limits of urban design strongly echo Jane Jacobs. Jacobs effectively challenged, from the outside, the very planning mentality that Bertaud challenges as an insider. I have no doubt that she would have delighted in his 2018 book, *Order Without Design*. Indeed, as a student of Jane Jacobs, it is easy for me to imagine that, if she had somehow been an urban planner herself instead of a public intellectual, she might have penned a tome very much like Bertaud's!

[14] See, for example, the United Nations figures at their website: https://www.un.org/development/desa/en/news/population/2018-revision-of-world-urbanization-prospects.html. Accessed 14 May 2023.

The number of possible topics I could explore here—e.g., revitalization of Pittsburg and Detroit, Singapore, and Shenzhen—is just too vast and would itself require a book-length treatment. Instead, I will draw on several examples of urban revitalization and city building that illustrate some possible ways forward.

We begin by looking at smaller-scale experiments that we might characterize as Market Urbanist and under the heading of urban revitalization. The last is a much more grandiose project in city building in Guatemala. First, a little background on public space as a common-pool resource.

3.1 Urban Revitalization

Elinor Ostrom, winner of the 2009 Nobel Prize in economics, spent a lifetime studying communities in culturally diverse locations around the world—including Spain, Switzerland, Japan, and the Philippines—that have found ways to solve "common pool resource" (CPR) problems. These problems arise when a valuable resource, such as a river or a forest, is not the private property of any person or group, a condition that can create powerful incentives for individuals ("appropriators") to overuse the CPR, to the long-term detriment of the entire community. In technical terms a CPR is a resource that is rival (i.e., my use interferes with your use) and nonexcludable (i.e., we can't keep anyone out). Each of us may realize self-restraint is in everyone's interest, but if we believe others will opportunistically free ride on our self-restraint, we too will be sorely tempted to do the same (Ostrom, 1990).

Ostrom found that in many (though not all) of the cases she studied, the appropriators themselves, mostly or entirely without help from their government, established rules and enforcement mechanisms effective enough to keep overuse and conflict to a minimum and flexible enough to adjust to changing circumstances over long periods of time, sometimes centuries (Ostrom, 1990). These governance arrangements were largely non-governmental and over time became self-regulating, based on local norms and conventions. These kinds of CPR situations appear in many places, including on the streets of a major metropolis. Which brings us to the concept of "shared streets."

3.1.1   Shared Streets

In the late twentieth century a radical way of addressing problems of traffic congestion, accidents, pollution, and mobility appeared on the scene. Urban streets are common-pool resources with multiple appropriators—cars, cyclists, and pedestrians—which are often notoriously overused, a.k.a. traffic jams. The policy of "shared streets" has been spreading across northern Europe, including the Netherlands, Sweden, and the United Kingdom, sometimes under the Dutch term *woonerf* (Jaffe, 2015). Shared streets calls for removing traffic lights and signage and marked pedestrian crossings; it recommends substituting traffic circles for traditional intersections and blending sidewalks seamlessly into streets. Motor vehicles, pedestrians, and bicyclists are given equal legal priority and must therefore find ways to peacefully share this particular public space. In principle a motorist or bicyclist could go through an intersection without stopping for anyone; a pedestrian could cross anywhere at any time. All are liable for any injury or damage their actions cause, of course, but no one would be guilty of a traffic violation insofar as there are no laws or regulations to violate.

Instead of chaos, the result has so far been fewer accidents and injuries, a smoother flow of traffic, even in busy London, and perhaps less pollution from needlessly idling vehicles.[15] Without signs to guide (or distract) them, drivers and cyclist need to be far more alert and careful than usual when approaching an intersection, and pedestrians more cautious when crossing the street. Common sense, self-preservation, and norms of civility have prevailed for the most part.

While there is less reliance on explicit rules and more on tacit rules, norms, and conventions, it is wrong to say, as a CNN news headline proclaimed, "Shared space, where streets have no rules" (Senthilingam, 2015). Indeed, the rules of shared streets are no less numerous, possibly even more numerous and complex, when the local authorities create the conditions that enable appropriate-but-unwritten rules to emerge and

---

[15] See, for example, Ruiz-Apilánez et al. (2017) and references therein.

play a greater role in coordinating movement.[16] Here, our earlier discussion of the nature of formal and informal rules is crucial, where the latter are norms and conventions that are often contextual and tacit.

Municipalities that have implemented shared streets have seen their accident rates and injuries decline (Project for Public Spaces, 2017). Although it is undoubtedly true that the first intersections were chosen for these experiments because of their greater potential for success, still we generally don't see pedestrians fearfully scampering across the street or cars dangerously bullying for the right of way.[17] On the contrary cars, walkers, and bicyclists rather routinely mingle, as equals, as they negotiate shared streets.

No one mandates the norms of civility people should observe in the traffic commons, nor what tacit and contextual rules of crossing they should observe. Instead, ordinary people simply use local knowledge and common sense to interact safely. Order emerges, like it did in those communities Ostrom studied that successfully preserve CPRs. The potential appropriators — the drivers and pedestrians — self-regulate because few want to cause an accident or to be a victim of one. It is well known that most of the rules of the road are unwritten anyway — which raises the question of how many of those rules really need to be written down at all. These are examples of Ostrom's principle of governing the commons, again with no or very little reliance on government intervention.[18]

Videos of shared streets remind me of when I was in Beijing in 1984 trying to cross one of those menacingly wide boulevards filled with a thick, endless stream of bicyclists. I stood paralyzed on the edge of the traffic until our guide told me that I should just start walking through, slowly but without stopping (like a cowboy wading through a herd), and the bicyclists would avoid us—and they did! Today, cars have largely replaced these swarms of bicycles, and I don't know how the norms may

---

[16] However, Karndacharuk et al. (2014) find there are specific rules, outlined by local governments, that are still needed.

[17] There is fear, although it is not clear whether the evidence supports it, that the visually impaired find shared streets more intimidating than traditional traffic arrangements. See, for example, this item from BBC news: https://www.bbc.com/news/uk-england-44971392. Accessed 14 May 2023.

[18] Naturally, if an accident occurs, the parties involved may have recourse to the judicial system, but whether that system needs to rely on government authority to operate effectively is equally debatable. Exploring this issue would take us well beyond the scope of this book, however.

have changed to fit the new circumstances. And in cities today where bicycles still dominate, as in Amsterdam, an entirely different set of rules may apply that have been adapted to suit the particular circumstances of time and place.

I am not suggesting that shared streets should be implemented globally right away. Rather, the point is to demonstrate that governance without government intervention is certainly possible in an area where many would find that surprising. And I don't claim that we could apply it safely overnight in the congested streets of Midtown Manhattan.[19] But with the success of shared streets, it may be easier now to imagine that someday we could. And with the concepts of tacit rules governing the traffic commons, it's easier to understand how it would work.

3.1.2   Sandy Springs, Georgia

Often, the problems a town might face are more narrowly financial. Although it's not unusual for some towns to contract with private providers for a limited number of municipal services, the town of Sandy Springs, Georgia, population about 94,000 in 2012, voted to privatize nearly all its services. According to its website:

> The city of Sandy Springs pioneered the Public-Private Partnership model for service delivery in 2005, using a private sector partner to provide general city services including Public Works, Community Development, Finance, IT, Communications, Recreation and Parks, Municipal Court, and Economic Development. With the exception of public safety personnel – police and fire – only eight members of the City Manager's executive staff were "city" employees.[20]

And according to the *New York Times*:

---

[19] Moody and Melia (2014) find that "some of the claims made on behalf of shared space have overstated the available evidence, and that caution is needed in implementing shared space schemes, particularly in environments of high traffic flows."

[20] On their website: https://www.sandyspringsga.gov/public-private-partnership. Accessed 14 May 2023.

To grasp how unusual this is, consider what Sandy Springs does *not* have. It does not have a fleet of vehicles for road repair, or a yard where the fleet is parked. It does not have long-term debt. It has no pension obligations. It does not have a city hall, for that matter, if your idea of a city hall is a building owned by the city. Sandy Springs rents.

The town *does* have a conventional police force and fire department, in part because the insurance premiums for a private company providing those services were deemed prohibitively high. But its 911 dispatch center is operated by a private company, iXP, with headquarters in Cranbury, N.J. (Segal, 2012)

In 2019 Sandy Springs elected to move from privately contracted services back to city-provided municipal services—retaining under private contract only Municipal Court Solicitors, City Attorney, and Non-Emergency Call Center—because it estimated a significant cost savings from doing so. So rather than sticking slavishly to one model or another, Sandy Springs uses whichever approach, or a combination of the two, it deems works best. Ultimately, then, flexibility may be the bottom-line virtue of their approach to governance, a willingness and ability to choose for-profit or not-for-profit provision of traditional municipal services as circumstances change.

You could argue that this flexibility to combine private operation with public governance works because Sandy Springs is a small town of about 94,000 persons. But if New York City were to first adopt a Jacobsian approach of subsidiarity, in which a district governments were granted the authority to provide a larger or smaller set of services under its jurisdiction, a genuine public-private solution (not to be confused with the PPP I critiqued in Chap. 8) might be scalable and workable alternative for certain of its funding problems.[21]

What other strategies might larger municipalities with deeper economic and social pathologies pursue?

---

[21] Not all such experiments have had Sandy Springs's success. Maywood, California, a town of about 27,000 persons, seems to have been unable to solve problems of poor financial practices, political corruption, and other civic maladies by contracting out. In this case, however, the reason for failure may lie elsewhere than with privatization. See Vives and Elmahrek (2018).

3.1.3   Cayalá, Guatemala City[22]

Guatemala City is a city of well over two million and growing. Outwardly, the capital of Guatemala is a vibrant metropolis with big-city traffic problems set amidst lush ravines in a mountain rain forest. On the street, however, it is a different story. Decades of civil war, natural disasters, and violent drug trafficking have left its public spaces dangerous places. Drivers tint their car windows black, and businesses large and small hire shotgun-wielding guards, all in the midst of an economy in which poverty exceeds 50 percent. As a result, genuine street life is rare and limited to a few promisingly emergent areas of the city. These include "Sixth Avenue" in Zone One, the oldest part of the city that was mostly abandoned after a terrible earthquake in 1976, and a few gentrifying streets in Zone Four. Less organic prosperity can be found in the lavish Oakland Mall in the safer (though still dangerous) Zone Ten, a.k.a. "Zona Viva."

Guatemala City, then, is a good candidate for some form of urban revitalization.

Amid this economic and social pathology, or rather on its outskirts, lies the New Urbanist development of Cayalá, designed by famed architect Léon Krier, who I have mentioned a few times before. Despite being designated "Ciudad Cayalá" or "Cayalá City"[23] on its website, a city it is not, at least not in the Jacobsian sense. It is at best a possible beginning of a major city revitalization project, a dramatic approach to a chronic urban problem, planned eventually to reach hundreds of hectares. Krier is one of the pioneers of New Urbanism, which I discussed in the last chapter, and it will be revealing to compare and contrast his ideas to that of Jacobs and Market Urbanism.

Some of Krier's ideas overlap Jacobs's. For example, he favors walkability over drivability (Krier, 2007: 128),[24] places similar value on street corners, intersections, and mixed uses, although more of the secondary diversity type than primary use (Ibid: 125), recognizes that "the feeling of

---

[22] This section draws from Ikeda (2022).

[23] See the official website for Cayalá, https://www.cayala.com/. Accessed 14 May 2023.

[24] Although even here he differs from Jacobs, who does not completely eschew cars or impose a strict norm as Krier does of "the pedestrian must have access to all the usual daily and weekly urban functions within ten minutes' walking distance, without recourse to transport" (Krier, 2007: 128).

security in public spaces increases with the efficiency and density of the street pattern" (Ibid: 129), appreciates the "fractal geometry" of urban patterns (Ibid: 131), values the dispersal of public and civic functions throughout urban quarters (Ibid: 155), warns against placing border vacuums (without using this term) in the midst of the urban core (Ibid: 129), and voices disdain for functional zoning (Ibid: 19).

Krier also favors the reform of traffic regulations in a way that appeals to advocates of shared streets: "The speed of vehicles should be controlled not by signs and technical gadgets (humps, traffic islands, crash barriers, traffic lights, etc.) but by the civic and urban character of streets and squares that is created by their geometric configuration, their profile, paving, planting, lighting, street furniture, and architecture" (Krier, 2007: 151, 130).

But Léon Krier is renowned for his adamant rejection of twentieth-century architectural modernism and city planning. Instead, he advocates a return to what he considers a more human-scale, traditional architecture that employs time-honored materials and techniques and an ethos that pays tributes to a location's history and character (Krier, 2007). One might think of Krier's architectural aesthetic (in contrast to his explicit design philosophy) as an emergent phenomenon that has withstood the test of time.[25] Thus:

Architecture finds its highest expression in the classical orders: a legion of geniuses could not improve them any more than they could improve the human body or its skeleton" (Krier, 2007: 179) [...] The generating principles of traditional architecture seem to have the same inexhaustible capacity for creating new and unique buildings and towns. The classical notions of stability and timelessness are clearly linked to the life-span of humanity—they are not metaphysical and abstract absolutes. In this context the age of the principle is irrelevant. (Krier, 2007: 183)

---

[25] Krier does write that "Traditional architecture is a pure invention of the mind (2007: 181)" but by this we might take him to mean that "It has greater universality than language for its elements are comprehensible to people everywhere without translation" (2007: 181). So in inventing new applications for traditional architecture, traditional architecture draws on a vocabulary that has emerged over time.

For Krier a successful city's morphology cannot be spontaneous but instead requires careful guidance by precise land-use and building regulations because "The beauty of an ensemble, of a city or landscape, represents an extremely vulnerable and fragile state of balance" (Krier, 2007: 207). Constructing and supporting this fragile balance requires strict adherence to a "masterplan" devised by a master architect and enforced by local authorities. In other words, Krier's ideal city must be "a work of art."

I am not qualified to comment on the aesthetics of Krier's architectural designs per se except perhaps to say that I personally like them very much, and that if I were planning to build, say, a villa of my own or a "mixed-use" development, I would seriously consider hiring a Krierian architect. I would not, however, wish him to attempt to build a living city in this way, which I regard to be literally impossible. But for Krier, a high degree of designed complexity is essential to achieve the urban norms of beauty, livability, and humane values he esteems in traditional cities. How should this be done? Krier begins with a masterplan.[26]

> The masterplan is to the construction of a city what the constitution is to the life of a nation. It is much more than a specialized technical instrument and is *the expression of an ethical and artistic vision.* (Krier, 2007: 113; emphasis added)

The masterplan to create this work of art has five major parts:

1. A plan of the city, defining the size and form of its urban quarters and parks, the network of major avenues and boulevards.
2. A plan of each quarter, defining the network of streets, squares and blocks.
3. The form of the individual plots on each urban block: number, shape and function of floors that can be built.

---

[26] It should be noted that the renowned urban planner Alain Bertaud is critical of many masterplan approaches, not because they are unnecessary but because of the overwhelming tendency on the part of politicians and urban planning departments to assume their job is done once the masterplan is in place and implemented. Bertaud argues that planning and implementation have to be monitored in an ongoing and data-driven process, not a one-and-done effort (2018: 353–72). This implies that a masterplan has to be simple enough for the relevant data to be effectively gathered.

4. The architectural code describing materials, technical configurations, proportions for external building elements (walls, roofs, windows, doors, porticoes and porches, garden walls, chimneys) and all built elements that are visible from public spaces.
5. A code for public spaces, defining the materials, configurations, techniques and designs for paving, street furniture, signage, lighting and planting. (Krier, 2007: 113)

The first two points of the plan are common to most municipal masterplans. The third appears reasonable, but the devil is in the details, as we will see shortly. The best examples of the fourth and fifth points can be found in districts of historic preservation and theme parks.

A city cannot be left in the hands of those of the market process, since "It is everywhere evident that private developers, private foundations and institutions, however well-intentioned, are incapable of building and preserving public spaces that are in any way the equal of European historic centers" (Krier, 2007: 117). Krier seems to take it for granted that government authorities implementing the masterplan will act largely in the interest of ordinary city dwellers and like Jacobs seems to assume that the government will be strong but limited, with effective state capacity. As a result, Krier like Jacobs appears to overlook how political interests will impact their policy advocacy.

Now, some details. Krier would ban most one-way streets (Krier, 2007: 163) because they promote vehicular interests over pedestrians; limit buildings to five stories to preserve human scale (Ibid: 157); and prohibit setbacks for buildings to preserve the visual distinction between public and private (Ibid: 139) and "the differentiation in scale, materials and volumes must be justified by the type and civic status of buildings and should not depend on the *mere fancy* of the architect or the owner or on purely technical imperatives" (Ibid: 141; emphasis added), unless perhaps approved by the Master Architect. The list goes on.

And unlike Jacobs, he would place strict limits on the size of a city.

Exactly like an individual who has reached maturity, a "mature" city cannot grow bigger or spread out (vertically or horizontally) without losing its essential quality. Just like a family of individuals, a city can grow only by reproduction and multiplication, that is, by becoming polycentric and polynuclear. (Krier, 2007: 124)[27]

That is, a city should grow by "reproduction" and "multiplication." The basic unit of urban growth should be the "urban quarter," from which the city expands modularly with an increase in population. Each urban quarter must be relatively autonomous, providing most of the services its inhabitants would typically require in a week, such as schools and grocery shopping, at no more than a ten-minute walk (Krier, 2007: 128).[28] In addition, Krier would ban buildings taller than five-stories to prevent "upward sprawl." The only way to achieve this result, according to Krier, is through a masterplan that caps building heights, mandates materials and construction methods, and dictates the size and location of public spaces as well as land-uses, especially secondary uses. Thus, Cayalá appears to be an attempt to revitalize Guatemala City by deliberately transforming it, quarter by quarter, into a "ten-minute city."

At the moment, however, Cayalá strikes one as an exclusive enclave for the wealthy, ungated but difficult to reach and too expensive to be much use for the majority of Guatemala City's poor. It appears to be another case of cataclysmic money, with the attendant visual, social, and economic homogeneity. And for now, safety and security seem to rely less on human "eyes on the street" and more on technological surveillance,[29] which is understandable given the high crime rates in the surrounding areas but not encouraging from the point of view of self-governance.

---

[27] As will become clear in a moment, "polycentricity" for as Krier uses the word is based on the idea that a city should consist of largely "autonomous" economic units in which residents should be able to obtain most of the weekly services they need within easy walking distance. For Jacobs "polycentric" refers to a subsidiarity-based administrative structure within the city as a whole. A city quarter in Krier's sense could be polycentrically administered, but he does not, at least in Krier (2007), argue for this administrative structure.

[28] This implicit structure reflects what Christopher Alexander would characterize as a "tree"—in which there is a hierarchy of uses without functional overlap—rather than a "semi-lattice" that allows for overlapping land-uses characteristic of actual, living cities (Alexander, 1965). And it also bears close resemblance to the currently popular idea of a "15-minute city"—see the website for this concept at https://www.15minutecity.com/. Accessed 14 May 2023.

[29] See https://www.asmag.com/showpost/24205.aspx. Accessed 14 May 2023. Extensive surveillance and policing is, as Jacobs noted, indicative of community failure.

Nevertheless, such level of control over design is profoundly at odds with the liberal Jacobsian and Market Urbanist approaches, despite being touted as "a public space created by the private sector."[30]

To succeed in the coming years as a living city, Cayalá must be knit into the rest of the urban fabric of Guatemala City and cannot remain an exclusive enclave. I have been told that this is just the beginning of a plan for quarter-by-quarter expansion over time and that for locals Cayalá is a kind of oasis and hopeful example of what is possible in this poverty-stricken country via private financing.[31] Perhaps time will tell. Likely, in the end it will become something very different from what its designers intended, which because a prime characteristic of a living city is its inherent unpredictability, could be a good thing.[32]

But a universal application of the Krierian approach to city building would not create a world of traditional cities; it would, on the contrary, undermine the dynamic processes that foster the kinds of beauty and values that future generations would venerate, in the same way Krier and people like myself today venerate the built achievements of a messy and spontaneous urban past. The problem with Krier's characterization of the urban problem is that it focuses too much on the form (e.g., skyscrapers, glass curtains, etc.) and not enough on what we have seen is the experimental, unplanned, unpredictable, and innovative, wealth-generating nature of a truly great city. The result, as Jacobs might say, is taxidermy.

3.2   City Building: Charter Cities and Startup Societies

Economist Mançur Olson argues that in a stable society certain people with common interests tend over time to organize groups to protect their status by crafting legal privileges for themselves, i.e., to engage in "rent

---

[30] Héctor Leal, engineer and general manager of the Cayalá project, quoted in "Crean ciudad privada" para los ricos en Guatemala" por ROMINA RUIZ-GOIRIENA, Associated Press, January 8, 2013.

[31] A colleague, an architect on the Cayalá project, related both the expansion plans and confirmation that the financing is totally private, although the city operates the streets and the developers work with city government for public thoroughfares.

[32] For a rosier evaluation of Cayalá by the Congress of the New Urbanism, see Steuteville (2021).

seeking" (Olson, 1984). This creates barriers between socioeconomic pathologies (e.g., crime, corruption, housing unaffordability) and their possible cures (e.g., regime change, land-use liberalization) that are difficult or impossible to dismantle from within. In such cases trying to work within the system is highly uncertain and if attempted likely to be disruptive economically and socially. Public protests, sometimes violent, could result. Examples aren't hard to find. Fundamental reform might also take place as a result of a systemic crisis, but the outcome could go either way (Ikeda, 1997).

In the past this has led some to pursue the risky, but potentially easier, route of establishing new settlements to start afresh. Historical examples include medieval *bastides*, colonies, or the spread of ancient Greek *polei* (Vance, 1990: 178; Gebel, 2018; Kitto, 1951; Pirenne, 1980). This is the motivation behind the so-called "Startup Society" movement. Rather than trying to reform entangled politico-economic systems within existing cities, the "city building" approach advocates basically starting from scratch.

3.2.1   Charter Cities

Paul Romer, winner of the 2018 Nobel Prize in economics, has proposed "Charter Cities" to jump-start chronically underdeveloped economies.

The Charter Cities[33] concept derives from the experience of politically autonomous cities, such as Hong Kong, located in countries other than their source of governance. The economic success of Hong Kong, a former British colony established on the Chinese mainland that was handed over to the People's Republic of China in 1997, spurred the PRC to create "Special Economic Zones" with "more liberal economic laws than those typically prevailing in the country" (Zeng, 2012), such as Shenzhen and Zhouhai. It also inspired Romer's Charter Cities concept. With the "host" country's blessing (e.g., the People's Republic of China), an economically developed "guarantor" country (e.g., Great Britain) or group of guarantor countries establishes a market-friendly legal framework

---

[33] See the Charter Cities website at https://chartercitiesinstitute.org/intro/. Accessed 14 May 2023.

patterned after their own, as well as some physical infrastructure, on leased territory in the host country. With the promise of a stable, market-friendly legal environment, the guarantors then arrange for private business investment from abroad to create jobs and housing for locals and immigrants in the Charter City.[34]

Charter Cities promise rapid economic development by allowing a portion of a less economically developed country to start off with a clean slate. The goal is to sidestep obstacles to reforming a system entangled in entrenched interests, excessive restrictions on business and immigration, and unpredictable political intrusions into domestic life. The concept promises a legal system already proven elsewhere that provides a relatively liberal economic environment along with the physical infrastructure necessary for economic development. It also holds the possibility of inculcating norms of behavior sympathetic to entrepreneurship, openness, and trade. Populated by those who self-select for ambition, tolerance, resourcefulness, and energy, a Charter City is seen as a way to more quickly and effectively overcome the challenges that typically block economic development.

But a Charter City confronts several other challenges, even assuming a host country and an agreeable foreign guarantor government can be paired. First, the entire concept smacks of colonialism, even if the host is not pressured to invite the guarantor government in. Suppose the concept is successful and gains popularity among governments worldwide. It is easy to imagine some governments chartering cities not to promote the economic interests of the citizens of the host and guarantor countries but strategically to invest in such cities for geopolitical reasons. Indeed, it seems naïve to think it would not be so. Similarly, such a scheme would seem to be vulnerable to rent-seeking businesses and politicians who vie for privileged investment positions in the provision of infrastructure or in establishing new businesses. On the other hand, there is the threat of "post-contractual opportunism" by the host government—i.e., appropriating the fixed assets of foreign investors—especially should the Charter

---

[34] Honduras began to implement the Charter City concept, although it ran into difficulties early on. See *The Economist* (2017) at https://www.economist.com/the-americas/2017/08/12/honduras-experiments-with-charter-cities. Accessed 14 May 2023.

City become, as it is hoped, a successful enterprise. From that perspective, private companies and productive workers would look like attractive cash cows to exploitive host countries. More seriously, if the host acts opportunistically toward investors who have sunk large sums in location-specific investments—say, by threatening to nationalize businesses—what response should we expect from the guarantor countries? Harsh language? An armada of warships? Indeed, the mere threat of this kind of opportunism could prevent the project from getting off the ground or getting very far if it does.

Finally, the Charter City proposal has troubling rationalist constructivist overtones. That is, we have seen that trying to design a complex system confronts Jacobs's problem of organized complexity. As with those of mice and men, the best-laid plans of even benevolent planners, to quote Robert Burns, "gang oft agly." How the host and guarantor countries respond to plan failure is critical, and their responses will probably be driven as much by political expediency as by considerations of the general welfare.[35]

3.2.2 Startup Societies[36]

The distinction between governance and government is especially relevant to proposals by classical liberal/libertarian thinkers who would like to see social cooperation and social order rely as much as possible on arrangements that do not entail governmental authority, even where the provision of infrastructure (e.g., roads, sewers, public safety) or the corresponding capabilities (e.g., mobility, waste removal, security) is concerned. The term "Startup Society" is sometimes used for specific approaches within this movement, but with apologies I will use this term generically to include various proposals such as "seasteading" and "free

---

[35] Appendix 2 to this chapter contains notes from a conversation with Alain Bertaud on the practical challenges of establishing Charter City-like settlements.

[36] There are many other challenges raised against Startup Societies than I discuss. Frazier and McKinney (2019) respond with possible solutions to many of them. My aim here is to focus on the deeper conceptual issues. Urban economist Vera Kichanova's as yet unpublished Ph.D. dissertation (Kichanova, 2022) takes a deep dive into the theory and current practice with respect to what she terms "free cities."

private cities." Each entail somewhat different financial arrangements—private investment versus government spending, purely voluntary associations versus governmental guarantors—and even within the private-investment approach some are more focused on marketing and profit-seeking while others explicitly prioritize liberty and autonomy,[37] although these ends are to some degree complementary. One example of the former is to treat a liberal "free city" as a commodity. As the father of seasteading Patri Friedman puts it (Friedman, 2019), why not treat "a city like an iPhone?" Another is an extension of the Charter City concept without the heavy reliance on guarantor governments.

To my knowledge, Jacobs has nothing to say about startup societies in general.[38] Nevertheless, I think the approaches are highly germane to Jacobsian social theory and economics.

Free Private Cities

As Frazier and McKinney (2019) describe them:

> Proponents of Free Private Cities advocate for-profit startup communities, where instead of paying taxes, individuals and companies would pay fees to a for-profit company. Free Private Cities are similar to Private Residential Communities in the way they manage infrastructure and services privately. Unlike a traditional private community, Free Private Cities would not just adopt the rules of the host jurisdiction. The city governs itself with its own charter document, rather than by a general law of a surrounding host government. Free Private Cities put a large emphasis on safeguarding personal liberty and property rights. (Frazier & McKinney, 2019: Loc. 1021–25)

Their independence from a guarantor government is the main difference from the original Charter City concept. This is true of seasteads, as well, but with a twist.

---

[37] Titus Gebel, for example, addresses his free city concept "for those who want to achieve liberty and self-determination during their lifetimes, but who have recognized that any transformation of existing systems from the inside is difficult to impossible" (Gebel, 2018).

[38] For a handbook on implementing a Startup Society, see Frazier & McKinney (2019). Gebel (2018) describes a free private city proposal and offers several examples of free cities throughout history, with particular emphasis on the German region.

Seasteading

Seasteads aim to be autonomous floating communities on the ocean, experimenting with new policies and institutional practices. Seasteads with modular designs would have a "dynamic geography" so residents can easily "detach" (i.e., exit) and form new communities.[39] The intended result is improving choice in governance and legal systems. Seasteads are meant to be a scalable form of an integrated Startup Society and offer depoliticized environments inspired by examples set in Free Economic Zones, such as Hong Kong (until recently) and private residential communities. Many seasteaders favor permanent dwellings outside any political jurisdictions, a reflection of a lack of faith that true variation in governance can occur on land.

The concept has evolved over time. The seasteading community now favors a gradualist approach that seeks host nations with which to partner in creating a free economic zone — a "SeaZone" — in their territorial waters. There, floating communities could provide tax-free or low-fee conditions for residents and businesses. In parallel, "LandZone" options would exist for local champions to gain free zone incentives for their own ventures on dry land. These initiatives hope to boost economic activity and awaken dormant assets in the SeaZone and LandZone areas (Frazier & McKinney, 2019: Loc. 1046–50). Currently, one such LandZone is being built in Roatán, Honduras.[40]

I believe Jacobs would share my reservations about any scheme that claims to build new "cities." Still, one of the purposes of *Death and Life* is "to introduce new principles of city planning and rebuilding" (Jacobs, 1961: 3). For Jacobs some of these include fostering multiple attractors to generate a greater diversity of land-use to lay the groundwork for a dynamic, complex divisions of labor, import replacement and shifting, and innovation. If the aim of Startup Societies is to create a dynamic city of innovation, I believe the chances of success increases if its proponents keep to these general principles and, most importantly, always remember

[39] For further details on seasteading, see the website of the Seasteading Institute at https://www.seasteading.org/. Accessed 14 May 2023.
[40] For the latest information on Prosperá, see their website at https://prospera.hn/. Accessed 14 May 2023.

that such a city is a spontaneous order, not a work of art. The concept of a Startup Society or free city is revolutionary, but its execution should be evolutionary. As Titus Gebel, an advocate for "free private cities," states:

> A private city is not a utopian, constructivist idea. Instead, it is simply a known business model applied to another sector, the market of living together. In essence, the operator is a mere service provider, establishing and maintaining the framework within which the society can develop, open-ended, with no predefined goal. (Gebel, 2016)

Such a settlement will tend to attract ideologically committed seekers of freedom, but what it will really need are people with diverse human capital, willing to work exceptionally hard. Fewer intellectuals, more people who can get things done. It will need people with complementary talents and tastes with the willingness and ability to fit them together. But it is not possible to know how all this will look down the road, because we don't know who will come and who will stay or what unexpected "pools of effective economic use" might be generated, a delight to some an offense to others. So, the gradual, modular approach, to the extent that the infrastructure is scalable,[41] is far preferable to the original Charter City mindset.

Some would approach a Startup Society as a business venture. I am uncomfortable with that idea, especially if the goal is to foster a living city and not simply a place to spend wealth we create somewhere else. If a living city is a spontaneous order then, as Gebel recognizes, it has no specific purpose, even to make a profit.

For example, if all the land of a settlement is owned by a single entity, where the users are leaseholders, then governance could be private, and as argued by anthropologist Spencer McCallum (1970), positive and negative externalities could mostly be internalized, as in a hotel or shopping mall. Certainly, hotels and malls turn a profit, and there is no reason why

---

[41] Among the unscalable infrastructure at present are airports, deep-water ports, sewer plants, water supply systems, main roads, and major administrative and social facilities. The last items might be scalable to the extent governance is done according to subsidiarity. It is worth exploring the extent to which the others might be scalable in an open-water setting à la seasteading. Again, it might be more helpful to think in terms of capabilities than specific kinds of infrastructure.

a settlement planned along the lines of McCallum or Friedman might not also, say, based on revenue from increasing land rents. In marketing terms, it makes sense to sell or lease the real estate as a commodity. But the city itself—the interaction of the physical and social—cannot be a commodity.

On the whole, then, I find the city-as-a-business concept to be off the mark. Friedman has said he appreciates that "something is lost" when treating a city in this way, something like "local identity" (Friedman, 2019), but it is more than that. What I fear is losing something closer to "civic culture," where genuine innovation and creativity thrive on messiness and livable congestion—where order stays just ahead of chaos. A "Startup Society as iPhone" is more Club Med than living city.

3.3   Other Examples of Startup Societies

Three other experiments deserve mention. The first is about as close to a fully spontaneously emergent city as you will find in modern times, notable for its rapid economic development and messiness. The second and third are examples of the exact opposite: mega-projects more in the line of Le Corbusier. The latter is currently under construction and just goes to show that Cartesian rationalism is indeed alive and well today.

3.3.1   Gurgaon, India

Gurgaon is a private city with massive problems. Despite all that, it has been strikingly successful.

In this city that barely existed two decades ago, there are 26 shopping malls, seven golf courses and luxury shops selling Chanel and Louis Vuitton. Mercedes-Benzes and BMWs shimmer in automobile showrooms. Apartment towers are sprouting like concrete weeds, and a futuristic commercial hub called Cyber City houses many of the world's most respected corporations. Gurgaon, located about 15 miles south of the national capital, New Delhi, would seem to have everything, except consider what it does not have: a functioning citywide sewer or drainage system; reliable electricity or water; and public sidewalks, adequate parking, decent roads or any citywide system of public transportation. Garbage is still regularly tossed in empty lots by the side of the road.

With its shiny buildings and galloping economy, Gurgaon is often portrayed as a symbol of a rising "new" India, yet it also represents a riddle at the heart of India's rapid growth: how can a new city become an international economic engine without basic public services? [...] In Gurgaon and elsewhere in India, the answer is that growth usually occurs despite the government rather than because of it. (Yardley, 2011)

Economists Alex Tabarrok and Shruti Rajagopalan, however, put these maladies in perspective. For example, while Gurgaon lacks a cohesive urban plan, "urban growth has vastly outpaced planning efforts in almost all Indian cities" and not Gurgaon, alone. Overall, Indian municipalities fail to provide effective infrastructure to their citizens (Tabarrok & Rajagopalan, 2015: 216). And while "public sewage provision in Gurgaon is appalling and in marked contrast to its gleaming private residences and workplaces, it is actually of above average quality by Indian standards" (Ibid).

Is Gurgaon a viable model for a Startup Society? Perhaps its most important function is to demonstrate that such a thing is even possible when no one thought it was. Or to put it another way, if the goal is to build apparently unscalable infrastructure—such as city-wide sewers and water provision, unified street grids, and so on—then using the political power of government may the most feasible, perhaps the only solution. But if the goal is to provide waste disposal, clean water, mobility, and so on, then Gurgaon demonstrates that this may not require massive, city-wide infrastructure investment.

Again, framing the problem in terms of capabilities rather than concrete assets can lead to finding solutions outside conventional planning strategies. Using conventional means in the past to achieve concrete objectives may have been efficient from a static point of view, that may not be the most useful approach to city planning in the future. This is true especially (1) if it comes with an easily corruptible, politically ossified administrative structure and (2) if, as in the case of Gurgaon, the city and the opportunities it creates would not have emerged within such a governance structure.

Taking a cue from the startup cities approach, instead of undertaking city building by first constructing a large government infrastructure, the solution may be to do just the opposite. As Tabarrok and Rajagopalan observe, Gurgaon suffers from a "tragedy of the commons," in which it is land that belongs to no one in particular that gets polluted the most. Dumping doesn't take place on private land (Tabarrok & Rajagopalan, 2015: 2020). From an economic perspective, the best way to address commons problems such as this is not to restrict private activity but to clearly define and enforce rights to private property. That way, we can avoid those problems in the first place through trade in land markets. In other words, where market imperfections exist in the form of negative externalities or lack of public goods, the solution may be to allow more, not less, private initiative to address them.[42]

3.3.2   Dubai, UAE, and Neom The Line

Here I will briefly mention two current megaprojects (the second probably qualifies as a true "giga-project"), both in the Arab world, that serve as excellent foils to Jacobsian urbanism: one begun earlier this century and other breaking ground as I write this. I will show my hand right now and say that if either is completed as planned, which is unlikely, it will at best be as a playground for the superrich, not as a living city.

Dubai's Island Archipelagos
In an effort to diversify its economy from petroleum exports, early in this century Sheikh Mohammed bin Rashid Al Maktoum led the creation of a free-trade zone to entice foreign investment, immigration, and economic expansion in Dubai, United Arab Emirates. According to Michael Strong and Robert Himber, "Dubai's ruler decided that the best strategy for jump-starting a world-class global financial hub would be to create a

---

[42] I would recommend the curious reader explore the large literature on the private provision of public goods, starting with economist Steven Cheung's pioneering article, "The Fable of the Bees" (Cheung, 1973).

legal environment based on British common law" (Strong & Himber 2009: 37), somewhat along the lines of a Charter City, though without the obligatory outside-guarantor country. In tandem with this change in legal structure, Dubai's planners embarked on a large-scale construction project unique in the history of modern city building: the creation of multiple sets of artificial archipelagos so large they could be seen from space—Google it and see for yourself—dubbed "Palm Islands."

Each Palm Island forms an outline in the shape of a stylized palm tree. The central trunk contains hotels, retail, and activity centers, and on each of the multiple fronds emanating from it are residential spaces for dozens of mansion-sized luxury dwellings priced in the millions of dollars. A crescent surrounds the islands to serve as a water break.

Construction of the first Island began in 2003 with Palm Jumeirah, which is now mostly completed, with a residential population of more than 10,000. Two even bigger Palm Islands were planned, with one, Palm Jebel Ali, now reportedly nearing completion after a years-long delay attributed to the 2008–2009 financial crisis (Arab Business, 2023). The other, Palm Deira, is still on the drawing board. If completed the Palms would have a surface area measuring over 60 square kilometers, about the size of Manhattan, New York. One other project, "The World"—consisting of clusters of some 300 islands each roughly the shape of a nation-state that together form a political map of the world—is planned to have 9.3 square kilometers of surface but was slowed by natural, financial, and legal problems (Burbano, 2022).

These islands were built for the rich and superrich and were never intended to be a city in any real sense. The entire project might best be described as a playground suburb built to serve tourism in the city of Dubai and as real a city as Disneyland.

Having built it, they may come, but will they stay? Probably not.

Neom, The Line
The Crown Prince of Saudi Arabia, Mohammed bin Salman (often referred to by his initials "MBS"), is also strategizing for a post-oil future for his country. But unlike Dubai's massive Club Med-like constructions, the Crown Prince's ambition is to build an actual city, dubbed Neom,

from a clean slate in a largely "uninhabited" desert region of his country. The official website for the project states MBS's grand vision:

> NEOM is an accelerator of human progress that will embody the future of innovation in business, livability and sustainability.
>
> NEOM offers many unique investment opportunities of different sizes across multiple industries.

According to the website,[43] "The Line" is only a single part of Neom,[44] but The Line intended to be the "city."

The Line's dimensions are truly breathtaking. It consists of a pair of parallel mirrored walls 200 meters apart, each 500 meters tall (taller than the Empire State Building), and extending eastward into the desert for 170 kilometers (100 miles)! The anticipated population when completed is nine million, the population of New York City. So instead of Le Corbusier's "towers in the park," we will have towering "mirrors in the desert."

The estimated cost of the entire Neom project is $500 billion, but some current estimates place that figure closer to $1 trillion, more than the current gross domestic product of Saudi Arabia. Excavation began in 2022 starting with The Line, while some attractions are scheduled to open as early as 2024, with the rest completed by 2030 (Jones, 2022).

The signs are not encouraging. As reported by *The Economist* magazine,

> Despite the high salaries, there are reports that foreigners [i.e. foreign consultants] are leaving the Neom project because they find the gap between expectations and reality so stressful. The head of Neom is said by his friends to be "terrified" at the lack of progress. (Pelham, 2022)

The Line can only exist as envisioned if it somehow manages to constrain the spontaneous complexity that will constantly push against its

---

[43] See the official website for Neom, The Line here: https://www.neom.com/en-us/regions/theline. Accessed 1 April 2023.
[44] Neo for "new" and M for the first initial of the Arabic word "Mustaqbal" for "future" and also for the first initial of MBS.

rigid design parameters, in which case it will drain the life out of the city and stunt its development. If successful as a utopia, it will fail as a city. Few want to live (and stay) in a place just because it has breathtaking architecture or boasts a superfast and sustainable transport system. What attracts us are the people there we hope to live and work with.

While The Line raises many obvious questions—Why a line? Who could afford to live there? Where will food come from and at what cost? Who will be displaced by the construction? How will this mirrored barrier affect wildlife and their migration?—our concern is with the problem of adaption with this construction. If it gets built, who or what determines where we should live or work, and how will the space constraint (as large as it is) adjust to the ever-changing needs of the population and the land-uses and densities that result? Will ordinary people even have much choice in the matter? How could they, given the intricacy, scale, and complexity of the imposed design?

Cartesian Rationalism, Again

Rather than dwell on the details of these constructions, let me simply remind the reader of the consequences of building so quickly on so massive a scale, where these include border vacuums, cataclysmic money, and pretended order substituting for emergent order. The trade-off between designed complexity and the spontaneous complexity of real, living cities that we have applied to Le Corbusier, Krier, etc., based on Jacobsian and Market Urbanist principles, applies no less to these contemporary schemes.

Though vastly different on the surface, these projects and some others discussed in this chapter are but manifestations of the same Cartesian rationalism that expands the range of decision-making to the point where S-judgments destructively displace O-judgments. They are high modernist utopias with a post-(or pre-)modernist veneer. And while their proponents may express concern with urban livability, sustainability, equity, and so on, there is scant appreciation for creative diversity, for messy trial and error, or for what we can learn about economics and social theory from Jane Jacobs.

4   What Then Might a City Be?

The nation-state is a relatively recent invention, a latecomer in the history of civilization (Parker, 2004). City and empire are far older. Political philosopher Pierre Manent, in his *Metamorphosis of the City*, writes:

> The two great political forms, the two mother forms of the ancient world, are the city and the empire. They are the mother forms, but they are also the polar forms: the city is the narrow framework of a restless life in liberty; the empire is the immense domain of a peaceful life under a master. (Manent, 2013: 105)

City-states have been around a long time, indeed.[45]

It would be folly to try to predict with any precision the global development of politico-economic systems, and the complex urban entities that will constitute them, decades from now. One trend may be a continuation of the age-old dream of political consolidation and the merging of nations into a global empire or super-state. But empires fade, while their capitals—Beijing, Athens, Rome, Cairo, Guatemala City, Baghdad, and London—live on. We have witnessed in modern times powerful forces of political disintegration, with the breakup of the Soviet Union and the exit of Great Britain from the European Union.[46] Those predicting the (re)emergence and dominion of the sovereign city-state could be right should these trends continue, heralded perhaps by the Startup Society movement or inspired by the city-states of Singapore, Dubai, and Monaco, which happen to be among the richest places in the world. There are economic forces at work here. As author and journalist Matt Ridley observes,

---

[45] A classic history of the city-state is Spruyt (1994).

[46] See, for example, the reporting on this trend here https://aeon.co/essays/the-end-of-a-world-of-nation-states-may-be-upon-us and here https://www.nytimes.com/1996/06/02/weekinreview/ideas-trends-the-return-of-the-city-state.html. Accessed 14 May 2023.

[such] fragmentation works best when it results in the creation of city states. These beasties have always been the best at incubating innovation: states dominated by a single city. (Ridley, 2020: 266)[47]

Independent, largely self-governing cities long preceded the ancient empires of China, India, Mesopotamia, and Egypt, just as they preceded the creation of the European states, centuries after the dissolution of the Roman Empire in the West (Pirenne, 1980; Weber, 1958; Vance, 1990). As we have noted, the city is a natural unit of economic analysis but evidently also of political governance. Historian Geoffrey Parker writes:

> Thus, ideally these nation-states are seen as being self-sustaining entities possessing their own independent internal structures. [...] However, analysis shows them to be largely artificial phenomena, the origins of which have lain in warfare and dynastic aspirations and the subsequent attempts of state governments to impose their own uniformity on pre-existing diversity. (Parker, 2004: 9)

Sociologist and historian Charles Tilly is blunter in his characterization of the nation-state:

> If protection rackets represent organized crime at its smoothest, then war making and state making – quintessential protection rackets with the advantage of legitimacy – qualify as our largest examples of organized crime. (Tilly, 1982: 169)

Contrary to Krier's notion of urban "maturity," cities have shown themselves to be "scale-free," capable of growth without upper bound in population, wealth, and other magnitudes that generally correlate with human well-being (as well as, of course, sometimes conflicts and disease).[48] The city has always been and will continue to be the driving force of

---

[47] Ridley also notes that "[o]ne of the peculiar features of history is that empires...are bad at innovation" (Ridley, 2020: 264).

[48] See, for example, the work of the Santa Fe Institute here https://www.santafe.edu/research/projects/cities-scaling-sustainability (accessed 14 May 2023) and reports on their work on the "superlinearity" of certain urban phenomena, also Krugman (1996).

cultural and economic change, even as the political authorities of nation-states have sought to contain it. But what can we say about the future?

Residents of a small, depopulated European town in 1000 CE, say Rome (population circa 25,000), would have had an accurate sense of what their "city" would look like and how it would operate in two or three generations, if they even bothered to wonder about such a thing. But residents of one of the growing number of new European settlements after the Treaty of Paris in 1229, *bastide* or imperial new town, would have had a harder time predicting the pattern of development in that same interval of time, even if the original settlement were planned very carefully. Just as Jacobs's hypothetical New Obsidian grew from a trading post into a large, diverse, and innovative city, new towns and the ancient cities in the Late Middle Ages would evolve in ways no one could have predicted nor in ways that everyone in them would have liked. The paths taken by the "once-startup societies" of Frankfurt am Main, Lübeck, Hamburg, Paris, Venice, and Hong Kong—their morphology, economy, society, culture, and politics—were and will continue to be inherently unpredictable, along with their progress or poverty, as long as they remain living cities.[49]

As we know, Jacobs herself proposes the careful disbanding of today's nation-states as a remedy for what she sees as the destabilizing and deadening economic consequences of the distorting feedback of national currencies and their exchange rates.

> The equivalent for a political unit would be to resist the temptation of engaging in transactions of decline by not trying to hold itself together. The radical discontinuity would thus be division of the single sovereignty into a family of smaller sovereignties, not after things had reached a stage of breakdown and disintegration, but long before while things were still going reasonably well. In a national society behaving like this, multiplication of sovereignties by division would be a normal, untraumatic accompaniment of economic development itself, and of the increasing complexity of economic and social life. Some of the sovereignties in the family would in their

---

[49] This open-endedness of urban evolution is nowhere more brilliantly illustrated on a smaller scale than the analysis of "Greene Street" in Lower Manhattan by development economist William Easterly. See this discussed at http://www.williameasterly.org/research. Accessed 14 May 2023.

turn divide as evidence of the need to do so appeared. A nation behaving like this would substitute for one great life force, sheer survival, that other great life force, reproduction.

As more of us appreciate the benefits or even the necessity of devolution, the transformation of nation-states into city-states or free cities, the highly improbable may become a reality. In this regard, I find the observation of Pasqual Maragall (the former Mayor of Barcelona) encouraging:

> A Europe, a world seen as a set of nations are [sic] slower, with more opposed languages, than a Europe and a world seen as a system of cities. Cities have no frontiers, no armies, no customs, no immigration officials. Cities are places for invention, for creativity, for freedom. (Quoted in Hughes (1992: 37))

What we can say about the living cities of the future, what they will be, is therefore extremely limited. Normatively, to ensure their continued existence, we can look to the kinds of things Jacobs points out, and that we have examined in this book, which are important, perhaps indispensable, ingredients for the emergence of complex social order, innovation, and prosperity, whatever forms these may take. Positively, there is even less we can say about how they will actually look or what they will feel like under our feet and nothing for certain about their morphology, culture, governance, or socioeconomic characteristics. The consequences of unpredictable changes in ethos, technology, demography, and political economy are of course themselves unpredictable.

But I will hazard to say that robust public spaces, even in the face of pandemics and other such traumas, will continue to manifest some form of Sasaki's urban tactility and Jacobs's intricate diversity, along with their necessary imperfections. Again, any living city will have things, perhaps very many things, to offend us. But by the same token, a living city of the future will have wonders, delights, and a greatness that we cannot now possibly imagine and that even its inhabitants will not fully appreciate.

354   S. Ikeda

Works Cited

Alexander, C. (1965). A City Is Not a Tree. *Architectural Forum, 122*(1), 58–62.

Arab Business. (2023, January 11). Dubai's Palm Jebel Ali in Final Stages of Construction, Nakheel Searching for Contractors: Report. https://www.arabianbusiness.com/industries/construction/dubais-palm-jebel-ali-in-final-stages-of-construction-nakheel-searching-for-contractors-report. Accessed 14 May 2023.

Beito, D. T., Gordon, P., & Tabarrok, A. (2002). *The Voluntary City: Choice, Community, and Civil Society*. Independent Institute.

Bertaud, A. (2018). *Order Without Design: How Markets Shape Cities*. MIT Press.

Beyer, S. (2022). *Market Urbanism: A Vision for Free Market Cities*. Market Urbanism Report.

Boettke, P. J. (1990). *The Political Economy of Soviet Socialism: The Formative Years, 1918-1928*. Kluwer Academic Publishers.

Burbano, L. (2022, October 18). What Happened to Dubai Man-Made Islands? *Tomorrow.City*. https://tomorrow.city/a/dubai-man-made-islands. Accessed 14 May 2023.

Cheung, S. (1973). The Fable of the Bees: An Economic Investigation. *The Journal of Law and Economics, 16*(1), 1–33.

de Jouvenel, B. (1956). Order Versus Organization. In M. Sennholz (Ed.), *On Freedom and Free Enterprise*. Van Nostrand.

Evans, P. B., Rueschemeyer, D., & Skocpol, T. (Eds.). (1985). *Bringing the State Back In*. Cambridge Univ. Press.

Frazier, M., & McKinney, J. (2019). *Founding Startup Societies a Step-by-Step Guide* (Kindle Edition). Creative Commons.

Friedman, P. (2019). Patri Friedman on Charter Cities, Investing, and Society. At Village Global Venture Stories, podcast: https://poddtoppen.se/podcast/1316769266/village-globals-venture-stories/patri-friedman-on-charter-cities-investing-and-society. Accessed 14 May 2023.

Gebel, T. (2016, April 22). Private Cities: A Path to Liberty. *The Freeman* Online. https://fee.org/articles/private-cities-a-path-to-liberty/?fbclid=IwAR0a43sBafXlbYeY8YK0vVoQJD28YWqC6sHCNQa4eG3ofiW8XFnMwfQ2Xcs. Accessed 14 May 2023.

Gebel, T. (2018). *Free Private Cities: Making Governments Compete for You*. Aquila Urbis. Kindle Edition.

Greif, A. (2006). *Institutions and the Path to the Modern Economy: Lessons from Medieval Trade*. Cambridge Univ. Press.

Hall, P. (1998). *Cities in Civilization*. Fromm International.

Hayek, F. A. (1942). Scientism and the Study of Society, Part I. *Economica, 9*(35), 267–291.

Hayek, F. A. (1944). *The Road to Serfdom*. Univ. of Chicago Press.

Hayek, F. A. (1948[1945]). The Use of Knowledge in Society. In *Individualism and Economic Order*. Univ. of Chicago Press.

Hayek, F. A. (1973). *Law, Legislation and Liberty: A New Statement of the Liberal Principles of Justice and Political Economy*. Univ. of Chicago Press.

Hayek, F. A. (1974). The Pretence of Knowledge. *Reprinted in American Economic Review, (1989), 79*(6), 3–7.

Hayek, F. A. (1978). The Errors of Constructivism. In *New Studies in Philosophy, Politics, Economics and the History of Ideas*. Univ. of Chicago Press.

Hughes, R. (1992). *Barcelona*. Vintage.

Ikeda, S. (1997). *Dynamics of the Mixed Economy: Toward a Theory of Interventionism*. Routledge.

Ikeda, S. (2022). Urban Planning and Urban Values. *Social Philosophy & Policy, 38*(2), 191–209.

Jacobs, J. (1961). *The Death and Life of Great American Cities*. Vintage.

Jacobs, J. (1969). *The Economy of Cities*. Vintage.

Jacobs, J. (1992). *Systems of Survival: A Dialogue on the Moral Foundations of Commerce and Politics*. Vintage Books.

Jacobs, J. (2000). *The Nature of Economies*. Modern Library.

Jacobs, J. (2004). *Dark Age Ahead*. Random House.

Jaffe, E. (2015, March 23). 6 Places Where Cars, Bikes, and Pedestrians All Share the Road as Equals. *Bloomberg CityLab*. https://www.bloomberg.com/news/articles/2015-03-23/6-places-where-cars-bikes-and-pedestrians-all-share-the-road-as-equals. Accessed 14 May 2023.

Jones, R. (2022, July 23). Inside Saudi Arabia's Plan to Build a Skyscraper that Stretches for 75 Miles. *The Wall Street Journal*. https://www.wsj.com/articles/inside-saudi-arabias-plan-to-build-a-skyscraper-that-stretches-for-75-miles-11658581201. Accessed 14 May 2023.

Karndacharuk, A., Wilson, D. J., & Dunn, R. (2014). A Review of the Evolution of Shared (street) Space Concepts in Urban Environments. *Transport Reviews, 34*(2), 190–220. https://doi.org/10.1080/01441647.2014.893038. Accessed 14 May 2023.

Kichanova, Vera (2022). Cities as Firms: The Coasian Case for Private Urban Development (Unpublished Ph.D. dissertation). Department of Political Economy, King's College London.

Kirzner, I. M. (1992). Prices, the Communication of Knowledge and the Discovery Process. In *The Meaning of the Market Process: Essays in the Development of Modern Austrian Economics*. Routledge.

Kitto, H.D.F. (1951). The Polis. Abridged in LeGates & Stout (1996).

Krier, L. (2007[1998]). *Architecture: Choice or Fate?* Papadakis Publisher.

Krugman, P. (1996). *The Self-Organizing Economy.* Wiley-Blackwell.

Lachmann, L. M. (1978). *Capital and Its Structure.* Sheed Andreews & McMeel.

Lang, G. (2021). *Jane Jacobs's First City: Learning from Scranton, Pennsylvania.* New Village Press. Kindle Edition.

Lavoie, D. (1985). *Rivalry and Central Planning: The Socialist Calculation Debate Reconsidered.* Cambridge Univ. Press.

Legates, R. T., & Stout, F. (1996). *The City Reader* (1st ed.). Routledge.

Manent, P. (2013). *Metamorphosis of the City: On the Western Dynamic.* Harvard Univ. Press.

McCallum, S. H. (1970). *The Art of Community.* Institute for Humane Studies.

Moody, S., & Melia, S. (2014). Shared Space: Research, Policy and Problems. *Research Repository*, University of the West of England: https://uwe-repository.worktribe.com/output/808489. Accessed 14 May 2023.

Moroni, S., Buitelaar, E., Sorelm, N., & Cozzolino, S. (2018). Simple Planning Rules for Complex Urban Problems: Toward Legal Certainty for Spatial Flexibility. *Journal of Planning Education and Research, 40*(3), 320–331.

Olson, M. (1984). *The Rise and Decline of Nations: Economic Growth, Stagflation, and Social Rigidities: Economic Growth, Stagflation and Social Rigidities.* Yale Univ. Press.

Ostrom, E. (1990). *Governing the Commons: The Evolution of Institutions for Collective Action.* Cambridge Univ. Press.

Ostrom, V., Tiebout, C. M., & Warren, R. (1961). The Organization of Government in Metropolitan Areas: A Theoretical Inquiry. *The American Political Science Review, 55*(4), 831–842.

Parker, G. (2004). *Sovereign City: The City-State through History.* Reaktion Books.

Pelham, N. (2022, 30 July–12 August). MBS: Despot in the Desert. *The Economist.* https://www.economist.com/1843/2022/07/28/mbs-despot-in-the-desert. Accessed 14 May 2023.

Pirenne, H. (1980[1925]). *Medieval Cities: Their Origin and the Revival of Trade.* Princeton Univ. Press.

Project for Public Spaces. (2017). What Is Shared Space? At https://www.pps.org/article/what-is-shared-space. Accessed 14 May 2023.

Ridley, M. (2020). *How Innovation Works: And Why It Flourishes in Freedom.* HarperCollins. Kindle edition.

Ruiz-Apilánez, B., Karimi, K., García-Camacha, I., & Martín, R. (2017). Shared Space Streets: Design, User Perception and Performance. *URBAN DESIGN International, 22*, 67–284.

Scott, J. C. (1998). *Seeing Like a State: How Certain Schemes to Improve the Human Condition Have Failed*. Yale Univ. Press.

Segal, D. (2012, June 23). A Georgia Town Takes the People's Business Private. *The New York Times*. https://www.nytimes.com/2012/06/24/business/a-georgia-town-takes-the-peoples-business-private.html. Accessed 14 May 2023.

Senthilingam, M. (2015). Shared Space, Where the Streets Have No Rules. *Future Cities/Transport* (CNN): https://www.cnn.com/2015/10/05/living/shared-spaces-future-cities/index.html. Accessed 14 May 2023.

Spruyt, H. (1994). *The Sovereign State and Its Competitors*. Princeton Univ. Press.

Steuteville, R. (2021, May 17). The Cayalá Effect in Guatemala City. *Public Square (A CNU Journal)*. https://www.cnu.org/publicsquare/2021/05/17/cayal%C3%A1-effect-guatemala-city. Accessed 14 May 2023.

Strong, M., & Himber, R. (2009). The Legal Autonomy of the Dubai International Financial Centre: A Scalable Strategy for Global Free-Market Reforms. *Economic Affairs, 29*(3), 36–41.

Tabarrok, A., & Rajagopalan, S. (2015). Lessons from Gurgaon: India's Private City. In D. Anderson & S. Moroni (Eds.), *Private Urban Planning: Opportunities and Limitations*. Edward Elgar.

Tilly, C. (1982). War Making and State Making as Organized Crime. In: Evans et al. (1985).

Vance, J. E. (1990). *The Continuing City: Urban Morphology in Western Civilization*. The Johns Hopkins Univ. Press.

Vives, R., & Elmahrek, A. (2018, February 26). A Tiny City with Huge Problems, Maywood Faces Its Biggest Scandal Yet. *Los Angeles Times*. https://www.latimes.com/local/lanow/la-me-ln-maywood-search-warrant-20180226-story.html. Accessed 14 May 2023.

von Mises, L. (1922). *Socialism: An Economic and Sociological Analysis*. Liberty Classics.

Weber, M. (1958). *The City*. Free Press.

Yardley, J. (2011, June 8). In India, Dynamism Wrestles with Dysfunction. *The New York Time*. https://www.nytimes.com/2011/06/09/world/asia/09gurgaon.html?pagewanted=all. Accessed 14 May 2023.

Zeng, D. Z. (2012). China's Special Economic Zones and Industrial Clusters: Success and Challenges. In *Lincoln Institute of Land Policy Working Paper*. Lincoln Institute of Land Policy.

Zipp, S., & Storring, N. (2016). *Vital Little Plans: The Short Works of Jane Jacobs*. Random House.

10

Coda

Throughout this book I have drawn attention to the social theory that underpins and unifies Jane Jacobs's economics, especially in relation to economic development and public policy. Nevertheless, I thought it might be useful to recapitulate the main elements of her overall analytical framework, as I see it, in terms of these three areas. In the final section of the chapter, I draw attention to particular topics I feel most deserve following up.

What in a nutshell, then, have we learned about economics and social theory from Jane Jacobs? The following lessons appear, not in the order in which Jacobs presents them or how they appear in this book but in an order that I think corresponds to their logical coherence.

1   Elements of Jane Jacobs's Social Theory

- Relevant knowledge is local and contextual. It is also imperfect and incomplete. This is the "knowledge problem."
- The knowledge problem means we must engage in trial and error to achieve success.

© The Author(s) 2024
S. Ikeda, *A City Cannot Be a Work of Art*,
https://doi.org/10.1007/978-981-99-5362-2_10

- Social networks and market prices, especially in cities, help to harness relevant knowledge and coordinate plans.
- The outcome of myriad interactions over time is a complex socioeconomic order whose precise details are largely unpredictable and that arises spontaneously within evolving social institutions and physical forms, without the need for overall conscious control. A "sidewalk ballet" that is more piazza than parade. A living city is a "spontaneous order," *par excellence*.
- A living city is the ideal incubator of new ideas and innovation because it attracts a disproportionate percentage of diverse, socially distant strangers having a wide range of knowledge, skills, and tastes in a safe environment. It promotes and accelerates the discovery and diffusion of new ideas.
- What generates land-use diversity and safety in public space are multiple primary attractors, street-level intricacy and granularity, affordable floor space, and population density (a.k.a. the "four generators of diversity").
- Norms of tolerance and inclusivity allow us to break strong ties and form weak ties to accommodate strangers into our social networks. "Weak ties" add dynamics to our networks, and "strong ties" stabilize them. The distinction between weak and strong ties implies two kinds of trust—cognitive and behavioral.
- Norms of tolerance need to include tolerance of change. This implies a tolerance for the messiness that accompanies trial and error.

2   Elements of Jane Jacobs's Economics

- Jacobs's main concern in economics is with economic development and innovation, and her relative lack of interest in efficiency is a consequence. The starting point is the knowledge problem.
- Social networks complement market prices in the competitive market process.
- The four generators of land-use diversity create "effective pools of economic use" in which entrepreneurs may discover complementarities that represent profit opportunities.

- The elements of these pools of use are in turn the diversity of people, places, and things; their creative use is enabled by the freedom of strangers to trust and contact one another in public space.
- City economies innovate and mutually develop through inter-city trade. "Import replacement" and "import shifting" are key stages in this process. Import replacement is entrepreneurship on the supply side of innovation, through altering and creatively extending the complex division of labor. Import shifting is entrepreneurship on the demand side of innovation, through broadening consumers' tastes and producers' uses of inputs.
- Innovation and the attendant creation of new work entail the constant creative destruction of parts of the division of labor, with the price system and social networks helping to coordinate the process.
- Profit-seeking through copycat investment can result in coarser land-use granularity, a commercial monoculture, and an endogenous "dynamics of decline" in innovation.

3 Elements of Jane Jacobs's Public Policy

- The legal setting and physical form of a city can promote or hinder peaceful, informal contact among strangers. When authorities are insensitive to the way the design of public space impacts social interaction, they risk hampering that essential contact.
- Because a great or living city is an incubator of ideas and attracts and retains so many anonymous strangers living close together, each seeking uncertain opportunities, the result can appear chaotic and indeed often is chaotic. But in a living city, where successes mingle with failures, order outpaces chaos and it is sometimes hard to tell them apart.
- In such an environment it is tempting, and perhaps occasionally justified, to address the perceived failures and the apparent chaos from the top down.
- The danger in doing so is to substitute a less visible emergent order with a "pretended order." Jacobs bases her critique of urban planning on these concerns, and her positive prescriptions are meant to ensure that interventions complement rather than displace spontaneous

orders. Designed complexity should not crowd out spontaneous complexity: more piazza, less parade!

- This entails placing limits on government intervention, where those limits depend on how sensitive authorities are to local knowledge and how well they can monitor the consequences of their interventions and adjust accordingly.
- This is the basis for her recommending "subsidiarity" as a governance structure.
- She cautions against constructing massive projects (private or public or public-private partnerships) in or near existing neighborhoods for fear of undermining local networks with cataclysmic money, border vacuums, and visual homogeneity, which erodes pools of economic use and stifles the ability of locals to utilize their resourcefulness.
- Functional zoning tends to block the interactions of the multiple "primary uses"—in combination with street intricacy, a range of building vintages, and population density—that generate the land-use diversity needed for safety, social networks, and the emergence of effective pools of economic use that is the basis for urban vitality and economic development. Functional zoning is unnecessary.
- In addition to regulating negative externalities, Jacobs would limit zoning to form-based zoning to combat vacuum-creating constructions.
- Jacobs's support for rent ceilings is limited because it does nothing to address the underlying causes of housing unaffordability. She recommends increasing the supply of housing through a "guaranteed rent method," which is a form of subsidy to the landlord. This reflects her appreciation for the signaling role of prices.
- The same goes with Jacobs's qualified support for tariffs to protect not infant industries but struggling regions against unfavorable changes in international currency exchange rates.
- This leads to perhaps her most radical, and self-described "utopian," suggestion: The deconstructing of nation-states into their economically relevant regional- or city-states.

4   Looking Ahead

I don't wish to give the impression that this book contains my final thoughts on the topics covered. Among them, the following I think most deserve further attention. (I suspect, and hope, that you may have a list of your own.)

The "Nature" of Economies Some readers familiar with Jacobs's later work may be disappointed to find relatively little on Jacobs's original ideas on the relation, indeed the identity, of the forces operating in the natural ecology and the social economy, as she treats in her book, *The Nature of Economies*. Actually, however, I have drawn significantly from it. Recall in particular her observations on the signaling role of prices, the parallels between her discussion of the growing complexity of an economy via "import stretching" and the concept of the "lengthening of the capital structure" of production, and the concept of dynamic stability as a potential alternative to the concept of economic equilibrium. At the same time, I have admitted to being unpersuaded by Jacobs's characterization of such ideas as exports as "discharges of economic energy" and uncomfortable with her vagueness about the nature of value.

To be honest, I don't have a better reason to give for not pursuing these ideas further other than my belief that doing so would have taken me beyond my goals of relating the core principles of her social theory and economics to market-process economics. The possibility remains, then, to link the social theory I have brought to light here to a more explicitly ecological approach to market systems.

Limits of Jacobs Density In my discussion of Jacobs Density (JD) I tried to refrain from using it as a normative benchmark in the sense that, ceteris paribus, a higher JD is always preferable to a lower one. Its positive use would simply be describing the impact of planning on systematically altering the potential for making diverse and socially distant contacts. JD would become a normative standard, however, if planners' objective is expressly to boost a city's liveliness or to increase the opportunities for creative discovery that may arise from enabling these kinds of contacts.

Also, as has been pointed out to me (HT to Alexander Schaefer), certain assumptions underlie my version of JD, namely, that Ego's ties to John or Mary (or whomever) in Figs. 5.4–5.6 are the same in terms of their strength or direction and that its practical usefulness is limited by its intent to measure potential rather than actual diversity and social distance—that once Ego makes direct contact with, say Morticia in Fig. 5.5, JD would actually fall, as the potential contacts reflected in a given JD become actual. Even under these assumptions I believe it can be a useful conceptual tool for evaluating the fecundity of action spaces, say, in different neighborhoods or in cyberspace. And speaking of action space…

Limits of Action Space While I believe the concept of action space offers a valuable lens through which to view social environments, especially with respect to urban dynamics, its usefulness depends on the kind of problem we are analyzing and is not always worth including. But I believe it can be useful, for example, as a way to conceptualize the link between the physical design of a space and the social interactions in it and the potential for entrepreneurial discovery—via the social networks, diversity of people, land-use granularity, and prevailing norms. Again, this is a question for further study.

The Metaverse I touched on this topic in Chap. 5, where I discuss the impact of new technologies, particularly apps that facilitate first contact with strangers, on urban agglomeration and how some of our urban concepts then need to adapt to these changes. (One of these adaptations is, of course, Jacobs Density.) I would like to add a few more thoughts on the subject.

People use the term "metaverse" fairly broadly (Ravencraft, 2022). It can refer to online platforms for gaming, social media, shopping, and entertainment of various kinds in "cyberspace." It can also refer to so-called augmented reality or virtual reality, in which some or all our senses are enhanced or replaced, so that I can take a tour of Berlin while comfortably seated in my home in Brooklyn (Greenwald, 2021). The latter technology seems to be the most immersive and therefore perhaps the most likely to replace some or all of our interactions in physical space. These days virtual classrooms and workplaces have become common, and the convenience of not having to commute long distances to school or work is huge. But as it stands now, there are significant drawbacks to this way of interacting.

To make my point, imagine a virtual technology so advanced it can recreate the sights, sounds, smells, and overall feeling of a concert hall. The three-dimensionality of the orchestra, stage, and music, the hues and spaciousness of the house, the pressure of the cushioned seat against our backs, the quiet struggle for elbow room on a narrow armrest, the fragrance of someone's cologne, and the smell and feel of our clothing; in short, everything exactly reproduced aurally, visually, and tactilely. We are transported from the physical reality of our living rooms to the virtual reality of the concert, and when it is over, we "materialize" instantaneously where we started (having never left).

The metaverse spares us the experience of traversing time and space, of getting dressed, navigating traffic or passersby, bundling against the evening chill, chatting up familiar concert-goers, waiting in line at the restroom, searching for a bar or restaurant to pop into, or dealing with strangers along the way. No checking out flashy cars and people on the street, deciphering the meaning of an overheard conversation, calculating the best way to squeeze through a crowd, or daydreaming while absently strolling. In short, we wouldn't have to experience the spontaneous complexity of the action spaces we would otherwise traverse.

Going to a concert is so much more than just being at the concert.

Some might say, "Good riddance!" Perhaps, but we wouldn't then have the chance to experience and discover the things, good and bad, we didn't know about the social cosmos.

Could such a complete metaverse be artificially created? Some maintain that the universe we actually experience is just such a metaverse. Possibly. But whatever the nature of our reality, to be an accurate reflection of it the metaverse would have to allow for the possibility of creativity, discovery, disappointment, and real danger, of genuine surprise and deep regret—experiences that are at the heart of what brings life to a city.

It shouldn't come as a shock that I don't think designed complexity can come close to simulating the social context needed to create such spontaneous complexity.

One day artificial intelligence and sensory technology might advance to the point where the metaverse could affordably replace our physical realities. Until that day arrives, however, no doubt we will live in cities. And if it does arrive? I would wager, even then, we would still want to dwell in real, living cities. Like X (formerly Twitter), Facebook, and Tinder today, the AR/VR technologies of the future will complement urban reality, not substitute for it.

*   *   *

Still, my mind is not completely made up about that. Indeed, I haven't stopped pondering most of the topics in this book, including those on which I have expressed an opinion or made a prediction. Like a living city, intellectual progress is driven by persistent trial and error and by radical tolerance and sincere criticism. And as with a living city, that process is characteristically messy and at times disagreeable. But the results can be unexpectedly pleasant and, often enough, enormously worthwhile. I look forward to your responses.

Works Cited

Greenwald, W. (2021, June 6). Augmented Reality (AR) vs. Virtual Reality (VR): What's the difference? *PC Magazine*. https://www.pcmag.com/news/augmented-reality-ar-vs-virtual-reality-vr-whats-the-difference. Accessed 20 May 2023.

Ravencraft, E. (2022, April 25). What is the metaverse, exactly? *Wired*. https://www.wired.com/story/what-is-the-metaverse/. Accessed 20 May 2023.

Appendix to Chapter 5

Calculating Social Average Distances

The following are long-hand calculations for the average distances in Networks A and B in Figs. 5.1 and 5.2, respectively

Network A

1 – 2: 1
1 – 3: 1 2 – 3: 2
1 – 4: 2 2 – 4: 1 3 – 4: 1
1 – 5: 3 2 – 5: 2 3 – 5: 2 4 – 5: 1
1 – 6: 4 2 – 6: 3 3 – 6: 3 4 – 6: 2 5 – 6: 1
1 – 7: 5 2 – 7: 4 3 – 7: 4 4 – 7: 3 5 – 7: 2 6 – 7: 1
1 – 8: 4 2 – 8: 3 3 – 8: 3 4 – 8: 2 5 – 8: 1 6 – 8: 2 7 – 8: 1
Total 20 + 5 + 13 + 8 + 4 + 3 + 1 = 64
64 ÷ 28 = 2.29

Network B

1 – 2: 1
1 – 3: 1 2 – 3: 2
1 – 4: 1 2 – 4: 2 3 – 4: 2
1 – 5: 2 2 – 5: 3 3 – 5: 3 4 – 5: 1
1 – 6: 2 2 – 6: 1 3 – 6: 3 4 – 6: 3 5 – 6: 2
1 – 7: 3 2 – 7: 2 3 – 7: 2 4 – 7: 2 5 – 7: 1 6 – 7: 1
1 – 8: 2 2 – 8: 3 3 – 8: 1 4 – 8: 3 5 – 8: 2 6 – 8: 2 7 – 8: 1
Total 12 + 13 + 11 + 9 + 5 + 3 + 1 = 54
54 ÷ 28 = 1.93

Appendix to Chapter 6

On the Need for Tariffs

There are strong and I think beneficial competitive forces among local, regional, or national currencies that tend toward, though perhaps never quite achieve, a single global currency. Throughout history, when multiple currencies circulate within a region, buyers and sellers in that region inevitably find this cumbersome, creating a strong incentive to alight on a single medium of exchange (Menger, 1981: 257–85). This works internationally as well, since a global currency lowers the cost of transacting among traders operating in different nations, in the same way the US dollar makes it easier for a person in Brooklyn, New York, to trade with someone in Mesa, Arizona, rather than having first to convert from one local currency into another. Sometime after World War II, the US dollar began serving as this kind of de facto near-global currency.

© The Author(s) 2024
S. Ikeda, *A City Cannot Be a Work of Art*,
https://doi.org/10.1007/978-981-99-5362-2

In *Cities and the Wealth of Nations* Jacobs objects to the use of a single currency over a large area, such as the United States, precisely because it means changes in the purchasing power of the American dollar vis-à-vis other national currencies do not adequately reflect significant differences in economic well-being among the country's various regions, thereby giving "false feedback" to weaker regions that do not influence international exchange rates.

For example, a strong dollar may reduce the foreign demand for coal mined in relatively poor Appalachia (i.e., it takes more of a foreign currency to buy a dollar). A foreign buyer in the Netherlands would have to take into account how many Euros (i.e., the currency used in the Netherlands and the rest of the European Union) it will take to purchase the dollars needed to buy a ton of Appalachian coal, which is denominated in dollars. Other things equal, a rise in the price of the American dollar against the Euro will depress the foreign demand for Appalachian coal. This means the demand for labor and other resources used in coal mining will also fall, resulting in lower wages and input prices in related industries. In the hypothetical long run, of course, and in the absence of further disturbances, all wages and prices will adjust back to their relationships prior to the exchange-rate change, so that in real terms (i.e., in terms of the purchasing power of these items) residents in these territories would be no better or worse off than before. But in the meantime, however, the adjustment could be painful.[1]

This false-feedback effect happens because the coal-mining industry is small relative to other industries and has little influence on the overall exchange value of the dollar against the Euro, compared to more-dominant American industries. These tend to be located in or near prosperous cities that have a very large overseas demand—e.g., in technology, financial services, or entertainment. Thus, a net increase in exports from the United States means foreign buyers of those exports will have to buy more dollars and, other things equal, increase the demand for and the price of dollars in terms of, say, the Euro. This makes the Euro "weaker"

---

[1] The situation is reversed in developing, predominantly agricultural or oil-rich, nations where urban residents are at the mercy of changes in the purchasing power of the currency resulting from the predominance of commodities industries in non-urban regions.

and the dollar "stronger." It could also make it cheaper at the margin to buy coal from abroad than in the United States.

That, as I understand it, is Jacobs's argument.

I find it plausible that a national currency could retard local innovation and growth in the manner Jacobs describes, and she offers many historical examples drawn from around the world, from ancient to modern times, where this appears to have taken place. Jacobs notes that some of the counter-examples she offers—e.g., Hong Kong and Singapore—are city-states that issue their own currencies and are therefore immune to this kind of false feedback (although in fact the Hong Kong dollar is currently pegged to the US dollar).

But the world is dominated by nation-states, most of which issue their own national currencies. In this case to counteract false feedback Jacobs favors permitting local city or regional governments to impose protective tariffs on imports. A local government would set the tariff high enough to offset the negative impact on nascent local industries of changes in a national currency's exchange rate. Although without the consent of Congress this violates the import-export clause of the US Constitution (Article I, § 10, clause 2), she argues doing so would stimulate local import replacement and lay a foundation, via a more complex division of labor, for local innovation and trigger a virtuous and expanding export-import cycle.

Jacobs recognizes that tariffs create their own problems, including retaliation, barriers to trade, and a bias toward city regions:

Jacobs recognizes that tariffs are far from an ideal remedy for faulty and deadening feedback to cities. Tariffs create obstacles of their own to volatile intercity trade. They are particularly hazardous for small countries, not only because they invite retaliatory barriers but also because, by their nature, the cities of small nations need heavy and volatile trade with cities across national boundaries. And in large nations or small, tariffs victimize rural economies lying outside of city regions (Jacobs, 1984: 168).

But Jacobs does seem unaware of or discounts the ability of politically connected special interests to lobby for tariffs simply to block more efficient competitors and, through higher prices, transfer wealth to themselves from unorganized consumers. Common legal privileges of this sort are a serious barrier to the very economic development Jacobs seeks to stimulate by erecting tariffs (Olson, 1982). (I discuss this blind spot in

Jacobs in Chap. 9.) Moreover, when governments sincerely try to practice "import substitution" (not to be confused with Jacobs's import replacement), they inevitably succumb to political pressures to "pick winners" that become chronically dependent on tariff protection. Weaning such industries off such privileges is politically tough.[2]

If protective tariffs are, at best, a second-best solution, what is Jacobs's first-best solution?

Jacobs argues that the radical remedy is to devolve nation-states into autonomous city-states that can better reflect the needs of local economic conditions:

> As far as I can see, there are no remedies at a city's or a nation's command, short of separations in the pattern of Singapore, for correcting the flaw I have hypothesized as leading to elephant cities while deadening others, and none for correcting the lack of feedback. (Jacobs, 1984: 180 – 181)

She advises that this should happen before nation-states engage in "transactions of decline" as "elephant cities" increasingly dominate national economies.

> The equivalent for a political unit would be to resist the temptation of engaging in transactions of decline by not trying to hold itself together. The radical discontinuity would thus be division of the single sovereignty into a family of smaller sovereignties, not after things had reached a stage of breakdown and disintegration, but long before while things were still going reasonably well. (Jacobs, 1984: 214)

Jacobs then suggests that the devolution (or subsidiarity?) of political authority opens the door to the possibility of city or regional currencies.

> A chief advantage, although not the only one, of this unlikely national behavior would be multiplication of currencies. The technical difficulties and inconveniences that would entail are surmountable, increasingly so with the aid of computers, instantaneous communications systems and such

---

[2] See this short blog post by Bryan Caplan (2021) on the infant-industry argument: "Infant industries and the dubious benefits of barriers" at Econlog Post (accessed 10 May 2023): https://www.econlib.org/infant-industries-and-the-dubious-benefits-of-barriers/

devices as credit cards which—even in their current rudimentary and limited uses—are already convenient for simultaneous transactions involving
currencies. On my card I can order, say, books from London payable in
pounds, shirts from the Boston city region payable in U.S. dollars, and garden seeds payable in my own currency, Canadian dollars, all the transactions
being equally convenient as far as I am concerned. Nor would multiple currencies that truly reflected the state of discrete economies be a step backward
from national currencies, or internationally pegged currencies, jumbling up
as they do apples, oranges and cucumbers in a meaningless chaos, and now
and again wildly inflating, then wildly devaluing. (Jacobs, 1984: 215)

Breaking up a nation-state with large differences in its regional economies into smaller autonomous city-states might mitigate Jacobs's false
feedback problem, as long as governments that oversee the currency resist
the temptation to debase or otherwise manipulate the value of their currencies to favor some areas or groups over others. Historically, in the case
of nation-states, this temptation is very strong indeed, even when there is
competition from other governments that issue their own currencies. If,
however, a local government prohibits its residents from using the currency of another locale in competition with its own (i.e., if there the local
currency is given a legal monopoly of local use), inter-city competition
among currencies would suffer because locals would be trapped into
using an inferior currency, unless they move to another jurisdiction—an
impracticable option for many.

Jacobs doesn't question the assumption that it must be a government,
at any level, that issues a currency, historical examples to the contrary,
and that the government must give that currency monopoly status. One
could say that a problem with Jacobs's proposal is that it is not radical
enough. Devolution of political and monetary authority is indeed a radical idea, but if she has gone this far why not a little further to solve these
additional problems?[3]

---

[3] On free banking see Lawrence H. White (1984), Free Banking in Scotland: Theory, Evidence,
Debate, 1800–1884, Cambridge Univ. Press; and George Selgin (2017), Money: Free and Unfree,
Cato Institute. Today, as cybercurrencies have taken center stage in the discussion about alternative
monies, geographically issued currencies have gotten less attention. One example is the Jacobs-
inspired "BerkShare," issued privately in upstate New York https://www.berkshares.org/. Wikipedia
also lists the following "community currencies" in the United States: https://en.wikipedia.org/wiki/
List_of_community_currencies_in_the_United_States. And for competitive currencies, see the
Canadian experience with free banking in Schuler (1992). (Both accessed 10 May 2023.)

It is interesting that her proposal to devolve political and monetary authority is very much in the spirit of proposals for "free banking" and "competing currencies," in which all private banks retain the right of issuing their own currencies, the stable purchasing power of which is kept in check by other banks that could cash in the notes of any competitor that overissues its currency. A local government might still issue its own currency, but without a legal monopoly to do so. In this way competition among the currencies of private banks of issue reduces the incentive for the local monetary authorities to manipulate the purchasing power of their currencies. Thus, one way of addressing the false-feedback problem that a national currency imposes on economically vulnerable regions would be to abolish the legal monopoly that nation-states grant to their national currencies and to permit local, private banks to issue competitive currencies if they wanted to.

Conventional wisdom has it that, unlike other goods and services that adjust to regional differences in supply and demand, free markets are incapable of providing currencies that adjust to these and other differences. Jacobs doesn't question this assumption, either. But if the Federal Reserve (the central banking authority of the United States) did not have an effective, legal monopoly on the issue of legal tender, and were the consequences of a uniform currency harmful enough over a long enough period, is it not likely that disadvantaged regions or cities would develop their own currencies to adjust to the flawed feedback mechanism of a national currency? In today's world, local currencies cannot emerge in local economies because national governments, like the United States, have a legal monopoly over currency issue.

What Jacobs is pointing out is a trade-off between the costs of national currencies in the form of false feedback and the cost of multiple local currencies that raise the cost of transacting inter-regional trade. Her second-best solution is a local protective tariff. But under free banking, competitive forces would tend to minimize those transaction costs. That is, instead of adopting an independent currency, a city or region could choose or adopt or peg their currencies to the "Appalachian dollar" or to some other currency, depending on the circumstances. Traders could use whatever currency they find convenient and switch from one to another as circumstances change. In time this would likely result in a dominant local or regional currency. In such a setup, the rationale for tariffs—false feedback—largely vanishes.

Moreover, according to Jacobs's logic, if a city-state that issues its own currency is itself very large and consists of multiple districts, some growing in economic strength and others declining, then the same problem arises at the urban level as in the case of a nation-state with a single currency, though on a smaller scale. In the great scheme of things this may not matter, except to those parts of the city that are chronically disadvantaged by the city's exchange rate vis-à-vis the currencies of other cities. But should this too become a problem, should neighborhoods then issue neighborhood currencies or erect trade barriers?

Again, if the feedback problem traces back to the exchange rate among different currencies, then wouldn't the feedback problem disappear because with a single, global currency there would be no exchange rate? This, indeed, has been the underlying tendency, sometimes swift but often slow, among international currencies since media of exchange first came into use. And it might have continued to evolve had not legal monopolies on note issue become a common practice among nation-states. Still, while the Euro and the US dollar today compete for global dominance, cyber-currencies and other technologies may one day overtake traditional money on a global scale and continue that historical tendency.

Appendix 1 to Chapter 9

Jane Jacobs and Classical Liberalism

What other evidence is there of Jacobs's classical liberal tendencies?

In her most "ideological" book, *Systems of Survival* (1992), Jacobs identifies what she concludes are the fundamental norms that ought to guide the private sector, "the commercial syndrome," and the public sector, "the guardian syndrome." They are as follows:

THE COMMERCIAL MORAL SYNDROME	THE GUARDIAN MORAL SYNDROME
Shun force	Exert prowess
Collaborate easily with strangers and aliens	Take vengeance
Be honest	Deceive for the sake of the task
Compete	Be exclusive
Respect contracts	Respect hierarchy
Use initiative and enterprise	Be obedient and disciplined
Be open to inventiveness and novelty	Adhere to tradition
Be efficient	Be ostentatious
Promote comfort and convenience	Show fortitude
Dissent for the sake of the task	Be loyal

(continued)

© The Author(s) 2024
S. Ikeda, *A City Cannot Be a Work of Art*,
https://doi.org/10.1007/978-981-99-5362-2

(continued)

Invest for productive purposes	Treasure honor
Be industrious	Make rich use of leisure
Be thrifty	Dispense largesse
Be optimistic	Be fatalistic

Jacobs's objective here is not to show preference for one moral syndrome over the other, but to make explicit the morals that, if adopted and practiced in each respective sphere, will result in a well-functioning society overall and to warn that applying the morals of the private sector to the public sector, or vice versa, will create "monstrous moral hybrids" that generate moral conflicts that will undermine the effectiveness of each sector. She has also said the guardian syndrome applies to people outside of government in activities such as the "free press" and "people who start movements." Overall, comparing the character of the norms that comprise the "guardian moral syndrome" to those of the "commercial moral syndrome," it is not going too far out on a limb to suggest that for Jacobs governance by the government should be strictly limited.

Further evidence of her liberalism is her tacit reliance on economic freedom, property rights, and free markets in *Death and Life*, which I have noted earlier in this book. Jacobs never advocated laissez-faire as such, but at a time when socialism was the dominant ideology among academics and intellectuals around the world as well as in the United States, Jacobs's recommendations for government intervention in 1961 were quite modest compared to equally prominent public intellectuals of the day of, say, John Kenneth Galbraith, Michael Harrington, or Rachel Carson.

But where in her writings she makes anti-business statements she always balances it with an equally strong condemnation of government, within a few pages or often in the very next breath. And *vice versa*. Examples aren't hard to find. What accounts for Jacobs's efforts to appear ideologically neutral? First, perhaps an honest effort on her part to be non-ideological and to see things in this balanced way. Second, although it may be that Jacobs's sympathies are on the ideological left, which my gut tells me is the case, perhaps her clear understanding of how markets work and profound appreciation for how they benefit the masses constrained her ideal vision of what government intervention can effectively do. Or in other words, as my late friend and colleague Steve Horwitz succinctly put it, "ought implies can."

Appendix 2 to Chapter 9

Alain Bertaud on the Practical Problems of City Building

The urban planner Alain Bertaud once related to me in a conversation[1] the multiple challenges with which anyone must contend who wishes to establish an ambitious, new settlement, whether a Charter City or Startup Society. The gist of those challenges is as follows:

- Cash flow is critical. Projects extending years or even decades into the future must generate sufficient revenue in the meantime to cover start-up costs of infrastructure and expansion. This is problematic given the levels of uncertainty involved.
- Timing is critical. Large projects run smoothly only if all the pieces come together at the right time, e.g., acquiring land, legal permissions, engineering issues of constructing infrastructure in proper sequence, and especially acquiring sufficient financing to cover the various stages of the project.

---

[1] The conversation took place on 6 October 2018 in Maspalomas in Gran Canaria, Spain, and was later followed up with written correspondence on 27–28 December 2018, 30 December 2018, and 4 January 2019.

© The Author(s) 2024   **381**
S. Ikeda, *A City Cannot Be a Work of Art*,
https://doi.org/10.1007/978-981-99-5362-2

- Any snags in the process create costly delays and jeopardize cash flow.

- Engineers like to build everything at once because it is easier that way and possibly cheaper in per unit cost, but it increases financial costs by creating long periods of negative cash flows. To decrease financial costs it is usually useful to generate revenues early in the project by selling or leasing land to end users. This assumes phasing the project so that some areas can be occupied early (e.g., water and sewer connected, schools operating). Even if the early net cash flow is negative, an early stream of revenue reassures lenders that there is demand for the project and that eventually the cash flow will at some point turn positive.

- It is usually more sensible to build these projects in slower, discrete stages to accommodate the actual inflow of immigrants with complementary skills. This, however, creates the problem of not getting a sufficient rate of return and cash flow in time to cover the cost of building out.

  - Again, any delay or interruption of the sequence in the stages of production can spell disaster.

- Most "charter cities" (not really in Romer's sense) situate themselves close to existing cities, i.e., as satellites, not in the hinterlands (such as The Line), to minimize the costs of transport and commuting and to draw on local skills.

  - Building in the hinterlands, on a large scale, is a costly and logistical nightmare.
  - These satellites may survive but never become living cities.

- New capital cities built by governments, like Brasilia, Islamabad, Canberra, Abuja, and Chandigarh, escape both the cash flow and the "viable population size" requirement because the state orders the civil servants to move at a set date and they have no choice if they want to keep their jobs. This already creates an immediate critical mass for services. The cash flow is financed by the treasury and is subsidized by the taxpayers of the entire country. There is never any problem of a bank refusing to roll over a loan because it finds the loan too risky. Typically, new capitals are constructed under very soft budget constraints, which undermines fiscal discipline. These soft budget constraints are fortunately not available to privately built cities.

- There has to be a "critical mass" of population size and complementarity of skills in the population in order to sustain supply and demand in enough markets to constitute a living city. Most new cities attract too many intellectuals and not enough carpenters!

  – In addition to encouraging ordinary markets, such a critical mass of people can help to cover fees and taxes for infrastructure and formal security services (as well as provide informal eyes-on-the-street safety and security, à la Jane Jacobs).

Index[1]

---

[1] Note: Page numbers followed by 'n' refer to notes.

© The Author(s) 2024
S. Ikeda, *A City Cannot Be a Work of Art*,
https://doi.org/10.1007/978-981-99-5362-2

Trial-and-error, 65, 77, 78, 82, 197,
    198, 206, 215, 252
Trust, 159, 216, 224, 240
    a bedrock attribute of a successful
        city, 172
    behavioral trust, defined, 163
    behavioral trust is not risk-
        loving, 165n22
    cognitive trust, defined, 159
    defined, 142
    paradox, 162
Turrentine, Jeff, 290
Twitter, 107, 108

U

Unintended consequences, 258, 259,
    285, 302
Unintended consequences of
        dynamic networks, 168–170
    diffusion of knowledge, 168
    external effects, 169
    increasing Jacobs Density, 170
    multiplex uses of ties, 168
    ties growing in strength, 168
Unplanned simplicity, 70n14
Unscalable infrastructure, 343n41
Upward sprawl, 336
Urban economics, 7
Urban interventions, 258, 259, 303
    that Jacobs criticizes, 259–279
Urbanization, 218, 220, 220n2, 252
    and its problems, 218–220
Urban planning, 219, 221, 222, 225,
    227, 230, 237, 247, 252
Urban renewal, 15
Urban revitalization, 327–337
    Cayalá, Guatemala City, 332–337

Sandy Springs, Georgia, 330–331
shared streets, 328–330
Urban sprawl, 282, 283, 303
Urban values, 173n28
Urban vitality, planning for,
    309, 311
The use of knowledge in
    society, 77
Usonia, 238

V

Vance, James E., 27, 182n3
Vaux, Calvert, 233
Ville Radieuse, see Radiant City
Virtual reality, 364
Visual homogeneity, 98
Visual order, 230–232, 239,
    241, 252
VIZ, see Voluntary
    inclusionary zoning
Voluntary inclusionary zoning
    (VIZ), 269, 269n10, 270
Vouchers, 275

W

Wagner, Richard E., 59
Walentas family, 111
Walker, Madam C.J., 186
Walras, Léon, 134
Ware, James E., 280
Warren, David, 325
Weak ties, 107–109, 186, 193
The Wealth of Nations, 194
Weber, Max, 8, 21, 74, 187
Wengrow, David, 185
West, Geoffrey, 21

Printed in the USA
CPSIA information can be obtained
at www.ICGtesting.com
LVHW052340031123
762902LV00013B/551